Words and the Word

Words
and the Word

Explorations in biblical interpretation
and literary theory

Edited by David G. Firth
and Jamie A. Grant

APOLLOS

APOLLOS (an imprint of Inter-Varsity Press)
Norton Street, Nottingham NG7 3HR, England
Email: ivp@ivpbooks.com
Website: www.ivpbooks.com

First published 2008

British Library Cataloguing in Publication Data
A catalogue record for this book is available from the British Library.

UK ISBN: 978-1-84474-288-2

Set in Monotype Garamond 11/13pt
Typeset in Great Britain by Servis Filmsetting Ltd, Stockport, Cheshire
Printed and bound in Great Britain by Ashford Colour Press Ltd, Gosport, Hampshire.

Inter-Varsity Press publishes Christian books that are true to the Bible and that communicate the gospel, develop discipleship and strengthen the church for its mission in the world.

Inter-Varsity Press is closely linked with the Universities and Colleges Christian Fellowship, a student movement connecting Christian Unions in universities and colleges throughout Great Britain, and a member movement of the International Fellowship of Evangelical Students. Website: www.uccf.org.uk.

CONTENTS

CONTRIBUTORS

Richard S. Briggs is the Director of Biblical Studies and Hermeneutics at Cranmer Hall, St John's College, Durham University, where he teaches Old Testament. He has written widely on the subject of biblical interpretation, including *Words in Action: Speech Act Theory and Biblical Interpretation* (T. & T. Clark, 2001) and *Reading the Bible Wisely* (SPCK, 2003).

Jeannine K. Brown (PhD, Luther Seminary) is Associate Professor of New Testament at Bethel Seminary, St. Paul, Minnesota. She is the author of *Scripture as Communication: Introducing Biblical Hermeneutics* (Baker, 2007) and *The Disciples in Narrative Perspective: The Portrayal and Function of the Matthean Disciples* (SBL/Brill, 2002).

David G. Firth is Old Testament Tutor and BA Course Leader at Cliff College, Derbyshire. He is the author of *Surrendering Retribution in the Psalms* (Paternoster, 2005) and co-editor of *Interpreting the Psalms* (Apollos, 2005).

Jamie A. Grant is Lecturer in Biblical Studies at the Highland Theological College, Dingwall, Scotland. He is the author of *The King as Exemplar* (SBL, 2004) and *The God of Covenant* (Apollos, 2005).

Grant R. Osborne is Professor of New Testament at Trinity Evangelical Divinity School, Deerfield, Illinois. He is the author of a number of books, including *The Resurrection Narratives* (Baker, 1984), *The Hermeneutical Spiral: A Comprehensive Introduction to Biblical Interpretation* (IVP, 1991, 2006), *Three Crucial Questions about the Bible* (Baker, 1994) and commentaries on Revelation, Romans and John.

Peter M. Phillips (PhD, Sheffield University) is New Testament Lecturer at Cliff College, Derbyshire, UK. In 2008 he becomes Director of Research at the new Centre for Biblical Literacy at St John's College, Durham. He is author of *The Prologue of the Fourth Gospel: A Sequential Reading*, Library of New Testament (T. & T. Clark, 2006).

S. D. (Fanie) Snyman is head of the Department of Old Testament Studies at the University of the Free State, Bloemfontein, South Africa. He is interested in the exegesis and theology of the Old Testament with a focus on the prophetic literature. His publications include 'Psalm 32: Structure – Genre – Intent and Liturgical Use', in D. J. Human and C. J. A. Vos (eds.), *Psalms and Liturgy*, JSOTSup 410 (T. & T. Clark International, 2004), pp. 155–167; and 'Eretz and Adama in the Book of Amos', in H. M. Niemann and M. Augustin (eds.), *Stimulation from Leiden: Collected Communications of the XVIth Congress of the International Organisation for the Study of the Old Testament* (Peter Lang, 2006), pp. 137–146.

Terrance R. Wardlaw, Jr., is a linguist with SIL International, and lives and works in Asia with his family. He is the author of *Conceptualizing Words for God within the Pentateuch: A Cognitive-Semantic Investigation in Literary Context*, LHBOTS (T. & T. Clark, forthcoming).

ABBREVIATIONS

1QM	*War Scroll*
4QSam^b	*Samuel^b* (second Samuel Scroll found in Cave 4, Qumran)
AA	*Argumentation and Advocacy*
AB	Anchor Bible
ABD	*Anchor Bible Dictionary*, ed. D. N. Freedman, 6 vols. (New York: Doubleday, 1992)
AcBib	Academia biblica
ACEBT	*Amsterdamse Cahiers voor Exegese en bijbelse Theologie*
ActSup	Acta theologica supplementum
AJSL	*American Journal of Semitic Languages*
AnBib	Analecta biblica
ANE	ancient Near East / ancient Near Eastern
ATSAT	Arbeiten zu Text und Sprache im Alten Testament
b. Ḥag.	*Babylonian Talmud Ḥagigah*
b. Yom.	*Babylonian Talmud Yoma*
BCOTWP	Baker Commentary on the Old Testament Wisdom and Psalms
BECNT	Baker Exegetical Commentary on the New Testament
BHK	*Biblia Hebraica*, ed. R. Kittel, 16th ed. (Stuttgart: Würtemburgische Bibelanstalt, 1973)

BHS	*Biblia Hebraica Stuttgartensia*, ed. K. Elliger and W. Rudolph (Stuttgart: Deutsche Bibelstiftung, 1983)
BI	*Biblical Interpretation*
Bib	*Biblica*
BIS	Biblical Interpretation Series
BL	*Bibel und Liturgie*
BTB	*Biblical Theology Bulletin*
BZAW	Beihefte zur Zeitschrift für die alttestamentliche Wissenschaft
CBET	Contributions to Biblical Exegesis and Theology
CBQ	*Catholic Biblical Quarterly*
CCC	*College Composition and Communication*
CEV	Contemporary English Version
CR:BS	*Currents in Research: Biblical Studies*
ECC	Eerdmans Critical Commentary
ESV	English Standard Version
ET	English Translation
EvT	*Evangelische Theologie*
ExpTim	*Expository Times*
GHAT	Göttinger Handkommentar zum Alten Testament
GNB	Good News Bible
HCOT	Historical Commentary on the Old Testament
Heb.	Hebrew
HeyJ	*Heythrop Journal*
HSS	Harvard Semitic Studies
JAAR	*Journal of the American Academy of Religion*
JAARSup	Journal of the American Academy of Religion Supplement
JAC	*Journal of Advanced Composition*
JBL	*Journal of Biblical Literature*
JBLMS	Journal of Biblical Literature Monograph Series
JETS	*Journal of the Evangelical Theological Society*
JLSM	Janua linguarum series minor
JLT	*Journal of Literature and Theology*
JNSL	*Journal of Northwest Semitic Languages*
JOTT	*Journal of Translation and Textlinguistics*
JR	*Journal of Religion*
JSNT	*Journal for the Study of the New Testament*
JSNTSup	Journal for the Study of the New Testament, Supplement Series

JSOT	*Journal for the Study of the Old Testament*
JSOTSup	Journal for the Study of the Old Testament, Supplement Series
JTS	*Journal of Theological Studies*
KR	*Kenyon Review*
Lat.	Latin
LB	The Living Bible
LCL	Loeb Classical Library
LHBOTS	Library of the Hebrew Bible / Old Testament Studies
LXX	Septuagint
LXX^B	Septuagint (Codex Vaticanus version)
MT	Masoretic Text
NBJ	Nouvelle Bible Jérusalem
NBS	Nouvelle Bible Segond
NEchtB	Neue Echter Bibel
Neot	*Neotestamentica*
NGTT	*Nederduitse Gereformeerde Teologiese Tydskrif*
NIB	*The New Interpreter's Bible*, ed. L. E. Keck, 12 vols. (Nashville: Abingdon, 1993–2002)
NICNT	New International Commentary on the New Testament
NICOT	New International Commentary on the Old Testament
NIGTC	New International Greek Testament Commentary
NIV	New International Version
NLH	*New Literary History*
NLT	New Living Translation
NovTSup	Novum Testamentum Supplements
NRSV	New Revised Standard Version
NS	New Series
NT	New Testament
NTS	*New Testament Studies*
OBO	Orbis biblicus et orientalis
OPTT	*Occasional Papers in Translation and Textlinguistics*
OT	Old Testament
OTE	*Old Testament Essays*
OTESup	Old Testament Essays, Supplement Series
POut	De Prediking van het Oude Testament
Presb	*Presbyterion*
Proof	*Prooftexts: A Journal of Jewish Literary History*
QJS	*Quarterly Journal of Speech*
RB	*Revue biblique*

RSV	Revised Standard Version
RTT	Research in Text Theory
SBL	Society of Biblical Literature
SBLDS	Society of Biblical Literature Dissertation Series
SBT	Studies in Biblical Theology
SemeiaSt	Semeia Studies
SHS	Scripture and Hermeneutics Series
SNTSMS	Society for New Testament Studies Monograph Series
SNTW	Studies of the New Testament and its World
SSN	Studia semitica neerlandica
StVTQ	*St. Vladimir's Theological Quarterly*
SubBib	*Subsidia biblica*
TNIV	Today's New International Version
TNTC	Tyndale New Testament Commentaries
TrinJ	*Trinity Journal*
TynBul	*Tyndale Bulletin*
UTPSS	University of Texas Press Slavic Series
VT	*Vetus Testamentum*
VTSup	Supplements to Vetus Testamentum
WBC	Word Biblical Commentary
WUNT	Wissenschaftliche Untersuchungen zum Neuen Testament
WW	*Word and World*
ZAW	*Zeitschrift für die alttestamentliche Wissenschaft*

INTRODUCTION

David G. Firth and Jamie A. Grant

Biblical studies has often looked for dialogue partners. And as it has conversed with other disciplines new questions have opened up regarding the Bible's interpretation, which at the same time have suggested new ways in which the Bible might speak to the world. The question, though, has often been who these dialogue partners should be.

In the early centuries, and even up to the time of the Reformation, the main collaborator was philosophy, especially as the biblical text was often relegated to the task of supporting established doctrine. Of course, great interpreters such as Augustine, Nicholas of Lyra or Calvin did considerably more than simply engage with philosophy or extract verses out of context to support doctrine. But it is impossible to read these authors without recognizing the extent to which they engaged with the dominant philosophical questions of their age. Theology was unavoidably drawn into the metaphysical debates of the day, and so these questions became the principal reference points for interpreters of the Bible throughout many generations.

Without abandoning philosophy altogether, a significant shift occurred with the advent of the Enlightenment . For biblical studies, increased historical awareness brought about crucial changes in the practice of academic theology, most obviously in the development of the so-called historical-critical method. This has given rise to significant debates about the Bible's historicity: can we trust its testimony and if so, to what extent?

One of the problems of historical criticism was its tendency to atomize texts and look at the world behind the text, often privileging hypothetical sources over the finished text. This is not to disparage historical inquiry into texts and how they develop, but it is perhaps akin to seeking to learn to drive a car by pulling it apart rather than understanding first how the whole works. The literary turn often associated with postmodernity changed this basic approach by beginning to look at texts as wholes, and this was not restricted to biblical studies. Whether or not postmodernity is really something new or simply the latter stages of modernity, clearly one important shift in recent years has been that scholars now more commonly foreground their methodological concerns. In line with other disciplines, biblical studies has become far more aware of the need to be conscious about the theory that underpins interpretation and how it shapes the questions we ask.

In making this move, we have also reached a point where, rather than philosophy or history dominating, biblical interpreters now draw on a plurality of disciplines, engaging with issues such as rhetoric, gender, postcolonialism and psychoanalytic theory.

In spite of this plurality, *literary theory* is a conversation partner of continued and increasing importance for biblical interpretation, though, as is clear from this collection, literary theory too takes multiple forms. Some of its aspects, such as *speech acts*, are strongly rooted in contemporary philosophy. Others, such as *rhetoric*, draw on a range of classical sources as well as modern theorists to understand how the text seeks to persuade. But whichever aspect of literary theory is emphasized, it is crucial that biblical interpreters have a proper understanding of this discipline if they are to draw fruitfully on its insights. This does not mean we must become expert in each of them, but we do need to have enough grounding in these theories to appreciate how they can contribute to the ongoing task of interpreting the Bible so we can hear its ancient message clearly today.

The contributors to this volume are united in their belief that a proper understanding of different aspects of literary theory can make a significant contribution to the interpretation of the Bible. Though none would claim to cover the whole of literary theory, since it is a sprawling and growing discipline, each brings expertise in a specific area. Therefore, those contributors discussing a particular method both outline the issues related to that method and show how it applies to the interpretative task. Thus we hope to integrate theory with practice so that the process of applying a set of analytical tools will expand the ways in which we understand them.

At the same time, these are only explorations in literary theory and biblical interpretation. There is considerably more that could be said about each approach, and there are also many more aspects of literary theory (such as metaphor, intertextuality, film theory) that could be considered. Guidance on these is offered in the opening chapters by Grant Osborne and Fanie Snyman, both of whom offer different, yet complementary, overviews on the relationship between literary theory and biblical interpretation.

We hope these essays will stimulate discussion of the importance of literary theory as applied to biblical studies, and at the same time encourage students to draw on the possibilities these methods suggest. Literary theory is not the only conversation partner for modern biblical interpretation, but these chapters suggest it is a vital one if we are to continue to hear the living word of the living God.

1. LITERARY THEORY AND BIBLICAL INTERPRETATION

Grant R. Osborne

Many Christians think of and read the Bible as if it were nothing but a series of propositional theological principles stated in epistolary form. They are so inured to and controlled by epistles like Romans and Corinthians that they fail to realize the richness and diversity of biblical expression. Few books contain the incredible diversity of genre and style exemplified in this Book of all books. Actually, *epistolary* material is among the smallest of the genres (about 9%). *Narrative* is by far the largest, representing over half of the biblical material. *Prophetic* material is second, followed by *legal* material, then *poetry* and then *wisdom* and *apocalyptic*. The point is that each type of literature has its own richness of expression and deeply theological message. Each needs to be read and allowed to function in its intended way on its own. The problem is that genre is a fluid form. Epistolary material contains poetry, apocalyptic portions, and several other types embedded in its works. Books like Revelation are composed not just of apocalyptic material but also epistolary and prophetic sections (see chapter 4 in this volume). Therefore, in analysing any portion of Scripture one cannot do justice to it without a sound knowledge of literary theory and a fairly sophisticated use of literary techniques.

This does not mean that the average layperson can no longer study the Bible, for the number of excellent commentaries and Bible study tools is growing. It does mean, however, that the previous dependence on pure inductive Bible study needs to be supplemented with an emphasis on deductive analysis as well, that is, with the tools such as dictionaries and commentaries to aid understanding. Inductive Bible study can degenerate into simply a more scientific way of being subjective when interpreting the Bible. There is no way we can navigate the twisted literary corridors of the complex biblical books on our own. We need the help of scholars who have walked these paths before us, who can guide us through the interpretative mazes. The purpose of this article and volume is to help the Bible student understand the literary process involved in the hermeneutical event.

The purpose of this chapter is to demonstrate the value and importance of literary theory for biblical interpretation. Yet let me go a step further. Interpretation, indeed reading, cannot be done without literary theory. The only question is whether it will be sound or flawed literary theory. As human beings, we engage in communication, which is fuelled by an innate sense of context and the development of sometimes correct and often incorrect understanding. My wife and I frequently mis-communicate, which is caused when we fail to understand the context and background behind what the other is saying. As we clarify and restate our previous point, we are using the shared literary assumptions with which we have grown up. Of course, that is oral communication, but similar assumptions guide our reading as well. In fact, it is far more difficult in Bible reading, for those works were written millennia ago in a culture long dead. How do we bridge the cultural distance in order to understand Scripture properly? That is what I would like to demonstrate in the ensuing pages.

Literary theory and general hermeneutics

Context

Every aspect of the hermeneutical process is infused and enriched with literary theory. Let us begin with the incredible importance of context. Those who have grown up in the church have probably been influenced by the memory-verse approach to theology. Since the infusion of Scottish common-sense realism in the latter part of the nineteenth century it has been thought that theological positions can be proved by quoting a few well-chosen verses, for example the security of the believer with John 10:27–28, Ephesians 1:13, 14, Romans 8:38–39, or the danger of losing one's salvation with Hebrews 6:4–6, James 5:19–20 and 2 Peter 2:20. People do not realize that the passages have to be interpreted and cannot be understood apart from the context in which they are embedded. Let me use as examples two verses commonly used for the process of salvation, Isaiah 1:18 ('though your sins are like scarlet' ESV) and

Revelation 3:20 ('I stand at the door and knock' ESV). However, examination of these in their context indicates that the first is about social justice and the second about church revival – neither is about evangelism!

Two recently developed disciplines guide the process by which context is studied: *rhetorical criticism* and *discourse analysis*. The first developed especially in the 1960s and 70s both as a study of the artistry employed in the poetic and stylistic construction of biblical texts[1] and as a study of the classical rhetorical patterns biblical authors utilized in developing their arguments.[2] The stylistic approach considers the techniques by which writers link and present their arguments.

I see five different types of stylistic relationships:[3] (1) *'Collection' relations*, often called rabbinic 'pearl-stringing', with messianic texts strung together as in Hebrews 1:4–14 (Ps. 2:7; 2 Sam. 7:17; Pss 97:7; 104:4; 45:6–7; 102:25–27; 110:1), or with ideas gathered around one concept, as in the 'salt' sayings of Mark 9:48–50. (2) *Cause–effect or problem–solution relations* consist of many types, as in prophetic situations when the sins of Israel are enumerated (e.g. Amos 2:6–13) and judgment is pronounced (2:14–16), or with Paul's use of the rhetorical question (presenting the false understanding of his opponents) followed by his answer to their error (Rom. 4:1–2; 6:1–2; 7:1–2, 13; 8:31–32; 9:19–24; 11:1–2). (3) *Comparison equates or contrasts ideas*, as in Paul's well-known first Adam / last Adam contrast of Romans 5:12–21, or in the wise–foolish contrast of Proverbs 1:7; 15:5. (4) *Description extends and clarifies a topic*, as in the extension of the Abrahamic blessing (Gen. 13:14–18) in Genesis 14:1–18, or Jesus' use of three parables on 'lost' things in Luke 15 to deepen the understanding of divine love and forgiveness. Under this might be placed the technique of inclusion, in which a writer repeats the opening idea in the conclusion

---

1. See especially A. N. Wilder, *Early Christian Rhetoric: The Language of the Gospel* (Cambridge, Mass.: Harvard University Press, 1964); and J. Muilenberg, 'Form Criticism and Beyond', *JBL* 88 (1969), pp. 4–8.

2. Two major works on this are G. A. Kennedy, *New Testament Interpretation through Rhetorical Criticism* (Chapel Hill: University of North Carolina Press, 1984); and B. L. Mack, *Rhetoric and the New Testament* (Minneapolis: Fortress, 1990). For recent presentations, see W. M. Roth, 'Rhetorical Criticism, Hebrew Bible'; D. F. Watson, 'Rhetorical Criticism, New Testament', in J. H. Hayes (ed.), *Dictionary of Biblical Interpretation* (Nashville: Abingdon, 1999), vol. 2, pp. 396–402; and chapter 7 in this volume.

3. G. R. Osborne, *The Hermeneutical Spiral: A Comprehensive Introduction to Biblical Interpretation*, 2nd ed. (Downers Grove: IVP, 2006), pp. 52–56.

for emphasis, as in the deity of Christ in John 1:1–18 (or in the chiasm in the trial before Pilate in John 18:28 – 19:16). (5) *'Shifts in expectancy'*, a general catch-all for ways the writer develops turning points and pivotal sections in the developing argument. For instance, in the healing of the demon-possessed child (Mark 9:14–29) the climax surprisingly occurs not with the exorcism but with the cry of the father, 'I believe; help my unbelief!' (v. 24 ESV), which is clearly the central point of the story and the antidote for the disciples' failure.

The argument for Hellenistic rhetorical forms in NT writings stems from the Hellenistic background of many of the NT authors (even Jewish writers like the authors of Hebrews and James), the formal nature of most of the writings, and the general knowledge of such forms in the first century, even in Palestine.[4] For instance, one could see the Sermon on the Mount (Matt. 5 – 7) organized along the lines of the *emcomium* or introduction establishing the ethical parameters (5:1–13); the *narratio* or proposition regarding Jesus' relationship with the law (5:17–20) and the explanation of it (5:21–48); the *partitio* or the particular concrete points arising from the proposition (6:1–18, applying to almsgiving, prayer, fasting); the *probatio* or logical arguments addressing specific issues (possessions, anxiety, judging others, asking and receiving in 6:19 – 7:20); and the *conclusio* or recapitulation and appeal to the emotions (7:21–27).[5] Many have found significant help from this method, yet questions must be raised:

1. Is there such a method, since its many practitioners disagree on any unified approach?
2. It must be made compatible with historical inquiry and centre upon the author's intention in producing the text.
3. It must overcome serious drawbacks in the tendency of many to lose sight of the text and impose their structure on it.
4. When supplementing other methodologies and made simply one part of literary analysis, it has immense potential.[6]

Discourse analysis is 'a process of investigation by which one examines the form and function of all the parts and levels of a written discourse, with the

---

4. See R. R. Melick, 'Literary Criticism of the New Testament', in D. S. Dockery (ed.), *Foundations for Biblical Interpretation* (Nashville: Broadman & Holman, 1994), p. 441.
5. See Kennedy, *New Testament Interpretation*, pp. 39–72; Mack, *Rhetoric*, pp. 82–85.
6. C. C. Black, 'Rhetorical Criticism', in J. B. Green (ed.), *Hearing the New Testament: Strategies for Interpretation* (Grand Rapids: Eerdmans, 1995), pp. 273–276.

aim of better understanding both the parts and the whole of that discourse'.[7]
There are three levels of investigation:

- the narrative's structure
- the communication of the author to the original readers
- the discourse between the text and the modern reader

Green believes the third level involves pragmatics, that is, a communicative act apart from historical concerns and involving multiple possible meanings in a semiotic sense.[8] I would argue that the author's intended meaning controls all three levels, and the modern reader appropriates the original meaning of the text and contextualizes it (see my *Hermeneutical Spiral*). By looking at the text in terms of its macro level (changes of genre and boundaries in the text as a whole) and its micro level (the structure and communication within each discourse unit within the larger structure), one can see how the author has organized and presented his or her developing argument.[9] For instance, Matthew 8 – 9 is the first extended narrative in Matthew and takes place between the Sermon on the Mount (5 – 7) and missionary discourse (10). An analysis of this finds three blocks of three miracles each (8:1–17; 8:23 – 9:8; 9:18–34) broken by discipleship sections (8:18–22; 9:9–13, 14–17). The first set concerns authority over illness, the second set over nature, demons and paralysis, and the third set over disabilities and death.[10] The primary thrust is Jesus' all-embracing power and authority, with a second theme being the place of faith in the process, seen in the leper, the centurion, the woman with the haemorrhage, and the two blind men.

Exegetical analysis

This includes grammar, semantics and syntax. Some might not think of grammar in terms of literary theory. However, grammar is the building block of the literary unit, and there can be no communication without it. The key

---

7. G. Guthrie, 'Discourse Analysis', in D. A. Black and D. S. Dockery (eds.),
   Interpreting the New Testament: Essays on Methods and Issues (Nashville: Broadman & Holman, 2001), p. 255.

8. J. B. Green, 'Discourse Analysis and New Testament Interpretation', in Green,
   Hearing the New Testament, pp. 276–279.

9. See Guthrie, 'Discourse Analysis', p. 260.

10. C. Keener, *A Commentary on the Gospel of Matthew* (Grand Rapids: Eerdmans, 1999),
    p. 258.

recent distinction for both grammar and semantics is that of the *synchronic* over the *diachronic*. It was Ferdinand de Saussure who first developed the distinction between diachrony (the historical development of a term) and synchrony (the use of a term in the current context), saying that what mattered was the use of the term in the present, not what led to the production of meaning.[11] Moreover, this is as true in grammar as in semantics.[12] Verbal aspect as developed by Porter and others considers not levels of time derived from the tenses but rather the ways that writers of Greek perceived the action as unfolding and chose tense forms for literary purposes, that is, to highlight various aspects of the action. Porter finds three 'planes of discourse' or action, with the aorist defining the 'background' behind the action, the present tense the 'foreground' or action featured or that climaxes the event, and the perfect tense the 'frontground' or single event featured.[13] This is an important contribution, though I disagree with Porter that aspect theory is a paradigm shift that replaces traditional theory. I prefer to consider it supplemental to traditional theory and to use the two side by side.[14] For instance, in Matthew 25:19 in the parable of the talents the two present tenses ('returns', 'settles accounts' after the aorists of vv. 15–18) are both historic presents and foreground the action, emphasizing the return of the master after a lengthy time away.

One of the newest disciplines is semantic analysis, which became a science only in the 1950s.[15] Even today it is common to hear word studies done in the light of the use of the word in Homer or Plato or with some 'root meaning' the term is supposed to have. James Barr coined perhaps the single most important phrase for these errors, 'illegitimate totality transfer', which means to transfer wrongly all the possible meanings a word can have into a single usage of it in one context.[16] A good example of this is discussion of

---

11. F. de Saussure, *Writings in General Linguistics* (Oxford: Oxford University Press, 2006).

12. S. E. Porter, *Idioms of the Greek New Testament* (Sheffield: JSOT Press, 1994), p. 15, says, 'I have taken a synchronic approach to the NT, treating it as consisting of representative Greek texts produced by actual language users of the first century AD.'

13. Ibid., p. 23.

14. See Osborne, *Hermeneutical Spiral*, pp. 68–69.

15. For the history of the discipline, see D. A. Black, 'The Study of New Testament Greek in the Light of Ancient and Modern Linguistics', in Black and Dockery, *Interpreting the New Testament*, pp. 230–252.

16. J. Barr, *The Semantics of Biblical Language* (Oxford: Oxford University Press, 1961), p. 218.

ekenōsen in Philippians 2:6, which has engendered all kinds of theories regarding what Jesus 'emptied' himself of, including the kenotic heresy in which he jettisoned his divinity. It is common today to say he 'emptied' himself of the prerogatives of deity. However, as Gerald Hawthorne has pointed out,[17] no content is specified, and the intransitive form of the verb means to 'pour himself out' or to 'make himself nothing' (TNIV). This fits the parallelism with 'took on the form of a slave' and 'humbled himself' in the context. The way you determine the meaning of a term is to note its semantic range (the number of possible meanings that term could have in the first century) and then to allow the context in which it is embedded to guide in selecting the use that best fits. The technical term for this is 'semotaxis', which means the influence of the surrounding terms in a literary context on the meaning of any given term in it. The meaning of any utterance is the sum total of all the factors/terms in it and how they relate to each other. This is the same with a sentence in a paragraph and with a paragraph in the developing argument of a text.

Literary theory and the discovery of meaning

Meaning is the 'embodied intention' seen 'in a stable verbal structure' that is 'enacted' by the author in order to be shared with the readers.[18] There are two levels: the author's *intended* meaning that is singular in essence, and what the text 'means' to *us*, which is potentially multiple depending on its significance for us at a given time. However, this is highly controversial, and literary theory over the last century has moved further and further away from the possibility of discovering intended meaning in a discourse.

The challenge: the author and the reader

An author creates a text, and a reader interprets that text. The question is: Who generates the meaning of the created text – the author, the text or the reader? From Schleiermacher to Bultmann it was always assumed that meaning centred on the *author*. Literary criticism, however, began moving away from an author-centred approach at the turn of the twentieth century. The school of 'New Criticism' emerged in the 1930s with movement away from the

17. G. Hawthorne, *Philippians*, WBC 43 (Waco: Word, 1983), pp. 85–86.

18. K. J. Vanhoozer, *Is There a Meaning in This Text? The Bible, The Reader, and the Morality of Literary Knowledge* (Grand Rapids: Zondervan, 1998), pp. 252–253.

historical dimensions of the text to its form and texture. Then in the 1950s came Wellek and Warren's *Theory of Literature* and Wimsatt and Beardsley's 'The Intentional Fallacy', both arguing that authorial intention was no longer tenable, for the author's meaning was private and inaccessible to later readers. Rather, they argued, texts are autonomous once they are written and become the vehicle for public understandings.[19] This entered biblical studies with Hans-Georg Gadamer's *Truth and Method*, which took an aesthetic approach to interpretation, arguing that studying a text was not a historical act of discerning original meaning but a leap into the stream of tradition, a 'fusion of horizons' in which the reader begins a dialectic with the text and awakens meaning when the interpreter's pre-understanding interrogates the text and is in turn interrogated by the text. The textual world has detached itself from past considerations and is open to new relationships with present readers.[20]

A brief school of thought that flourished in the late 1960s and early 1970s was *structuralism,* a theory that arose in France with the waning of existentialism and believed that meaning takes place in the 'deep structure' world or unconscious systems that lay behind the structure of texts, namely those binary oppositions such a light/darkness, inside/outside, male/female. The interpreter studies the actantial movements in a text, those codes that underlie it in order to discover the mythopoetic message underneath it. However, the absence of a strong philosophical base and the vast overstatement regarding a closed system of signs, among other weaknesses, quickly led to its displacement by 'post-structuralism', the view that predominates in many circles to this day. Building on Saussure's notion that all terms are arbitrary signs, this movement states that the relationship between the signifier (the word) and the signified (the interpretation) is not closed but open and demands that the reader rather than the text complete its meaning. The text becomes a playground in which readers are free to play their own way and to provide their own rules for understanding. The result is 'polyvalence' or multiple meanings, a 'second-order system' that compels each reader to determine the thrust of the unstated signified (the meaning of the text) rather than the text/signifier itself.[21]

---

19. R. Wellek and A. Warren, *Theory of Literature* (New York: Harcourt, Brace & Wold, 1956); and W. K. Wimsatt and M. C. Beardsley, 'The Intentional Fallacy', in D. Newton-deMolina (ed.), *On Literary Intention* (Edinburgh: Edinburgh University Press, 1976), pp. 1–13.

20. H.-G. Gadamer, *Truth and Method* (New York: Seabury, 1976), pp. 353–357.

21. See S. Wittig, 'A Theory of Multiple Meanings', *Semeia* 9 (1977), pp. 75–103.

Two schools of thought complete this movement from author to ι. The leading voice of our day, Jacques Derrida, published his three mι works in one year, 1967 (*De La Grammatologie; L'Écriture et la différence;* and ι *Voix et le phenomena*), and gave his first address in America at Johns Hopkins University in 1966. Yet his impact was not felt until the 1980s. His is the ultimate expression of post-structuralist thought and his approach is called 'deconstruction'. Building on the nihilistic world view of Nietzsche, the radical scepticism of Freud and the ontology of language of the later Heidegger, Derrida wants to free philosophy from the restraints of Western metaphysical philosophy. He asserts that philosophy like all language deconstructs itself, because it consists of an endless chain of significations that decentres itself and is characterized by instability. Logic pretends to be rational but is actually metaphorical, and all language is rhetorical at the core. Since metaphor controls both the external sign system behind language and the internal meaning that results, the whole process of coming-to-understanding must be deconstructed. Derrida argues that speech is characterized by 'absence' and 'difference', and with a French play on words language both 'differs' (the opposition between signifier and signified) and 'defers' (meaning is 'deferred' by the endless play between text and reader). Thinking is writing on the mind and therefore autonomous from the start.[22] In short, since there is no external referentiality, since texts point to other texts (intertextuality) and words to other words (metaphoricity), the reader is free from the constraints of the Western demand for final meaning in a text. For Derrida, we have been liberated to construct our own readings, our own understandings.

If Derrida is the deep French philosopher, Stanley Fish is the American pragmatist, the major voice behind reader-response criticism, which posits not only the autonomy of the text but the phenomenological union between text and reader in the act of reading. Fish does not believe there is any epistemological choice between alternate understandings of a text but only an ontological union between reader and text. In his *Is There a Text in This Class?* Fish states that there is, but it is not the book on the table but rather the reader in the chair. The text has no prior existence before the act of reading; it disappears, and the meaning is 'created' in the mind of the reader. This occurs on the basis of the 'interpretative strategies' each reader forms from the interpretative communities (similar to Gadamer's 'traditions') of which they are a part. His thesis is, 'the form of the reader's experience, formal

---

22. J. Derrida, *Writing and Difference*, tr. A. Bass (Chicago: University of Chicago Press, 1978), pp. 29–30.

units, and the structure of intention are one, that they come into view simultaneously, and that therefore the questions of priority and independence do
not arise'.[23] It is the community that is pre-existent, not the text, and the
reader as part of that community produces meaning in the act of reading. In
the beginning there was the community! For instance, in the debate over pre-
destination in Romans 9 – 11, Derrida and Fish would say there is no final
meaning, and both answers are correct depending on whether your community is Reformed or Wesleyan-Arminian. In fact, there are many other possible interpretations, and any of the multiple possible meanings are equally
viable in the long run.

A mediating solution

There are many valid points in the movement away from text to reader as the
generating force in the creation of meaning. While authors create texts, it is
readers who interpret and come to understand them. Indeed, most of what
Derrida and Fish argue actually occurs in the average church, which becomes
the interpretative community for its members and pretty much determines
their understanding of Scripture. If we were honest, most of us would have
to say, 'How do I know? My pastor told me so,' rather than 'The Bible told
me so.' Vanhoozer speaks of the place of the 'Rule of Faith': 'It carries the
venerable weight of ancient tradition and appeals to postmodern sensibilities (the authority of interpretive communities, interpretation as a mode of
identity construction) besides.'[24] So for many (perhaps most) Christians, the
Bible is filtered largely through their church's teaching. There is no denying
the place of the reader and the community in the process of interpretation,
and these challenges have corrected an error in traditional hermeneutics.
Moreover, language is indeed metaphorical at the core. Every title of God in
the Bible is a metaphor, and every theological doctrine consists of metaphors
and models that are heuristic and must be continually refined.[25] However,
such radical scepticism is neither necessary nor helpful. It is interesting that
while Fish has so negative an attitude toward author and text, he has so
uncritical an attitude toward interpretative communities. Freeplay is one
thing, but the deterministic and binding authority of the community is quite

---

23. S. Fish, *Is There a Text in This Class? The Authority of Interpretive Communities*
    (Cambridge, Mass.: Harvard University Press, 1980), p. 177.
24. K. J. Vanhoozer, *First Theology: God, Scripture and Hermeneutics* (Downers Grove: IVP;
    Leicester: Apollos, 2002), p. 288.
25. See Osborne, *Hermeneutical Spiral*, pp. 387–394.

another. Where is the critical apparatus that enables (indeed requires) dialogue between communities?

Thiselton provides a fourfold critique of deconstructionism:[26] (1) While it is true that there is no fixed or final reading of a text, and that internal factors play a critical role in the reading of a text, this by no means demands a continual flux, nor does it mean that outside factors (e.g. other community understandings) play no part in interpretation. (2) The idea of 'an infinite chain of signs' is not demanded by semiotic theory, for *langue* (the system) is nothing more than potential until it is activated by *parole* (spoken language) 'which presupposes *human choice and judgment*' (italics his); Wittgenstein's 'public criteria of meaning' is the answer. (3) There is a 'speaking subject' in a text that communicates in a decipherable way, and interpretation does not need to swim in a sea of subjectivity but is part of public communication of meaning and asks for human judgment. (4) 'Textual play' in terms of texts as aesthetic objects like a concert or a painting does fit some kinds of texts (even some biblical ones) but hardly fits the majority of texts; such an approach constitutes literary hedonism, seeking play without licence.

In the light of this, we need to develop a theory of meaning based on literary theory. Let us consider three figures who develop the later Wittgenstein's theory of language.

First, J. L. Austin developed the three dimensions in which language (and literary theory) operates: the *locutionary* level, namely what a sentence means as a proposition; the *illocutionary* level, namely what the sentence accomplishes (assertion, question, command); and the *perlocutionary* level, namely what effect the sentence has on the reader.[27] Texts do not merely communicate meaning; they act and guide the readers in reacting. It is not the reader but the text that generates meaning.

Secondly, John Searle says that 'speaking a language is engaging in a (highly complex) rule-governed form of behavior'.[28] He develops three 'axioms' of reference to bridge from the utterance to its meaning: (1) *existence*, presupposing that the object referred to exists in the textual world and the rules of the language game; (2) *identity*, assuming the predication of the utterance is true of the object; (3) *identification*, assuming that the act of the utterance will provide

---

26. A. C. Thiselton, *New Horizons in Hermeneutics* (Grand Rapids: Zondervan, 1992), pp. 124–132.

27. J. L. Austin, *How to Do Things with Words* (Oxford: Clarendon, 1962), pp. 101–119.

28. J. Searle, *Speech Acts: An Essay in the Philosophy of Language* (New York: Cambridge University Press, 1969), p. 80.

both the conditions for understanding and 'excluders' that guide the reader in deciphering the referential meaning.[29]

Thirdly, Vanhoozer applies this to biblical literature and notes four areas of agreement between speech-act theologians: (1) Language is not just referential but is transformative, containing pragmatic as well as semantic aspects; (2) it is not indeterminate, so the author is a critical factor in coming-to-understanding; (3) action as well as representation are critical components of language, so there is both promise and covenant in the act of reading; (4) readers are not free to manipulate texts and read whatever they want into their meaning.[30] In other words, John 1:1 ('In the beginning was the word') asks us both to understand its meaning and to act on it.

An epistemological theory[31]

Yet we still need a theory that can guide us in the discovery of meaning in literary texts. Let me begin with the sociology of knowledge, which studies the effects of culture, societal values and world view on the attainment of knowledge. This calls for a 'critique of ideology', namely an awareness of the extent to which ideological factors control the process of communication. Every text is a product of a world view and attempts to control readers and draw them into that social world. Interpreters need to be aware of this on the part of both the text and themselves, then, in the words of Habermas, must free the text from 'systematically distorted communication' via a 'scenic understanding' that analyses the forces behind a particular language game in terms of competence and viability.[32] At first glance, this seems a challenge to our theory, but in reality it recognizes the viability of not only detecting the intended meaning of a text but also of discerning the ideological purposes of the text, that is, its illocutionary and perlocutionary purposes. This is indeed the case. When reading 1 Corinthians 1 – 4, we understand not only that Paul is challenging the secular sophistry and conflict within the Corinthian leadership but also that he is impelling us today to forgo our pride and commit ourselves to the scandal of the cross.

Let us bring into our discussion the role of interpretative communities in decision-making. Four factors combine to construct a theological belief

---

29. Ibid, pp. 42–56, 80.

30. K. J. Vanhoozer, *The Drama of Doctrine: A Canonical/Linguistic Approach to Christian Theology* (Louisville: Westminster John Knox, 2005), pp. 164–167.

31. Here I shall be drawing from Osborne, *Hermeneutical Spiral*, pp. 505–516.

32. J. Habermas, *Knowledge and Human Interests*, tr. J. J. Shapiro (Boston: Beacon, 1971), pp. 190–203.

system: *Scripture, tradition, community* and *experience*, with the latter three constituting our pre-understanding. Of these, the community is the determining factor, mediating the tradition we inherit and helping us cope with our experiences. The question is whether the paradigm community we belong to determines our understanding or merely guides it. Some take the former view, arguing that change in science and literature occur when a community of scholars with the same shared values come to consensus on a new paradigm.[33]

However, it is more and more realized that change occurs not with paradigm leaps but with micro changes of understanding and especially when competing paradigm communities engage in critical dialogue and learn from one another. In this Ian Barbour provides a helpful model for constructing theories: (1) all data may be value laden, but rival theories are not incommensurable; (2) paradigms do resist falsification, but observation still maintains some control over the process; (3) no final rules for paradigm shift exist, but there are independent criteria for assessment, and even metaphysical assumptions are open to change. Community dialogue and tradition or 'revelatory events' must be combined with critical reflection so that subjective features like pre-understanding and resistance to change can be influenced by objective features like data, critical evidence and reason.[34] Competing communities often do not dialogue, but they can, and that is a critical factor in coming to truth.

The issue is whether polyvalence is always the natural result of interpretation (since every community or reader will have a different understanding), or whether the original intention of the author in a text is in any sense a viable goal. This is a problem of distanciation, that is, the great gap between the original production of a text (especially the Bible, written from 2,000 to 3,500 years ago) and the modern reader. How can we ever understand what Isaiah or Paul wrote in a culture no longer accessible to us? Yet, while it is difficult, it is not an insurmountable obstacle. In the next section there will be a methodology for discerning the author's intended meaning. Here it is critical mainly to establish the viability of this enterprise. In contemporary dialogue we interact with the communities of the present, in ancient studies we do so with the communities of the past, that is, we consult commentaries, dictionaries and other study tools to establish the viable theories regarding the original meaning of the text and then critically examine the theories in terms of which best

---

33. For instance, T. S. Kuhn, *The Structure of Scientific Revolutions* (Chicago: University of Chicago Press, 1970).

34. I. Barbour, 'Paradigms in Science and Religion', in G. Gutting (ed.), *Paradigms and Revolutions* (Notre Dame: University of Notre Dame Press, 1980), pp. 75–95.

enumerates the whole context. G. B. Caird concludes that (1) words have the sense the writer intended them to have; (2) the author's intention determines the rules of the language game; and (3) a word has the referent the writer intended.[35] The main point is that the attempt to elucidate the original meaning is a viable goal.

It is important to realize that we do so on the basis of probability rather than certainty. It is the demand for certitude that fuels much of radical scepticism and the hermeneutics of suspicion that results. W. V. Quine states that the 'observation sentence' in knowledge theory seeks to be both 'subjectively observable' and 'generally adequate . . . to elicit assent'. This then is subjected to query and evidence leading to predication within 'a narrow spectrum of visible alternatives', which leads to revision of the theory. Then the process of 'refutation and correction' depends on the recognition of probability as the basis for decisions.[36] Philosophy since the 1950s has turned more and more to probability as the basis for decisions, and this has opened up many fruitful dialogues, not least the viability of seeking the intended meaning of a text.

The means by which we make interpretative decisions is critical realism. 'Realism' is the belief that there is something 'real' in the text to be ascertained, and the way it is elucidated is by 'critical' reflection. N. T. Wright separates this from both the 'naïve realism' of positivism (the belief that we can have definite objective knowledge) and the pessimism of phenomenalism (believing in the inaccessibility of knowledge) and says that critical understanding occurs when 'initial observation is challenged by critical reflection but can survive the challenge and speak truly of reality'. This occurs as observation leads to hypotheses, which are then refined by critical reflection that leads to verification/falsification.[37] There is a tentativeness in all interpretative decisions, but this does not mean that all such are equal and that one cannot demarcate which are more likely and which are not. Critical analysis of the data utilizing probability theory can enable the interpreter to ascertain the likely original meaning.

The simple fact is that the Bible claims to contain propositional truth. This does not mean that every part of the Bible is propositional, for much of the

---

35. G. B. Caird, *The Language and Imagery of the Bible* (London: Duckworth, 1980), pp. 37–61.

36. W. V. Quine, 'The Nature of Natural Knowledge', in S. Guttenplan (ed.), *Mind and Language* (Oxford: Clarendon, 1975), pp. 73, 81 (cf. pp. 67–81).

37. N. T. Wright, *The New Testament and the People of God* (Minneapolis: Fortress, 1992), p. 36 (cf. pp. 32–37).

Bible is narrative, and much of the rest is poetry, wisdom or apocalyptic. Still, since Scripture claims to be divine revelation, it obviously intends to communicate eternal truth to finite humankind. As a literary text, it is a communication event, and its authors demand to be understood, obviously expecting its readers to do just that. So at least in terms of its original audience, it claims to be knowable. Yet even figurative speech communicates itself as non-literal. In this light, let us consider metaphor. Theological statements by nature are highly metaphorical, as are the titles of God. 'Yahweh' is a covenant metaphor for the never-changing God who is always in an 'I–thou' relationship with his people.[38] Metaphors are not so much 'rule-governed' as 'rule-changing' parts of speech, tensive symbols that transform one's understanding of a thing. Yet they are not open-ended and necessarily polyvalent, devoid of referential content. Metaphors communicate indirectly by way of semantic opposition, that is, they state one thing in terms of another, such that the meaning is expanded through the interplay of ideas. Still, they communicate ideas and are accessible and verifiable when they are embedded in a context. Soskice develops a referential theory of metaphor in terms of the difference between *sense* (possible meanings) and *reference* (the actual meaning in a certain context). So as part of a whole speech act in an individual context, metaphors communicate and have truth value in a referential way.[39]

Hermeneutics and literary theory in the construction of meaning

We have established that it is viable to seek the author's intended meaning in a literary work, but it remains to establish practical guidelines for doing so to demonstrate not only its viability but its pragmatic possibility. The basic solution is to establish a trialogue between *author*, *text* and *reader*. The author has produced the text and embedded certain messages in the literary interplay of semantic forces in the text. Readers study the text and try to allow the intrinsic genre (Hirsch) and rules of the language game (Wittgenstein) in the text to guide them in the process of coming-to-understanding. 'The text then guides the reader by producing certain access points that point the reader to the proper language game for interpreting that particular illocutionary act. The reader thereby aligns him- or herself with the textual world and propositional content, thus coming to understand the intended meaning of the text.'[40]

---

38. See D. W. Baker, 'God, Names of', in T. D. Alexander and D. W. Baker (eds.), *Dictionary of the Old Testament: Pentateuch* (Downers Grove: IVP, 2003), pp. 362–364.

39. J. M. Soskice, *Metaphor and Religious Language* (Oxford: Clarendon, 1985), pp. 51–53.

40. Osborne, *Hermeneutical Spiral*, p. 516.

The first thing a student must do is come to grips with her pre-understanding, especially presuppositions and prejudices. Bultmann was correct: neutral exposition is impossible. At the same time, it is possible to bracket our a priori understandings and make certain the text has priority over them. In other words, we want to do exegesis aware of our background, training and theological preferences. My pre-understanding is a positive 'friend' in my interaction with the biblical text, for it allows me to understand and arrange the nuances of the text theologically, but if my pre-understanding becomes presupposition, then my system places a grid over the text and Stanley Fish is right: my interpretative community rather than the text determines its meaning. The key is to place my preferences consciously in front of the text rather than behind it, that is, to allow the text to create its own meaning and then to challenge, and if necessary correct, my theological system. I must not only address the text but allow the text to address me (the hermeneutical circle).

'Structural linguistics' refers to the fact that the sense of a term is dependent on its place in the structure of the sentence, the sentence draws meaning from its place in the paragraph and so on. Silva assigns 'a *determinative* function to context; that is, the context does not merely help us understand meaning; it virtually *makes* meaning' (italics his).[41] Without a structural context, words and phrases have only potential meaning. Consider 'the love of Christ' (*tē agapē Christou*). The thrust could be possessive (Christ's love) or descriptive (Christlike love) or source (love from Christ) or sphere (love in Christ) or epexegetical (Christ is love) or possessive (Christ loves us) or objective (we love Christ). Each is possible, and only the context can decide. For instance, in 2 Corinthians 5:14 ('Christ's love compels us' NIV) most translations make it possessive, but commentators take it as either objective ('our love for Christ', taken by a few) or subjective ('the love Christ showed') taken by most because the context centres on Christ's death as 'evidence of his self-sacrificial love'.[42]

Sawyer speaks of the 'linguistic environment' that draws meaning from stylistic concerns, that is, from the preferences of both different authors and different genres for particular types of expression (idioms, technical phrases, habitual ways of saying things).[43] For instance, John in his Gospel is well

---

41. M. Silva, *Biblical Words and Their Meaning: An Introduction to Biblical Semantics* (Grand Rapids: Zondervan, 1983), p. 139.

42. M. J. Harris, *The Second Epistle to the Corinthians*, NIGTC (Grand Rapids: Eerdmans, 2005), pp. 418–419.

43. J. F. A. Sawyer, *Semantics in Biblical Research: New Methods of Defining Hebrew Words for Salvation* (London: SCM, 1972), pp. 10–28.

known for using synonyms theologically: two words for 'know', two words for 'send', four words for 'see'. Therefore in John 21:15–17 (ESV), when Jesus says, 'Simon, son of John, do you love (*agapaō*) me', and Peter responds, 'Yes, Lord; you know that I love (*phileō*) you', there are not two different meanings for the terms 'love', as if Jesus were asking for divine love and Peter was giving him human affection. Rather, the two terms are synonyms (in fact there are four word pairs in those three verses: two words for 'love', two for 'know', two for 'tend', and two for 'sheep'). Jesus is not trying to upgrade the depth of Peter's love. Rather, Jesus is giving him his apostolic marching orders! There are two reasons for the threefold repetition: (1) Peter is being reinstated after his three-fold denial, and, more importantly (2) the three commands to 'tend my flock' make it the ultimate pastoral responsibility of all those in mission. The context of John 21 is mission, and saying something three times makes it a superlative emphasis (cf. 'holy, holy, holy' in Isa. 6:3; Rev. 4:8). This passage is about the pastoral mission of the disciples (and us), and the message is, 'If we love Christ, we must feed his sheep.'

While historical backgrounds are not normally discussed as part of literary theory, a word must be said about the importance of background analysis for understanding ancient literary texts. It is impossible to interpret any past text without uncovering its ancient cultural and linguistic heritage. Postmodernists, though, do so because of their separation of the real from the implied author. They commonly say, 'The text contains all the meaning there is,' and, like Gadamer, believe that all interpretation centres on the text as a present entity with its own world. Yet this is a mistake. The author shared certain information with his original readers, and that is discernible in the text.

> The implied author is the conscious representation of the real author in the text. As such, it provides an access point to the historicality of the text and its message, anchoring interpretation in the ancient world. The implied reader was the focus of the conscious direction of the text and as such provides the access point to the fusion of horizons. The original author had a certain audience in mind, and the text addresses itself to these implied readers.[44]

Background studies trace the shared assumptions between the original author and readers in their culture and times. The literary text points behind itself to what could be called one aspect of the 'deep structure' behind the text (along with the biblical theology also utilized by the author). Moreover, such

---

44. Osborne, *Hermeneutical Spiral*, p. 519.

sociological description is not as elusive as we think. We know just as much about the sociological background of the first century as we know about the grammar and semantics of Koine Greek.[45] We can use that information with as much precision as we do our knowledge of grammar and semantics.

Moreover most of the recent major commentaries on various biblical books utilize such information well, so the average Bible student has access to deep information. Our knowledge in these areas has at least tripled since the 1950s, so we are able to speak with ever greater precision in these areas. For example, people for centuries puzzled over the letter to Laodicea when Jesus tells that church, 'I know your deeds, that you are neither cold nor hot. I wish you were either one or the other! So, because you are lukewarm – neither hot nor cold – I am about to spit you out of my mouth' (Rev. 3:15–16 TNIV). Readers always wondered why Jesus prefers Christians to be cold spiritually than lukewarm. We now realize that he is likening their church to their water supply. Laodicea was perfectly situated at the apex of two trade routes for making money, but the town had no source of water. They had to pipe it in from several miles way, and it arrived lukewarm and so mineral-laden that to drink it was to vomit. Yet 6 miles north lay Hierapolis, famed for its hot mineral springs, and 10 miles to the east lay Colosse, well known for its cold, pure drinking water.[46] So Jesus is in effect saying, 'I wish you were spiritually healing like the hot springs of Hierapolis and spiritually refreshing like the cold pure water of Colosse. But you're neither. Instead, you are just like your water, and you make me sick!'

Finally, it is absolutely critical to listen and learn from the competing schools of thought. So long as we interpret texts entirely within our own paradigm communities (e.g. Calvinistic or Lutheran exegesis, or dispensational, charismatic or Anabaptist thought), we are proving Fish and Derrida correct. I can only be lifted out of my reading strategy when I allow myself to be challenged by other competing schools. This forces me to re-examine the text anew and to consider other possible interpretations, thereby allowing me to step outside my pre-understanding and give the text priority over the reading community influencing

---

45. See e.g. C. A. Evans and S. E. Porter, *Dictionary of New Testament Background* (Downers Grove: IVP, 2000). IVP is planning to publish a similar volume on Old Testament backgrounds in the near future.

46. See C. J. Hemer, *The Letters to the Seven Churches of Asia in their Local Setting*, JSNTSup 11 (Sheffield: JSOT Press, 1986), pp. 187–191. He shows that Jesus in all the letters addresses the seven churches using imagery drawn from the city of which they are a part.

my interpretation. I can as a result be more honest in my conclusions. It must be admitted that this too rarely happens. Let me give an example. I am an Arminian teaching at a school that is primarily Calvinistic; through the years I believe I have learned a great deal from my colleagues and refined my position a great deal. I recently contributed to a volume on the warning passages of Hebrews, one of two Arminians along with two Calvinists.[47] As I was exegeting the passages, my whole purpose was to make a case for the Arminian position and both to present my paper and respond to the other papers. How open could I be to the other positions? My basic approach was that of D. A. Carson's, a 'functional non-negotiable';[48] that is, I sought to learn from the other papers and be open to their evidence and positions, but after my years of study was fairly convinced of my position. Still, I tried to remain open and willing to change. I believe that enabled me to work with the text from a fresh perspective and move closer to the author's intended meaning.

A test case: narrative theory

Narrative theory lies at the heart of 'literary criticism'. So this is the perfect model for demonstrating the effect of literary theory on biblical interpretation. Literary criticism began in the early 1980s with the work of Robert Alter and quickly eclipsed redaction criticism as the major approach to biblical narrative.[49] Its major premises are the centrality of the final form of the text (over reconstructed 'early' forms) and the view of biblical story as 'art' and 'poetry'. It centres on the 'fictive' element in narrative, that is, the presence of plot, dialogue, point of view and characterization.

Introduction: the character of biblical narrative
At the outset biblical narrative consists of the Pentateuch and historical books of the OT, the Gospels and Acts in the NT. Also, there are narrative components in several others, like Job and Daniel, Philemon and Revelation. Each book provides its own unique perspective on the events

---

47. H. W. Bateman (ed.), *Four Views on the Warning Passages of Hebrews* (Grand Rapids: Kregel, 2007).

48. D. A. Carson, 'A Sketch of the Factors Determining Current Hermeneutical Debate in Cross-Cultural Contexts', in D. A. Carson (ed.), *Biblical Interpretation and the Church* (Nashville: Nelson, 1984), pp. 12–15.

49. R. Alter, *The Art of Biblical Narrative* (New York: Basic, 1981).

it chronicles. This is best exemplified by the Synoptic Gospels or
Samuel/Kings–Chronicles. They tell pretty much the same stories but from
widely different vantage points with different details in the same stories. They
are not meant to be thrown together into a so-called Life of Christ but are
intended to be studied as individual works with a divinely inspired perspective on the life and impact of Jesus. In these works, there is a combination of
history and theology, that is, they tell what happened but make redactional
(editorial) choices in terms of what to omit and what to include in order to
bring out the theological import of the events. This is best demonstrated in
the differences between Samuel–Kings and Chronicles or in the four Gospels
when they tell the same story but from different theological perspectives.
This will be explored further later.

The primary issue here is how we can have both history and theology in biblical narrative. Since Bultmann (who followed Martin Kähler) and his followers, many have said that where one has the 'historic biblical Christ' one cannot
have 'the historical Jesus'. The former is the product of the early church and
by definition is not history. A great disjunction has been placed between
history and theology. Since stories like the temptation narrative or the resurrection contain theological assertions they must be divorced from history.
However, is such a radical dichotomy valid? J. D. G. Dunn argues that the above
is a fundamental misunderstanding of Kähler's point. 'The idea that we can see
through the faith perspective of the NT writings to a Jesus who did *not* inspire
faith or who inspired faith in a different way is an illusion. There is no such
Jesus.'[50] Wright adds, 'There is no reason in principle why the question, what
precisely happened at Easter, cannot be raised by any historian of any persuasion.'[51] Since the 1970s the trend has been away from such dogmatic declarations. Yet the simple fact is that one cannot study history or any other aspect
of the world we live in with complete objectivity. History must be interpreted,
and interaction with the ancient world demands involvement in the implications of those events. The temptation story or the resurrection of Jesus of
Nazareth in this sense are no different than the death of Julius Caesar. We are
asking what event lay behind the interpretative details, and that is a historical
question.

The 'myth' that theology (*Geschichte*) must be separated from history
(*Historie*) began to be exploded with I. Howard Marshall's *Luke: Historian and*

---

50. J. D. G. Dunn, *Jesus Remembered* (Grand Rapids: Eerdmans, 2003), pp. 126–127 (his
    emphasis).

51. N. T. Wright, *The Resurrection of the Son of God* (Minneapolis: Fortress, 2003), p. 21.

Theologian in 1970, and that was followed in subsequent years by Martin, Smalley and France.[52] All argued that the evangelists were theologians who wrote history and tried to be faithful to the original events even while interpreting them. Then, in the series *Gospel Perspectives* from 1980 to 1986, Richard Bauckham wrote that the evangelist's 'traditions, however "midrashic" his procedure may be, could be historical in origin'.[53] There is simply no reason for saying that theological interpretation must obviate historical viability. The task of the historian is to make exactly that type of decision. As Meir Sternberg has said, 'From the premise that we cannot become people of the past, it does not follow that we cannot approximate to this state by imagination and training – just as we learn the rules of any other cultural game – still less that we must not or do not make the effort.'[54]

We are living in an age of far greater openness to historical Jesus studies. With the rise of the third quest in the 1980s and its proof for a Jewish Jesus, the radical scepticism of the last century has been replaced by both a narrative theology and a search for the plausible Jesus who fits his times. Theology is now seen as not only viable as a vehicle for historical study but as an actual aid in the enterprise. It is no longer isolated snippets of material here and there that are regarded as historical. The form-critical assumptions of independent transcription of individual traditions has given way to a narrative approach. Now narrative is seen as the vehicle and goal of historical research (see below). History comes to us as story, and since the 1980s the studies have centred on the Jesus story, for example Jesus the social revolutionary of Horsley, the counter-cultural sage of Crossan, the marginal Jew of Meier, the return from exile of Wright. This is seen in the very meaning of 'Gospel', for the verb form is *euangelizomai*, 'preach', showing that the Gospels are 'theological history', or 'history with a message'.

---

52. I. H. Marshall, *Luke: Historian and Theologian* (Grand Rapids: Zondervan, 1970); R. Martin, *Mark: Evangelist and Theologian* (Exeter: Paternoster, 1972); S. Smalley, *John: Evangelist and Interpreter* (London: Paternoster, 1978); R. T. France, *Matthew: Evangelist and Teacher* (London: Paternoster, 1989).

53. R. Bauckham, 'The *Liber Antiquitatum Biblicarum* of Pseudo-Philo and the Gospels as "Midrash"'', in R. T. France and D. Wenham (eds.), *Gospel Perspectives III: Studies in Midrash and Historiography* (Sheffield: JSOT Press, 1983), p. 67.

54. M. Sternberg, *The Poetics of Biblical Narrative: Ideological Literature and the Drama of Reading* (Bloomington: Indiana University Press, 1985), p. 10. For more on this issue, see G. R. Osborne, 'History and Theology in the Synoptic Gospels', *TrinJ* NS 24 (2003), pp. 5–22.

Biblical narrative as literature: history or fiction

Another misconception on the part of many is that biblical narrative by definition must be fictive, a view especially many literary critics hold. Robert Alter spoke for many when he said, 'prose fiction is the best general rubric for describing biblical narrative'.[55] V. P. Long traces this bias to a view of literature as linked with poetry and fiction, and a view of history in a positivistic way as part of the natural sciences. Both aspects are wrong.[56] Wright even claims that first-century people 'understood more about the real nature of history, that is, about the complex interaction of "event" and "meaning", than has been grasped by the ardent proponents of "scientific history" in comparatively recent times'.[57] It is the task of historical research to ascertain the historical facts behind the interpreted story, but the point here is that this is a viable enterprise.

Moreover, it is hermeneutically possible to differentiate historical from fictive writing. Clarence Walhout says the difference-maker is 'authorial stance', that is, the fictive stance of the novelist and the assertive stance of the historian, as 'the historian claims – asserts – that the projected world (the story) of the text together with the authorial point of view counts as a story and an interpretation of events as they actually occurred'.[58] In other words, history and theology can be determined and demarcated. Anthony Thiselton speaks of 'extratextual factors', especially the illocutionary stance of the author that either creates an imaginary world or ties the reader to the real world implied in the text.[59] Walhout provides three criteria for doing so: (1) The world behind the text is factually accurate, presenting events it claims actually occurred; (2) the author's 'techniques of presentation', for example phrasing, genealogies and so on fit the state of affairs at that time; (3) there is an atmosphere of history (factually conceived) behind the details.[60] In short, historical narrative

---

55. Alter, *Art of Biblical Narrative*, pp. 23–24.

56. V. P. Long, *The Art of Biblical History* (Grand Rapids: Zondervan, 1994), pp. 151–152.

57. N. T. Wright, *The New Testament and the People of God* (Minneapolis: Fortress, 1992), p. 122.

58. C. Walhout, 'Texts and Actions', in R. Lundin, A. C. Thiselton and C. Walhout, *The Responsibility of Hermeneutics* (Grand Rapids: Eerdmans, 1985), p. 69. John Searle says, 'roughly speaking, whether or not a work is literature is for the readers to decide, whether or not it is fiction is for the author to decide' (J. Searle, 'The Logical Status of Fictional Discourse', in *Expression and Meaning: Studies in the Theory of Speech Acts* [Cambridge: Cambridge University Press, 1979], p. 59).

59. Thiselton, *New Horizons*, pp. 372–373, building on Searle.

60. Walhout, 'Texts', pp. 72–73.

will 'tell it like it was' and interpret events written as they happened, while fiction will build an imaginary world, often with background details that fit the period, but with a quite different stance. In fact, one can disagree with the interpretative stance of the historian and yet recognize the historical facts behind the narration. While there is theological assertion in the biblical narratives, that does not obviate their basic historical stance.

Biblical narratives contain both narrative and historical elements. As narrative, they exemplify real/implied author and reader, point of view, story time, plot, characterization and dialogue. As history, they attempt to trace what actually happened. A good definition will help:

> 'Narrative history' involves an attempt to express through language . . . the meaning . . . – that is, a particular understanding/explanation . . . – of the relationship of a selected sequence of actual events from the past . . . and to convince others through various means, including the theological force and aesthetic appeal of the rendering . . . , that the sequence under review has meaning and that this meaning has been rightly perceived.[61]

The modern reader accomplishes this by comparing the historical story to external data on the event in history and thereby evaluating the event portrayed in terms of its contribution to historical knowledge. By ascertaining the implicit commentary and point of view, one can see how the author is not only telling what happened but also developing the significance and moral content of the story. 'It is clear that in the historical narratives of the Scriptures, the authors believed they were retelling the historical past of Israel and the early church so as to solidify the self-conscious identity of the people in their present time. In other words, there was a historical purpose throughout.'[62] Again, we must establish a trialogue in the hermeneutical enterprise between an *author* who constructs a story and adds interpretation, a *text* that embeds this story conceived by the author, and a *reader* who attempts to enter the world of the story and reconstruct both the historical nucleus and the original theological interpretation (see above). This is accomplished by allowing the illocutionary force of the text to communicate its meaning. The story has a performative function and draws the reader into its narrative world, thereby communicating the intended meaning, that is, either an imaginary fictive world

---

61. I. Provan, V. P. Long and T. Longman III, *A Biblical History of Israel* (Louisville: Westminster John Knox, 2003), p. 84.

62. G. R. Osborne, 'Historical Narrative and Truth in the Bible', *JETS* 48 (2005), p. 684.

or a reconstructed historical world. The historical narrative in Scripture (and the early church) claims to announce events that actually happened (Luke 1:1–4; John 19:35; 21:24; 1 Cor. 15:6; 2 Pet. 1:16–18), and these claims should be taken seriously.

The components of biblical narrative

Certain aspects of narrative must be considered in any literary reading. These have long been chronicled by scholars.[63] The first is *point of view*, which refers to the perspective taken by the author, the 'shape' given to the story, and the intended effect on the readers. There are several kinds of point of view:[64]

- 'psychological', as in the Samson story in which his carnal, self-centred nature is featured
- 'ideological', as in the contrast between the leaders of Israel (blind) and the man given sight (then finding spiritual insight) in John 9
- 'spatial', as in the travel narrative of Luke 9 – 19 (and the Emmaus story in Luke 24)
- 'temporal', when the story is related in the present tense and the reader is drawn into it (as in the call of Jeremiah, Jer. 1:4–9)
- 'phraseological', when dialogue is featured, as in the conversation between Haman, his wife and friends in Esther 5:12–14

A second feature is *narrative or story time*. This is not chronological, because it relates to the order of events in the developing work as a whole rather than the historical progression of them. This is important because the Gospels do not try to be chronological. A good example is the order of events in Mark 1:21–45 and the fact that Matthew reverses the healing of Peter's mother-in-law (Mark 1:29–34 // Matt. 8:14–17) and the healing of the leper (Mark 1:40–45 // Matt. 8:2–4). A study of a synopsis will show many similar examples. In keeping with ancient historiography, the Gospels were not concerned with the chronological order of events but rather wished to show the meaning and impact of Jesus' life. So they organized the events in such a way as to provide a theological portrait of Jesus' life and impact. More on this will be said later.

---

63. For instance, S. Chatman, *Story and Discourse: Narrative Structure in Fiction and Film* (Ithaca: Cornell University Press, 1978), p. 6. See also Osborne, *Hermeneutical Spiral*, pp. 203–212.

64. Osborne, *Hermeneutical Spiral*, pp. 151–158. See also A. Culpepper, *The Anatomy of the Fourth Gospel: A Study in Literary Design* (Philadelphia: Fortress, 1983), pp. 20–34.

Thirdly, there is *plot development*. This looks at the sequence of events in terms of conflict and climax. In all biblical stories there is the fight between good and evil, the macro narrative in which God is at work bringing rebellious humanity back to himself and overcoming sin with salvation. Below we shall see how plot functions at both the macro (the large unit) and the micro (the individual story) levels. It is in the plot that a great deal of theology arises. For instance, in John 5 – 10 there are two primary themes, the major aspect, the conflict between Jesus and the Jewish people centring on their rejection of their Messiah; and the minor aspect, Jesus fulfilling the Jewish feasts (the Sabbath in ch. 5, the Passover in ch. 6, Tabernacles in chs. 7–9, and the Feast of Dedication in ch. 10).

Fourthly, there is *characterization and dialogue*. The success of any story depends somewhat on whether the characters in it are interesting and meaningful. The Bible is remarkably forthright about the foibles of its characters: Samson's carnality, David's lust, Elijah's cowardice in running from Jezebel just after his great victory on Mount Carmel, the disciples' self-centredness. Often there is a great contrast between the immutability and holiness of God and the finiteness of his people, between Christ's victory on the road to Jerusalem alongside the disciples' frequent failures (e.g. Mark's placing of their misunderstanding and desire for greatness directly after each passion prediction [8:31–34; 9:30–35; 10:32–45]).

Fifthly, there is the *implied reader*.[65] Every book is written with a specific audience in mind, and the Gospels are no exception. There is some debate on this, for it has been common to believe that each Gospel was written for the *Sitz im Leben Kirche* (the 'situation in the life' of a few specific 'churches'), but Bauckham has shown that the Gospels had the church as a whole in mind.[66] Still, we, the 'real reader', should study what the author was asking the original readers to do with the story and align ourselves with that illocutionary intention. This is called 'reader identification' and guides us to the proper contextualization or application of biblical narrative for today. As Culpepper says, 'As the reader adopts the perspectives thrust on him or her by the text, experiences

---

65. R. Fowler, 'Who Is the "Reader" in Reader Response Criticism', *Semeia* 31 (1985), pp. 5–23, prefers to call this 'the ideal reader', for he believes this figure is created in the mind of the real reader, but, as stated above, I would argue that the implied reader is created by the author in the text and so prefer to call this 'the implied reader'.

66. R. Bauckham, 'For Whom Were Gospels Written?', in R. Bauckham (ed.), *The Gospel for All Christians* (Grand Rapids: Eerdmans, 1998), pp. 9–48.

it sequentially, has expectations frustrated or modified, relates one part of the text to another, and imagines and works out all the text leaves for the reader to do, its meaning is gradually actualized.'[67] Exegesis allows us to get at the locutionary or propositional aspect of the text, and the implied reader allows us to get at the perlocutionary or commissive aspect of the narrative.

Let us consider the interesting parable of the friend at midnight (Luke 11:5–8) as an example. A villager has an unexpected guest arrive at midnight (due to the extensive heat, travel was often at night) but has no food left (bread made without yeast did not last long, and a 'loaf' was usually enough just for one person). So he goes next door to borrow food. Middle Eastern laws of hospitality meant that the whole village was responsible to care for visitors. Still, the neighbour was asleep with his children; the average home was a single room, and the family slept together. To get up and get food would wake the children and ruin the night, so he was reluctant to get the bread. The thrust of the parable is dependent on one Greek word in the last verse (*anaideia*), which the TNIV and NLT take as 'shameless boldness': 'because of his (the knocker's) boldness'. If so, the implied reader is called to persistent prayer, preparing for verse 9 ('keep on asking/seeking/knocking' NLT). However, the normal meaning of the word is 'avoidance of shame', and if that is the meaning here, we would translate, 'because of his (the neighbour's) desire to avoid shame', and the implied reader is asked to reflect on the character of God as stated in the Lord's Prayer in verse 2, 'May your name be kept sacred.' If the former, the parable looks forward to the persistent prayer of verse 9; if the latter, it looks back on the character of God in verse 2. Due to the prevalence of the 'avoidance of shame' understanding of this noun in Koine Greek,[68] I believe the latter is the better understanding, so my 'reader identification' is to realize that the very name of God is at stake in his answering my prayers.

In this final section we shall centre on the four Gospels as a prime example of biblical narrative. Two preliminary issues should be discussed at the outset. (1) Source criticism has found a huge consensus over the last century in favour of Markan priority, that is, that Mark was the first Gospel written and that Matthew and Luke used Mark as well as Q (a source [either oral or written] of

---

67. Culpepper, *Anatomy*, p. 209. He does not give 'authorial intention' the same emphasis I do, but this description is still apt.

68. See A. F. Johnson, 'Assurance for Man: The Fallacy of Translating *Anaideia* by "Persistence" in Luke 11:5–8', *JETS* 22 (1979), pp. 123–131. Recent commentaries by John Nolland and Joel Green have also taken this approach.

Jesus' quotations that are common to Matthew and Luke). John is independent from the Synoptics. (2) Form criticism recognizes that the Gospels contain several subgenres (parables, miracle stories, poetry, pronouncement stories, chreia, wisdom sayings, apocalyptic utterances) that need to be considered when interpreting the complex interlocking grid of Gospel pericopae. Each has its own peculiar set of hermeneutical principles that must be considered.

Study the plot at the macro level

Each Gospel has its own unique metanarrative and plot development. One of the difficult tasks in any serious study is to determine the major and minor points of the plot, ascertain the structural development and decide on the plot of the major sections. The difficulty is shown by the fact that if you consult ten commentaries, you will on average discover six to seven different structures between them. So in the end you must do the work yourself and see which outline fits best. The most helpful tool for this is text-linguistics, which is part of discourse analysis (see above). By considering introductory particles, changes of verbal aspect or mood, and shifts of focus we try to demarcate the shifts of emphasis. Then we look at the major section as a whole and map these changes into a literary structure, tracing the plot of the whole.

Let me use Mark 6:30 – 9:9 as an example. There are two interlocking structures in this passage. First, there is the central unit, 6:30 – 8:21, with the key being the two feeding miracles (6:30–44; 8:1–10). These both introduce sections on discipleship failure, producing an A–B–A pattern of Failure (6:30 – 7:23) > Faith (7:24–37) < Failure (8:1–21). The two feeding miracles exemplify the message 'God will provide', and, after both, the disciples exemplify the failure to appropriate that truth but instead have 'hardened hearts' (7:52; 8:17). Also, the hardened disciples are like the Jewish leaders ('hardened' in 3:5), who also fail in 7:1–23, 8:11–13.

Throughout Mark, faith is shown by what are called the 'little people' (characters who appear only once),[69] who show the way to true discipleship by depending entirely on Christ. Here these are the Syro-Phoenician woman and the deaf mute in 7:24–37; they surrender themselves entirely to Jesus, while the disciples centre only on themselves. The second structure in the passage revolves around the healing of the blind man in 8:22–26 (only in Mark).

First, we notice that in Jesus' challenge to the disciples in 8:18 he accuses them of being blind and deaf; yet surrounding that passage Jesus heals a deaf

---

69. See D. Rhoads and D. Michie, *Mark As Story: An Introduction to the Narrative of a Gospel* (Philadelphia: Fortress, 1982).

man (7:31–37) and a blind man (8:22–26), showing that if he can heal the physically blind and deaf, he can heal the spiritually blind and deaf (the disciples). Secondly, we also notice that the healing of the blind man is a two-stage miracle, and this is programmatically worked out in the ensuing section, where he heals the disciples' misunderstanding in two stages, first in Peter's confession at Caesarea Philippi, where Peter sees Jesus in a blurred fashion (8:27–33 // 8:24), and then in the transfiguration, when the inner circle of disciples see Jesus clearly (9:1–9 // 8:25).

Study the plot at the micro level

Here we do the same type of structural analysis, but of the individual story. The same text-linguistic principles are used but in the smaller passage. We are looking for the primary sections where the focus changes to a new unit and then are determining the plot of the individual story. An excellent example here would be John 20, the first of two chapters John uses to tell the resurrection narrative.[70] This chapter is a great example for inductive Bible study. It breaks up neatly into four stories, *the race to the tomb* (20:1–10), *Mary Magdalene* (20:11–18), *the Eleven* (20:19–23) and *Thomas* (20:24–29). Moreover, each story has the same subplot: (1) in each the faith gets lower (the beloved disciple's great faith, Mary's sorrow, the disciple's fear, Thomas' cynical doubt). (2) In each case Jesus meets their need in ever-increasing ways (John needs no help; Mary needs the voice of the Good Shepherd; the disciples need to see his wounds; Thomas needs to touch them). (3) The results get greater in each instance (John does nothing with his faith in v. 10; Mary is made the first herald of the resurrection tidings; the disciples are given the incredible mission mandate in vv. 21–23; Thomas is the first to recognize the deity of Christ in v. 28). The basic plot or proposition is powerful: no matter how low our faith, Jesus will meet our need right where it is, turn our life around, and make of us something greater than we ever thought we could be!

Study the redactional (editorial) changes

Redaction criticism, which developed in the 1960s and 1970s, centres on the way the Gospels used their sources. By noting the changes between Matthew, Mark and Luke, we can see more clearly how they organized their individual works and the theological intentions they had in doing so. Of course, the the-

---

70. See G. R. Osborne, *John*, Cornerstone Commentaries (Carol Stream, Ill.: Tyndale House, 2007), where I argue first that ch. 21 was originally part of John and then develop the structure of ch. 20.

ology flows out of the whole of the literary passage, but the changes guide us in seeing how they structured their material. Robert Stein suggests looking at the seams between episodes, insertions, arrangement and modification of material, introductions, vocabulary, Christological titles, selection or omission of material, and conclusions.[71] The student studies what the author selected for his rendition of the story, how he organized it, what context he placed it in, and what the theological implications are. For the example of this, let us consider the walking-on-water miracle in Mark 6:45–52 and Matthew 14:22–33.

Both follow the feeding of the five thousand. As stated above, the feeding miracle demonstrated that 'God will provide' for his people, yet when the disciples were sent across the lake and the storm arose, they forgot all about that and feared for their lives. In Mark 6:48 (only in Mark) we are told that Jesus 'intended to pass them by', which demonstrates that Christ is Lord of the water, that is, as Yahweh passed by at Sinai (Exod. 33:18ff.) and Mount Horeb (1 Kgs 19:11ff.), so Jesus does likewise.[72] His purpose is to assure them that God is with them and will care for them. Yet they miss the signal entirely, look at Jesus walking on the water and think he is a ghost. They are probably thinking, *What he is represents what we are going to be in another minute – ghosts!* Mark stops the story there and deliberately (most likely) draws his conclusion: the disciples failed because 'they had not understood about the loaves; their hearts were hardened' (v. 52 TNIV).

Matthew follows Mark to that point and denotes their failure but goes on. After the episode of Peter walking on the water and failing, the disciples then conclude, 'Truly you are the Son of God' (Matt. 14:32 TNIV). There could not be a greater polarity than the conclusions of Mark and Matthew, from hardened hearts to a Christological affirmation greater than the disciples ever do in Mark (they never get beyond 'Messiah')! Yet the conclusions do not contradict one another, for Matthew recognizes the failure but passes on to the later victory. The difference is in their theological purposes. Mark, for the rest of his Gospel, centres on their repeated failures (true discipleship is seen in 'the little people'; see above), while Matthew recognizes failure but wants to show that the presence of Jesus makes the difference and allows the disciples to find victory. This is seen also after the feeding of the four thousand in both Gospels; Mark ends with 'Do you still not understand?' (8:21 TNIV), while Matthew with 'Then they understood' (16:12 TNIV). This is in keeping with the

---

71. R. Stein, 'Interpreting the Synoptic Gospels', in Black and Dockery, *Interpreting the New Testament*, pp. 349–351.

72. J. Marcus, *Mark 1–8*, AB (New York: Doubleday, 2000), p. 426.

discipleship themes in their respective Gospels, as Mark centres on their failure
while Matthew centres on their growing understanding.[73]

Study the characters and dialogue

As shown above, characterization is essential to all biblical narrative. As we
see the interaction between the characters and between the characters and
God/Jesus, the themes come to the fore. In all four Gospels, the basic story
centres on the impact between Jesus and four groups (disciples, crowds,
leaders, demons) in a descending order of growing opposition to Jesus. Let me
give two examples of this.

The first is the cosmic encounter with the demon-possessed man at the synagogue in Capernaum in Mark 1:23–28. That this is the first episode in Jesus'
ministry in Mark is telling, for it establishes a tone. The dialogue with Jesus and
the demon is critical. While some think the demon's 'What is it to us and to
you (lit.) . . . I know who you are, the Holy One of God' is just supernatural
knowledge of Jesus on the part of the demon, it is more likely that this is spiritual warfare. Marcus says that in ancient magical texts a magician says 'I know
you' to a god in order to gain control over it.[74] Jesus' 'Be silent' then forces the
submission of the demonic realm to himself. The dialogue shows that spiritual warfare is taking place, and the exorcism is a 'binding of Satan' (cf. 3:27).

Secondly, let us examine Jesus and the Samaritan woman in John 4. First,
we are told that Jesus 'had' (dei, divine necessity, v. 4) to go there, and so his
whole purpose was to confront the woman with the kingdom news. Then he
took the initiative, asking her for water, shocking her since she was a woman
and also because she was a Samaritan; Jesus would have been rendered unclean
by such a thing. His speech is fraught with ambiguity and double meaning, both
Johannine traits. Jesus offers her 'living water' (vv. 10, 13–14), referring both to
the bubbling spring in the well and the life-giving water of God (here it refers
to salvation and the Holy Spirit, the thrust of the water symbol in 3:5; 7:37–
39). Throughout Jesus is speaking heavenly truths, while she understands him
on the earthly plane, like Nicodemus in chapter 3. He is confronting her (the
key Johannine theme, namely the encounter of every person with the message
of salvation; cf. 1:4, 7, 9) at ever deeper levels, beginning with the giving of
water and her Samaritan heritage and then moving on to her personal situation

---

73. For Matthew's discipleship theme, see J. K. Brown, *The Disciples in Narrative
    Perspective: The Portrayal and Function of the Matthean Disciples*, AcBib 9 (Boston: Brill,
    2002).

74. Marcus, *Mark 1–8*, p. 193.

(vv. 15–19) to the very worship of God (vv. 20–24) and finally to the messianic nature and ministry of Jesus himself (vv. 25–26). Her conversion is never described (as is true of the disciples in ch. 1 and Nicodemus in ch. 3), another literary trait (called a 'gap') used to draw the reader into the world of the story.[75] But her witness ('Could this be the Messiah?', v. 29) leads to the conversion of many in the village (v. 39). In John dialogue and characterization are raised to a high art.

Study the implied reader and perform reader identification

The significance of narrative texts for us cannot be understood until we have studied how the authors intended to draw their original readers into the story (the illocutionary aspect), and what they wanted them to do with it (the perlocutionary aspect). We then consciously align ourselves with that original message and ascertain what the parallel situation is with that today, in other words, 'If certain biblical authors were here in my congregation, what issues would they address in their text?' (reader identification). To illustrate this, let us consider the temptation narrative (Matt. 4:1–11 // Luke 4:1–13). This used to be a sermon I had my students write in my Gospels course, until I realized hardly any of them got it right. Now I use it as my example in class. They made two mistakes: first, they had always heard this taught as a discipleship passage, that is, if we memorize Scripture we can defeat the devil any time. Secondly, they neglected to study seriously the passages Jesus quoted against the devil. Let us take these one at a time.

First, if we look at this passage in context, it is the final preparatory event in Jesus' ministry (after his baptism), and the major theme is Jesus as Son of God. Luke 4 demonstrates this best; Jesus is proclaimed God's 'beloved Son' at his baptism (3:23) and then Luke inserts the genealogy here, running in opposite order to the genealogy in Matthew and going all the way to Adam, who is called finally 'the son of God' (3:38), thereby preparing for the temptations, with the first being, 'If (a condition of fact meaning virtually "since") you are the Son of God' (4:3). Satan knows Jesus is Son of God and tempts him to selfishly prove it to the world.

Secondly, all three of Jesus' quotes stem from Deuteronomy 6 – 8, and each time the quote occurs at that place in Deuteronomy where Israel failed in the very test Jesus is enduring. In other words, Jesus is saying to Satan, 'I know what you are doing; it worked with Israel, but it will not work with me.' So the thrust of the temptation is quite clear: it is Christology, not discipleship. Jesus

---

75. See Sternberg, *Biblical Narrative*, pp. 265–270.

begins his ministry by taking on Satan in open combat and defeating him, thereby proving himself to be Son of God. The reader is called to worship, to recognize Jesus as Son of God. There may be a secondary application, as the reader says, 'I shall not fail like Israel did,' but the primary thrust is that victory comes through recognizing Jesus to be Son of God.

Conclusion

Every aspect of the hermeneutical process is immersed in literary theory because every part of Scripture is literature. I could have used any genre in the Bible (law, poetry, wisdom, prophecy, parable, epistle, apocalyptic) but chose narrative as the most prevalent form. At each level of the study of biblical literature, literary features determine the meaning and significance of the text. In terms of general hermeneutics, this is true of all three aspects of exegetical analysis: context, grammar, semantic analysis. The process of deep Bible study is an exciting one. It is like digging for buried treasure. Each level yields richness, and the deeper you go the greater the reward. The tools for digging deep are literary and historical ones: grammars, dictionaries, encyclopedias, background studies, commentaries. As in excavation work, they are costly but ultimately rewarding.

The goal of literary interpretation is always the 'meaning' of the text, but who generates that meaning? The twentieth century saw a movement away from author to text and then to the reader as the creative force in finding meaning, therefore leading to a polyvalent or multiple-meaning approach to hermeneutical theory. Since the 1970s this has climaxed with post-structuralism and reader-response criticism, with their denial that anything but the reader generates meaning in a text. I have proposed an alternate literary theory derived from the successors of Wittgenstein, namely that all utterances, oral or written, guide the hearers/readers of the text into the rules of the language game by the intrinsic genre of each text. Thus a trialogue is established between the author who produced the text, the text as a historical document open to historical analysis, and the reader who studies and interprets the text via historical axioms of interpretation, namely the historical-grammatical method. Through this critical-realist approach based on probability principles, the most likely original meaning of a text can be discovered. Of course the results of such analysis are heuristic, demanding constant reappraisal by the community of scholars, but still the results are available to any who wish to do a deep Bible study of the text by utilizing this literary theory.

My model for this literary approach is biblical narrative, particularly the four Gospels. We cannot begin to understand the actual import of these works without the aid of literary theory. First, I would argue that biblical narrative is composed of history and theology, actually of historical theology or 'history with a message'. No biblical writer simply gives the brute facts. Rather, each interprets the historical events and selects (or omits) details in order to show the significance of those events for Israel and the early church. Both what it meant (the original meaning of the text) and what it means (the significance of the text for today) are discovered through this process. At each level (word, sentence, paragraph, section) the text is studied according to literary principles to see how it functions and the meaning it produces. When all are utilized, the multifaceted thrust the author gave the text comes through in all its depth, and the reader is enriched by the process. Finally, the intended meaning and significance are open (not closed) to the reader, though the process takes time and effort. The thesis of this chapter is that the results are worth it!

Select bibliography

BARR, J., *The Semantics of Biblical Language* (Oxford: Oxford University Press, 1961).

BLACK, D. A., and DOCKERY, D. S. (eds.), *Interpreting the New Testament: Essays on Methods and Issues* (Nashville: Broadman & Holman, 2001).

CAIRD, G. B., *The Language and Imagery of the Bible* (London: Duckworth, 1980).

CHATMAN, S., *Story and Discourse: Narrative Structure in Fiction and Film* (Ithaca: Cornell University Press, 1978).

DERRIDA, J., *Writing and Difference*, tr. A. Bass (Chicago: University of Chicago Press, 1978).

FISH, S., *Is There a Text in This Class? The Authority of Interpretive Communities* (Cambridge, Mass.: Harvard University Press, 1980).

GADAMER, H.-G., *Truth and Method* (New York: Seabury, 1976).

GREEN, J. B. (ed.), *Hearing the New Testament: Strategies for Interpretation* (Grand Rapids: Eerdmans, 1995).

HAYES, J. H. (ed.), *Dictionary of Biblical Interpretation*, 2 vols. (Nashville: Abingdon, 1999).

KENNEDY, G. A., *New Testament Interpretation through Rhetorical Criticism* (Chapel Hill: University of North Carolina Press, 1984).

MACK, B. L., *Rhetoric and the New Testament* (Minneapolis: Fortress, 1990).

OSBORNE, G. R., *The Hermeneutical Spiral: A Comprehensive Introduction to Biblical Interpretation*, 2nd ed. (Downers Grove: IVP, 2006).

PORTER, S. E., *Idioms of the Greek New Testament* (Sheffield: JSOT Press, 1994).

SEARLE, J., *Speech Acts: An Essay in the Philosophy of Language* (New York: Cambridge University Press, 1969).

SILVA, M., *Biblical Words and Their Meaning: An Introduction to Biblical Semantics* (Grand Rapids: Zondervan, 1983).

SOSKICE, J. M., *Metaphor and Religious Language* (Oxford: Clarendon, 1985).

STERNBERG, M., *The Poetics of Biblical Narrative: Ideological Literature and the Drama of Reading* (Bloomington: Indiana University Press, 1985).

THISELTON, A. C., *New Horizons in Hermeneutics* (Grand Rapids: Zondervan, 1992).

VANHOOZER, K. J., *Is There a Meaning in This Text? The Bible, the Reader, and the Morality of Literary Knowledge* (Grand Rapids: Zondervan; Leicester: Apollos, 1998).

2. A STRUCTURAL-HISTORICAL APPROACH TO THE EXEGESIS OF THE OLD TESTAMENT

S. D. (Fanie) Snyman

Introductory remarks

Before enrolling for a theology degree, students read and understand the Bible without engaging exegetically with the biblical text in a technical sense. In a seminary or faculty of theology the student is confronted with exegesis and the methodology of exegesis, and may ask why a methodology of exegesis is necessary for Bible interpretation. Why not just keep reading the Bible the way we always have? How does the exegesis we do when studying theology differ from ordinary Bible reading? Professional exegetes and theologians all too often take biblical exegesis for granted, while newcomers to theological study have to face these questions for the first time.

Clearly, a differentiation can be made between *ordinary* Bible reading, which can be referred to as a 'pre-scientific' or 'naive' understanding of the Bible, and *exegesis*, which indicates a more 'scientific' understanding of the Bible.

A pre-scientific/naive understanding of the Bible usually means that

- such Bible readers cannot justify their interpretation of the text
- the interpretations presented are difficult to test
- there is a danger of assigning additional meaning to the text

- a text is read selectively, which means that only sections that match existing convictions are read.[1]

Exegesis, a scientific approach to the Bible, entails more than the above. The concept of exegesis is derived from the Greek word *exēgeomai*, 'to lead out'. The noun *exēgēsis* can be translated as 'explanation', 'elucidation', 'interpretation'. A person embarking on an exegesis of a text therefore seeks to understand and interpret the text. Thus a person engaged in the exegesis of the OT is serious about trying to get to grips with the meaning of a text as accurately as possible.

Although 'exegesis' is a technical name for what is simply the elucidation or interpretation of a text, we often engage in exegesis in our daily lives: we interpret news reports, newspapers and literary works; we try to understand the meaning of an article, a poem or a novel. These acts essentially amount to exegesis, for by them we seek the meaning of the texts we engage with.

By nature, a television news report is an interpretation of an event: the angle from which the report is presented is either sympathetic or critical towards the televised issue. This implies that the news staff interpret each event they report on. Plus we do not merely read newspaper reports – we interpret them. We therefore sometimes agree with a newspaper's view of an event, and at other times disagree with it. We are thus taking the stage of interpretation one step further by reinterpreting the text the newspaper has already tried to interpret for us. When the main heading on the newspaper's front page reads, 'Extremist forces clash with government forces', we in turn may reinterpret this as 'Freedom fighters clash with the forces of tyranny' (depending on our world view).

Since a scientific understanding of events originates in our everyday and pre-scientific world, exegesis also begins with the reading of a text, but goes beyond the mere naive understanding of that text.[2] But what exactly does 'exegesis' mean, and why should scientific exegesis be the approach we take in reading the Bible?

---

1. H. L. Bosman, 'Die Ontstaan en Verstaan van die Ou Testament', in F. E. Deist and W. S. Vorster (eds.), *Woorde wat Ver Kom*, Die Literatuur van die Ou Testament (Cape Town: Tafelberg, 1986), pp. 8–9.
2. Ibid., p. 9.

Why exegesis?

Exegesis intends to bring the conversation about the meaning of biblical texts to the level of a scientific argument.[3] There are at least five reasons why exegesis is essential for a correct understanding of the biblical text.

Historical distance

Around 2,500 years (or longer) have elapsed between present-day readers and the writers of the OT, so it is virtually impossible to understand the OT text with a twenty-first-century mindset. The OT originates from a cultural world unfamiliar to the modern reader (many customs in the OT are strange or even at first sight incomprehensible to us) and it is written in a language no longer spoken today (modern Hebrew differs considerably from biblical Hebrew). Thus, exegesis becomes essential.[4] Exegesis begins at the point where the immediate meaning of a text is no longer understood.[5]

Not only do the historical distance and the historical context make interpretation of the OT text essential; there is also a historical distance *within* the OT itself. There is a world of difference between the time before the Babylonian exile of 586 BC and the period after the exile. Far-reaching changes took place in the political and social circumstances of the Israelites from the time before the exile to the period of exile among the Babylonians, as well as the period after the exile, which the Persians and Greeks dominated.

A great variety of interpretations

In view of the above, it is understandable that a great variety of interpretations of a specific text have developed. Differences in the interpretation of sections of the Bible result not only from theological arguments, but Bible translations often differ to such an extent that it is necessary to return to the original biblical languages to try to understand what is meant by a specific passage. Any *translation* of the Bible is also an *interpretation* of the Bible. The existence of so many Christian denominations can often be traced back to their differing interpretations of specific texts.

---

3. F. E. Deist and J. J. Burden, *'n ABC van Bybeluitleg* (Pretoria: J. L. van Schaik, 1980), p. 5.
4. G. Wanke, 'Notwendigkeit und Ziel der Exegese des Alten Testaments', in G. Fohrer and H.-W. Hoffmann (eds.), *Exegese des Alten Testaments: Einführung in die Methodik*, Uni-Taschenbücher 267 (Heidelberg: Quelle & Meyer, 1976), p. 267.
5. A. H. J. Gunneweg, *Understanding the Old Testament* (London: SCM, 1978), p. 31.

Most literary texts, including the Bible, contain unclear or ambiguous aspects. Word meanings do not always remain static over a period of a few hundred years. The same word can thus have different meanings in different historical contexts, which makes correct interpretation essential.

Ideological indoctrination

When people interpret the Bible, their ideological thought patterns play a role. Ideological interpretation includes attitudes and convictions regarding racism, classism, sexism, imperialism and elitism.[6]

Ideological indoctrination is not unique to our day. Kugel, for instance, points out how early interpreters said that (1) the Platonic notion of ideas occurs in the Bible as well (Gen. 1 recounts the creation of the *ideal* human, while Gen. 2 describes the creation of the *earthly* human), or (2) the prophets predicted the fall of the Roman Empire (the reference to 'Edom' in Obad. 1:1 must ultimately refer to Rome), or (3) the crucifixion of Jesus was predicted in detail in the OT (the ram that entangled its horns in a bush according to Gen. 22:13 is a symbolic prediction of Jesus' crown of thorns).[7] Thus, whoever seeks to understand the Bible, in whatever historical period, must guard against the ideological indoctrination that consciously or unconsciously influences Bible interpretation.

The text of the Bible invites interpretation

The Bible has been interpreted since the earliest times. In fact, there are indications in the OT itself of text interpretation. For example, we read in Daniel 9:2 that 'in the first year of his reign, I, Daniel, understood from the Scriptures, according to the word of the LORD given to Jeremiah the prophet, that the desolation of Jerusalem would last seventy years' (NIV). The author of the book of Daniel uses this text from the book of Jeremiah to bring his message home to his readers/listeners.

Equally, the NT interprets the OT. The NT contains numerous allusions to the OT. Jesus interprets sections of the Ten Commandments in the Sermon on the Mount, Paul in his letter to the Galatians refers to Abraham, the letter to the Hebrews contains numerous references to the OT's sacrificial practices,

---

6. E. M. Conradie, L. C. Jonker, D. G. Lawrie and R. A. Arendse, *Op Soek na Jona: Verskillende Benaderings tot die Interpretasie van die Bybel*, Teks en Konteks 6 (Bellville: University of the Western Cape, 1995), p. 9.

7. See J. L. Kugel, *The Bible As It Was* (Cambridge, Mass.: Harvard University Press, 1997), pp. 53–82, 177–178.

which are interpreted against the background of the events surrounding Christ, the symbolism in the book of Revelation is derived from the OT, and further examples of the NT interpreting the OT abound.

Precise reading of the text of the Bible gives rise to textual questions that must be answered, and the answers to these essentially amount to interpretation. For example, according to Exodus 16:4, God caused food to rain down from heaven for the Israelites, confirmed by Psalm 105:40:

> They asked, and he brought them quail,
> and satisfied them with the bread of heaven. (NIV)

The question the text raises is: What is food/bread from heaven? Some of the earliest interpreters of the OT argued that this could not be earthly bread, since the text expressly states it came from heaven. According to Psalm 78:25, the manna was nothing less than the food eaten by *angels*. In fact, the respected NIV, translates the text as 'bread of angels'. Interestingly, the CEV (one of the most recent English Bible translations) translates this section as 'special food'. So what exactly was the manna in the desert? Was it food eaten by the angels in heaven, or should we interpret it differently? Of course, this single question can be multiplied a thousand times when other textual issues arise.

Understanding a text

One can also say that the purpose of exegesis is for understanding a text or, in the words of the late Professor Ferdinand Deist, '[T]he Bible is read to get to the meaning of a specific section, to understand something of the world of religious symbols of which the text is part'.[8] Why should we want to understand the biblical text? Because as Christians we assume or profess that the text is still relevant for today. We believe the text has a message for us, as we profess that the Bible is God's Word to us.

The function of exegesis

In the light of the preceding argument, exegesis has at least three important functions:

1. *To verify.* The minute we begin reading a text, we are interpreting that text. After all, we are reading the text to make sense of it. Exegesis

---

8. F. E. Deist, 'Eksegese as Leeskompetensie: Oor die Onderrig in Skrifuitleg', *NGTT* 30.1 (1989), pp. 56–63.

verifies our reading of the text, and our first impressions of the text can be confirmed or changed.

2. *To give reasons for a specific understanding of the text.* Since such a long period of time has elapsed between us and the text's authors, with the result that a great variety of interpretations of that text have developed, exegesis makes it essential for us to give reasons why we understand the text a particular way.

3. *To weigh up alternatives.* Alternative interpretations of the text are weighed up against one another, and reasons must be given for preferring one interpretation.[9] Some exegetical approaches and results are simply more satisfying than others, although different interpretations are also possible within the same approach. A responsible exegesis must thus endeavour to give reasons why a specific interpretation is favoured.

Situating the exegetical scene

In oversimplified terms, and for the sake of convenience, the modern exegetical scene consists of the following four categories.[10] (1) *Historical-critical* methods, where the emphasis falls on the growth and development of the text over a period of time. (2) *Literary* methods, which require the text itself to be studied without considering its history and origins. Barton points out that other terms can also be used for the two main schools of thought in the exegesis of the OT (historical-critical vs. literary): *diachronic* versus *synchronic, historical* versus *literary, objective* versus *subjective, empirical research* versus *literary theory,* what the text *meant* versus what it *means* today.[11] The history of the practice of OT studies has at times been described as a 'story of two ways', with the one way representing the historical-critical approaches, and the other the text-

---

9. Deist and Burden, *ABC,* p. 3.

10. The oversimplification results from the so-called reader-directed approach being included with the other literary approaches, when it should be in a category of its own. Recently the exegetical scene in South Africa (the vantage point from which I write) has become more diverse than being merely a simple dichotomy between historical-critical and literary approaches.

11. J. Barton, 'Historical Criticism and Literary Interpretation: Is There Any Common Ground?', in S. E. Porter, P. Joyce and D. E. Orton (eds.), *Crossing the Boundaries: Essays in Biblical Interpretation in Honour of Michael D. Goulder,* BIS 8 (Leiden: Brill, 1994), pp. 3–16.

directed or synchronistic approaches.[12] (3) *Reader-oriented* methods, where the emphasis falls on the role of the reader in the process of interpretation. (4) *Hermeneutical* methods, such as feminist interpretations of the text or approaches from a liberation theology perspective or political and ideological readings of a text.

While in some circles historical-critical approaches to the text of the OT still represent the dominant exegetical approach to the OT, in other circles text-oriented approaches, such as for example the text-immanent and synchronic, have acquired a firm footing. Whereas earlier evaluations of the two types of methodology tended to be in an either–or direction, today the value of both for the understanding of the text is acknowledged to a far greater extent.

Various factors have played a role in the rise of specifically text-oriented exegetical approaches.

The Old Testament as literature
Without denying for one moment that the OT is part of the canon of Scripture, the Word of God, it is equally true that the OT is literature that can be read and studied *as literature*. This observation has lead biblical scholars to conclude that insights from literary theory may prove fruitful in illuminating the OT. This has been a major trend in exegetical circles especially in South Africa.[13]

The distinction between synchrony and diachrony
This is regarded as one of the most important and influential insights gained from literary theory. *Synchrony* has to do with the text itself irrespective of its historical growth. *Diachrony* has to do with the historical growth and development of a text over the course of history. Text-oriented exegetical methods lean to a synchronic emphasis, while historical-critical methods lean to a diachronic one.

Insight into the value of each method has resulted in an increased awareness of the one-sidedness of each. Thus, for example, historical-critical approaches have been accused of moving away too quickly from the final form

---

12. J. H. Le Roux, *A Story of Two Ways, Thirty Years of Old Testament Scholarship in South Africa*, OTESup 2 (Pretoria: Verba Vitae, 1993).

13. F. E. Deist, 'Die Ou Testamentiese Eksegese en Algemene Literatuurwetenskap', *NGTT* 14 (1975) pp. 75–81; Le Roux, *Story of Two Ways*; D. J. Human, 'Die Literêr-Historiese Lees van 'n Teks', *Skrif en Kerk* 20.2 (1999), pp. 354–368.

of a text to a (supposed) historical layering of the text, which, in turn, has led to an atomizing of the text.[14]

A criticism of text-oriented approaches, on the other hand, is that they underemphasize, or even ignore, the essential historical dimension of a text. The result is that what was supposed to be a synchronic approach in fact becomes an *achronic* approach, with all the dangers inherent in such a process. Van Zyl speaks of a historically naive point of view where a text-oriented reading of a passage dismisses recourse to any historical awareness of the text's setting.[15] Deist especially voices this kind of criticism against text-oriented methods. He draws attention to the growing dissatisfaction with immanent methods, which detach texts from their cultural-historical and religious-historical roots, thereby opening the way for an uncritical and fundamentalist use of the Scriptures.[16] He warns against an overinterpretation of the form of a text which results in separating that text from its history, and argues that no literary work can be understood unless attention is paid to its historical context.[17]

A positive aspect of the text-oriented approaches is their strong focus on the text itself. But this strength can simultaneously become a weakness because the focus falls so strongly on a single text that one tends to lose sight of its wider context. Combrink points out that the shift in exegetical method towards a synchronic one constitutes an acknowledgment that justice is not always done to a text if it is approached from only one perspective.[18] Synchronic exegesis has also been accused of analytical positivism, with the criticism being levelled that those who practise this procedure believe absolutely in their methods.[19]

However, we must recognize that text-oriented approaches have arisen

---

14. This is, of course, not the only criticism of the historical-critical method. Vigorous opposition has come from various sides.

15. H. C. Van Zyl, *Die Vervreemdings- en Toe-Eieningstaak van die Eksegese* (Bloemfontein: University of the Free State, 1991), p. 10.

16. F. E. Deist, 'Onlangse Konsepte in Teksuitleg en hulle Konsekwensies vir die (Gereformeerde) Teologie', *In die Skriflig* 28.2 (1994), pp. 165–178, esp. 167.

17. F. E. Deist, *Ervaring, Rede en Metode in Skrifuitleg: 'n Wetenskapsteoretiese Ondersoek na Skrifuitleg in die Ned. Geref. Kerk 1840–1990* (Pretoria: RGN, 1994), p. 296.

18. H. J. B. Combrink, 'Die Krisis van die Skrifgesag in die Gereformeerde Eksegese as 'n Geleentheid', *NGTT* 31.3 (1990), pp. 325–335, esp. 333.

19. E. J. van Wolde, *Words Become Worlds: Semantic Studies of Genesis 1–11*, BIS 6 (Leiden: Brill, 1994), p. 202.

because of a growing dissatisfaction with the historical-critical methods of exegesis. Historical-critical methods, which have been accused of fragmenting the text into too many pieces, have became so technical that only well-trained exegetes dare to perform a proper exegesis of a text. Plus the historical-critical approach presupposes a pre-literary phase for almost all OT texts, and is of little use for those interested in the theological meaning of texts.

Recently, a vigorous debate has arisen about whether, and to what extent, synchronic and diachronic approaches can be reconciled. In 1994, for example, the joint congress of the Dutch and South African OT Societies held in Kampen in the Netherlands was devoted wholly to the issue of synchrony and diachrony in OT exegesis. The problem is also widely discussed in academic theses[20] and journal articles.[21]

Scholars hold widely divergent opinions on the matter. While some believe the two methods should be followed independently, without searching for points of contact, other scholars would like to see the two approaches complementing each other. Professor Bob Becking from Utrecht in the Netherlands holds the following opinion: 'When it comes to the process of interpretation two features are equally important: On the one hand texts should be read to get an insight in the text-internal dynamics. On the other hand the historical setting of the text should be designed from evidence outside the text.'[22] Synchronic and diachronic exegesis should thus complement one another.[23]

---

20. E. Talstra, *Solomon's Prayer: Synchrony and Diachrony in the Composition of I Kings 8,14–61*, CBET 3 (Kampen: Kok Pharos, 1993); L. C. Jonker, 'Exclusivity and Variety: A Typological Study towards the Integration of Exegetical Methodologies in Old Testament Studies' (DTh diss., University of Stellenbosch, 1993).

21. J. Barton, 'Reading the Bible as Literature: Two Questions for Biblical Critics', *JLT* 1.2 (1987), pp. 135–153; F. H. Polak, 'Het Bijbels Verhaal als Palmpsest: Over de Rol van de Diachrone in de Structurele Analyse', *ACEBT* 9 (1988), pp. 22–34; S. Boorer, 'The Importance of a Diachronic Approach: The Case of Genesis–Kings', *CBQ* 51.2 (1989), pp. 195–208; W. S. Vorster, 'The In/compatibility of Methods and Strategies in Reading or Interpreting the Old Testament', *OTE* 2.3 (1989), pp. 53–63; P. R. Noble, 'Synchronic and Diachronic Approaches to Biblical Interpretation', *JLT* 7.2 (1993), pp. 130–148; Barton, 'Historical Criticism'.

22. B. Becking, 'A Plea for a Historical Critical Approach in the Study of the Old Testament'. Paper read at the Congress of the IOSOT in Oslo, Norway, 1998, p. 4.

23. Human, 'Literêr-Historiese Lees', p. 362.

The method I propose here constitutes an attempt to place a text analysed for its literary meaning within a specific historical framework. A literary reading of a text does not exclude a historical reading of the same text in a single exegetical exercise. All biblical texts originated within history and meant something specific to people within a particular historical context. Thus the historical foreignness of the Bible, its historical distance from us today, must be acknowledged.[24] The trend towards an achronic exegesis within an exegetical framework that claims to be synchronic is actually a contradiction. To work synchronically indeed implies that a text cannot be viewed achronically, but must be read and understood within the context of a specific period.[25]

The historical dimension of a text has a significant influence on the understanding and interpretation of that text. To read Deutero-Isaiah as if it were a pre-exilic book would result in the reader understanding it quite differently than if it were read in a post-exilic context. Whether we read the book of Daniel as if it were written during (and for) the period of Babylonian exile or within the context of the time of Antiochus Epiphanes will determine the theological meaning we attach to the book. Such examples can be multiplied. We thus cannot escape the historical dimensions of a text. To deny or fail to appreciate a text's historical dimension impoverishes the text theologically. Furthermore, the objection that the dating of texts in the OT is often of such a hypothetical nature that so many divergent opinions exist about the matter as to render it a meaningless exercise is not a decisive argument. Of course, the careful exegete should avoid historical recontructions that are simply beyond all probability. All exegetical work (e.g. the analysis of the structure of a pericope, and any historical reconstruction of the time frame of a text) is hypothetical and provisional.

The etymology of a word

The distinction between synchrony and diachrony has had an effect on the study of the etymology of words. For a long time in the practice of exegesis it was thought that investigating the etymology of a word could lead to the so-called 'original' meaning of that word, which would then be its 'true' meaning. But contemporary exegetical practice has largely abandoned such a notion. Kremer maintains that 'to explain the meaning of a word, one does not enquire

---

24. Van Zyl, *Vervreemdings-*, p. 7.

25. F. E. Deist, 'The Bible as Literature: Whose Literature?', *OTE* 7.3 (1994), pp. 327–342, esp. 328.

into its etymology anymore; one rather determines the meaning of a word by establishing the immediate context of the word' (my tr.).[26]

The eminent British scholar James Barr criticized the study of word etymology. His famous statement 'the main point is that the etymology of a word is not a statement about its meaning but about its history . . . [I]t is quite wrong to suppose that the etymology of a word is necessarily a guide either to its "proper" meaning in a later period' is often quoted in discussing procedures of Bible interpretation.[27] The meaning of words, according to Barr, does not primarily reside in their *history*, but in the *context* in which they are used. Barton agrees: 'Words or sentences in a language do not have any "inherent" meaning: this is an absolutely fundamental principal in the modern study of language.'[28]

Language is structured

When one uses language, one does so in coherent sentences, paragraphs and even larger units. This means that all language is structured in order to be meaningful. Du Toit remarks that 'this structuring may be striking or unnoticed, deliberate or spontaneous, firm or loose, successful or less successful, yet structuring remains an irrefutable fact whether at a word or sentence or more comprehensive level'.[29]

A structural-historical approach to the exegesis of the Old Testament

Exegesis of the Old and New Testaments has become a highly scientific enterprise. The approach explained here is meant to provide the non-technical exegete with ample tools to reach exegetical results in a responsible manner. Pastors are often pressed for time to produce a sermon for the next Sunday's service. They are keen to exegete a text, but cannot dwell on technical detail at

---

26. J. Kremer, 'Alte, Neuere und neueste Methoden der Exegese', *BL* 53.1 (1980), pp. 3–12.

27. J. Barr, *The Semantics of Biblical Language* (Oxford: Oxford University Press, 1969), p. 109.

28. J. Barton, *Reading the Old Testament: Method in Biblical Study* (London: Darton Longman & Todd, 1984), p. 10.

29. A. B. Du Toit, 'The Significance of Discourse Analysis for New Testament Interpretation and Translation: Introductory Remarks with Special Reference to I Peter 1:3–13, in Linguistics and Bible Translation', *Neot* 8 (1977), p. 55.

length. Practising exegesis that arrives at tenable results is important, and the approach explained here seeks to meet this need.

My choice of 'approach' indicates a broad framework for OT exegesis. Plus 'structural' will indicate the text-*internal*, and 'historical' the text-*external*, relations of a pericope. A pericope cannot be understood solely on its own terms. To make it intelligible, the exegete must refer to matters, events, people and so on outside the text and relate them to it. The term 'historical' also implies that the text to be interpreted must be placed within a historical framework. But 'historical' is not equivalent to 'diachronic', because 'diachronic' refers to the *development* of a text over a period of time.

Moreover, the terms 'text-internal' and 'text-external' are not exclusive or mutually incompatible. The exegete's knowledge of Hebrew in order to recognize structures within a text, or the skill of textual criticism, or of recognizing literary techniques used in a text, are text-external matters used to get to grips with the text (text-internally). The *Gattung* (literary genre) of a text is also both a text-internal and a text-external matter. On the one hand, the *Gattung* of a specific text must be determined (text-internally), but at the same time criteria for the *Gattung* are imported from outside the text (text-externally). The terms 'text-internal' and 'text-external' are also not the only ones used. Deist speaks of a 'grammatical-historical' approach to exegesis,[30] while Prinsloo distinguishes between 'intratextual' and 'intertextual' aspects of an exegetical study.[31] Van Wolde adds the term 'extratextual'.[32] I use 'text-internal' and 'text-external' here to avoid confusion with an intertextual approach.

The phases of a structural-historical investigation

The term 'phase' is used to distance ourselves from the idea that exegesis can be done according to a rigid series of steps. Exegesis instead is a series of *phases* in each of which theoretical steps take place. And the emphasis should fall on the logical rather than chronological distinctions that are part of the task of literary-historical exegesis. A structural-historical study can be divided into four phases: (1) preliminary phase, (2) text-internal study, (3) text-external study and (4) concluding phase.

---

30. F. E. Deist, 'Again: Method(s) of Exegesis', *OTE* 1 (1983), pp. 73–88.

31. G. T. M. Prinsloo, "n Literêr-Eksegetiese Analise van die Boek Habakuk' (DD thesis, University of Pretoria, 1989), p. 52.

32. E. J. van Wolde, 'Van Tekst via Tekst naar Betekenis: Intertekstualiteit en haar Implicaties', *TvT* 30.4 (1990), pp. 333–361.

Preliminary phase
The reading and translation of the text   Exegesis of a text starts with the reading of
the text, initially in the language in which the exegete feels at home. However, a
single translation offers only one perspective, so a text should be read in various
translations. Accessing more than one translation delivers a number of benefits:
reducing the restrictions imposed by a single source of meaning, showing
different nuances of meaning and highlighting the bias of translations. We
should also make our own 'working' translation if we have access to the original languages. In fact, the preponderance of translations and the questions that
arise at repeated rereading of the text and different translations compel the
exegete to turn to the original language of the text. To study Shakespeare's
Macbeth in a language other than English always remains an inferior option!

Questioning the text and one's own context   Questioning a text is important to arrive
at its correct meaning. A critical awareness that results from moving away from
a naive and pre-scientific reading is cultivated by putting questions to the text.
To interrogate the text one also has to read carefully. Textual questions may
include the following: Why do the translations differ? Who is speaking here?
Who are the addressees? Is there any indication of when this prophecy or
psalm was uttered? Are the customs referred to in the text clear? Why would
an author utter these words?

During the preliminary reading and interrogation of the text, exegetes must
remain constantly alert to the fact that they do not read a text neutrally. Exegetes'
denominational background, political convictions, economic position and a
whole range of other factors influence their reading of a text.[33] To put it
differently: unbiased exegetes do not exist. Thus, not only must the text under
scrutiny be questioned, but exegetes must simultaneously interrogate *themselves*.

Text-internal study
A text-internal study comprises the following three facets.

Demarcation of the pericope   Before one can proceed to work with a specific text,
the passage must be demarcated in an accountable manner. Prinsloo says that
'Before one can start expounding a text it needs to be demarcated.'[34] Von Rad
says that 'a great deal depends on correct determination . . . in particular on

---

33. Conradie et al., *Op soek na Jona*, pp. 20–31.
34. W. S. Prinsloo, 'Isaiah 14:12–15: Humiliation, Hubris, Humiliation', *ZAW* 93.3
    (1981), p. 433.

the correct delimitation of the beginning and end of the unit under discussion. To add a verse from the unit which follows, or to omit one which properly belongs to the close of an oracle, can alter the whole meaning.'[35]

A passage defined in this manner is called a 'pericope'. A pericope is a demarcated structural and semantic unit based on characteristics encountered in a specific text. Furthermore, the demarcation of a pericope must be done on the basis of insights offered by *Literarkritik* (literary criticism).

The differentiating of a pericope or pericopes is an important stage in the process of exegesis. What an author wishes to communicate is not expressed in isolated words, but in word relations that convey meaning, that is, in sentences constructed in specific ways. What an author wishes to say is therefore expressed in sentences and in the sequence of sentences, so the exegete must work with such combinations of sentences or pericopes.[36]

A second reason why the demarcation of a pericope is important is that neither the division of chapters nor the *perashim* (separations) of the *BHS* or *BHK*, nor the chapter divisions of the Greek NT, can be regarded as reliable demarcation points. The book of Malachi, for instance, has good examples of a misleading division of chapters. For example, verse 17, the last verse of Malachi chapter 2, introduces a new pericope. Malachi 2:1 also does not introduce a new pericope, but forms part of a pericope that starts with Malachi 1:6.

A third reason why the demarcation of a pericope is essential for exegesis is that the various translations and commentaries differ regarding the division and demarcation of pericopes. In order to make a responsible choice for a specific division of pericopes, the ability to make a reasoned demarcation of textual contexts is vital.

With the help of insights derived from *Literarkritik*[37] a variety of formal and content-based criteria are used to demarcate pericopes. Huber remarks that the first task of the literary critic is to determine the beginning and end of a text. Thus traditional demarcations of pericopes are either confirmed or new conclusions reached.

The following criteria are usually used to demarcate pericopes. Richter regards *duplications* and *repetitions* as the most important criteria for the

---

35. G. von Rad, *Old Testament Theology*, vol. 1 (London: SCM, 1975), pp. 38–39.

36. J. A. Loader, 'Gedagtes oor Gekontroleerde Eksegese', *Hervormde Teologiese Studies* 34.1–2 (1978), p. 7.

37. Here the term *Literarkritik* is not used in its usual sense: where the issue of a passage's 'authenticity'/'inauthenticity' (*Einheitlichkeit/Uneinheitlichkeit*) plus the possibility of sources and comments in a unit are discussed.

demarcation of pericopes.[38] The two stories of creation at the beginning of Genesis are good examples of this. However, not all repetitions and duplications necessarily serve as an indication of the start of a new pericope. If a repetition is used as an instrument of style in a passage and is often repeated (cf. e.g. Gen. 1 and Amos 1 and 2), it naturally does not serve as an indication of a new pericope.[39] This is probably why Huber prefers to speak of 'disrupting' repetitions as an indication of the start of a new pericope.[40]

Tensions in a passage are also a sign of a new pericope (cf. once again the two stories of creation in Gen. 1 and 2). Sometimes different words are used for the same places or persons; for example, Sinai and Horeb, which refer to the same mountain, and different names for God used in successive pericopes.

A stereotyped introductory formula usually indicates the start of a new pericope; for example, the well-known 'Thus says the LORD' formula or the expression 'The word of the LORD that came to', which occurs frequently in the OT.

A significant change in vocabulary can serve as an indication of a break with the previous pericope. A classic example is the change of vocabulary found in Genesis 1 and 2. Although both chapters deal with the theme of creation, there are major differences in vocabulary, which indicates two different accounts of creation.

A difference in the names of persons and places can serve to indicate that a new pericope is starting. A change of scene and a changeover to new central characters are also criteria that indicate the opening of a new pericope.[41]

Not all the above criteria can be applied to each text – the passage under the spotlight provides the relevant criteria. The list is also incomplete. See Richter for a much fuller exposition.[42]

Textual criticism   Textual criticism is an essential facet of exegetical work. For various reasons corruption of the text during the transcription of manuscripts resulted in the text sometimes becoming incomprehensible. But the aim of textual criticism is not to reconstruct the so-called original reading: 'The discipline investigating the vicissitudes of a text in so far as these pertain to its genesis we call Literary Criticism. Textual Criticism, on the other

---

38. W. Richter, *Exegese als Literaturwissenschaft: Entwurf einer alttestamentlichen Literaturtheorie und Methodologie* (Göttingen: Vandenhoeck & Ruprecht, 1971), p. 51.

39. Ibid., p. 55; F. Huber, 'Literarkritik', in Fohrer and Hoffmann, *Exegese des Alten Testaments*, p. 50.

40. Huber, 'Literarkritik', p. 50.

41. Ibid., p. 47.

42. Richter, *Exegese als Literaturwissenschaft*, pp. 50–62.

hand, investigates the vicissitudes of a text in so far as these pertain to the transmission of the final text, whether transmission by copying or by translation.'[43]

Although the MT is taken as the point of departure for the OT, it is essential for a pericope to be subjected to a text-critical study in accordance with the principles that apply to the discipline of textual criticism:

- Manuscripts are *weighed, not counted.* A reading from a good manuscript will carry more weight than a lot of other manuscripts.
- The *more difficult reading* is preferred. It is more likely that a reading would be made easier than vice versa.
- The *shorter reading* is preferred. A scribe would lengthen rather than shorten a text.
- The *explicable reading* is the weaker reading. If reading B can be explained as a corrupted form of reading A, but A not as a corrupted form of B, then reading A is to be preferred.[44]

Analysis of the structure of the pericope   A text-internal study of a demarcated pericope proceeds from the point of departure that a linguistic expression consists of a network of connections or relations and that the relations jointly help to determine the meaning of the pericope. During analysis of the structure of the pericope, this network of internal relations is studied, so a whole range of syntactic and stylistic characteristics or techniques can be used in a pericope.

Syntactic techniques consist of features such as the following: the occurrence of the waw consecutive, introductory formulas that introduce direct speech, pronominal inclusion through suffixes, pronouns and finite verbs contained in the verb, imperatives, jussives, interrogative sentences, particles, prepositions, correspondence and variation with regard to the form of the verb, the significant repetition of words and/or groups of words, changing of the subject, changing of the object, similarity and so on.

At a stylistic level one finds techniques such as parallelisms, chiasms, inclusio, antithetical word pairs, synonymous word pairs, *figura etymologica*, lists, deletion, figures of speech such as paronomasia, metonymy, litotes,

---

43. F. E. Deist, *Towards the Text of the Old Testament* (Pretoria: Dutch Reformed Church Booksellers, 1978), p. 25.

44. F. E. Deist, *Witnesses to the Old Testament: Introducing Old Testament Textual Criticism*, The Literature of the Old Testament 5 (Pretoria: Dutch Reformed Church Booksellers, 1988), p. 203.

hyperbole, merism, metaphors, comparisons, imagery, irony and so on.[45] Acoustic phenomena such as alliteration, assonance and rhyme must also be taken into account in pericope analysis. Identifying the function of syntactic, stylistic and other techniques that occur in a pericope help the exegete to determine the structure of a pericope. This, in turn, clarifies a train of thought and helps him or her to gain a deeper insight into the text.

Analysis of a pericope's structure is not an instrument for unlocking its meaning. However, analysis does provide parameters within which a specific interpretation would be valid.

Text-external study

A text or pericope is not only understandable in relation to itself; external factors also determine its meaning.

Investigation of the literary type (Gattung) *and situation in life* (Sitz im Leben) Study of the structure of a pericope reveals the form of the text.[46] Such a form can, however, exhibit similarities with the form of other pericopes. When different forms exhibit certain similarities, such a group of pericopes are considered a *Gattung*. As we saw earlier, the German term *Gattung* means 'literary type' or 'genre', and a variety of these are found in the OT.

Genres typical of the latter prophets include prophecies of doom, prophecies of salvation, call narratives of prophets, visionary material, symbolic actions performed by a prophet, historical accounts, wisdom sayings or geneaologies. In the Psalms are psalms of praise, psalms of lament, psalms of wisdom, wedding songs, liturgical material and so on.

It is important to determine the function of a particular genre in a pericope because, for example, a poem needs to be read differently from a historical narrative. This insight of the OT scholar Hermann Gunkel linked the concepts *Gattung* and *Sitz im Leben. Sitz im Leben* means the typical

---

45. G. Wanke, 'Sprachliche Analyse', in Fohrer and Hoffmann, *Exegese des Alten Testaments*, pp. 66–69; E. Zenger, 'Ein Beispiel exegetischer Methoden aus dem Alten Testament', in J. Schreiner (ed.), *Einführung in die Methoden der Biblischen Exegese* (Würzburg: Echter, 1971), pp. 97–148; Richter, *Exegese als Literaturwissenschaft*, pp. 79–89; W. S. Prinsloo, 'A Comprehensive Semiostructural Exegetical Approach', in P. J. Botha, H. L. Bosman, J. J. Burden and J. P. J. Olivier (eds.), *Understanding the Old Testament in South Africa*, *OTE* 7.4, Special Edition (Pretoria: OTSSA, 1994), p. 81.

46. See chapter 4 in this volume.

sociological life situation within which one would expect a specific *Gattung* to be used.

The typical situation within which a *Gattung* functions must not be understood as an ahistorical or supra-temporal situation. The determination of the *Sitz im Leben* of a pericope on the basis of the *Gattung* must also lead to the historical setting of the pericope. In what kind of historical situation would such a *Gattung* have been appropriate? The establishment of the *Sitz im Leben* via the *Gattung* helps to situate the pericope historically. However, sometimes it is impossible to determine the historical placement of a text (e.g. the Psalms or wisdom literature) beyond doubt.

Determining the genre and the typical historical situation are important facets of an exegetical process. One can hardly use a psalm of lament in a sermon that attempts to get a congregation to praise the Lord! Equally, a preacher would not normally expound a prophecy of doom in proclaiming the promises of God's redemption.

Investigation into traditional material   A pericope studied exegetically does not exist in isolation from other pericopes. The fact that a pericope forms part of a larger whole impels investigation of the relationship between that pericope and the rest of the OT. Within the OT certain 'schools of thought' can be distinguished: theological convictions that determined the direction of the OT. These schools of thought can be called 'traditions'. The traditions of the OT are anchored in history, meaning that the dominant traditions tell the story of God's deeds of salvation in the history of his chosen people. The following traditions are usually identified in the OT: creation, the Patriarchs, the exodus, the wilderness wandering, the events that took place at Sinai, the promise and conquest of the land, and the Davidic and Zion traditions.[47] The exegete should have a firm knowledge of these in order to integrate it meaningfully into the exegetical process.

Investigation of traditional material aims to establish whether any of the stereotyped traditions occur in the text, and, if they do, to determine their function in the specific pericope(s). A tradition is used to legitimate theological convictions, as, for example, the Zion tradition in Psalm 46. A tradition can also be used to criticize theological convictions, as, for instance, in Deutero-Isaiah, where the questions regarding the seeming absence and impotence of Yahweh are criticized on the basis of the creation tradition, which emphasizes Yahweh's omnipotence.

The investigation into the traditional material contained in a pericope is an

---

47. Von Rad, *Old Testament Theology*, vol. 1.

important facet of the structural-historical approach. It opens a window on to the world of thought of the pericope and also places the pericope within the broader framework of the rest of the OT.

Investigation into redactional activity   Within the historical-critical paradigm, 'redaction criticism' proceeds from the point of departure of multiple authorship, indicated in the Literarkritik. Redaction criticism compares the text in its earliest written form against the background of its evolution.

Within an exegetical framework that proceeds from the final form of the text, without enquiring about its prehistory, little attention is devoted to the possibility of redactional text editing. It may, however, be the case that there are such clear indications of a redaction of the text that even a structural approach cannot ignore this. An analysis of the make-up of the text's structure can also pinpoint breaks that indicate redaction.

Concluding phase

The 'concluding phase' of an exegesis clarifies obscurities that may still remain in the text.

Detailed exegesis   Concepts, words, expressions, customs, place names about which doubt may still exist can now be elucidated. During this phase the historical foundation (bedding) of the text must also receive attention. Are there indications in the text that point out its historical placement? Within which historical circumstances would the text have made (most) sense? Are there indications in the text that it could have been read sensibly either earlier or later than its apparent historical placement? Help can be found in commentaries, theological dictionaries, concordances, atlases, insights derived from archaeology, geography, the history of Israel and the ANE, archaeological discoveries and so on.

Establishment of the theological intention of the pericope   The aim of exegesis is to discover the theological intention of a pericope under investigation – exegesis ultimately exposes a pericope's theology. What theological sense does the pericope make? A pericope's theological intention is formulated in the light of all the data mined from the exegetical process. Theological insights are gained as a result of the interplay between the internal/literary features of a text and its external/historical dimensions. Plus an ancient pericope must be understood in contemporary terms. This part of the investigation can thus be called the 'hermeneutical' phase. However, it must be borne in mind that the *whole* exegetical process is a process of hermeneutics. Therefore the exegete must be sensitive to factors that steer the understanding of a text in a certain direction right from the start of the exegetical process (see the section 'Text-internal study' above).

The theological message or intention of the pericope is, however, not simply read at surface level from the data collected during the process of exegesis. Formulation of the message is a *creative act*, which means the interpreter recreates the message with the help of the available exegetical data. Exegesis is therefore both a science and an art. As a *scientific* discipline the exegesis of a text proceeds according to the rules of literary and textual investigation; as an *art*, allowance must be made for the exegete's creative input.[48] In the same way an artist chooses not merely to reproduce a scene as it appears in a photo, but to paint it as he or she sees it, or to emphasize certain elements, the exegete, in determining its message, also has the freedom to highlight parts of a pericope. Therefore preachers can deliver different but equally valid sermons on the basis of the same text or pericope. The important thing is merely that the correlation or relationship with the text must not be relinquished.

Exegesis can also be likened to the metaphor of a musical performance. The 'text' of the performance is the musical composition. But although different orchestras render the works of great masters differently, whatever the quality of a performance, it must still be recognizable as the work of a certain composer. However, whereas the quality of a musical performance is judged by music critics, the quality of a pericope's exegesis is judged by the interpreting community (fellow exegetes, ministers etc.).

Deist is, therefore, correct in stating that exegesis should not be regarded as a number of steps to be executed in the correct sequence in order to achieve the desired result.[49] Exegesis and the formulation of the theological intention of a pericope are rather something that happens. The different facets of an exegetical investigation can be compared to a number of tentacles that emerge from the head of the exegete that then, as it were, attach themselves to the text. The various bits of information obtained thus correlate simultaneously. The facets of an exegetical study are therefore also not the theology of a text, but data by means of which the theology of that text is formed (created) in the head of the exegete.

Conclusion

Text-immanent exegesis of the OT is in danger of neglecting the historical dimension of the text. In this chapter I have argued that an exegetical approach

---

48. M. Vervenne, *Bijbelwetenschap: Inleiding oud Testament* (Louvain: Catholic University of Louvain, 1992), p. 15.
49. Deist, 'Eksegese as Leeskompetensie', pp. 56–63.

which aims to be synchronic must guard against the danger of ignoring the historical dimension, for in doing so it becomes an *achronic* approach. My aim in this chapter has been to indicate that a text-immanent approach, where emphasis is laid on the text itself, need not and indeed should not exclude the historical dimension. The challenge for text-immanent approaches is to take the historical dimension seriously.

Literary or synchronic approaches have brought exegetes back to the text as the primary focus of exegetical endeavour. The text in its final form does make sense, which obviates the need to trace hypothetical pre-literary phases.

Bibliography

ADAM, G., KAISER, O., and KUMMEL, W. G., *Einführung in die exegetischen Methoden* (Munich: Chr. Kaiser, 1975).

BARR, J., *The Semantics of Biblical Language* (Oxford: Oxford University Press, 1969).

BARTON, J., 'Historical Criticism and Literary Interpretation: Is There Any Common Ground?', in S. E. Porter, P. Joyce and D. E. Orton (eds.), *Crossing the Boundaries: Essays in Biblical Interpretation in Honour of Michael D. Goulder*, BIS 8 (Leiden: Brill, 1994), pp. 3–16.

——, 'Reading the Bible as Literature: Two Questions for Biblical Critics', *JLT* 1.2 (1987), pp. 135–153.

——, *Reading the Old Testament: Method in Biblical Study* (London: Darton Longman & Todd, 1984).

BECKING, B., 'A Plea for a Historical Critical Approach in the Study of the Old Testament'. Paper read at the congress of the IOSOT in Oslo, Norway, 1998.

BOORER, S., 'The Importance of a Diachronic Approach: The Case of Genesis–Kings', *CBQ* 51.2 (1989), pp. 195–208.

BOSMAN, H. L., 'Die Ontstaan en Verstaan van die Ou Testament', in F. E. Deist and W. S. Vorster (eds.), *Woorde wat Ver Kom*, Die Literatuur van die Ou Testament (Cape Town: Tafelberg, 1986), pp. 8–9.

BOTHA, P. J., BOSMAN, H. L., BURDEN, J. J., and OLIVIER, J. P. J. (eds.), *Understanding the Old Testament in South Africa*, OTESup 7.4, Special Edition (Pretoria: OTSSA, 1994).

COMBRINK, H. J. B., 'Die Krisis van die Skrifgesag in die Gereformeerde Eksegese as 'n Geleentheid', *NGTT* 31.3 (1990), pp. 325–335.

CONRADIE, E. M., JONKER, L. C., LAWRIE, D. G., and ARENDSE, R. A., *Op Soek na Jona: Verskillende Benaderings tot die Interpretasie van die Bybel*, Teks en Konteks 6 (Bellville: University of the Western Cape, 1995).

CRYSTAL, D. A., *Dictionary of Linguistics and Phonetics*, 3rd ed. (Oxford: Blackwell, 1992).

DEIST, F. E., 'Again: Method(s) of Exegesis', *OTE* 1 (1983), pp. 73–88.

——, 'The Bible as Literature: Whose Literature?', *OTE* 7.3 (1994), pp. 327–342.

DEIST, F. E., 'Eksegese as Leeskompetensie: Oor die Onderrig in Skrifuitleg', *NGTT* 30.1 (1989), pp. 56–63.

——, *Ervaring, Rede en Metode in Skrifuitleg: 'n Wetenskapsteoretiese Ondersoek na Skrifuitleg in die Ned. Geref. Kerk 1840–1990* (Pretoria: RGN, 1994).

——, 'Onlangse Konsepte in Teksuitleg en hulle Konsekwensies vir die (Gereformeerde) Teologie', *In die Skriflig* 28.2 (1994), pp. 165–178.

——, 'Die Ou Testamentiese Eksegese en Algemene Literatuurwetenskap', *NGTT* 14 (1975), pp. 75–81.

——, *Towards the Text of the Old Testament* (Pretoria: Dutch Reformed Church Booksellers, 1978).

——, *Witnesses to the Old Testament: Introducing Old Testament Textual Criticism*, The Literature of the Old Testament 5 (Pretoria: Dutch Reformed Church Booksellers, 1988).

DEIST, F. E., and BURDEN, J. J., *'n ABC van Bybeluitleg* (Pretoria: J. L. van Schaik, 1980).

DU TOIT, A. B., 'The Significance of Discourse Analysis for New Testament Interpretation and Translation: Introductory Remarks with Special Reference to I Peter 1:3–13, in Linguistics and Bible Translation', *Neot* 8 (1977), pp. 54–79.

FOHRER, G., and HOFFMANN, H.-W. (eds.), *Exegese des Alten Testaments: Einführung in die Methodik*, Uni-Taschenbücher 267 (Heidelberg: Quelle & Meyer, 1976).

GUNNEWEG, A. H. J., *Understanding the Old Testament* (London: SCM, 1978).

HOFFMANN, H.-W., 'Verlauf der Exegese', in FOHRER and HOFFMANN, *Exegese des Alten Testaments*, pp. 23–30.

HUBER, F., 'Literarkritik', in FOHRER and HOFFMANN, *Exegese des Alten Testaments*, pp. 44–57.

HUMAN, D. J., 'Die Literêr-Historiese Lees van 'n Teks', *Skrif en Kerk* 20.2 (1999), pp. 354–368.

JONKER, L. C., 'Exclusivity and Variety: A Typological Study towards the Integration of Exegetical Methodologies in Old Testament Studies' (DTh diss., University of Stellenbosch, 1993).

KREMER, J., 'Alte, Neuere und neueste Methoden der Exegese', *BL* 53.1 (1980), pp. 3–12.

KUGEL, J. L., *The Bible As It Was* (Cambridge, Mass.: Harvard University Press, 1997).

LE ROUX, J. H., *A Story of Two Ways, Thirty Years of Old Testament Scholarship in South Africa*, OTESup 2 (Pretoria: Verba Vitae, 1993).

LOADER, J. A., 'Gedagtes oor Gekontroleerde Eksegese', *Hervormde Teologiese Studies* 34.1–2 (1978), pp. 1–40.

NOBLE, P. R., 'Synchronic and Diachronic Approaches to Biblical Interpretation', *JLT* 7.2 (1993), pp. 130–148.

POLAK, F. H., 'Het Bijbels Verhaal als Palmpsest: Over de Rol van de Diachrone in de Structurele Analyse', *ACEBT* 9 (1988), pp. 22–34.

PRINSLOO, G. T. M., ''n Literêr-Eksegetiese Analise van die Boek Habakuk' (DD thesis, University of Pretoria, 1989).

PRINSLOO, W. S., 'A Comprehensive Semiostructural Exegetical Approach', in BOTHA et al., *Understanding the Old Testament*, pp. 78–83.

——, 'Isaiah 14:12–15: Humiliation, Hubris, Humiliation', *ZAW* 93.3 (1981), pp. 432–438.

RAD, G. VON, *Old Testament Theology*, 2 vols. (London: SCM, 1975).

RICHTER, W., *Exegese als Literaturwissenschaft: Entwurf einer alttestamentlichen Literaturtheorie und Methodologie* (Göttingen: Vandenhoeck & Ruprecht, 1971).

SCHREINER, J. (ed.), *Einführung in die Methoden der Biblischen Exegese* (Würzburg: Echter, 1971).

TALSTRA, E., *Solomon's Prayer: Synchrony and Diachrony in the Composition of I Kings 8,14–61*, CBET 3 (Kampen: Kok Pharos, 1993).

TOV, E., *Textual Criticism of the Hebrew Bible* (Philadelphia: Fortress, 1992).

UTZSCHNEIDER, H., and NITSCHE, S. A., *Arbeitsbuch literaturwissenschaftliche Bibelauslegung: Eine Methodenlehre zur Exegese des Alten Testaments* (Gütersloh: Gütersloher Verlagshaus, 2001).

VAN ZYL, H. C., *Die Vervreemdings- en Toe-Eieningstaak van die Eksegese* (Bloemfontein: University of the Free State, 1991).

VERVENNE, M., *Bijbelwetenschap: Inleiding oud Testament* (Louvain: Catholic University of Louvain, 1992).

VORSTER, W. S., 'Aischunomai en Stamverwante Woorde in die Nuwe Testament' (DD thesis, University of Pretoria, 1974).

——, 'Concerning Semantics, Grammatical Analysis and Bible Translation, in Linguistics and Bible Translation', *Neot* 8 (1974), pp. 21–41.

——, 'The In/compatibility of Methods and Strategies in Reading or Interpreting the Old Testament', *OTE* 2.3 (1989), pp. 53–63.

WANKE, G., 'Notwendigkeit und Ziel der Exegese des Alten Testaments', in FOHRER and HOFFMANN, *Exegese des Alten Testaments*, pp. 9–13.

——, 'Sprachliche Analyse', in FOHRER and HOFFMANN, *Exegese des Alten Testaments*, pp. 57–81.

WATSON, W. G. E., *Classical Hebrew Poetry: A Guide to its Techniques*, JSOTSup 26 (Sheffield: JSOT Press, 1984).

WOLDE, E. J. VAN, 'Van Tekst via Tekst naar Betekenis: Intertekstualiteit en haar Implicaties', *TvT* 30.4 (1990), pp. 333–361.

——, *Words Become Worlds: Semantic Studies of Genesis 1–11*, BIS 6 (Leiden: Brill, 1994).

WÜRTHWEIN, E., *The Text of the Old Testament: An Introduction to the Biblia Hebraica* (Grand Rapids: Eerdmans, 1979).

ZENGER, E., 'Ein Beispiel exegetischer Methoden aus dem Alten Testament', in SCHREINER, *Einführung in die Methoden*, pp. 97–148.

3. SPEECH-ACT THEORY

Richard S. Briggs

Introduction

Speech-act theory is concerned with the many and various things done with words. It is common to begin discussions of speech-act theory and biblical interpretation with lengthy and technical accounts of the theoretical aspects of speech-act theory, before adducing the occasional (everyday or biblical) example to illustrate what is meant by some such concept as an 'illocutionary act'. The result is often massive conceptual complexity for somewhat limited exegetical insight. Although we shall in due course come to the theory, I choose a different route here, and begin with an interpretative thesis: The Bible itself is persistently and seriously concerned with the many and various things that can be done with words. As a result, it will be worth our while to invest in an interpretative approach that can give us facility with handling how words are used.

This is a small nod in the direction of allowing that our hermeneutical sophistication might be theologically wiser if it is itself informed by the kinds of burdens and agendas that occupy the Scripture we seek to interpret. In later sections of this chapter I shall endeavour to show that speech-act theory helps us to reconceptualize the task(s) of biblical interpretation in such a way as to avoid the familiar stand-off between 'theological interpretation' and other forms of interpretation (be they literary, historical, sociological or whatever). In the course of making such an argument, it will be necessary to explore what is perhaps the most important point about speech-act theory for biblical interpretation, namely that it offers an *integrative* and *balanced* account of all the many factors that go into a text's being encountered by a reader. The resultant hermeneutic I call a 'hermeneutic of self-involvement'. Whether the reader is thus self-involved with the text, the human author or the divine author of Scripture turns out to be one of the areas where speech-act integration offers a more compelling account than a false polarization between alternatives.

The goal of hermeneutics, in any case, is not to demonstrate the superiority of any one method for obtaining 'correct' readings, but is rather to facilitate the evaluation of public criteria for whichever method is to hand.[1] More than this would be unfair to expect of any hermeneutical approach. If the biblical texts are themselves to be taken seriously, then it should be evident that hermeneutical dexterity is not the key to the kingdom of God. Nevertheless, it should also be clear that hermeneutics can still help us to provide a coherent account of the nature and significance of acts of reading and interpreting within that kingdom. That is the goal here.

The significance of 'things done with words' in the Bible

In this section we shall survey some of the many things words do in the biblical texts, in a somewhat unsystematic way conceptually, but with one eye on gathering some of the relevant examples for our discussion of speech-act theory. In the process I hope to demonstrate the interpretative thesis set out above, and begin to raise, by way of pre-theory-laden examples, the kinds of issues speech-act theory is concerned to address.

The first act of Scripture is a speech act: 'Then God said, "Let there be light"; and there was light' (Gen. 1:3).[2] By the end of the chapter God has commanded, commissioned and commended the components of creation, and blessed its human inhabitants. Blessing, as we shall see, is an archetypal speech act. In Genesis 2 the *'ādām* (human) names the animals, up to and including the *'iššâ* (woman) who is taken out of the *'îš* (man). Naming is an act

---

1. See my discussion in 'What Does Hermeneutics Have to Do with Biblical Interpretation?', *HeyJ* 47.1 (2006), pp. 55–74.

2. I am assuming the NRSV reading of Gen. 1:1, but even if one opts for 'In the beginning God created the heavens and the earth', it is still the case that the first such creative act recorded is in v. 3. (All quotations in this chapter are from the NRSV.)

that makes substantial and permanent difference to the early days of the world. In chapter 3 the snake arrives, and immediately begins with the classic hermeneutical question: 'Did God say . . .?' A prototypical argument about interpretation follows. God calls, then critiques, and even curses the ground ('ādāmâ), while the humans argue and blame. Again all acts are performed by and in words, and all this before we have even left the garden.[3]

The creation accounts are followed by further narratives where words play a key role. The Babel story of Genesis 11 is an obvious example, as the confusion of human language is understood to be a separating marker between humanity and God. Promises and blessings loom large throughout Genesis, as well as playing a key role in the Balaam narratives of Numbers 22 – 24. The book of Exodus records the 'ten words' given to Israel. They are to be recited always (Deut. 6:7). In canonical review of the Torah, at Joshua 1:8, we read, 'This book of the law shall not depart out of your mouth'. The idea here is not so much that the Torah is *read*, as that it is recited and 'performed' in spoken meditation, with the hope that as Israel speaks so shall it do. Within the Torah there is the repeated emphasis that the priest shall *say*, and the people shall *respond*. The right words create the right liturgical context for engaging with God. When the words are especially memorable, they are recorded as psalms for future use, and these psalms can then in turn be acts of praise or lament, blessing or invocation, or many other kinds of performative act. Upon return from exile the Book of the Law is read, and produces responses of first weeping and then rejoicing (Neh. 8:8–12). Something about this text is encountered as transformative, and yet the nature of the transformation depends both on the content and the understanding of the effect it is designed to achieve. These are already some of the key themes of speech-act theory.

In addition to all the narrated and recorded examples of the significance of words and speech, the book of Proverbs draws thematic attention to the issue: 'Communication is a large subject in the book of Proverbs. The proper use and reception of words was critically important to the sages.'[4] It is worth pausing, however, to note in what sense this is true. Some proverbs gathered in chapter 12 suggest the following:

---

3. An account that emphasizes 'wordplays in the garden', including a use of speech-act theory as it does so, is B. J. Stratton, *Out of Eden: Reading, Rhetoric, and Ideology in Genesis 2–3*, JSOTSup 208 (Sheffield: Sheffield Academic Press, 1995), esp. pp. 109–168.

4. T. Longman III, *Proverbs*, BCOTWP (Grand Rapids: Baker, 2006), p. 570.

Whoever speaks the truth gives honest evidence,
    . . . the tongue of the wise brings healing.
Truthful lips endure for ever.
(12:17–19)

Each verse also contrasts such speech with opposites: falsehood, deceitfulness, lying. Nevertheless, the sense of 'truth' here, I would suggest, is not 'that wise words match external reality' where 'words can at least adequately represent reality outside of ourselves'.[5] Rather, we might observe that words hook up 'truthfully' to the world in a variety of significant ways: by referring back to what has happened (or what is now the case); by relating internally to what is going on inside us; or by invoking a world created by what we say, a world 'in front of' the text, as I shall describe it later. On the whole, Proverbs is not particularly interested in the first of these. Even 12:17–19 is fundamentally concerned with faithful witness,[6] and the point of this is that one's words have implications for the way the world *will be*, which are both related to but not the same as the way the world is or is represented. The problem with lying, in general in Proverbs, is not that it speaks falsely about what has happened, though this is indeed so, but that in doing so, it sets up a false framework for the world in which we live, or relationships within it, which will have future consequences.

To anticipate the terms I shall be developing, lying is a form of wilful *mis-*construction of the world. Thus a lying witness, described as 'testifying falsely', is at fault because he or she 'sows discord in a family' (6:19). Lying destroys relationships (cf. 10:18). And most interestingly, where lying is an abomination to Yhwh, it is contrasted with 'those who act faithfully' (12:22): the difference is between those who move ahead in wisdom and those who make it difficult (if not impossible?) for others to move ahead in wisdom. The ability of words to construct fundamental aspects of the world remains a persistent theme throughout Proverbs, and longer collections of sayings such as 15:1–5 and 25:11–15 draw out many aspects of this theme, culminating in the memorable image that 'a soft tongue can break bones' (25:15).

---

5. Thus *pace* the otherwise most helpful treatment of Longman both in his Proverbs commentary (see previous note) and in the thematic study of 'Wise Words, Foolish Words', in his *How to Read Proverbs* (Downers Grove: IVP, 2002), pp. 145–155 (quotes from p. 147).

6. The 'false witness' of 12:17b may suggest a court setting.

The nature of prophetic speech, in both OT and NT, probably deserves its own full study from a speech-act perspective.[7] Typically the prophets announce words of judgment or vindication, doom or comfort. These are pronouncements with intended effects, as declared by Yhwh through Isaiah:

> [S]o shall my word be that goes out from my mouth;
>   it shall not return to me empty,
> but it shall accomplish that which I purpose . . .
> (Isa. 55:11)

This concept is not as straightforward as it looks: what if the purpose of the prophetic word is to sketch a future scenario with the intent that the hearers will be shocked into not letting it come about?

This of course is exactly what happens in Jonah 3 – 4, where the prophet wastes no time in complaining to God that he knew it was pointless to preach judgment on Nineveh, because the result would be mercy and not judgment. With a sense for postmodern irony worthy of Jonah himself, literary critic Terry Eagleton once used this story to conclude that 'All good prophets are false prophets, undoing their own utterances in the very act of producing them. . . . [They] produce a state of affairs in which the state of affairs they describe won't be the case.'[8]

The converse, and probably more serious, case occurs in Jeremiah 23:22, where Jeremiah appears to say that if a prophet is really speaking from Yhwh, then the hearers 'would have turned from their evil way', which in Jeremiah's case of course they had not, thereby apparently suggesting that Jeremiah has failed his own test for prophetic validity.[9]

In fact, both these cases require us to find a way of articulating a meaningful distinction between what prophets intend to happen by way of their prophetic announcement, and the actual result of their prophetic declaration. Speech-act theory is interested in precisely this distinction, as we shall see

---

7. The nearest to such a thing is W. Houston, 'What Did the Prophets Think They Were Doing? Speech Acts and Prophetic Discourse in the Old Testament', *BI* 1 (1993), pp. 167–188.

8. T. Eagleton, 'J. L. Austin and the Book of Jonah', in R. Schwartz (ed.), *The Book and the Text: The Bible and Literary Theory* (Oxford: Blackwell, 1990), p. 233.

9. This verse, and relevant interpretations of it, are fully discussed in R. W. L. Moberly, *Prophecy and Discernment* (Cambridge: Cambridge University Press, 2006), pp. 83–88.

when we come to define 'illocutionary' and 'perlocutionary' acts. Armed with this framework, Houston's analysis is precisely to the point:

> [A]s long as the prophets' hearers understood that they were warning them, calling for repentance or whatever the particular speech act might be, and understood the content of the warning or whatever it might be, then the prophets had *done* what they set out to do, even if they had not achieved the effect they had hoped for.[10]

Other prophets, meanwhile, continue to prophesy 'Peace! Peace!' when there is no peace (Jer. 6:14/8:11), an act Jeremiah describes as 'treating the wound of [God's] people carelessly'. Again, the point is less that the words of the (other) prophets are a false record of what is the case, but rather that they promise a false way ahead, with damaging (future) consequences for those who are deceived. What is done with the words is inappropriate, but it is not a failure to report accurately.

Some of these same concerns with the power of words and care needed in their deployment resurface in the NT in the book of James. 'Not many of you should become teachers' (Jas 3:1), not because there is an especial burden on teachers to make accurate statements, because this would be a proper concern of all, but because the tongue is an untameable fire, in disproportionate significance to its size (3:5–8), and thus teachers stand to achieve wide-ranging performative effects of perhaps unpredictable consequences. Indeed, in 1:26 the control of the tongue is one of the two main tests by which true service of God may be discerned. As one commentator notes, it tells us more about our concerns than James's that interpretation of James today tends to focus almost exclusively on the other test, concern for the poor, while speech ethics languishes in relative obscurity.[11]

Much of the relevant NT data, however, as was the case with the OT, occurs in narrative and other contexts. The parables of Jesus spin their perplexing web around those with or without ears to hear, and early Christian preaching places speech once again central to the nature of

---

10. Houston, 'What Did the Prophets Think?', p. 177.

11. See the brief but programmatic comments of R. Bauckham, *James*, New Testament Readings (London: Routledge, 1999), pp. 203–205. We may note too William Baker's discussion of speech ethics in the epistle of James, which somewhat surprisingly makes no substantial use of the insights of speech-act theory: W. R. Baker, *Personal Speech-Ethics in the Epistle of James*, WUNT 2.68 (Tübingen: Mohr, 1995).

Christian discourse. Telling parables and preaching sermons are widely recognized as significant acts performed by words.[12] There is the problem that ever since C. H. Dodd's influential work on 'the apostolic preaching', it has been common to draw too heavy a distinction between teaching (*didachē*) and the powerful summons of preaching (*kerygma*).[13] However, an example such as 1 Corinthians 15:1–11 clearly shows how one could be teaching at the same time as having the content of the teaching serve as the basis of the proclaimed message (*kerygma*). To oversimplify, all teaching keeps summons in view; and all forms of summoning expect and hope to be explained and understood.[14]

The purpose of this survey, of course, is not to be comprehensive, but some awareness of the scope for further exploration may easily be obtained. We may note that the kinds of acts in view are exactly what Wittgenstein called 'language games', such acts as confessing, forgiving, pardoning, repenting, proclaiming, teaching, preaching, praying, interceding, lamenting, rejoicing, boasting, prophesying . . . A convenient way of reviewing the variety of these kinds of language games in the NT is provided by consulting the United Bible Societies' lexicon, which is organized, with a linguistic sensitivity rare in reference works, according to semantic domains rather than alphabetically. In their section on 'Communication', editors Louw and Nida gather the data on some fifty-six different kinds of acts performed with words, providing a veritable encyclopedia of speech acts in the NT.[15] They note too the various and unruly

---

12. On parables, see the selection of pieces collected in A. C. Thiselton, *Thiselton on Hermeneutics: The Collected Works and New Essays of Anthony Thiselton*. Part 5: 'Parables, Narrative-Worlds and Reader-Response Theories' (Aldershot: Ashgate, 2006), pp. 397–521, esp. 417–440. On preaching, note T. M. McNulty, 'Pauline Preaching: A Speech-Act Analysis', *Worship* 53 (1979), pp. 207–214, though this does not really get to the heart of the matter.

13. C. H. Dodd, *The Apostolic Preaching and its Developments* (London: Hodder & Stoughton, 1936), pp. 7–8.

14. This paragraph summarizes an argument explored in R. S. Briggs, *Words in Action: Speech Act Theory and Biblical Interpretation* (Edinburgh: T. & T. Clark; New York: Continuum, 2001), pp. 201–202, based on the work of J. I. H. McDonald, *Kerygma and Didache: The Articulation and Structure of the Earliest Christian Message*, SNTSMS 37 (Cambridge: Cambridge University Press, 1980).

15. J. P. Louw and E. Nida (eds.), *Greek–English Lexicon of the New Testament Based on Semantic Domains*. Vol. 1: *Introduction and Domains*, 2nd ed. (New York: United Bible Societies, 1989), §33, 'Communication', pp. 388–445.

interrelationships between these acts, which are not susceptible to neat subclassification. One might also suggest, in the light of speech-act theory, that the title 'Communication' does not quite do justice to the many and various 'things done with words' listed in this section, but in any case, the value of this resource for speech-act analysis far outweighs the inevitable problems it raises regarding classification.

It is worth noting that the significance of 'things done with words' in the biblical writings is derived from the fact that words can in general be performative and effective in language use, and does not derive from some supposed special or 'primitive' biblical view that a word was a kind of 'thing' endowed with automatic and mysterious efficacious power.[16] The fact that *dābār* can mean both 'word' and 'thing' in Hebrew is irrelevant to our concerns. The point is simply that the effects of words are of considerable significance in many biblical passages. Before we turn to an analysis of why this is so, I shall clarify some of the issues at stake by exploring one type of example in more detail, the example of blessing (and cursing).

We use the language of blessing easily. We say 'God bless you!' or pray the Aaronic blessing of Numbers 6:24–26 over those we care about: 'The Lord bless you and keep you . . .' But what is blessing, and what happens when we bless?[17]

'Blessing' is one of those words we all understand but find hard to define. Louw and Nida observe that 'in a number of languages the closest equivalent of "to bless" is "to pray God on behalf of" or "to ask God to do something good for"'.[18] To bless is to convey some kind of benefit, but the focus is less on the benefit and more on the life or relationship thus benefited. Indeed, blessing can sometimes be the enriching of a life by the very act of stating or emphasizing a relationship.[19] In their dynamic celebration of 'theology as praise', Hardy and Ford write movingly of what it means to bless God:

> Blessing is the comprehensive praise and thanks that returns all reality to God, and so lets all be taken up into the spiral of mutual appreciation and delight which is the

---

16. This contrast was first and programmatically made by A. C. Thiselton, 'The Supposed Power of Words in the Biblical Writings', *JTS* 25 (1974), pp. 282–299.
17. An excellent overview is offered by K. Grüneberg, *Blessing: Biblical Meaning and Pastoral Practice*, Grove Biblical Books B27 (Cambridge: Grove, 2003).
18. Louw and Nida, *Greek–English Lexicon*, p. 442.
19. See K. H. Richards, 'Bless/Blessing', *ABD* 1: 753–755.

fulfilment of creation. For the rabbis of Jesus' time, to use anything of creation without blessing God was to rob God. Only the person receiving with thanks really received from God . . .[20]

Several aspects of blessing are in the foreground here, mutuality and receptivity among them. To receive a blessing may involve material things or offspring, but even these would only be a blessing if accompanied with the transformation of spirit and attitude that allows them to be received with thanks.[21]

When we read biblical texts of blessing in the light of this, we may understand how they work as speech acts. If one prays 'the LORD lift up his countenance upon you, and give you peace' (Num. 6:26), then this is the expression of a desire that the person prayed for will receive peace (šālôm) as they go through the day. This is not an automatic guarantee of peace, but in the very wishing of it upon someone it does contribute to the possibility of their experiencing peace as they go on their way. In general, we may say that whether something or some event is a blessing depends significantly (though not exclusively) on how it is perceived. This is even true of the archetypal elements of OT blessing, land and offspring.

The story of Isaac's blessing of his sons in Genesis 27 is a case where a speech-act analysis highlights what is happening. Isaac offers to bless Esau (v. 4) but Rebekah contrives to have Jacob appear before him under the pretence of being Esau in order to acquire for himself this paternal blessing. Isaac is fooled (vv. 21–27), though only just, and as a result gives his blessing to Jacob, including the declarative

> Let peoples serve you,
> and nations bow down to you.
> Be lord over your brothers . . .
> (v. 29)

---

20. D. W. Hardy and D. F. Ford, *Jubilate: Theology in Praise* (London: Darton Longman & Todd, 1984), p. 81. In a later work Ford adds, 'God blesses and is blessed, we bless and are blessed, creation blesses and is blessed, and a glorious ecology of blessing is the climactic vision of the Kingdom of God' (D. F. Ford, *Self and Salvation: Being Transformed* [Cambridge: Cambridge University Press, 1999], p. 156).

21. Grüneberg, *Blessing*, pp. 9–11, is very helpful on the significant but limited role of material blessing, and the recognition that it does not work 'mechanically'.

At which point, enter Esau, and Jacob's deception is uncovered. 'Bless me, me also, father!' cries Esau (v. 34), but in a move that has long puzzled interpreters, Isaac replies, 'Your brother came deceitfully, and he has taken away your bless-ing' (v. 35). Esau immediately spots the problem any reader of the passage feels: given that this is so unfair of Jacob, why can't his father simply reverse or restore the blessing to its intended recipient, and, failing that, can he at least have another blessing in any case? It is this last, least satisfactory, option that Isaac feels able to bestow.

Why? If an Olympic medal is awarded today to someone who is later dis-covered to have cheated (e.g. taken proscribed drugs), then the medal is stripped from them and awarded to someone else. The difference between the two situations is not to be found in a supposed primitive view of word magic, but in the fact that different conventions are in place that circumscribe the pos-sibilities differently in each case. In the Olympics, awards can be given and taken away, as Job might have said. But in Genesis 27, no convention was apparently in place for the withdrawal of the blessing, and one reason for this is that with Jacob having fled the scene it is not actually possible for him to be recalled to account in order to be told that he has acted deceitfully. As noted in Thiselton's study of word power in the OT, 'to give the same blessing to Esau would be like saying "I do" to a second bride',[22] an example that happens to make it very clear that such an impossibility is socially constructed (given the existence of polygamous practice, and indeed given Esau's subsequent action in Gen. 28:9!).

Jacob, however, has escaped with an ill-gotten blessing, which, rather like stolen cash, is not useless, but is difficult to deploy as part of a life of praise and thanksgiving to God, with all the self-involving implications that has for him. One implication the narrator surely intends us to notice is that when Jacob finds himself in the east, at Uncle Laban's house, he works seven years to wed the attractive Rachel, only to wake the next morning and find he has wed Leah instead, presumably after a day of some merrymaking. But just as the performa-tive act of blessing cannot be undone, neither can the performative act of enter-ing into a marriage covenant, at least not then, nor even today on the morning after the vows. It is interesting that commentators have tended to find this less puzzling than the incident in chapter 27. This is surely because the conventions of saying 'I will' (or its ancient equivalent) are better understood than the con-ventions of blessing, but in each case the speech act presupposes, and then in turn creates, aspects of the social context that explain it and make it possible.

---

22. Thiselton, 'Supposed Power', p. 294.

Many other aspects of blessing could usefully be explored under a speech-act rubric.[23] Indeed, a comparable analysis of cursing would also be productive, though clearly it can on one level be understood as a form of negative blessing, and it is not difficult to see how curses such as those recorded in Deuteronomy 28:16–20ff. would have a certain self-fulfilling disastrous predictive sense.[24] While the power to bless and to curse is largely presupposed in the NT, it is not always explored; the kind of passing reference in James 3:10 being typical.

It has been a deliberate choice to speak, up to this point, of 'how things are done with words'. This is intended to call to mind the founding text of contemporary speech-act theory, J. L. Austin's *How to Do Things with Words*, which to some extent was a non-technical discussion of how language is used for a whole lot more purposes than the making of statements. It therefore followed that whether an assertion was true or false was only one of several potentially interesting avenues of enquiry in assessing a use of language. Did it convince me? Were certain circumstances of my life changed by it (as e.g. with the reading of a will)? Did it alienate? Was it energizing or energy-sapping? Language uses can radiate down all these possible lines of evaluation, as well as being (in certain cases) true or false.

Why would the Bible be concerned with how language is used? The answer to this, I suggest, is that the biblical writers were well aware that many of the most significant aspects of human life are governed in profound ways by language and its uses and effects. To the child who has been upset by taunts and name-calling we may say, 'Sticks and stones may break my bones / but names can never hurt me.' We do this, however, precisely because name-calling *can* hurt, and many of the most cruel ways in which children interact are in fact linguistic. The 'scars' are not physical but can be real enough to affect the rest of the child's life. This example, by focusing on children, is designed to soften us up for the broader point: many aspects of our human interactions are irreducibly linguistic in nature. This is true whether we are talking about the umpire in sport ('That's out!'), the judge in the courtroom ('You're guilty'), or the regulation of a professional exam ('You must stop writing'). It is fashionable, in some circles, to talk of the social construction of reality, and in other

---

23. A speech-act analysis of Gen. 12:1–3 would be an important example. There are pointers towards the themes it might employ in the suggestive, if theoretically complex, reading offered by H. C. White, *Narration and Discourse in the Book of Genesis* (Cambridge: Cambridge University Press, 1991), esp. pp. 107–112 and 169–173.

24. See the useful survey of W. J. Urbrock, 'Blessings and Curses', *ABD* 1: 755–761.

circles to deride this as trendy nonsense. I would argue that the notion of a socially constructed reality is a profound half-truth. Some things are there regardless, stubbornly and objectively, while others we make by our conventions. John Searle, a leading speech-act theorist in his time, helpfully suggests recasting the point at issue as *The Construction of Social Reality*, and offers the following memorable example: 'Part of being a cocktail party is being thought to be a cocktail party; part of being a war is being thought to be a war. This is a remarkable feature of social facts; it has no analogue among physical facts.'[25] Clear-headedness on this issue would be of inestimable benefit to biblical studies, which still too often operates with questions like 'Did it happen?' rather than 'What is at stake (or how far am I invested) in describing an incident in such-and-such a manner?'

It is these ideas, and more, formalized to some or other extent, that make up the burgeoning literature of speech-act theory. It needs to be acknowledged that many writers in the subject seem to take an undue delight in heavyweight terminological definitions and the classification of ever more narrowly defined cases and concepts. It is my judgment that there is a place for such conceptual clarity, but that it needs to be balanced by regular review of why it is that speech-act theory is worth pursuing in the first place for those interested in biblical interpretation. The preceding examples have already attempted to pave the way for this claim. In the remainder of this chapter, I propose to summarize the results of the detailed discussions elsewhere with some brevity, aware that at every turn a myriad of qualifications and footnotes might have been added, before moving on to a more extended account of what is, I think, the important issue foregrounded by speech-act theory, which I shall call 'a hermeneutic of self-involvement'.

Speech-act theory: a glossary of key terms and why they matter for biblical interpretation

I have argued at length elsewhere that one reason for confusion among biblical interpreters is that speech-act theory has been developed in a variety of contrasting ways.[26] One might say that there is no one 'canonical' account of it, and a simple reason for this is that J. L. Austin's *How to Do Things with Words*

---

25. J. R. Searle, *The Construction of Social Reality* (London: Penguin, 1995), p. 34.
26. The following account is extracted and considerably simplified from Briggs, *Words in Action*, pp. 31–72.

was in fact a posthumous publication of lecture notes.[27] Austin's text is wonderfully readable, a rare philosophical text that one can recommend without hesitation to non-philosophers. It is full of lecturer's asides and unexpected notes that 'It is time then to make a fresh start on the problem,'[28] at which point, well over halfway through the book, one realizes we haven't really begun yet. Nowhere is the informality of the book more significant than in its final brief chapter, which sets out five different types of speech act.[29] The result of this 'work in progress', left unfinished by Austin's death in 1960, is that it has become possible to develop his insights in a variety of directions. The philosopher most commonly credited with picking up his cloak and inheriting a double portion of his performative spirit is John Searle, whose *Speech Acts* is perhaps the second most significant text in the field, and whose various other studies have produced quite a body of work essentially concerned to systematize a theory of speech acts.[30] Much of the more recent philosophical and linguistic work in speech-act theory is still in essence attempting to articulate the nuances and implications of the basic positions sketched out by Austin and Searle.[31]

Rather than offer yet another full account of this development and diversity, I shall instead simply provide working definitions of key terms, and in the process try briefly to indicate their significance.

Illocutionary act

On the occasion of the utterance of a sentence we may say that three 'acts' are performed. The *locutionary* act is the act of saying, pure and simple. The *illocutionary* act is performed in saying something: in saying 'I promise to be there

---

27. J. L. Austin, *How to Do Things with Words*, ed. J. O. Urmson and M. Sbisà, 2nd ed. (Oxford: Oxford University Press, 1975).

28. Ibid., p. 91.

29. Ibid., pp. 148–164.

30. See J. R. Searle, *Speech Acts: An Essay in the Philosophy of Language* (Cambridge: Cambridge University Press, 1969); *Expression and Meaning: Studies in the Theory of Speech Acts* (Cambridge: Cambridge University Press, 1979), esp. its opening chapter, 'A Taxonomy of Illocutionary Acts' (pp. 1–29); and his article 'How Performatives Work', in his *Consciousness and Language* (Cambridge: Cambridge University Press, 2002), pp. 156–179.

31. Witness the clear and up-to-date editorial overview of the discipline provided in the 'Introduction' to D. Vanderveken and S. Kubo (eds.), *Essays in Speech Act Theory*, Pragmatics and Beyond NS 77 (Amsterdam: John Benjamins, 2001), pp. 1–21.

tomorrow' I actually promise, rather than just saying those words. The promise, in this instance, is itself the illocutionary act. The results of the act, which will depend on a whole bundle of contextual circumstances, are the *per-locutionary* effects. The distinction is sometimes (and usually fairly) approximated by saying that the three acts are '*of* saying' (locution), '*in* saying' (illocution) and '*by* saying' (perlocution).

Confronted with a sentence in our printed biblical text, textual criticism is (approximately) the art of discerning the locution. Rhetorical criticism (arguably) is concerned with the perlocution, or perhaps better the intended perlocution, which concept is largely undeveloped by Austin and Searle, although Vincent Brümmer has suggested that it would be useful to develop it and call it the 'per-illocution': 'evoking an intended response in a hearer by performing an illocution'.[32] Speech-act theory, I hereby advocate, is most usefully concerned with the illocution. Because this is so, some writers use the term 'speech act' to discuss what might technically be called illocutions, although in context this rarely causes confusion.

We have seen several examples of the significance of illocutions in our survey of biblical texts. The prophets preach the need to repent: this address is illocutionary, and is a separate point at issue from the perlocutionary one, which is whether anyone repents or not. In Acts 23:6, Paul says to the gathered Sanhedrin, 'I am on trial concerning the hope of the resurrection of the dead.' The locution is clear, but the illocution, if we credit Paul with the deliberate desire to get out of a tight spot by creating dissension between the Pharisees and Sadducees present, appears to be something more to do with foregrounding a subject of controversy than of saying why he was on trial.[33] The perlocutionary effect, in any case, is something of a mini-riot, which probably ran beyond what Paul had hoped (or intended?) to achieve, but still solved his immediate problem.

Performative utterance

Sometimes certain types of illocution are called 'performative utterances' for historical reasons that need not detain us. A performative utterance is typically a present-tense first person indicative sentence ('I name this ship!'), though this is neither a necessary nor sufficient condition. Searle's definition

---

32. V. Brümmer, *Theology and Philosophical Inquiry: An Introduction* (Philadelphia: Westminster, 1982), p. 11.

33. See e.g. I. H. Marshall, *Acts*, TNTC (Leicester: IVP, 1980), p. 360, who says explicitly that Paul 'successfully divided the assembly by claiming . . .' – thus a perlocution par excellence.

will suffice: '[S]ome illocutionary acts can be performed by uttering a sentence containing an expression that names the type of speech act, as in, for example, "I order you to leave the room." These utterances, and only these, are correctly described as performative utterances.'[34] The point is clearer set against the alternatives, 'I can't fry an egg by saying, "I fry an egg," but I can promise to come and see you just by saying, "I promise to come and see you." '[35]

Divine performatives are of particular interest in Scripture, from 'Let there be light' through to 'Your sins are forgiven.' The difference between divine and human performatives is not fundamentally a matter of *how* they function as language, so much as the different capacities of the performer of the action, a point somewhat surprisingly made by philosophers with no avowed interest in biblical interpretation at all: '[A]ny verb at all that names an intentional action could be uttered performatively. All depends on facts about how the world works and not on the meaning of action verbs. Because of His supernatural powers, God can use performatively many more verbs than we can.'[36] Thus the difference between 'Let the dry land appear' and 'Let there be a coffee break'. Francis Watson has offered a helpful account of Genesis 1 as what he calls 'the *speech-act model* of divine creativity', where at least on days 1 and 3 (vv. 3, 9 and 11) there appears to be no intermediate act between God commanding 'Let there be . . .' and its being so.[37]

Types of illocutionary act

How many different types of illocution are there? The answer to this depends on many conceptual and contextual factors, but one almost universally adopted schema is Searle's fivefold view that 'there are a rather limited number of basic things we do with language: we tell people how things are, we try to get them to do things, we commit ourselves to doing things, we express our feelings and attitudes and we bring about changes through our utterances'.[38] These classifications are often known as

---

34. Searle, 'How Performatives Work', p. 158.

35. Ibid., p. 156.

36. Vanderveken and Kubo, 'Introduction', in Vanderveken and Kubo, *Essays in Speech Act Theory*, p. 8.

37. F. Watson, *Text, Church and World: Biblical Interpretation in Theological Perspective* (Edinburgh: T. & T. Clark, 1994), pp. 140–151, esp. 140–142, where he compares this model with 'fabrication' and 'mediation' models.

38. Searle, *Expression and Meaning*, p. 29. I offer an extended critique of the *necessity* of this view in Briggs, *Words in Action*, pp. 50–58.

- assertives
- directives
- commissives
- expressives
- declaratives (or declarations)

The first four can all be performed declaratively too, in a hybrid fashion.[39] Most of the standard and clearest examples of 'speech acts', on this classification, are 'assertive declarations', where the act of asserting makes it so. One study of speech acts classifies over 270 'performative verbs' under these various headings, and analyses how the speaker and hearer are related in them, according to which of these five basic categories of illocutionary act is performed.[40]

Such terminology is useful for the biblical interpreter in so far as it serves to clarify discussion, and the kinds of case study noted above can be helpful for illuminating examples of illocutions in the biblical text. In many cases, the correct illocutionary classification is *the* question of interpretation. What act is performed by 'I permit no woman to teach' (1 Tim. 2:12), an expressive (a personal preference) or a declarative ('It shall not be done')? Note too that this is a question about illocution and not perlocution, the (illocutionary) point of the verse, not its actual effect(s). To take another example, a complex question of classification is raised by saying 'I forgive you': is this a declarative that is successful by virtue of being said, or is it a description of some other act that needs to be performed in order to be true? The interpretation of several texts concerning forgiveness depends on how we relate the spoken words to the ongoing nature of the relationship involved.[41]

---

39. So J. R. Searle and D. Vanderveken, *Foundations of Illocutionary Logic* (Cambridge: Cambridge University Press, 1985), p. 175. Note the quote in the previous note actually continues, 'Often, we do more than one of these at once in the same utterance.'

40. D. Vanderveken, *Meaning and Speech Acts*. Vol. 1: *Principles of Language Use* (Cambridge: Cambridge University Press, 1990), pp. 166–219. It is this kind of analysis that is needed to supplement the cataloguing of Louw and Nida, *Greek–English Lexicon*; see n. 15 above.

41. This is a complex and theologically important example, or set of examples, and I do not wish to do it the injustice of too rapid summary or simplification. I have offered some aspects of a speech-act analysis of forgiveness in Matthew's Gospel in Briggs, *Words in Action*, pp. 217–255.

Brute and institutional facts

We have seen above that speech acts create states of affairs, or, more simply, some facts are facts because we say so. John Searle defines a fact that depends on human agreement as an 'institutional fact', whereas facts that are so whether anyone believes them or not he defines as 'brute facts'. Alternatively, brute facts operate outside any human institutions, whereas institutional facts exist only within them, and most exist within some and not others. An additional category is the 'social fact', which is an institutional fact derived from a collective intentional agreement.[42]

These categories are of immense use to any theological analysis of the world, if only because the church (or any defined gathering of believers) constitutes an institution in this sense. Further, most questions of whether something is 'allowed' or not are actually questions about how the institution manages its boundary. Are practices allowed, accepted or prohibited? It depends on how the (social) institution is constructed.[43]

How does all this relate to speech-act theory? Here, I think, is one area where the implications of speech-act theory have still not been adequately explored in biblical and theological interpretation. Searle demonstrates that the fundamental building block of 'social reality' is the decision to count one thing as something else in certain situations. Money is an obvious example: we count this kind of piece of paper as £10 in the British economy. Searle's formula is 'X counts as Y in context C'. In speech-act theory, locutions count as illocutions under certain conditions. These words constitute a *promise*. Those words count as a *blessing*. This speech is taken as a *kerygmatic sermon*. That word is a *violent and offensive act*, and to say it would have (social/institutional/personal) consequences.[44] These are just the sorts of examples we have tracked through the scriptural texts above. If Searle is right, then what is happening in these situations is that a form of social reality is being created, sustained and developed by the performance of illocutionary acts. It is important to see that it is *illocutions* which do this: they operate the conventions of the day and are, if one may

---

42. We rapidly run into the controversial aspects of Searle's thesis whereby much of his understanding of language is built on his philosophy of mind and a particular view of intentionality and collective intentionality. This need not concern us here. The above definitions are most easily found in Searle, *Construction of Social Reality*, pp. 1–3, 26, and esp. 27–29.

43. This turns out to be one of the issues related to forgiveness (e.g. with respect to binding and loosing in the church in Matthew's Gospel). See n. 41 above.

44. Thus 'if you say "you fool" you will be liable to Gehenna', Matt. 5:22 (NRSV fn.).

say it this way, effective before one necessarily knows what has been said. Jacob has married Leah, and cannot say, 'I don't.' The act is performed in the saying of the words. The ways in which this process operates in and through specifically biblical texts brings in the question of canon, to which we return below, but in essence it means that the world created in front of *these* texts carries more theological weight than any other, for those who accept the significance of the canon.[45]

A note is needed to tidy up one major implication of what has just been said. If it is true that texts count as certain illocutionary acts, and thus that biblical exegesis involves the appropriate discernment of textual illocutions, then what is to stop people taking locutions in other ways, or arguing that it all depends on how you take something? Has this not handed over all the interpretative 'power' to readers and their decision about how to construe the text? The short answer is that there is a whole spectrum of responses to this question, ranging from those who think that speech-act theory does precisely this (i.e. it leaves the author at the mercy of the interpreter) through to those who think it offers a description of communicative action that respects both author and reader.[46] I have argued elsewhere that this spectrum is in fact appropriate: there are texts where the reader may 'take' or 'count' the text as something quite other than its locutionary appearance would suggest, while there are others where we 'read' or 'see' texts in ways that offer little scope for such a strong construal. This, in fact, is one area where the application of speech-act theory to written texts as communicative acts does introduce further dimensions of complexity, owing to the 'distanciated' nature of communication through texts as against through face-to-face speech. Speech-act theory

---

45. Of course, those who accept it would also say that the theological weight applies to those who do not accept it too, but that this latter group do not *realize* it. Accounts of canonical authority in terms of social construction are thus not necessarily 'sectarian' or reduced to 'it works for us', though obviously this does not mean they will not be contested by those with differing views.

46. For the former, see most famously S. Fish, *Is There a Text in This Class? The Authority of Interpretive Communities* (Cambridge, Mass.: Harvard University Press, 1980), esp. pp. 197–245 and 268–292; and J. Derrida, *Limited Inc*, ed. G. Graff (Evanston: Northwestern University Press, 1988). For the latter, note K. J. Vanhoozer, *Is There a Meaning in this Text? The Bible, the Reader, and the Morality of Literary Knowledge* (Grand Rapids: Zondervan; Leicester: Apollos, 1998), drawing on the work of Searle and also of J. Habermas, *The Theory of Communicative Action: The Critique of Functionalist Reason*, 2 vols. (Boston: Beacon, 1984, 1987).

describes the issue of how texts are construed as acts, but it does not offer a simple resolution to it.[47]

We conclude this section with an example designed to show the benefits of recognizing that language is not necessarily in the business of describing reality but may equally be concerned to construct reality. This may be illustrated with respect to changing perceptions of the social location and function of the book of Revelation. It was commonplace to argue, based on a certain theory of apocalyptic literature, that the book of Revelation represented a form of resistance under persecution. To be precise it was dated to the Domitianic persecution of AD 95–6, deduced from Eusebius' brief remarks in his *Ecclesiastical History* (3.19.1–20.7). It is far from evident, however, why Eusebius need be taken at face value, given the various competing claims of apologists of later Roman rulers.[48] Taking his cue from the performative view of language suggested by speech-act theory, Leonard Thompson's study of Revelation argued that in fact the text was designed to provoke crisis among a readership too easily accommodated to the Roman Empire. Jonathan Knight summarizes as follows:

> John *encourages* his readers to see themselves in conflict with society as part of his
> distinctive vision of the world that he communicates to the churches. The
> Apocalypse *creates* the notion of conflict through its choice of genre, where conflict
> and world-negation are prominent themes, and also through the language and
> imagery as the different visions unfold.[49]

This is not a report of a state of affairs, but a performative call to construe a certain state of affairs where it is not perceived. Are the seven churches of Revelation 2 – 3 in a state of 'crisis'? Not obviously, on any straightforward reading of the text. In any case, suggests Thompson, we would really need to define what we meant by 'crisis' before such a claim would be worth making, and he cites approvingly those who have observed that 'Crisis is defined by a

---

47. See Briggs, *Words in Action*, pp. 73–103, on whether the theory applies to written
     texts, and pp. 105–143 on how the construal of texts as particular actions may
     operate.

48. L. L. Thompson, *The Book of Revelation: Apocalypse and Empire* (New York: Oxford
     University Press, 1990), pp. 95–115, and *passim*. For a reading of the book based on
     this programmatic thesis, see J. Knight, *Revelation*, Readings (Sheffield: Sheffield
     Academic Press, 1999), esp. pp. 21–28.

49. Knight, *Revelation*, pp. 26–27.

set of variables as perceived by the decision maker.' In other words, a crisis is
a social fact, and the decision to call a situation a crisis is a self-involving one.[50]

Reading scriptural texts in the light of speech-act theory

Having acquired this much theory relating to speech acts, we must now reconsider some of the hidden hermeneutical issues in the opening discussion of
the significance of words in the biblical accounts. The preceding discussion of
speech-act theory and its significance for questions of biblical interpretation
has, in the interests of defining and illustrating key points, glossed over one
rather central question. This is what difference it makes, if any, that the texts
in question are *biblical* ones? In other words, is what has been described so far
an approach to texts that could equally well unlock the powerful impact of the
novels of Jane Austen on today's reader, or the works of Josephus or Aquinas
or Dan Brown? Some of the concerns of speech-act theory seem to me to
offer some helpful ways ahead here.

Put simply, an emphasis on speech acts in biblical interpretation invites a
variety of possible ways of understanding who is doing what and to whom
with words:

1. Characters within biblical narratives, to each other.
2. The authors of biblical texts, to their readers.
3. The collectors/editors/compilers of these texts, to *their* readers (which
   includes readers all the way from 'then' to 'now', including us).
4. God, in, by or through any or all of the above.

One cannot necessarily map these different performative levels to different
speech acts. A narrated blessing in the midst of Genesis may at one and the
same time be a blessing to the reader and a blessing by God, or not, as the case
may be.

Different writers tend to emphasize one or the other type of speech acts.
Thus the burden of Nicholas Wolterstorff's much-discussed book *Divine
Discourse* is to explore how God appropriates for his own communicative purposes the human discourses of Scripture. The book is essentially a programmatic attempt to 'introduce the concept of double-agency discourse, thereby
enabling us to understand how it might be that God speaks – that is, performs

---

50. Thompson, *Book of Revelation*, pp. 28 and 215 (n. 10).

illocutionary acts – by way of the writing and speaking of the biblical writers'.[51] He is less clear on how we might actually know what has been divinely said (or performed).[52]

Probably the most thorough investigation to date of this whole area is Kevin Vanhoozer's substantial chapter on 'Scripture Acts', in which he argues that 'understanding consists in recognizing illocutionary acts and their results', and that 'interpretation is the process of inferring authorial intentions and of ascribing illocutionary acts'.[53] When it comes to the specific case of interpreting the Bible, Vanhoozer suggests a concept of 'canonical illocution', which is something like taking into account the genre of a whole text (rather than one act within it), and asking what act is performed by the text in its canonical context.[54] He gives the example of the book of Jonah, where the key issue of interpretation is not working out what the individual sentences or even component narratives mean, but what constitutes the 'illocutionary act performed on the level of a literary whole'. For Vanhoozer, the canonical illocutionary act performed by the book of Jonah is that of satirizing religious complacency while also critiquing a kind of ethnocentrism.[55] This is a good example of the

51. N. Wolterstorff, *Divine Discourse: Philosophical Reflections on the Claim that God Speaks* (Cambridge: Cambridge University Press, 1995), esp. pp. 183–222. The quote is from his later reflection on the book, 'True Words', in A. G. Padgett and P. R. Keifert (eds.), *But Is It All True? The Bible and the Question of Truth* (Grand Rapids: Eerdmans, 2006), p. 36.

52. An interesting debate regarding how reliable his criteria are, focusing on the question of knowing a trustworthy God before one comes to the biblical text, is set out (but not resolved) in N. Wolterstorff, 'The Promise of Speech-Act Theory for Biblical Interpretation', in C. G. Bartholomew, K. Möller and C. Green (eds.), *After Pentecost: Language and Biblical Interpretation*, SHS 2 (Grand Rapids: Zondervan; Carlisle: Paternoster, 2001), pp. 73–90; and M. Hesse, 'How to Be a Postmodernist and Remain a Christian: A Response to Nicholas Wolterstorff', in Bartholomew, Möller and Green, *After Pentecost*, pp. 91–96. I offer a brief critique of the relevant issues in my 'Speech-Act Theory', in K. J. Vanhoozer (gen. ed.), *Dictionary for Theological Interpretation of the Bible* (Grand Rapids: Baker, 2005), pp. 763–766.

53. K. J. Vanhoozer, 'From Speech Acts to Scripture Acts: The Covenant of Discourse and the Discourse of Covenant', in *First Theology: God, Scripture and Hermeneutics* (Leicester: Apollos, 2002), pp. 180, 182, the fifth and sixth of the ten 'theses' defended in the chapter.

54. This is a simplified account of ibid., pp. 188–199.

55. Vanhoozer, 'Speech Acts', p. 192.

kind of issue at stake in reading a scriptural book for its illocutionary point, which is not necessarily linked on the level of meaning (or content) to the individual illocutions at work in the text.

Two points may perhaps be made here. First, Vanhoozer offers his 'reading' of Jonah in a footnote, more or less, and there are few interpreters of Jonah today who are not asking basically this question, though with considerably more nuanced readings of the text.[56] In this sense it is not that speech-act theory is offering an insight heretofore unavailable, but rather that it is refining the conceptuality of the question being asked. In particular, we may now go further than asking, 'What is the *point* of the Jonah story?', and see that the communicative analysis offered by Vanhoozer, in passing, can easily distinguish between the *illocutionary* (canonical) act, which is a matter of an intended and/or conventional effect, and the actual results of reading Jonah, which have occurred down through the centuries (the *perlocutionary* effects).[57]

Secondly, it is important not to move too fast with the claim that a divine illocutionary act relocates the focus of the interpreter on to a supposed 'world in front of the text', where God deals with the theologically envisioned narrative world the text displays. A speech-act hermeneutic will enable us to realize fairly easily that different texts will have different relationships between states of affairs 'behind' the text and 'in front of' the text. Some texts report, others suggest, others still imagine, and many operate in a variety of modes. Anthony Thiselton picks up this point when he observes the overwhelming tendency of some biblical interpreters to subsume all biblical texts to one or another fashionable literary theory: Jonah may be a 'self-contained satire', but 'to fail to look "behind" the text of 1 Corinthians, or "behind" *as well as* "within" the world of the Gospels would fatally detach text from the extra-textual world of reality'.[58] As one speech-act theorist memorably expressed it, locutionary acts

---

56. For one recent example, along with discussion of others, see R. W. L. Moberly, 'Jonah, God's Objectionable Mercy, and the Way of Wisdom', in D. F. Ford and G. Stanton (eds.), *Reading Texts: Seeking Wisdom: Scripture and Theology* (London: SCM, 2003), pp. 154–168.

57. On which, see the remarkable survey of Y. Sherwood, *A Biblical Text and its Afterlives: The Survival of Jonah in Western Culture* (Cambridge: Cambridge University Press, 2000).

58. A. C. Thiselton, '"Behind" and "In Front of" the Text: Language, Reference and Indeterminacy', in Bartholomew, Möller and Green, *After Pentecost*, p. 100. This article is a helpful analysis of the metaphors of 'behind' and 'in front' as applied to textual worlds.

'stage' illocutionary ones, and in order to discern 'the real pragmatic activity of the actors, as opposed to the characters they play on stage, one had better look behind the scenes'.[59] In other words, any text could be interpreted as a self-contained literary (staged/'in front') world, but to determine whether this does justice to the text involves judgments about extra-textual factors such as the nature of the illocutions involved.

Now, are all of these concerns and categorizations relevant only to biblical texts, or do they illuminate other works too? I think it is possible to answer this question without presenting a full analysis of Jowett's famous contention that we should read the Bible like any other book, or indeed of the current debate about the nature of 'theological' interpretation of scripture.[60] Speech-act theory, I suggest, sets up exactly the right framing questions for what is involved in the broadly conceived process of interpreting a text.[61] The construal of any text includes assessing which illocutionary acts are being performed, which, as Recanati puts it, involves looking 'behind the scenes'. The judgments concerned, then, will be of a nature relevant to the particular text being interpreted. Judgments about whether the God of the Genesis narrative is the God of the Christian church today will make a difference to how the various narratives are construed as performing acts upon the reader. Indeed, the debate about Jonah seems to illustrate this too: it is on the level of the 'canonical' and/or theological framing of the book that these judgments come into their own, but they are not separable from the question of what illocutions are at work in specific sentences of the text. What is being done to the reader, for instance, when the

---

59. F. Recanati, *Meaning and Force: The Pragmatics of Performative Utterances* (Cambridge: Cambridge University Press, 1987), p. 266.

60. Cf. B. Jowett, 'On the Interpretation of Scripture', in *Essays and Reviews*, 7th ed. (London: Longman, Green, Longman & Roberts, 1861), pp. 330–433, for the famous contention that one should interpret the Bible 'like any other book'.

61. Thus it is that there is a literature relating to how it works in general literary terms, even if it sometimes seems too easily sidetracked by other ideological issues. For two of the best examples, see M. L. Pratt, *Toward a Speech Act Theory of Literary Discourse* (Bloomington: Indiana University Press, 1977); and S. Petrey, *Speech Acts and Literary Theory* (New York: Routledge, 1990). This is also the place to note a route not explored here, that of working with Paul Grice's pragmatics-oriented principles of 'conversational implicature', politeness, relevance and so forth, which are occasionally bracketed under the heading of 'speech-act theory', though the concerns seem significantly different. See P. Grice, *Studies in the Way of Words* (Cambridge, Mass.: Harvard University Press, 1989).

sailors cry out, 'Please, O Yhwh, we pray, do not let us perish . . .'? (Jon. 1:14). Who recognizes Yhwh in this book, and how does that relate to how inter-preters discern Yhwh at work in and through this book?

But having said all this, I am not persuaded that these questions are funda-mentally different *hermeneutically* from the questions raised by interpreting other texts too. Thus Jane Austen's 'It is a truth universally acknowledged that a single man in possession of a good fortune must be in want of a wife' is at one and the same time a whole raft of illocutionary acts, each discernible only to differing levels of extra-textual judgment. At the very least the narrator of *Pride and Prejudice* is giving voice to Austen's ironic critique of her social world. Likewise, much of the discussion of Dan Brown's *Da Vinci Code* turns on pre-cisely the question of how much non-narrative-world backing is implied in the claims of some of the characters, with regard to, say, non-canonical gospels or reconstructions of events in the life of Jesus.

To summarize, speech-act theory offers a way of thinking about the com-municative dynamics of all texts, but the specific nature of the biblical texts serves to intensify the issues at stake. In particular, the ways in which the God of biblical texts is related to the God of Christians today, and remains a God interested in communicating through these particular texts, gives us a com-municative dynamic of unusual complexity, as well as requiring us to pay careful attention to the nature of the scriptural illocutions effective among us.

A hermeneutic of self-involvement[62]

Enough has been said, I hope, to demonstrate that speech-act theory has both significant resources as well as significant limitations as one hermeneutical tool among many in interpreting biblical texts. In particular, it invites us to seek out the best way of juggling the various claims of author, text and reader in

---

62. Cf. Briggs, *Words in Action*, pp. 147–182, and *passim*. As per its subtitle, this book pointed '*toward* a hermeneutic of self-involvement', and was a conscious attempt to build upon and develop the original speech-act analysis of D. D. Evans, *The Logic of Self-Involvement: A Philosophical Study of Everyday Language with Special Reference to the Christian Use of Language about God as Creator* (London: SCM, 1963). See also the significant study of A. C. Thiselton, 'The Hermeneutics of Self-Involvement: From Existentialist Models to Speech-Act Theory', ch. 8 of his *New Horizons in Hermeneutics: The Theory and Practice of Transforming Biblical Reading* (London: HarperCollins, 1992), pp. 272–312.

biblical interpretation. I shall now turn to one way in which we might understand this task.

The resources of speech-act theory for biblical interpretation, as described above, do not constitute an interpretative method by means of which one may generate 'speech-act readings' of biblical texts in general or deploy 'speech-act criticism' alongside other types of approach.[63] Some attempts to do just this seem to run aground somewhat on cataloguing large numbers of assertions amid more 'interesting' cases.[64] Rather, speech-act theory highlights the ways in which the biblical text is drawn into the life of the reader, as illocutions are discerned amid the locutions. While on one level, this can of course be done with any text, the fact of the matter is that many stretches of text are more or less straightforward ways of, for example, moving the narrative to the next point of interest or tension. For this practical reason, if for no other, it seems worthwhile to distinguish between 'strong' and 'weak' illocutions. All illocutions operate with and through conventions in place at the time of utterance, but sometimes these conventions are only linguistic conventions (e.g. that words count in certain ways). A weak illocution, then, is one that requires only linguistic conventions in order to function. This is the case with many assertions. A strong illocution (such as a promise, curse or confession etc.) requires certain non-linguistic conventions to be in place before it can function. Applications of speech-act theory to biblical interpretation that have taken this distinction on board, even without the terminology of 'strong' and 'weak', have tended to produce correspondingly more interesting and substantive results.[65]

In this section I want to try to offer a straightforward account of what I call 'a hermeneutic of self-involvement', which is operative in cases of texts that

---

63. See further Briggs, *Words in Action*, pp. 73–104 and 293–298 in particular.

64. Thus e.g. J. E. Botha, *Jesus and the Samaritan Woman: A Speech-Act Reading of John 4:1– 42*, NovTSup 65 (Leiden: Brill, 1991), who analyses fifty different utterances in John 4 but ends up classifying no fewer than forty-two of them as 'constative'. Many such examples are working with the 'Gricean' model not explored here. See n. 61 above.

65. I have surveyed them up to 2000 in my 'The Uses of Speech-Act Theory in Biblical Interpretation', *CR:BS* 9 (2001), pp. 229–276. The interesting work of B. Gilfillan Upton, *Hearing Mark's Endings: Listening to Ancient Popular Texts through Speech-Act Theory*, BIS 79 (Leiden: Brill, 2006), which makes its own attempt to demarcate appropriate texts for such an analysis, came to my attention too late for consideration here.

carry strongly self-involving illocutions. It is here, I think, that the benefits of a speech-act analysis are most significant, although it is true to say that there have not yet been many such studies. Our goal, then, is to draw together the threads of the discussion so far, and see how speech-act theory can highlight certain theologically important dimensions of the function of biblical texts, and then give one or two examples of this analysis at work.

The issue at hand is how this (biblical) text transforms its readers. Ever since the rise of historical criticism, this has been a difficult issue to articulate. As Hans Frei noted, 'The relation between historical criticism and hermeneutics has remained an unresolved issue ever since its inception in the eighteenth century.'[66] All too often, the solution was to separate out 'meaning' as the matter of the text, and then regard any personal, affective or transformational dimension as an extra step, almost detachable or hermeneutically optional. Indeed, the standard genre of 'biblical commentary' seems to exemplify exactly this divide. As the modern consensus has begun to evaporate, it has become apparent that this account of biblical interpretation is insufficient for allowing us to analyse the dimension of 'self-involvement' that the church's experience of reading the Bible so often encounters.

We can understand 'self-involvement' from a variety of everyday experiences. We receive a letter from a loved one: this is read with more intense investment in its contents than a letter explaining a change in one's electricity bill. Though even then, if money is tight and the bill is going up, there is a fair degree of involvement. Likewise we hear on the news of troubles in some far country, and are attentive but not perhaps struck. When the troubles occur in a city where we have friends and relatives, we sense that the news is suddenly addressing us personally. A text is posted on the wall. It turns out to be notice of redundancy. One cannot read this without a form of (very negative) personal transformation occurring in the reading.

The point about speech-act theory and biblical interpretation is that the reading of the biblical text is just such a self-involved and transformative act, and that it is so (at least in part) because of the illocutions operative in Scripture. We are not required to remove transformation to a separable and second stage in the hermeneutical process. Rather, with a strongly self-involving illocution, the transformative effect is a part of the successful function of the illocutionary act. Recall that with illocutions the effect is not how

---

66. H. W. Frei, *The Eclipse of Biblical Narrative: A Study in Eighteenth and Nineteenth Century Hermeneutics* (New Haven: Yale University Press, 1974) p. 56. Frei's book is effectively a prolegomenon to sorting out this very issue.

the text turns out to affect us, but it is a transaction completed in the very reception of the text, or perhaps better, in the understanding of the text.

The strongly self-involving illocution of confessing one's sin, for example, is possible only from a self-understanding that acknowledges sin. In 1 John 1:9 we read, 'If we confess our sins, he who is faithful and just will forgive us our sins . . .' This text is designed to highlight the self-involving nature of confession. Many of us, much of the time, are not in a position to acknowledge our sin. If however we are so inclined, then that says something about our nature, and what the text promises is that these sins are forgiven by God. Both confession and forgiveness are illocutionary acts. 1 John is full of these kinds of examples, and has been the subject of an illuminating and rewarding study by Dietmar Neufeld, who argues that 'The power of the written word to transform the orientation of the readers does not lie in carefully argued theological propositions, but in acts of speech with the power to change the self of the speaker.'[67]

The key issue (at least theologically) is transformation, but the problem with calling this a 'hermeneutic of transformation' is that 'transformation' is ambiguous with respect to whether the effects on the reader are illocutionary or perlocutionary in nature. While this is of little theological import on one level, on another level it makes a big difference. Texts can have all sorts of effects for all sorts of reasons, and just because a text has an effect does not always mean that something good or relevant to God's (communicative) purposes is happening. If rhetorical criticism does not convince us of this, then our experience of the practical use of the Bible from certain pulpits and in certain social situations should certainly suggest it. The difference in the case of illocutionary effects is that the results of the speech act are inherent in the communicative act itself. In terms of Frei's view cited above, in the case of illocutions, historical criticism and hermeneutics are two sides of the same coin, a conclusion manifestly untrue in general, which has in turn caused the largely unhelpful stand-off between 'historical' and 'theological' interpretation referred to at various points above.

Since it has become increasingly clear that the concerns of Christian reading of biblical texts are not met by a hermeneutic reduced to the analysis of historical conditions of production, there have indeed been several calls for more than this in recent years. Perhaps the programmatic attempt was Walter Wink's pointed analysis of the 'bankruptcy' of historical criticism and his call for an

---

67. D. Neufeld, *Reconceiving Texts as Speech Acts: An Analysis of 1 John*, BIS 7 (Leiden: Brill, 1994), p. 134.

engagement with the psychologically transformative nature of biblical texts instead.[68] In more recent years, the best analysis of this problem is Schuyler Brown's suggestive study of *Text and Psyche*, significantly subtitled 'Experiencing Scripture Today'.[69] Brown, as Wink before him, turns to psychology to try to show how the Bible can transform the human soul, and develops what he calls 'biblical empirics' in order to look at 'the impact of scripture upon the heart'.[70] He suggests that while literary criticism makes some significant advances on 'doctrinal' and 'historical' paradigms, it is ultimately only a knowledge of psychology that will really allow us to transcend the dichotomy of cognitive and affective approaches to the text.[71]

Brown's study, I have said, is the best analysis of the problem. I am unpersuaded, though, that it offers an answer. He chooses to follow Carl Jung, himself the son of a pastor, down an increasingly mystical route, toward a conclusion (of sorts) that sees fully fledged gnostic exegesis as exemplifying the appropriate aspects of affective transformation.[72] This may seem a long, long way from speech-act theory, but in fact it is close to the heart of the matter. Brown's (and Wink's) psychological intuitions, as well as Frei's hermeneutical sophistication, are both pressed right up against the central nature of the Bible's transformative language without exploring the point that it can be cashed out in performative and illocutionary terms. The cognitive and the affective are two dimensions of a multi-dimensional speech-act approach, and speech-act theory is in fact specifically concerned with the question of how these dimensions interrelate in the various kinds of speech act performed.

Understood rightly, speech-act theory is not a methodology one can employ in order to talk about how some texts are performative, but it is the laying bare of the transformative effects of illocutionary acts, which cannot properly be described in the traditional categories of rhetoric or the newer language of psychology or of postmodern persuasion. These other categories are perfectly good for describing the phenomena around which they themselves are organized (rousing rhetoric, a transformed self-image, ironic detachment and many more), but none of these is illocutionary, and all therefore risk the constant blurring of transformative effect into 'being per-

---

68. W. Wink, *The Bible in Human Transformation: Toward a New Paradigm for Biblical Study* (Philadelphia: Fortress, 1973).

69. S. Brown, *Text and Psyche: Experiencing Scripture Today* (New York: Continuum, 1998).

70. Ibid., p. 118; cf. pp. 31–57.

71. Ibid., p. 37.

72. Ibid., pp. 114–135.

suaded' or 'feeling changed'. Over against all of these, a hermeneutic of self-involvement says: for certain types of text, which are strongly self-involving illocutions, the personal transformation effected is a result not of perlocutionary effect, but of successful performance of the illocution, that is, it is due to certain states of affairs, and the status of the one performing the act, and the nature of the reader who can rightly construe the illocutionary act performed.

Examples of a hermeneutic of self-involvement are, in the nature of the case, difficult to find. This is not primarily due to the complexities of speech-act theory, though doubtless that is a factor. It is even more due to the fact that interesting examples will involve self-transformation in the construal of scriptural illocutions, with the relevant questions of perspective and self-involvement foregrounded. This can make it time consuming to explore even a relatively straightforward example. Furthermore, even the most probing analyses of biblical texts rarely stop to reflect on the self-involving nature of key claims, and I am not about to suggest I have to hand a large stock of either probing analyses or transformative and self-involved readings of biblical texts no one else has spotted, which is one traditional temptation for those mounting hermeneutical arguments. Walter Moberly's recent study of 'Prophecy and Discernment' is focused most helpfully on how to discern the ways of God in and amidst human (prophetic) speech, and thus sees the issues with an unusual clarity. He has it exactly right when he notes that 'To speak of Yhwh and His presence and protection is self-involving language, which commits those who would speak thus to live in accordance with Yhwh's own priorities.'[73] Nevertheless, the hermeneutical implications of reading performative texts in speech-act terms are not the focus of his study.

By way of example, therefore, we turn to Alexandra Brown's perceptive work on 1 Corinthians, *The Cross and Human Transformation*.[74] 1 Corinthians is certainly fertile ground for the benefits of speech-act theory, owing to the confluence of a number of factors: it is a directed and directive text, in which an author about whom we have historical information is attempting to effect certain types of changed behaviour in his hearers, but in the context of decrying the ways in which behaviour can be changed by skilful rhetoric (2:1–5). What Paul is therefore seeking is a change in behaviour driven by a change of perception regarding the Corinthians' status before God. This is exactly the

---

73. Moberly, *Prophecy and Discernment*, p. 61.

74. A. R. Brown, *The Cross and Human Transformation: Paul's Apocalyptic Word in 1 Corinthians* (Minneapolis: Fortress, 1995).

kind of situation in which illocutionary speech acts may be expected to provide the key to how hearers/readers should be transformed by the text.

Brown sets up her discussion in terms of Paul's 'apocalyptic epistemology': the claim that in the revelation of Christ, Paul has discerned a new way of seeing the world, which he wishes to preach by way of 'apocalyptic language [which] not only says something but does something in the saying'.[75] The focus of her study is 1 Corinthians 1:18 – 2:16, where 'Paul uses the discourse on the cross to bring about effects in his hearers, the most obvious being the effect of reconciliation.'[76] By way of the ironic citation of various epistemological terms and slogans in use in Corinth, Paul gradually begins to undermine the ways in which the Corinthians understand their world. In contrast, he then sets up an understanding of the world that is designed to help the Corinthians grasp the word of the cross as the alternative way of understanding the world. Brown highlights three kinds of performative language in 1 Corinthians 1 – 2:

1. Language that reflects *what* Paul preaches (the 'Word of the Cross').
2. Language that reflects the 'worlds' that allow the Word of the Cross to be heard.
3. Language that reflects the 'perceptual predispositions and transpositions' that accompany the preaching of that Word.[77]

The climax of the argument is reached in 2:16, with 'But we have the mind of Christ'. In contrast to the Corinthian concerns with status, power and privilege, Paul here offers a transformative word based on the cross. Brown's conclusion is worth citing at length:

> he [Paul] speaks a performative word if that word, in fact, is received by the hearer as the culmination of the larger speech act in which Paul has been engaged. For here, the cross, the *pneuma*, and the noetic self are joined in an image that defines a new social relationship. One who receives this mind perceives anew who God is, that is, the self-giving God of the cross, and is thus reorientated toward reconciling service to God and the world.[78]

---

75. Ibid., p. 15; cf. pp. 8–12, where she draws on the arguments of J. L. Martyn, whose relevant essays are now conveniently gathered in his *Theological Issues in the Letters of Paul*, SNTW (Edinburgh: T. & T. Clark, 1997), esp. pp. 89–156.

76. Brown, *Cross*, p. 19.

77. Ibid., pp. 65–66.

78. Ibid., p. 146.

Note here that the transformation (which involves all the practical implications of 'reconciling service') is immediate upon the self-involved grasping
of the point, because the point is illocutionary, fundamentally to do with a
reconstruing of one's place in the world and before God. In Corinth, where
there is much ado about rhetorical power, this is a different way with words.
As Thiselton notes, the illocutionary dimension of Paul's preaching as highlighted by Brown underlines 'the distinction between the nature of *apostolic*
rhetoric and the *pragmatic, audience-determined rhetoric of Corinth and of a postmodern world* shaped by social construction alone'.[79] In a later article he expounds
the considerable significance of the word 'alone' in this quotation, citing 'the
divine sovereign initiative of . . . grace', which is 'a conscious address to challenge the scope of human or social construction'. This is in the context of
drawing upon just this kind of analysis of 1 Corinthians to show how the
overlapping natures of pre- and postmodern perlocution (among other
things) allow a positive answer to his title question, 'Can a Pre-Modern Bible
Address a Postmodern World?'[80] If speech-act theory is truly the laying bare
of human (and divine) communicative action, then this is one sense in which
one might expect biblical *address* to be capable of analysis within any social
framework.

We might reflect particularly here on the fact that such a 'hermeneutic of
self-involvement' is not so much an *alternative* to a historical-critical reading as
a form of reading that integrates historical-critical insights into a broader
canvas that allows transformative effect and interpersonal dynamic to play a
full part in assessing the nature and function of the biblical text. As Neufeld
observes in his speech-act study of 1 Corinthians 6, 'Clarity about the historical situation will help to locate the conventions and circumstances that determine the illocutionary force of "rebuke" and "admonition" [his chosen speech
acts]. Linguistic communication is governed by extra-textual rules, often
unspoken and conventional.'[81] What we are observing here relates to
Recanati's point about 'looking behind the scenes'. Speech-act theory, in this
example, draws together the historical context, the transformational effect and

---

79. A. C. Thiselton, *The First Epistle to the Corinthians*, NIGTC (Grand Rapids:
    Eerdmans; Carlisle: Paternoster, 2000), p. 51.

80. A. C. Thiselton, 'Can a Pre-Modern Bible Address a Postmodern World?', in P.
    Gifford, D. Archard, T. Hart and N. Rapport (eds.), *2000 Years and Beyond: Faith,
    Identity and the 'Common Era'* (London: Routledge, 2003), p. 146.

81. D. Neufeld, 'Acts of Admonition and Rebuke: A Speech-Act Approach to 1
    Corinthians 6.1–11', *BI* 8 (2000), pp. 375–376.

the communicative dynamic of the text, exemplifying what I have several times referred to as its 'integrative' nature.

Conclusion

Speech-act theory provides us with the concepts and criteria for analysing the performative functions of scriptural texts. We began with the claim that 'how to do things with words' is a proper subject of concern for the biblical interpreter. The biblical texts themselves are concerned with a wide variety of performative acts, and even more to the point these texts are themselves performative acts of address. Some are strongly self-involving directive acts, attempting to obtain direct 'results'. Some are more 'gentle', addressing by way of telling a story or reciting a poem, but still addressing with a purpose. The dual nature of biblical texts as human literature and divine address, we then noted, was also susceptible to the descriptive flexibility of speech-act theory. Armed with this orientation and the conceptual tools of speech-act theory, we have then explored a hermeneutic of self-involvement, whereby readers are drawn into the transformative effects of texts as they construe textual illocutions. We have contrasted this with other types of transformative effect, such as the psychological and the rhetorical.

Speech-act theory is designed to give us just the right language and conceptual tools to express these certain kinds of hermeneutically interesting readings. Of course, it matters relatively little whether the language (or jargon) of speech-act theory is used in such hermeneutical analysis – what matters is that texts of transformation can effect their self-involving responses, and not on the basis of the kinds of 'plausible words of speech and proclamation' Paul has in his sights in 1 Corinthians 2:4. Nevertheless, the conceptual tools, or hermeneutical frameworks, we bring to the text do have a tendency to serve as filters on what we are able or willing to perceive there, and if speech-act theory is the best model we have to hand of how communicative action works, then it should commend itself to us as one more valuable tool for the many and various tasks of biblical interpretation.

Bibliography

AUSTIN, J. L., *How to Do Things with Words*, ed. J. O. Urmson and M. Sbisà, 2nd ed.
  (Oxford: Oxford University Press, 1975).

BAKER, W. R., *Personal Speech-Ethics in the Epistle of James*, WUNT 2.68 (Tübingen: Mohr, 1995).

BARTHOLOMEW, C. G., MÖLLER, K., and GREEN, C. (eds.), *After Pentecost: Language and Biblical Interpretation*, SHS 2 (Grand Rapids: Zondervan; Carlisle: Paternoster, 2001).

BAUCKHAM, R., *James*, New Testament Readings (London: Routledge, 1999).

BOTHA, J. E., *Jesus and the Samaritan Woman: A Speech-Act Reading of John 4:1–42*, NovTSup 65 (Leiden: Brill, 1991).

BRIGGS, R. S., 'Speech-Act Theory', in K. J. Vanhoozer (gen. ed.), *Dictionary for Theological Interpretation of the Bible* (Grand Rapids: Baker, 2005), pp. 763–766.

——, 'The Uses of Speech-Act Theory in Biblical Interpretation', *CR:BS* 9 (2001), pp. 229–276.

——, 'What Does Hermeneutics Have to Do with Biblical Interpretation?', *HeyJ* 47.1 (2006), pp. 55–74.

——, *Words in Action: Speech Act Theory and Biblical Interpretation* (Edinburgh: T. & T. Clark; New York: Continuum, 2001).

BROWN, A. R., *The Cross and Human Transformation: Paul's Apocalyptic Word in 1 Corinthians* (Minneapolis: Fortress, 1995).

BROWN, S., *Text and Psyche: Experiencing Scripture Today* (New York: Continuum, 1998).

BRÜMMER, V., *Theology and Philosophical Inquiry: An Introduction* (Philadelphia: Westminster, 1982).

DERRIDA, J., *Limited Inc*, ed. G. Graff (Evanston: Northwestern University Press, 1988).

DODD, C. H., *The Apostolic Preaching and its Developments* (London: Hodder & Stoughton, 1936).

EAGLETON, T., 'J. L. Austin and the Book of Jonah', in R. Schwartz (ed.), *The Book and the Text: The Bible and Literary Theory* (Oxford: Blackwell, 1990), pp. 231–236.

EVANS, D. D., *The Logic of Self-Involvement: A Philosophical Study of Everyday Language with Special Reference to the Christian Use of Language about God as Creator* (London: SCM, 1963).

FISH, S., *Is There a Text in This Class? The Authority of Interpretive Communities* (Cambridge, Mass.: Harvard University Press, 1980).

FORD, D. F., *Self and Salvation: Being Transformed* (Cambridge: Cambridge University Press, 1999).

FREI, H. W., *The Eclipse of Biblical Narrative: A Study in Eighteenth and Nineteenth Century Hermeneutics* (New Haven: Yale University Press, 1974).

GILFILLAN UPTON, B., *Hearing Mark's Endings: Listening to Ancient Popular Texts through Speech-Act Theory*, BIS 79 (Leiden: Brill, 2006).

GRICE, P., *Studies in the Way of Words* (Cambridge, Mass.: Harvard University Press, 1989).

GRÜNEBERG, K., *Blessing: Biblical Meaning and Pastoral Practice*, Grove Biblical Books B27 (Cambridge: Grove, 2003).

HABERMAS, J., *The Theory of Communicative Action: The Critique of Functionalist Reason*, 2 vols. (Boston: Beacon, 1984, 1987).

HARDY, D. W., and FORD, D. F., *Jubilate: Theology in Praise* (London: Darton Longman & Todd, 1984).

HESSE, M., 'How to Be a Postmodernist and Remain a Christian: A Response to Nicholas Wolterstorff', in BARTHOLOMEW, MÖLLER and GREEN, *After Pentecost*, pp. 91–96.

HOUSTON, W., 'What Did the Prophets Think They Were Doing? Speech Acts and Prophetic Discourse in the Old Testament', *BI* 1 (1993), pp. 167–188.

JOWETT, B., 'On the Interpretation of Scripture', in *Essays and Reviews*, 7th ed. (London: Longman, Green, Longman & Roberts, 1861), pp. 330–433.

KNIGHT, J., *Revelation*, Readings (Sheffield: Sheffield Academic Press, 1999).

LONGMAN, T., III, *How to Read Proverbs* (Downers Grove: IVP, 2002).

——, *Proverbs*, BCOTWP (Grand Rapids: Baker, 2006).

LOUW, J. P., and NIDA, E. (eds.), *Greek–English Lexicon of the New Testament Based on Semantic Domains*. Vol. 1: *Introduction and Domains*, 2nd ed. (New York: United Bible Societies, 1989).

McDONALD, J. I. H., *Kerygma and Didache: The Articulation and Structure of the Earliest Christian Message*, SNTSMS 37 (Cambridge: Cambridge University Press, 1980).

MCNULTY, T. M., 'Pauline Preaching: A Speech-Act Analysis', *Worship* 53 (1979), pp. 207–214.

MARSHALL, I. H., *Acts*, TNTC (Leicester: IVP, 1980).

MARTYN, J. L., *Theological Issues in the Letters of Paul*, SNTW (Edinburgh: T. & T. Clark, 1997).

MOBERLY, R. W. L., 'Jonah, God's Objectionable Mercy, and the Way of Wisdom', in D. F. Ford and G. Stanton (eds.), *Reading Texts: Seeking Wisdom: Scripture and Theology* (London: SCM, 2003), pp. 154–168.

——, *Prophecy and Discernment* (Cambridge: Cambridge University Press, 2006).

NEUFELD, D., 'Acts of Admonition and Rebuke: A Speech-Act Approach to 1 Corinthians 6.1–11', *BI* 8 (2000), pp. 375–399.

——, *Reconceiving Texts as Speech Acts: An Analysis of 1 John*, BIS 7 (Leiden: Brill, 1994).

PETREY, S., *Speech Acts and Literary Theory* (New York: Routledge, 1990).

PRATT, M. L., *Toward a Speech Act Theory of Literary Discourse* (Bloomington: Indiana University Press, 1977).

RECANATI, F., *Meaning and Force: The Pragmatics of Performative Utterances* (Cambridge: Cambridge University Press, 1987).

RICHARDS, K. H., 'Bless/Blessing', *ABD* 1: 753–755.

SEARLE, J. R., *The Construction of Social Reality* (London: Penguin, 1995).

——, *Expression and Meaning: Studies in the Theory of Speech Acts* (Cambridge: Cambridge University Press, 1979).

——, 'How Performatives Work', *Consciousness and Language* (Cambridge: Cambridge University Press, 2002), pp. 156–179.

——, *Speech Acts: An Essay in the Philosophy of Language* (Cambridge: Cambridge University Press, 1969).

SEARLE, J. R., and VANDERVEKEN, D., *Foundations of Illocutionary Logic* (Cambridge: Cambridge University Press, 1985).

SHERWOOD, Y., *A Biblical Text and its Afterlives: The Survival of Jonah in Western Culture* (Cambridge: Cambridge University Press, 2000).

STRATTON, B. J., *Out of Eden: Reading, Rhetoric, and Ideology in Genesis 2–3*, JSOTSup 208 (Sheffield: Sheffield Academic Press, 1995).

THISELTON, A. C., ' "Behind" and "In Front of" the Text: Language, Reference and Indeterminacy', in BARTHOLOMEW, MÖLLER and GREEN, *After Pentecost*, pp. 97–120.

——, 'Can a Pre-Modern Bible Address a Postmodern World?', in P. Gifford, D. Archard, T. Hart and N. Rapport (eds.), *2000 Years and Beyond: Faith, Identity and the 'Common Era'* (London: Routledge, 2003), pp. 127–146.

——, *The First Epistle to the Corinthians*, NIGTC (Grand Rapids: Eerdmans; Carlisle: Paternoster, 2000).

——, *New Horizons in Hermeneutics: The Theory and Practice of Transforming Biblical Reading* (London: HarperCollins, 1992).

——, 'The Supposed Power of Words in the Biblical Writings', *JTS* 25 (1974), pp. 282–299.

——, *Thiselton on Hermeneutics: The Collected Works and New Essays of Anthony Thiselton* (Aldershot: Ashgate, 2006).

THOMPSON, L. L., *The Book of Revelation: Apocalypse and Empire* (New York: Oxford University Press, 1990).

URBROCK, W. J., 'Blessings and Curses', *ABD* 1: 755–761.

VANDERVEKEN, D., *Meaning and Speech Acts*. Vol. 1: *Principles of Language Use* (Cambridge: Cambridge University Press, 1990).

VANDERVEKEN, D., and KUBO, S. (eds) *Essays in Speech Act Theory*, Pragmatics and Beyond NS 77 (Amsterdam: John Benjamins, 2001).

——, 'Introduction', in VANDERVEKEN and KUBO, *Essays in Speech Act Theory*, pp. 1–21.

VANHOOZER, K. J., 'From Speech Acts to Scripture Acts: The Covenant of Discourse and the Discourse of Covenant', in *First Theology: God, Scripture and Hermeneutics* (Leicester: Apollos, 2002), pp. 159–203.

——, *Is There a Meaning in This Text? The Bible, the Reader, and the Morality of Literary Knowledge* (Grand Rapids: Zondervan; Leicester: Apollos, 1998).

WATSON, F., *Text, Church and World: Biblical Interpretation in Theological Perspective* (Edinburgh: T. & T. Clark, 1994).

WHITE, H. C., *Narration and Discourse in the Book of Genesis* (Cambridge: Cambridge University Press, 1991).

WINK, W., *The Bible in Human Transformation: Toward a New Paradigm for Biblical Study* (Philadelphia: Fortress, 1973).

WOLTERSTORFF, N., *Divine Discourse: Philosophical Reflections on the Claim that God Speaks* (Cambridge: Cambridge University Press, 1995).

——, 'The Promise of Speech-Act Theory for Biblical Interpretation', in BARTHOLOMEW, MÖLLER and GREEN, *After Pentecost*, pp. 73–90.

——, 'True Words', in A. G. Padgett and P. R. Keifert (eds.), *But Is It All True? The Bible and the Question of Truth* (Grand Rapids: Eerdmans, 2006), pp. 34–43.

4. GENRE CRITICISM AND THE BIBLE

Jeannine K. Brown

[G]enre is based on what people already know and do . . . It is the intriguing job of genre scholars to figure out what lies behind what everyone already knows.

(A. J. Devitt, *Writing Genres*)

Difficulty arises because texts do not identify themselves.

(T. Longman III, *Literary Approaches to Biblical Interpretation*)

Even a cursory look at the Bible reveals that it contains many different kinds of writing. Narratives appear all over the Old and New Testament. Poetry circumscribes many OT books, while poetic forms can also be found within the Gospels and NT letters. Letters make up the majority of the NT books. Other kinds of literary types, or genres, in the biblical canon include law, prophetic writings, wisdom literature and apocalyptic. Most readers of the Bible traverse these different genres by intuitively adjusting their reading expectations and strategies. We read a psalm differently from an epistle of Paul. This is right. The pressing question for Bible readers today, however, is whether we are making the right intuitive shifts, given that the genres we meet in Scripture are not contemporary ones. The ancient genres of the Bible often exhibit differing conventions from their contemporary counterparts.[1] For example, modern English poetry in many ways does not act like ancient Hebrew poetry. How are we to know when we should leave our 'intuitive' expectations at the door and when these expectations may actually be helpful for interpretation? To answer this question well shall require an exploration, not only of ancient genres, but also of the concept of genre itself.

The study of the ancient genres represented in the Bible is not a new endeavour. Biblical criticism of the modern period has had a keen interest in studying the Bible's diverse genres. In the latter part of the nineteenth and early part of the twentieth centuries, form critics paid concerted attention to the individual literary forms evident in the Old and New Testaments, often drawing on studies of ANE or classical Greek genres and forms. The discipline of form criticism focused for the most part on those forms that were oral in origin (e.g. lament psalms or Jesus' parables). Scholars like Gunkel in the OT and Dibelius and Bultmann in the New worked to identify and define these relatively short literary forms, asking the question of function in their original (oral) settings.

More recently, the literary-critical turn in biblical studies has focused attention on ways the biblical text reflects the genres of its socio-historical contexts at a more holistic level – that is, at the level of biblical books. These studies also include significant comparative work with ANE or Greco-Roman materials to assist in genre identification.[2] In addition, a growing number of books are being written to describe the contours of the various genres of the Bible for a general population of Bible readers.[3]

---

1. This presumes the presence of literary counterparts; some biblical genres would seem to have no contemporary counterpart; e.g. apocalyptic literature. As Giese states, 'Though we bring a knowledge of English literary forms with us to the biblical text, and this is helpful, in some cases this will mislead us, and in other cases it is simply not enough since modern forms are so different from the ancient ones' (R. L. Giese, Jr., 'Literary Forms of the Old Testament', in D. B. Sandy and R. L. Giese, Jr. [eds.], *Cracking Old Testament Codes: A Guide to Interpreting the Literary Genres of the Old Testament* [Nashville: Broadman & Holman, 1995], p. 24).

2. E.g. D. E. Aune, *The New Testament in Its Literary Environment* (Philadelphia: Westminster, 1987); and T. Longman III, 'Israelite Genres in Their Ancient Near Eastern Context', in M. A. Sweeney and E. Ben Zvi (eds.), *The Changing Face of Form Criticism for the Twenty-First Century* (Grand Rapids: Eerdmans, 2003), pp. 177–195.

3. J. L. Bailey and L. Vander Broek, *Literary Forms in the New Testament: A Handbook* (Louisville: Westminster John Knox, 1992); G. D. Fee and D. Stuart, *How to Read the Bible for All Its Worth*, 3rd ed. (Grand Rapids: Zondervan, 2003); W. W. Klein, C. L.

Yet, despite occasional forays into literary genre theory, biblical studies has not generally taken advantage of all that contemporary genre theory offers. In fact, there seems to be a growing gap between literary and rhetorical theorizing on genre and the work being done in biblical studies. This arises in part from the difficulty of keeping up with the ever-expanding discourse of modern genre theory. Biblical scholars, who invest much of their time and energy in their own already-diverse areas of study, may find it time-prohibitive and even a bit daunting to wade into wide-ranging discussions of genre in the fields of literature and rhetoric. A second barrier arises from the perceived irrelevance of some of these discussions for studying *ancient* literature, including the literature of the Bible. For example, a crucial strand of the literary discussion focuses on re-evaluating the search for and esteem of pure genres, which has been a hallmark of past eras. Biblical scholars, on the other hand, focus on historical analysis of the Bible's genres rather than a search for the notion of genre purity.

If there is a growing gap between these fields, it is a central goal of this chapter to describe the direction of contemporary genre studies and then assess areas of particular value for biblical studies. After giving a theoretical lie of the land that includes a brief historical sketch of genre theory, issues of defining genre and evaluating the role of genre criticism in interpretation are addressed. Along the way, I provide examples from the Bible to illustrate the payoff of genre awareness for interpretation. In addition, it is my hope that readers will gain greater insight into their own inclinations about genre and how these inclinations impact their reading of the Bible.

Historical survey of genre theory and practice

Ancient genre theory
We can look to Plato and Aristotle for the origins of ancient reflection on genre as a literary phenomenon. Plato (c. 429–347 BC) assumed a connection between genres and the expression of one's character, 'tak[ing] it for granted that different individuals will work in genres suited to their respective

---

Blomberg and R. L. Hubbard, Jr., *Introduction to Biblical Interpretation* (Dallas: Word, 1993); G. R. Osborne, *The Hermeneutical Spiral: A Comprehensive Introduction to Biblical Interpretation*, 2nd ed. (Downers Grove: IVP, 2006); Sandy and Giese, *Cracking Old Testament Codes*; and R. H. Stein, *A Basic Guide to Interpreting the Bible: Playing by the Rules* (Grand Rapids: Baker, 1994).

characters'.[4] Whether one wrote a hymn or a satire depended, for Plato, upon the kind of person they were, so that genre is not so much about choice as about nature. Aristotle (c. 384–322 BC), who drew upon Platonic theory, understood literature as imitation (*mimesis*) and proposed the following as criteria for literary genres: the means of representation (e.g. metre and rhythm), the objects of representation (the subject matter), and the manner of representation (the work's perspective).[5]

Aristotle's theorizing led the way among subsequent writers and philosophers. In their discussions about genre, clear boundaries between genres were emphasized (the major genres or generic modes being epic, tragedy and comedy). Cicero (c. 106–43 BC), among others, expressed what was implicit in Aristotle, namely the affirmation of genre purity as opposed to the mixing of forms and generic purposes.[6] In addition, ancient explicit discussion of genre tended to idealize certain genres. For example, tragedy was considered nobler than comedy. The notions of purity and hierarchy in genre were captivating ones upheld in later discussion by Horace (65–8 BC) and Quintilian (c. AD 35–95).[7] Horace was the first to speak of 'the law of genre' – which communicated the emphasis that genres constrain authors.[8] For Horace, form and content must be properly related in any particular genre.[9] Yet in practice ancient writers belied the commitment to genre purity by mixing genres, even while affirming the ideal of purity in their more explicit commentary. Farrell demonstrates this with examples from Horace and from Latin love elegy, showing that theoretical genre boundaries were readily 'transgressed' in actual literary practice.[10]

---

4. J. Farrell, 'Classical Genre in Theory and Practice', *NLH* 34 (2003), p. 384; cf. Plato, *Republic* 394e–395a.

5. Aristotle, Poetics 1.1. R. J. Connors, 'Genre Theory in Literature', in H. W. Simons and A. A. Aghazarian (eds.), *Form, Genre, and the Study of Political Discourse* (Columbia: University of South Carolina Press, 1986), p. 26.

6. R. Colie, 'Genre-Systems and the Functions of Literature', in D. Duff (ed.), *Modern Genre Theory* (Harlow, UK: Longman, 2000), p. 151.

7. For an example of genre hierarchy in poetry, see Quintilian, *Institutio* 10.1.63.

8. *Ars poetica*, line 135. Farrell, 'Classical Genre', p. 394.

9. D. A Russell, *Criticism in Antiquity* (Berkeley: University of California Press, 1981), p. 153.

10. Farrell, 'Classical Genre', pp. 394–395, 396–402. Farrell concludes, 'the "implied theory" instantiated in ancient poetry is far more sophisticated than the explicit theory developed by philosophers and literary critics and apparently espoused by

Renaissance to modern genre theory

The Renaissance, with its renewed interest in all things classical, saw a revival of Aristotelian values toward literature. Consequently, the notions of genre purity and hierarchy were again embraced. It was the case that authors were judged on their adherence to genre parameters; genre in neoclassicism was 'a criterion of critical discrimination'.[11] This way of viewing genre as prescriptive as well as descriptive, as having clear and impenetrable boundaries (at least prescriptively), typified eighteenth century neoclassical literary theory. Yet even during this period, a new genre, the novel, was being developed that provided a challenge to neoclassical genre categories.[12]

The Romantics of the nineteenth century reacted against prescriptive genre categories, emphasizing the individual work as unique and autonomous.[13] Yet Romantic interest in genre theory continued. 'What the romantics argued against was any *privileged* or *elitist* genre, any attempt to exclude works from consideration because they did not meet rigid expectations of class.'[14] This initiated a movement in genre theory from genre as taxonomy to a more functional view of genre, though the perspective of genre primarily as a precise classificatory system continued to be influential well into the twentieth century.[15]

In practice, the Romantic rejection of neoclassical genre categories did lead some to ignore or reject genre altogether. This can be seen in

---

the poets themselves in their manifestos and programmatic declarations' (p. 402). Cf. also Aune, *New Testament*, p. 23. Pearson and Porter emphasize that ancient discussion of genre categories should be used judiciously, given that such discussion is 'generally concerned with the *creation* of literature, not its *interpretation*' (B. W. R. Pearson and S. E. Porter, 'The Genres of the New Testament', in S. E. Porter [ed.], *Handbook to Exegesis of the New Testament* [Leiden: Brill, 1997], p. 136).

11. J.-M. Schaeffer, 'Literary Genres and Textual Genericity', in R. Cohen (ed.), *The Future of Literary Theory* (New York: Routledge, 1989), p. 168. This was the case in France and Italy more so than in England, according to Connors ('Genre Theory in Literature', pp. 30–31).

12. Connors, 'Genre Theory in Literature', p. 34.

13. G. R. Osborne, 'Genre', in K. J. Vanhoozer (gen. ed.), *Dictionary for Theological Interpretation of the Bible* (Grand Rapids: Baker, 2005), p. 252.

14. Connors, 'Genre Theory in Literature', p. 36 (italics in original).

15. P. Ricoeur, 'The Hermeneutical Function of Distanciation', in *Exegesis: Problems of Method and Exercises in Reading (Genesis 22 and Luke 15)*, tr. D. G. Miller (Pittsburgh: Pickwick, 1978), p. 308.

the work of Benedetto Croce. Croce disavowed the legitimacy of genre as a category for true aesthetic reflection. For Croce, the true artist is never bound by the chains of genre but breaks free in the creative process.[16] The rejection of genre as a legitimate critical category has led to a common contemporary perspective that 'there is no intermediate entity between the unique individual work and literature as a whole, the ultimate genre'.[17]

Yet not all genre theory followed this trajectory. There was also a reaction to Romanticism during the Victorian age, influenced by Darwinism and determinism. This reaction brought about a more systematized categorization of genres as well as a developmental perspective on genres through time.[18] With the rise of the new criticism in the earlier part of the twentieth century (1920s onward), genres were understood as 'informing devices that tie together literary traditions with human expectations' rather than prescriptive rules placed upon authors.[19] It was also during this time that two distinct strands of genre theory emerged, one growing out of literary studies and the other arising from the discipline of rhetorical studies.

Contemporary genre criticism
In literary criticism
In literary studies, a wide spectrum emerged during the twentieth century. On one side of that spectrum, literary critics continued to reflect upon categories of abstract genres, assessing texts and genres across the Western literary canon. Northrop Frye, in his foundational work *Anatomy of Criticism*, proposes a theory of genres, an archetypal criticism that 'attempts to fit poems into the

---

16. Connors, 'Genre Theory in Literature', p. 39. Cf. B. Croce, *Aesthetic as Science of Expression and General Linguistic* (London: Macmillan, 1922).

17. T. Todorov, *Genres in Discourse* (Cambridge: Cambridge University Press, 1990 [French original 1978]), p. 13. Todorov goes on to argue against this viewpoint, which characterizes one stream of literary criticism.

18. Connors, 'Genre Theory in Literature', p. 37.

19. Ibid., p. 40. The new criticism tended to downplay the role of genre analysis, since in new criticism the individual work was paramount. For example, T. S. Eliot speaks of the tendency (in the era of new criticism) to value 'those aspects of [a poet's] work in which [s]he least resembles anyone else' (T. S. Eliot, 'Tradition and the Individual Talent', in *Selected Essays* [London: Faber & Faber, 1932], p. 14).

body of poetry as a whole' (and poetry or literature as part of all civilization) by studying generic conventions.[20]

On the other end of the spectrum, in contrast to Frye and others, are literary critics who question the legitimacy of an overarching genre theory. White, for example, claims that no such compelling genre theory has ever been developed, even while acknowledging the possibility of studying genres from a historical angle.[21] Derrida argues for a dialectic of genre, a breaking down of genre as a category: '[A]t the very moment that a genre or a literature is broached, at that very moment, degenerescence has begun, the end begins'.[22] Along with this 'deconstruction' of genre theory, some theorists have emphasized the ideological nature of genre theory: 'If genre is resistant to theory, it is certainly not resistant to use by bias, prejudice, and preconception.'[23]

Contemporary literary studies offers a number of contributions to genre theory. First, by questioning the value of genre purity, literary critics have been able to show the reality and artistic value of genre mixing in both ancient and modern literature. In doing so, they have begun to unmask the implicit ideologies in genre theory as well as ideologies or points of view embedded in genres themselves.[24] In addition, since literary genre analysis has tended to focus on the ability of authors to transcend the 'strictures' of genre, literary critics have pushed for a much more flexible understanding of genre. It is certainly the case that literary work on genre has moved away from an essentialist model. Genre is no longer viewed as a formal container into which content

---

20. N. Frye, *Anatomy of Criticism: Four Essays* (Princeton: Princeton University Press, 1957), pp. 99, 105. Frye's work offers a theory of discerning how it is we implicitly read and understand literature via archetypal genres.

21. H. White, 'Anomalies of Genre: The Utility of Theory and History for the Study of Literary Genres', *NLH* 34 (2003), p. 597.

22. J. Derrida, 'The Law of Genre', tr. A. Ronell, *Critical Inquiry* 7.1 (autumn 1980), p. 66. The very act of paying attention to similarities invites comparison of differences as well, thus introducing the dialectic of genre.

23. White, 'Anomalies of Genre', p. 599. See also Todorov, *Genres in Discourse*, p. 19. For Devitt, genres often have 'unrecognized ideological power' because they are both widespread and inevitable. In addition, genres by their very nature simplify experience and so can be potentially (ideologically) harmful (*Writing Genres*, pp. 158–159).

24. For example, a genre theory might 'play favourites' by implying the superiority of one genre over another. Alternately, an emphasis on genre purity could have the effect of supporting the status quo, by valuing standardization versus innovation.

is poured. Instead, current literary theory argues for a synthesis of form and content in literary works.[25]

In rhetorical criticism

In the early twentieth century, the study of genre from the perspective of rhetorical criticism became an area of inquiry in its own right. Wichelns, in his 'The Literary Criticism of Oratory' (1925), was an early rhetorical critic who called attention to genre analysis arising from the study of rhetoric and oratory as distinct from the literary study of genre.[26] Since it derives from study of non-literary genres (primarily oral ones), rhetorical genre analysis has emphasized that genres emerge and develop within recurring rhetorical situations. In other words, genres (recurring forms) are closely connected to recurring situations. A genre is a way of responding to a typified situation.[27] For instance, a rhetorical genre critic might study political speeches to observe the ways that characteristic political situations call for recurring patterns of rhetoric.

Other non-literary genres that have been studied by rhetorical genre critics include such divergent forms as eulogies, tax documents and science lab reports. The goal in each case is to learn more about the use of such 'ordinary' genres and what they tell us about their related human activity and expectations.[28] According to Campbell and Jamieson, a number of genre affirmations are common to even divergent rhetorical-critical perspectives. These include

---

25. Ricoeur, 'Hermeneutical Function', p. 309. The contributions delineated in this paragraph are expanded and illustrated in subsequent discussion.

26. K. K. Campbell and K. H. Jamieson, 'Form and Genre in Rhetorical Criticism: An Introduction', in K. K. Campbell and K. H. Jamieson (eds.), *Form and Genre: Shaping Rhetorical Action* (Falls Church, Va.: The Speech Communication Association, 1978), p. 12. Campbell and Jamieson provide a helpful overview of the modern history of rhetorical criticism in relation to genre analysis (pp. 12–18). In her essay comparing literary and rhetorical genre theories, Devitt refers to the latter category as *rhetoric-composition*, pointing to the origins of reflection from the study of written composition as well as from the study of rhetoric (A. J. Devitt, 'Integrating Rhetorical and Literary Theories of Genre', *College English* 62 [July 2000], pp. 696–718).

27. Campbell and Jamieson, 'Form and Genre', pp. 12–16.

28. While some literary critics view 'ordinary' texts as so distinct from literary works as to require a different theory of interpretation, there is good reason to view both under the rubric of 'communicative act'. See J. K. Brown, *Scripture as Communication: Introducing Biblical Hermeneutics* (Grand Rapids: Baker, 2007), p. 71.

the notion of genre as 'a constellation of substantive, situational, and stylistic elements' and the dual affirmation that genre criticism uncovers both conventional and unique aspects of literary works.[29]

To these contributions of rhetorical genre analysis offered by Campbell and Jamieson, we can also add an understanding of genres as socially and culturally embedded and an emphasis on the functionality of genres.[30] In addition, while literary theorists typically emphasize the author's ability to transcend genre parameters, rhetorical critics tend to focus on the ways genres constrain communication in order to enable it to be successful.[31]

Applying genre theory to the Bible

Given the many different and often divergent ways genre has been understood in the history of genre theory and even in contemporary genre reflection, it might be tempting to marginalize genre theory or analysis for interpretation of literary works, including the literature of the Bible. Yet the overwhelming chorus of genre theorists and practitioners maintain that genre is an inevitable facet of literature, even of life. 'The attempt to understand phenomena by referring them to other phenomena both similar and dissimilar is one of the basic human conceptual activities.'[32] In relation to literature specifically, the consensus holds that genres are inevitable.[33] And as the history of genre theory has shown, 'the establishment of generic classifications (in any form whatsoever) is a constant fact of literary history, and it would be ridiculous to deny its importance'.[34]

If this is the case, then those of us engaged in biblical interpretation will want to pay attention to how genres impact textual meaning and how genre

---

29. Campbell and Jamieson, 'Form and Genre', p. 18.

30. Devitt, 'Theories of Genre', p. 703.

31. Ibid., pp. 704–705: 'Where rhetorical genre theorists often seek texts that typify a genre . . . literary genre theorists are more likely to seek texts that break the rules of a genre.'

32. Connors, 'Genre Theory in Literature', p. 25.

33. R. Cohen, 'Introduction: Notes Toward a Generic Reconstitution of Literary Study', *NLH* 34 (2003), p. v; Ricoeur, 'Hermeneutical Function', p. 306; M. M. Bakhtin, *Speech Genres and Other Late Essays*, ed. C. Emerson and M. Holquist (Austin: University of Texas Press, 1986), p. 78; Longman, *Literary Approaches*, p. 77; and T. Pavel, 'Literary Genres as Norms and Good Habits', *NLH* 34 (2003), p. 202.

34. Schaeffer, 'Literary Genres', p. 181. Cf. also Campbell and Jamieson, 'Form and Genre', p. 25.

awareness impacts interpretation.[35] A crucial preliminary discussion to this topic is the very definition of genre, which is discussed and debated by contemporary theorists. What is genre and how does our understanding of it impact our ways of reading?

Definitions of genre

As we have seen, it has been the tendency of traditional genre theory to view genre as a kind of formal container that then holds the content or meaning of a work. This formal framework is then standardized across any number of works and becomes the means of classifying such works. Yet genre theorists, both literary and rhetorical, have found this definition less than adequate. In particular, they have questioned genre as 'container', genre as taxonomy (i.e. as a precise classification tool), genre purity and any unexamined hierarchy of genres. If these categories for understanding genre have been deemed less than adequate, how might we draw a more helpful and holistic definition of genre?

The spectre of arriving at a definition for genre might be a bit daunting, given that a brief glance at contemporary genre theory illustrates that there are almost as many definitions of genre as there are theorists! Yet there are common themes in this definitional work that can helpfully guide our thinking about genre. An obvious starting point is understanding genre as *convention* or *codification*.[36] Genre is centrally about commonality in a group of texts or discourses. These common or conventional textual features do not, however, establish rigid class categories that function essentially as laws for writers and speakers. Instead, they might be more helpfully described as 'predominances' or even 'family resemblances'.[37]

---

35. For a theoretical model of textual meaning in relation to the Bible and its interpretation, see Brown, *Scripture as Communication*, ch. 2.

36. While Todorov speaks of genre as 'codifications of discourse' (Todorov, *Genres in Discourse*, pp. 10, 18), Frye uses the language of 'convention' for genre (Frye, *Anatomy of Criticism*, pp. 96–99).

37. Respectively, C. Brooke-Rose, 'Historical Genres/Theoretical Genres: A Discussion of Todorov on the Fantastic', *NLH* 8 (autumn 1976), p. 157; and A. Fowler, 'The Future of Genre Theory: Functions and Constructional Types', in Cohen, *Future of Literary Theory*, p. 298.

Recent discussion has also emphasized the *functional nature of genres*. For example, Ricoeur views genre as less than static in his affirmation that genres are competencies.[38] He proposes that '[g]enre is generative process ending in the performance of a singular work.'[39] In recent work by rhetorical scholars, who draw upon linguistic developments like speech-act theory, genre as action is also emphasized. For example, Miller defines genres as 'typified rhetorical actions based in recurrent situations'.[40] This definition focuses attention on a genre as a purposeful and dynamic situational response. As Devitt notes in this regard, 'Genres help people do things in the world.'[41]

Positing genre as action points to the *contextualized nature of genre*, since human actions are best, and sometimes only, understood within their social (cultural, political and religious) contexts. As Miller's definition indicates, genres are responses to recurring rhetorical situations. In explicating this notion, Devitt argues that culture is 'an element in the dynamic construction of genre'.[42] Todorov refers to societal involvement in and even determination of genres and genre categories: '[T]he choice a society makes among all the possible codifications of discourse determines what is called its *system of genres*'.[43] While this affirmation does not necessarily rule out similarities of literary forms across cultural and language boundaries, it does locate genre actions primarily within societal and cultural contexts. It also implies that generic boundaries and usages are more fluid and flexible than rigid and impermeable.

---

38. We might define generic competence as authorial capacity to use and adapt generic particulars, and the capacity of genre to be used and adapted.

39. 'Ricoeur, Hermeneutical Function', p. 310. See also M. Gerhart, 'Generic Studies: Their Renewed Importance in Religious and Literary Interpretation', *JAAR* 45 (1977), p. 317.

40. C. R. Miller, 'Genre as Social Action', *QJS* 70 (1984), p. 159. As Simons and Aghazarian put it, 'It is the result of the recurrence of situations – their typicality – that rhetorical practices recur, are emulated, and sometimes become conventionalized' ('Introduction', in *Form, Genre*, p. 5).

41. Devitt, *Writing Genres*, pp. 13–14.

42. Ibid., pp. 25–26. Devitt goes on to modify and extend Miller's definition by proposing that genre be understood 'as a nexus between an individual's actions and a socially defined context' (p. 31). For Fowler, 'genres exist as cultural objects' ('Future of Genre Theory', p. 296).

43. Todorov, *Genres in Discourse*, pp. 10, 19.

Drawing upon these broad yet fruitful definitional discussions about genre, I would suggest the following working definition of genre. *Genre is a socially defined constellation of typified formal and thematic features in a group of literary works, which authors use in individualized ways to accomplish specific communicative purposes.*[44]

Genre as constellation

As we examine and illustrate this definition in some detail, we shall first want to ask what it means that genre is a *constellation* of typified features. Drawing upon Campbell and Jamieson who propose the language of constellation, we can productively view genre as typified features 'bound together by an internal dynamic'.[45] This means that, beyond simply the presence of various formal and thematic features in a work, the *arrangement, priority and coherence* of these features are generically significant.[46] Ricoeur, referring to a 'topology of discourse', suggests 'that to understand a text is not to add partial meanings to one another. The text as a whole has to be "construed" as a hierarchy of topics, of primary and subsidiary topics.'[47] This may be affirmed not only for topical features but also for more formal and stylistic features of a text. In other words, various features of a work will be prioritized in a certain way given the text's generic shape. As a result, these features *in their arrangement* function as indicators of genre to the reader.

For example, it is not the presence of sound devices in poetry that 'makes' it poetry. It is the *prominence and arrangement* of such sound devices as rhythm, alliteration, assonance, onomatopoeia and wordplay in a work that

---

44. The attention to form, theme (viewed broadly) and function/purpose in this definition concurs with many other definitions, from Aristotle to the present, that draw on these three aspects in some way for understanding genre. For example, Aristotle's reference to the means, objects and manner of presentation correspond roughly to formal features, thematic features and textual purposes.

45. Campbell and Jamieson, 'Form and Genre', p. 21. Ricoeur also speaks of genre 'establishing a common *dynamics* capable of ruling both the production of discourse . . . and its interpretation' ('Hermeneutical Function', p. 309).

46. Aune's definition of genre is helpful in this regard: 'a group of texts that exhibit *a coherent and recurring configuration* of literary features involving form, . . . content, and function' (*New Testament*, p. 13; my italics). Collins speaks of generic elements being part of a 'paradigm [that] is internally coherent'(J. J. Collins, 'Introduction: Towards a Morphology of a Genre', *Semeia* 14 [1979], p. 12).

47. 'Ricoeur, Hermeneutical Function', pp. 307–308.

point to its likely affinity with this genre. For instance, the presence of alliteration and assonance in Philippians 2:15, where Paul speaks of believers
shining as stars (*phainesthe hōs phōstēres*) does not argue for Philippians as a
poetic book. Rather, Paul, drawing on language and imagery from the
poetry of Deuteronomy, shapes his prosaic language alliteratively (cf.
Deut. 32:5 LXX). Other features, such as the thematic feature of doxol-
ogy (praise), are of greater prominence in Hebrew poetry, while still
being a possible feature in other genres (as in Paul's epistle to the Romans,
11:33–36).

By focusing on genre as a constellation of features, we avoid the temptation to define a genre by the mere *presence* of certain features. Their place in
the overall arrangement and coherence of a work becomes a key genre index.
In addition, the converse temptation is avoided: that is, the temptation to
'require' each and every work in a particular genre to include certain features.
While it may be the case that some generic features are so definitive of a
genre that they necessarily characterize all works of that genre (a simple
example being the presence of conflict in narratives), others may appear in
some but not all works categorized in the same genre. As Fowler notes,
'Recognition of genre depends on associating a complex of elements, which
need not all appear in one work.'[48] An often-repeated example is the fairy tale,
which typically begins and ends with highly stylized formulas: 'Once upon a
time . . .' and 'They all lived happily ever after.' Yet these stylistic features
found in many fairy tales are not required of all fairy tales. We recognize fairy
tales because of the prominence, arrangement and coherence of a number
of formal (e.g. narrative structure) and thematic features (e.g. presence of
magical qualities).

Genre as formal and thematic features
If genre is understood as a constellation of typified features, it will be helpful
to delineate the nature of these typified features. What kinds of features recur
in texts that show them to participate in a particular genre?[49] I have delineated
both formal and thematic features as those that recur in genre. It has been
common to focus primarily on formal features when defining a genre, features

---

48. A. Fowler, 'The Life and Death of Literary Forms', *NLH* 2 (winter 1971), p. 202.

49. 'Participation' is Derrida's language: 'Every text participates in one
or several genres, there is no genreless text; there is always a genre
and genres, yet such participation never amounts to belonging' ('Law
of Genre', p. 65).

like plot in narrative and metre or rhythm in poetry.[50] Although formal features are important indicators of genre, other features, what we might term thematic features, also constitute a genre.[51] Thematic features, broadly conceived, include (but also go beyond) what are often referred to as aspects of the content of a text.[52] Thematic features include mood, topic (motif), setting and point of view.[53] In a genre, thematic features fuse with formal features to function in typified ways.

An example of a thematic feature in biblical law is the provision of a motive for following a particular instruction.[54] 'You shall have only a full and honest weight; you shall have only a full and honest measure, so that your days may be long in the land that the Lord your God is giving you' (Deut. 25:15).[55] The second half of this verse provides a motive for the instruction concerning honest weights. Yet it is often the case that thematic features cross genres more easily than do formal features. Given this, we shall need to be careful not to tie particular thematic features too strictly with particular genres (such as the presence of motives as always indicating the genre of law, since, for example, they

---

50. Wellek and Warren delineate metre, stanza and structure as formal aspects of genre, what they term 'outer form' (R. Wellek and A. Warren, *Theory of Literature* [New York: Harcourt, Brace, 1949], p. 243). We might also include stylistic features in this category; cf. Bailey and Vander Broek (*Literary Forms*, p. 12), who delineate style in addition to form, content and function as aspects of genre.

51. My definition draws from Damrosch, who refers to 'the thematic and formal shaping of the text' (D. Damrosch, *The Narrative Covenant: Transformations of Genre in the Growth of Biblical Literature* [New York: Harper & Row, 1987], p. 38).

52. I prefer the language of 'thematic features' to 'content', since I want to avoid the notion that we can neatly separate form and content. Formal features fuse with thematic ones, which together (along with context) bring about meaning. As Miller puts it, 'A particular kind of fusion of substance and form is essential to symbolic meaning . . . [F]orm becomes a kind of meta-information, with both semantic value (as information) and syntactic (or formal) value' ('Genre as Social Action', p. 159). Or, as Ricoeur puts it, 'Content and form – to use inadequate categories – are "generated" together' ('Hermeneutical Function', p. 309).

53. Wellek and Warren speak of the 'inner form' of a genre as comprising its attitude, tone and purpose (*Theory of Literature*, p. 241). Longman includes in this category mood, setting, function, narrative voice and content (*Literary Approaches*, p. 80).

54. P. T. Vogt, *Interpreting the Pentateuch: An Exegetical Handbook* (Grand Rapids: Kregel, forthcoming).

55. Bible quotations in this chapter are from the NRSV.

are also a prominent feature of proverbial wisdom).[56] Again, it is the constellation of features that brings clarity regarding the genre of a text.

Genre as social construct

Let's revisit our definition again: Genre is a *socially defined* constellation of typified formal and thematic features. We have already seen that contemporary genre theorists emphasize the contextual nature of genres: genres as social acts embedded in socio-rhetorical contexts. This has been rather obvious to those whose task it is to study ancient texts like the Bible, since these ancient genres often 'act' in ways unfamiliar to readers distant from the Bible by time, language and culture. Biblical apocalyptic literature, for example, is quite dissimilar from any contemporary, Western genre and, as a result, it often befuddles contemporary readers. Yet the original audiences of Daniel and of Revelation, which are in part apocalyptic writings, would have been familiar with the ways these books showed their participation in the genre of apocalyptic. Jewish apocalyptic literature exists outside the Bible, and its conventions and aims would have been understood by the biblical audiences.[57]

Yet even those biblical genres that seem more 'transparent' to modern readers (i.e. that appear to transcend the ancient-to-modern cultural divide) will require closer scrutiny within their original contexts to avoid our misunderstanding them. The Gospels are a case in point. A common assumption brought to the Gospels is that they provide strict chronological information about Jesus' ministry. This assumption comes from our familiarity with modern biography or historiography. Yet the Gospels often follow the pattern of Greco-Roman biography, which was frequently constructed according to thematic rather than chronological concerns. 'Concern for chronological order was not characteristic of ancient biographical writing. As a stylistic technique, presentation of biographical material *per species* [according to topics] is much more common.'[58] Reading with this thematic interest (this convention) in mind will help us understand better what the individual Gospel writers are communicating. For instance, Luke places the account of Jesus preaching in his home

---

56. Fowler, 'Life and Death', p. 203; Pavel, 'Literary Genres', p. 205.

57. Examples of Jewish apocalyptic include *1 Enoch* and 2 Esdras. See Collins for discussion of the parameters of apocalyptic literature ('Morphology of a Genre', pp. 1–20).

58. G. Stanton, *Jesus of Nazareth in New Testament Preaching* (New York: Cambridge University Press, 1974), p. 121. See also Brown, *Scripture as Communication*, pp. 158–159.

town at the very beginning of the ministry of Jesus (Luke 4:16–30), while Mark and Matthew place this story further into their telling of Jesus' ministry after a number of miracles and teachings (Mark 6:1–6; Matt. 13:54–58). One result of the front placement of this account in Luke's arrangement is that the reader hears this story as emblematic for Jesus' ministry, particularly the way the Isaiah texts read by Jesus in the synagogue describe his own ministry. Jesus comes to fulfil the role of the servant of the Lord who preaches good news to the poor and ministers to the oppressed (both significant Lukan themes). Placement points to thematic emphases rather than to strict chronology, a fact that will not surprise us if we attend to the conventions of Greco-Roman biography.

Genre as action

The final part of my definition focuses on genre as it *functions in communication*: Genre is a socially defined constellation of typified features in a group of literary works, both formal and thematic, *which authors use in individualized ways to accomplish specific communicative purposes*. It is in this part of my definition that genre as authorial action is underscored. Genres are not containers that hold textual meaning; rather, they are social actions that accomplish social purposes.[59] As Vanhoozer puts it, they are 'communicative practices'.[60] Putting the emphasis on genre as activity or practice will keep us attentive to the truth that

different genres communicate in distinct ways. While in an epistle an author seeks to persuade through a course of reasoning that is fairly explicit and often linear,

---

59. There is significant consensus that part of what constitutes a genre is its purpose(s) or function(s). In other words, authors draw upon particular genres to fulfil particular purposes, and discerning these purposes is helpful for interpretation. Cf. Fowler, 'Future of Genre Theory', p. 295; Aune, *New Testament*, p. 13; Giese, 'Literary Forms', p. 11; Damrosch, *Narrative Covenant*, p. 39; Bailey and Vander Broek, *Literary Forms*, p. 12. As Devitt states, '[f]ollowing the generic "rules" enables one to achieve a goal; not following them potentially leaves some important function unfulfilled' (*Writing Genres*, p. 147). I do not include function as one of the features of genre (along with form and theme) because it is not so much that function sits alongside formal and thematic features. Rather, it is the formal and thematic features *in constellation* (i.e. as a whole) that function to fulfil certain purposes.

60. K. J. Vanhoozer, *The Drama of Doctrine: A Canonical-Linguistic Approach to Christian Theology* (Louisville: Westminster John Knox, 2005), pp. 213, 283.

narrative authors do their 'persuading' most often implicitly, through story and point of view. Poets, in contrast, use sounds and images to somehow speak of the unspeakable and evoke emotions. By paying attention to the genre choice made by an author, we will be in a better position to understand that author's communication.[61]

A crucial question that follows genre as communicative practice is: *How does a genre communicate?* [62] To illustrate, we might ask this question of the narratives of Scripture. How does narrative specifically communicate? First, the mode of communication in narrative genre is most often indirect. Authors of story often show rather than tell. They let their settings, characters and action speak for them. An author's point of view comes across through the way he or she sets and arranges the story, through characterization (what characters say and do and how readers are led to view those words and actions) and through thematic emphasis. For example, the book of Ruth highlights the theme of loyalty, both the God of Israel's covenant loyalty to Naomi and Ruth, as well as the importance of human loyalty to God and to other people. This is not achieved by simple assertions that such loyalties are important. Rather, the author shows us the value of human loyalty in Ruth's decision to follow Naomi back to Israel and in Boaz's choice to enfold Ruth and Naomi into his family and care. It is through the words and actions of these two characters that the author brings out this theme. Boaz's transaction at the city gate to commit himself to caring for Ruth (4:7–8) and Ruth's words in chapter 1 make it clear that such loyalty should typify not only these characters but the readers/hearers of Ruth as well:

> Do not press me to leave you
> or to turn back from following you!
> Where you go, I will go;
> where you lodge, I will lodge;
> your people shall be my people,
> and your God my God.
> (Ruth 1:16)

Authors of narrative use indirect means to communicate their messages. This is part of the power of narrative as a genre, since readers

---

61. Brown, *Scripture as Communication*, p. 140. The question of *what* a text communicates continues to be important, yet that question cannot be fully answered without attention to *how* a text communicates.

62. Ibid., p. 140.

who may not listen to a sermon on loyalty may be drawn into a narrative about it.

In addition to communicating indirectly, biblical narratives communicate theologically. Biblical narratives mean to show us who God is. In fact, biblical writers are most often interested in communicating about God, and secondarily about people:

> [B]iblical narratives are primarily about God and God's redemptive activity among humanity, and their authors claim to reveal God truthfully. This may seem like a truism, but we often focus our attention on the ethical dimensions of narrative rather than on its theological dimension. In other words, it is too easy to ask the question of narratives, what should I be like? rather than, what is God like? or what is God doing? The ethical question is not inappropriate. Yet our primary interpretive focus should be theological. Our first question ought to be the 'God question.'[63]

We have looked at the extended genre example of narrative to illustrate the active ways genres communicate. Narrative genre communicates in particular ways, most often in indirect fashion through the patterns of the storyline. Biblical narratives communicate theologically as well. Other biblical genres communicate in ways often distinct from narrative, so in interpretation we shall want to attend to the question of *how a genre communicates*.

To summarize, it is interpretatively profitable to view genre as *a socially defined constellation of typified formal and thematic features in a group of literary works, which authors use in individualized ways to accomplish specific communicative purposes.* Let us turn now to the implications of such a definition for interpreting the Bible.

Genre and biblical interpretation

Preliminary issues regarding biblical genres

Having developed a working definition of genre, we now turn to the question of genre and interpretation. How does recognizing the genre of a text assist in its interpretation? Our focus in this discussion will be on how genre intersects with the interpretation of the Bible. An initial observation, in this regard, has to do with the historical nature of genre analysis of the Bible. When we

---

63. Ibid., p. 162. See also J. Goldingay, 'Biblical Narrative and Systematic Theology', in J. B. Green and M. Turner (eds.), *Between Two Horizons: Spanning New Testament Studies and Systematic Theology* (Grand Rapids: Eerdmans, 2000), p. 137.

read the Bible, we implicitly bring our own knowledge of contemporary literary genres with us. Yet if we rely only on what we know about the genres of our own culture, we shall inevitably misunderstand at least some features of the genres of Scripture. What we need is a *historical understanding* of the genre represented in any particular book of the Bible. For the genres represented in the Bible are obsolete; they are no longer utilized in our contemporary cultures, even if similar genre types exist. Hebrew wisdom literature is not practised today, although proverbial genre is a part of many contemporary cultures. The interpreter's job in this case will be to learn the contours of OT wisdom literature especially as it differs from any analogous genre that might be culturally familiar to the interpreter.

One of the issues genre theorists face as they study ancient literature is how to categorize texts. Longman describes two approaches to genre classification. *Emic classification* refers to an attempt to follow indigenous or native classifications for literature.[64] Problematic for this approach is that some ancient contexts have no explicit genre theory, as in the case of the ANE.[65] And as we saw in our historical survey of ancient Greek genre theory, even when a genre theory was espoused, it did not always cohere with the actual practice of writers of that cultural tradition, especially in relation to genre purity. So, contemporary interpreters of the Bible will need to rely on etic as well as emic classifications of texts. An *etic classification* arises from theorizing that comes from outside the culture in which a text was written.[66] Whatever the disadvantages of relying on etic classifications, those who study the Bible cannot avoid non-indigenous categorizations. In fact, it is possible that careful attention to *similar features in constellation* between texts may very well illuminate generic parameters that truly reflect ancient conventions and not simply the generic grid of the interpreter. As Simons and Aghazarian put it, 'The fact is . . . that certain of our literary and rhetorical genres "exist" as cultural artifacts, and not just in the minds of classification-happy academics.'[67] The challenge in approaching the Bible's genres is that we must reconstruct these cultural artefacts from study of the Bible and other ancient texts.

---

64. Longman, 'Israelite Genres', pp. 180–181.

65. Damrosch, *Narrative Covenant*, p. 38. He notes that the only categorization we can observe is not based on 'specific genre qualities of form or content but rather on the media of performance or inscription'; e.g. 'song' used to designate epics as well as hymns (p. 38).

66. Longman, 'Israelite Genres', p. 181.

67. Simons and Aghazarian, 'Introduction', in *Form, Genre*, p. 11.

A second issue that arises far more from biblical than modern genres is the orality of much of the Bible. By this I mean first that some parts of the Bible were orally composed. Examples of this include psalms and other songs, many prophetic oracles, and parables and other teachings of Jesus. In addition, even those parts of the Bible that were written compositions from their conception were meant to be read aloud to their intended audiences.[68] As interpreters, we must attend to this feature of the biblical text and its genres. For example, the seemingly abrupt shift that occurs at Philippians 3:1–2 has in the past caused some scholars to argue against the unity of this Pauline letter. Yet in an oral culture, the words of closure expressed at 3:1 ('finally', *to loipon*) may be better understood as an aural clue to a topical shift (which would need to be more pronounced in an oral reading context than in a modern written document, which has paragraph markers and punctuation to assist in such signalling).[69]

Genre as constraint or creativity?

The nature of the relationship between genres and texts has been a central issue for genre theory throughout its history. Do genres constrain authors and their texts? And if so, to what extent? Or are authors (at least the best authors) free from virtually all constraints? The answers to these questions will indicate the importance of genre for those who come to interpret texts.

A helpful starting point is the recognition that our understanding of a genre comes only from our interaction with specific texts:

> Genres are abstractions from particular texts. Similarities are highlighted as literary texts are placed into groups. Genres are not categories that are fixed in nature, but

---

68. This was the case even when the intended audience was primarily an individual as in Philemon. See Brown, *Scripture as Communication*, p. 132. Stein discusses this phenomenon: 'Even private reading was generally performed out loud' (R. H. Stein, 'Is Our Reading the Bible the Same as the Original Audience's Hearing It? A Case Study in the Gospel of Mark', *JETS* 46 [2003], p. 68).

69. P. J. Achtemeier, '*Omne Verbum Sonat*: The New Testament and the Oral Environment of Late Western Antiquity', *JBL* 109 (1990), p. 26. Achtemeier's helpful discussion may be complemented by the comprehensive method for attending to 'oral residue' in NT texts, as proposed by C. W. David, *Oral Biblical Criticism: The Influence of the Principles of Orality on the Literary Structure of Paul's Epistle to the Philippians*, JSNTSup 172 (Sheffield: Sheffield Academic Press, 1999).

rather are based on the observation of textual similarities of a number of different types. The fluidity of genres derives from the fact that a researcher/reader can attend to a small number of similarities, thus producing a large category, or a large number of similarities, which will result in a small category of texts.[70]

Genres are flexible categories because they are generalizing, fluid constructs.

This realization allows for the unique elements that authors bring to their writings, while still granting the inevitability of genres in all communication, including literary communication. In this area, maintaining the tension between the constraints of a genre and an author's freedom to individualize her work is crucial. Devitt argues for understanding this tension as dialectic rather than dichotomy: 'both constraint and choice are necessary and therefore [both are] positive components of genre'.[71] This means that, as interpreters, we must give 'detailed attention to the interplay between abstract categories and the originality of their instantiation'.[72] Texts exhibit generic and unique features, so attention to both genre and individualization in interpretation is necessary.

Let's look at one practical outworking of proper consideration of this dialectic or tension between genre constraint and artistic choice. Devitt notes that an author 'can foreground innovation because of the background of the expected'.[73] Genre conventions are by definition 'the expected'; therefore, when an author stretches or breaks a particular convention, readers will rightly perceive an emphasis in what has been foregrounded. This seems to be the case in Psalm 92. The presence of poetic parallelism is commonplace in this psalm as in Hebrew poetry generally. Note that in the following assessment there is only one non-parallel line (monocolon) in the psalm (92:8). (Parallel lines have been grouped without spacing; the single line is italicized.)

> It is good to give thanks to the LORD.
>> to sing praises to your name, O Most High;
>> to declare your steadfast love in the morning,

---

70. Longman, 'Israelite Genres', p. 183. As Schaeffer puts it, 'our knowledge goes from texts to genres much more than from genres to texts' ('Literary Genres', p. 176).

71. Devitt, *Writing Genres*, pp. 130–140.

72. Pavel, 'Literary Genres', p. 202. Pavel goes on to note, 'Writers, who like most human beings know their best interest, tend to follow [literary] customs and habits' ('Literary Genres', p. 206).

73. Devitt, *Writing Genres*, p. 154.

and your faithfulness by night,
to the music of the lute and the harp,
   to the melody of the lyre.
For you, O LORD, have made me glad by your work;
   at the works of your hands I sing for joy.
How great are your works, O LORD!
   Your thoughts are very deep!
The dullard cannot know,
   the stupid cannot understand this:
though the wicked sprout like grass
   and all evildoers flourish,
they are doomed to destruction for ever,
   but you, O LORD, are on high for ever.
For your enemies, O LORD,
   for your enemies shall perish;
   all evildoers shall be scattered.

But you have exalted my horn like that of the wild ox;
   you have poured over me fresh oil.
My eyes have seen the downfall of my enemies;
   my ears have heard the doom of my evil assailants.

The righteous flourish like the palm tree,
   and grow like a cedar in Lebanon.
They are planted in the house of the LORD;
   they flourish in the courts of our God.
In old age they still produce fruit;
   they are always green and full of sap;
showing that the LORD is upright;
   he is my rock, and there is no unrighteousness in him.

By moving outside the more expected use of parallelism, the psalmist seems to be foregrounding this poetic line. If this is the case, then it is probably no accident that this line highlights Yahweh as eternally reigning in the midst of a psalm that contrasts the quick (though not immediate) demise of the wicked with the flourishing of God's faithful, righteous ones by the hand of God.[74]

---

74. D. Howard, 'A Contextual Reading of Psalms 90–94', in J. C. McCann (ed.), *The Shape and Shaping of the Psalter*, JSOTSup (Sheffield: JSOT Press, 1993), p. 113.

Genres as heuristic tool

Another way of maintaining this balance between genre as constraint and genre as opportunity for creativity is to view genres as heuristic devices. This means attending to broad genre types for interpretative help, while maintaining a close reading of specific texts that allows for their ability to 'transgress' genre boundaries. As Hirsch states, 'broad, heuristic type concepts are just as essential as intrinsic genres. It is by means of them that new intrinsic genres are able to come into existence and are capable of being understood' (Hirsch's definition of intrinsic genre is akin to the individuation of a specific literary work).[75] For Hirsch, genre concepts are best used as heuristic devices that give a provisional lie of the land from which to understand individual texts. Genre typifications provide 'conceptual wedges' into texts.[76]

Understanding genres heuristically, as entrance points for interpretation, can keep interpreters from overly constraining authors via genres. For instance, many commentators have noted how Paul expands the typical thanksgiving section of the ancient Greek letter from a brief, (polite) expression to extended, theologically shaped prayers on behalf of his recipients. To limit Paul merely to the conventional parameters in this regard would be wrong-headed. In addition, Paul chooses to omit this section of his letter when

75. E. D. Hirsch, Jr., *Validity in Interpretation* (New Haven: Yale University Press, 1967), p. 104. Hirsch provides at least two distinct definitions of intrinsic genre. He first defines intrinsic genre as the 'entire, complex system of shared experiences, usage traits, and meaning expectations which the speaker [or author] relies on' in communication (p. 80). He also states that intrinsic genre is '*that sense of the whole [textual meaning] by means of which an interpreter can correctly understand any part in its determinacy*' (p. 86; italics in original). Hirsch's use and definition of intrinsic genre, especially in the latter definition, is idiosyncratic; no other author I have consulted delineates *genre* as the textual meaning viewed holistically. This appears in Hirsch's definition of extrinsic genre as 'a wrong guess' about genre, while an intrinsic genre is 'a correct one' (p. 88). Pearson and Porter interpret Hirsch's unique way of using the terms 'intrinsic' and 'extrinsic' genre as 'obviat[ing] the need for genre as an important interpretive tool' ('Genres', p. 134). This seems to do a disservice to Hirsch's statements elsewhere in *Validity in Interpretation*, which indicate the necessity of larger, heuristic genre categories not only for interpretation but also for textual production (e.g. *Validity in Interpretation*, p. 104).

76. Hirsch, *Validity in Interpretation*, p. 116. The heuristic use of genres is affirmed by many theorists, including Schaeffer, 'Literary Genres', p. 177; Todorov, *Genres in Discourse*, p. 17, n. 9; and Bakhtin, *Speech Genres*, pp. 78–79.

writing to the Galatians. This creative move has interpretative implications. The Galatian Christians would have felt the shaming effect of this omission, even if contemporary readers do not automatically register this. Authors are free to poke and nudge at generic conventions to accomplish their own communicative purposes. So interpreters will want to allow for the creative movement of authors within typical genre parameters.

A provisional, heuristic use of genre categories accomplishes two quite helpful tasks for the interpreter. First, it eliminates any number of false expectations for a text.[77] By making an initial genre hypothesis, the interpreter rules out a wide range of unlikely genre conventions. It is true that the interpretative process can and often should include various revisions of the genre hypothesis first made. Interpretation is, in the end, 'dependent on the last, unrevised generic conception' of the interpreter.[78] Nevertheless, the process of refining generic conception helpfully rules out a wide array of extraneous conventions. For example, some readers of Revelation identify its genre as eschatological history, containing rather straightforward predictions of events to come. Other interpreters note the apocalyptic convention of framing past history as future event and so understand events framed as future to be portraying past ones. Viewing Revelation through one of these genre lenses will necessarily rule out the other possible reading strategy.[79]

Secondly, the heuristic use of genre categories 'prompts[s] a reading strategy'.[80] As Bakhtin notes, '[W]hen hearing others' speech, we guess its genre from the very first words; we predict a certain length (that is, the approximate length of the speech whole) and a certain compositional structure; we foresee the end; that is, from the very beginning we have a sense of the speech whole, which is only later differentiated during the speech process'.[81] This provisional sense of the whole guides the interpreter's reading strategy, which will expect certain features and will interpret these within the presumed generic conception. As the provisional genre is confirmed, rejected or modified, an interpreter adjusts the reading strategy used. For example, when technological advances first led to the ability to do mass mailings with per-

---

77. Longman, *Literary Approaches*, p. 83.

78. Hirsch, *Validity in Interpretation*, p. 76.

79. Murphy traces historical understandings of Revelation via these two categories (F. A. Murphy, 'Revelation, Book of', in Vanhoozer, *Dictionary for Theological Interpretation*, pp. 682–686).

80. Longman, *Literary Approaches*, p. 83.

81. Bakhtin, *Speech Genres*, p. 79.

sonalized information atop a form letter (e.g. name and address), genre confusion resulted. People (like me) often confused these form letters for the
genre of individualized business letters, and this led to a reading strategy that
expected relational elements and situationally specific information. Yet when
this information was lacking, the true genre became clear. The seemingly
individualized letter was actually intended to address a large number of
people with the same message, but did so with a more personalized touch
that would presumably draw in the reader (and keep her from tossing out the
letter without reading it!). A change in genre identification affects one's genre
reading strategy.

It will be helpful to raise one qualification at this juncture. While authors
who want to communicate with their readers follow generic conventions, it
is not the case that *all aspects* of a text are genre-dependent.[82] As we have seen
in our definition of genre, some thematic and even some formal features occur in more than one genre. In addition, some aspects of a text are
not specified by genre. 'Within any genre, there is a great deal of "free"
variation.'[83]

The benefits of larger genre categories

Given the argument for a provisional, heuristic use of genre in interpretation,
it also follows that larger genre categories are often more helpful for interpretation than narrower ones. The larger the genre category, the fewer and usually
more pronounced the similarities that characterize texts from that genre as distinguished from other major genre categories.[84]

---

82. Hirsch, *Validity in Interpretation*, p. 77.

83. Devitt, *Writing Genres*, p. 149.

84. As we move from larger to narrower genre categories, which are often derived
    from fewer textual clues, less interpretative weight should be given to any proposed
    category (Fowler, 'Future of Genre Theory', p. 302). For example, the Psalms fit
    the broad category of Hebrew poetry. Beyond this, they are examples of the use of
    poetry in song and/or prayer. We can attend to further groupings of psalm types
    with their own generic features, such as praise psalms, laments and wisdom psalms.
    Yet when we move to this level of specificity, the generic signals may become less
    clear. For example, Ps. 89 exhibits clear characteristics of a royal psalm from 89:1
    to 89:37. Yet this psalm concludes with classic lament features (89:38–52), although
    the royal emphases do not disappear (89:39, 49). In the end, it is not that reference
    to narrower categories is illegitimate but that the larger, more comprehensively
    attested, category should receive greater interpretative weight.

> Differences of kind that make a difference can be found among very large [genre]
> categories . . . When readers apply the conventions of 'satire' to 'apologues' . . . or the
> conventions of 'represented actions' . . . to satire, maimed readings result – readings
> that may seem satisfying but that collapse as soon as someone points to all the
> elements that have had to be ignored to make the reading seem coherent. Though
> actual readers will make of works whatever their generic expectations enable them to
> make, works themselves work very hard, as we might say, to put up 'dead end' signs
> and directional arrows that actually *work*.[85]

Literary works themselves guide the reader toward their generic affinities. The larger the generic category, the greater the number of signals ('dead end signs' and 'directional arrows', as Booth terms them) communicated to the reader.

OT prophetic writings, for example, incorporate Hebrew poetry and in some cases narratival frames or inclusions (e.g. Jeremiah's prologue and concluding chapter). So formal poetic features, such as line parallelism and metaphorical language, are prominent. We can see both in Zephaniah 2:1–2, which consists of four lines of poetry with the final three being parallel to each other in a kind of thought progression. The use of simile is also present in the second line:

> Gather together, gather, O shameless nation,
> before you are driven away like the drifting chaff,
> before there comes upon you the fierce anger of the LORD,
> before there comes upon you the day of the LORD's wrath.

Such poetic features, in fact, provide a 'directional arrow' indicating that Zephaniah is a prophetic writing. Other generic indicators include a book opening that identifies the prophet, the prophetic oracle as a basic unit of thought, and the use of cosmological language for God's activity in human history.

The book of Zephaniah also puts up dead-end signs that indicate *what Zephaniah is not* generically. For example, Ecclesiastes is a book categorized as wisdom literature that shares features with prophetic writings such as the use of Hebrew poetry and a book opening identifying the writer. Yet these common features occur in decidedly different constellations in each genre;

---

85. W. C. Booth, *The Rhetoric of Fiction*, 2nd ed. (Chicago: University of Chicago Press, 1983), p. 435 (italics in original).

and it is the features in constellation that define a genre. Though both poetic, Zephaniah's use of prophetic oracles, rather than proverbial reflection, re-directs the reader away from the category of wisdom literature toward the genre of prophetic writing. By looking for such genre indicators, the inter-preter can helpfully draw upon genre categories for understanding a specific biblical text.

As we use larger genre categories in interpretation, we must be careful to avoid the conclusion that genre categories absolutely define and subsume indi-vidual texts. As Hirsch notes, 'The larger genre concepts represent something real only to the extent that they represent norms and conventions that were actually brought into play. Used in this way, the terms are valid even if they are not adequately definitive.'[86] As we have already affirmed, authors can draw upon existing genre conventions while significantly recasting some of their features in the artistic process. For example, Damrosch argues that the histor-ical writing of the Hebrew Bible arose from 'a far-reaching transformation' of the earlier Mesopotamian genres of historical chronicle and poetic epic.[87] Allowing for such transformations of existing genre parameters will be import-ant for nuanced interpretation.

Attending to genre complexity and fluidity

Genre complexity

As we interpret the Bible, we should pay attention to what genre critics have affirmed about the complexity and fluidity of genres. In addition to the com-plexity of genres as constellations, genres generate further complexity when they contain any number of 'subgenres' or when they are a mix of two or more genres.

Genres may 'contain' any number of shorter literary forms. Bakhtin distin-guishes these shorter forms from the genres that include them as primary and secondary forms, respectively. It is this type of embedding of primary forms within secondary forms, or genres, that contributes to the complexity of genres and their interpretation.[88] As a result, interpreters will want to identify

---

86. Hirsch, *Validity in Interpretation*, p. 109. See also Simons and Aghazarian, 'Introduction', in *Form, Genre*, p. 53. As Hirsch further clarifies, 'the larger genre . . . is at best a partial and provisional classification, though it is a necessary one' (p. 110).

87. Damrosch, *Narrative Covenant*, p. 41.

88. 'Secondary (complex) speech genres – novels, dramas, all kinds of scientific research, major genres of commentary, and so forth – arise in more complex and

primary forms (or subgenres) within the biblical books they are studying and become aware of the conventions of these forms. It is at this level of inter-pretation that attention to orality is crucial, since many of the primary forms embedded in various books of the Bible were first oral compositions. Habakkuk is a case in point. While at book level it participates in the genre of OT prophetic writings, it also contains a number of primary forms with an oral cast to them (whether their origin is oral or written), including the woe oracle (Hab. 2) and the psalm (Hab. 3).

An example of the significant placement of a primary form occurs within the letter of 1 Peter. The Petrine household code is centrally located and takes up over a chapter of this letter; thus it merits close attention (2:13 – 3:7). The house-hold code was a typical form used within Greco-Roman philosophical discus-sions prior to and around the time of the NT. Allowing for inevitable variability, such household codes usually addressed three relationships in the household: master and slaves, husband and wife, and father and children.[89] The addressee of the household code was typically the male householder, that is, the one who was master, husband and father. He was expected to maintain order in his house-hold and, according to Aristotle, to 'rule over wife and children' (*Politics* 1.5.1–2). Knowing some of the typical formal and thematic features of ancient household codes helps us as we turn to 1 Peter. First, we note that the author begins the household code by enjoining submission to governing rulers (2:13–17). Although not typically a part of household codes, this move makes sense in the context of 1 Peter. There seems to be an uneasy relationship between believ-ers and outsiders, who are speaking against Christians and their allegiances (2:11–12; 3:13–17; 4:3–4, 14–16). In this context, the author indicates via the household code that Christians should avoid any hint of insurrection that might

---

Footnote 88 (*continued*)

comparatively highly developed and organized cultural communication (primarily written) that is artistic, scientific, sociopolitical, and so on. During the process of their formation, they absorb and digest various primary (simple) genres that have taken form in unmediated speech communion' (*Speech Genres*, p. 62). I have chosen to use the term 'genres' for more complex, secondary forms (typically, on the level of the whole book) and (primary) 'forms' for simpler literary forms. Various theorists identify the distinctions between genres and literary forms differently. See the discussion in Pearson and Porter, 'Genres', p. 134.

89. J. K. Brown, 'Silent Wives, Verbal Believers: Ethical and Hermeneutical Considerations in 1 Peter 3:1–6 and Its Context', *WW* 24 (autumn 2004), p. 399; e.g. Aristotle, *Politics* 1.2.1; Eph. 5:21 – 6:9; Col. 3:18 – 4:1.

compromise the gospel. A second observation: slaves and wives are directly addressed in the Petrine household code (2:18; 3:1), though this is not the usual form of household codes outside the NT. By modifying convention, the author 'implies that both [slaves and wives] have a measure of moral responsibility and choice unprecedented in Greek thought'.[90] Finally, the inclusion of a missional purpose in the exhortation to wives of unbelieving husbands stretches the boundaries of the household code form: 'Wives, in the same way, accept the authority of your husbands, so that, even if some of them do not obey the word, *they may be won over without a word by their wives' conduct*' (3:1; my italics). Given traditional expectations that women would follow the gods of their husbands, the implicit contradiction of this expectation adds 'a subversive element to the otherwise traditional contours of this part of the household code'.[91]

The Gospels provide another illustration of primary forms embedded in secondary ones. In addition to their overarching narrative genre (consisting of both narration and discourse), the Gospels contain such literary forms as parables, proverbs, genealogies, prayers, pronouncement stories and call narratives.[92] The interpreter will certainly want to understand the conventions of these various primary forms as they study the Gospels. Nevertheless, the history of NT interpretation since the early twentieth century reveals a tendency to isolate these primary forms. Early form critics focused almost exclusive attention on the forms in isolation from their literary contexts, seeking to identify the forms, their conventions and their life situation in the oral traditions of the early church. In addition, modern preaching practices also tend to isolate Gospel stories, so that congregations may be given little idea of where a story or saying of Jesus fits in the wider telling of a Gospel. Since both recent history of interpretation and much preaching has resulted in atomizing the Gospel stories, it will be especially important to integrate study of any specific primary form into our understanding of the whole Gospel we are interpreting.[93] Paying attention to *where a parable occurs* in the flow of Matthew's narrative, for instance, will contribute to understanding Matthew just as much as attending to how individual parables communicate and function.[94] In the end, both interpretative tasks are crucial.

---

90. K. H. Jobes, *1 Peter*, BECNT (Grand Rapids: 2005), p. 204.

91. Brown, 'Silent Wives', p. 400.

92. For a catalogue of such subgenres for the Gospels, see J. L. Bailey, 'Genre Analysis', in J. B. Green (ed.) *Hearing the New Testament: Strategies for Interpretation* (Grand Rapids: Eerdmans, 1995), p. 207; Bailey and Vander Broek, *Literary Forms*.

93. See Brown, *Scripture as Communication*, pp. 212–217.

94. I give the example of Jesus' parables, because they have been and continue to be

In addition to the embedding of primary forms within genres, the complexity of genres also arises from the mixing of genres in a text.[95] This is a common enough occurrence despite the traditional preference for genre purity. Biblical studies has historically followed ancient and neoclassical sensibilities in this preference. Longman points out that Gunkel applied an already obsolete model from literary genre theory to his study of forms, one that idealized genre purity and saw later forms as corruptions of earlier ones.[96] We can see this tendency in Mowinckel's reference to the 'disintegration' of earlier forms evident in some psalms.[97] Yet poets and other literary artists, ancient and modern, often *mix genres to good effect*. As Osborne notes, an author's choice to mingle genres does not invalidate the notion of genre parameters, since the recognition of such combinations presupposes the categories being mixed.[98]

Since authors regularly mix genres, interpreters will need to be aware of this tendency and will want to attend to the complexities of such mixing in any particular book of the Bible. Damrosch's claim that the historical books of the OT are a 'combination of many of the values, themes, and formal properties of historical chronicle with those of poetic epic' has interpretative implications.[99] One implication Damrosch underscores is the appropriateness of drawing upon ANE literary evidence as an interpretative backdrop for the OT,

---

Footnote 94 (*continued*)

separated from their contexts more than most primary forms in the Gospels. For an examination of how Matthew's parables function in the five major discourses of Matthew, especially their culminative function, see J. K. Brown, 'Direct Engagement of the Reader in Matthew's Discourses: Rhetorical Techniques and Scholarly Consensus', *NTS* 51 (2005), pp. 32–33.

95. This may happen when two genres combine into a hybrid genre or when an author extends an existing genre into a new type. Cf. Hirsch, *Validity in Interpretation*, p. 105; Devitt, *Writing Genres*, p. 151. According to Todorov, 'A new genre is always the transformation of an earlier one, or of several: by inversion, by displacement, by combination' (*Genres in Discourse*, p. 15).

96. Longman, 'Israelite Genres', p. 181.

97. S. Mowinckel, *The Psalms in Israel's Worship*, vol. 2 (Oxford: Basil Blackwell, 1962), p. 77.

98. G. R. Osborne, 'Genre Criticism – *Sensus Literalis*', in E. D. Radmacher and R. D. Preus (eds.), *Hermeneutics, Inerrancy, and the Bible* (Grand Rapids: Academie, 1984), p. 170.

99. Damrosch, *Narrative Covenant*, p. 41.

recognizing that biblical authors may borrow, adapt and even subvert generic conventions of neighbouring peoples.[100]

The determination of the genre of the Gospels has had a long and hotly debated history.[101] One of the difficulties of arriving at their genre is their mixed nature. While Burridge has made a compelling case for the Gospels as *bios*, that is, Greco-Roman biography,[102] it is also the case that their Jewish character is pronounced. Thus it may be that understanding the Gospels as a generic combination of *bios* and Jewish historiography will be conceptually helpful for their interpretation. As Wright concludes:

> [The Gospels] are, in fact, Jewish-style biographies, designed to show the quintessence of Israel's story played out in a single life . . . What Jesus has done, the evangelists are saying, is to bring to its climax not simply the chain of the stories of individual faithful Jews but the whole history of Israel. The gospels are therefore the story of Jesus *told as the history of Israel in miniature*.[103]

Genre fluidity

Genres are both complex and fluid; they are 'soft concepts', as Schaeffer puts it.[104] As we have seen, this is the case because genres are categories constructed from observations about texts; and authors of texts are both constrained by and free to adapt existing genres. One aspect of genre fluidity is that genres change over time.[105] Since they are cultural constructs, this should come as no

---

100. Damrosch notes that dichotomizing epic and chronicle has sometimes led to an undue disregard of ANE evidence (ibid., pp. 41, 87).

101. Early form critics thought the Gospels to be *sui generis* (a wholly new genre). There is, however, more continuity between the Gospels and already existing genres than these scholars acknowledged. Bailey puts it well: '[The gospel genre] borrows features from ancient biography and historiography but finally presents a new mixed literary genre as a way to express the surprising quality of Jesus' ministry, death, and resurrection' ('Genre Analysis', p. 202).

102. R. A. Burridge, *What Are the Gospels? A Comparison with Graeco-Roman Biography*, 2nd ed. (Grand Rapids: Eerdmans, 2004).

103. N. T. Wright, *The New Testament and the People of God* (Minneapolis: Fortress, 1992), p. 402 (italics in original).

104. Schaeffer, 'Literary Genres', p. 178.

105. Cohen, 'Generic Reconstitution', pp. vi–vii; Fowler, 'Future of Genre Theory', pp. 298, 301; Schaeffer, 'Literary Genres', pp. 173, 175; Todorov, *Genres in Discourse*,

surprise. What the interpreter will want to watch for is the status of a genre at the point in time of the text being studied.[106]

Another aspect of genre fluidity is the potential for overlap between categories of genres. Since genres are groupings of texts based on similarities, it is possible that a single text could be identified with more than one genre type, if it shares significant similarities with multiple categories. The book of Job is often included in the genre category of wisdom literature, which features poetic, proverbial reflection on life as God has ordered it. Yet Job has also been categorized as 'lawsuit' or 'dramatized lament'.[107] When more than one genre is applied to a single book, it is helpful to notice what varying identifications say about the book in question. In this case, the narrative framework of Job as well as its thematic focus on the portrayal of a righteous sufferer compelled to defend his piety complicate its genre identification as wisdom literature, at least for some.[108] Noticing genre fluidity usually boils down to noticing textual flexibility. Texts can straddle the genre categories that scholars have delineated, given the overlapping characteristics between genres. This does not make genre categories illegitimate; it does, however, call interpreters to a more flexible understanding of genres.

What is helpful in cases like these is to understand a genre in relation to other genres. That is, a genre is defined in part by *what it is not* as well as by what it is. As White suggests, '[W]e might profitably consider the problem of genre by identifying each genre's conceptual "other" rather than by simply classifying genres according to a principle of similarity and difference'.[109] I have attended to this briefly in my example of Zephaniah as prophetic writing and not wisdom literature. Here the generic signals

---

Footnote 105 (*continued*)

 p. 20. 'Logically, since they reflect their cultural, situational, and generic contexts, and since those contexts change over time, genres, too, must change over time' (Devitt, *Writing Genres*, p. 89).

106. Pearson and Porter, 'Genres', p. 133.

107. R. L. Schultz, 'Form Criticism and the Old Testament', in Vanhoozer, *Dictionary for Theological Interpretation*, p. 235.

108. Part of the issue may be wisdom literature as a genre. For a discussion of OT wisdom literature and the difficulties of defining and delineating it generically, see R. C. Van Leeuwen, 'Wisdom Literature', in Vanhoozer, *Dictionary for Theological Interpretation*, pp. 847–848.

109. White, 'Anomalies of Genre', p. 610; Cohen, 'Generic Reconstitution', p. xiv; Devitt, *Writing Genres*, p. 27.

are pretty clear. In the case of Job, which has been viewed as more generically ambiguous, comparing typical features of wisdom literature with the genre of poetic laments might clarify the ways in which Job participates in wisdom literature but also pushes at the 'boundaries' of that genre. Collins does this same kind of genre comparison when he clarifies the parameters of apocalypse by comparing it to oracle, testament and revelatory dialogue, each of which contains eschatological material similar to that found in apocalypses.[110]

Addressing genre impact

Our exploration of genre and interpretation has focused on how we might learn the conventions of biblical genres in order to respond to Scripture according to its authors' intentions.[111] Genres are *active skill sets* authors employ, which they expect their readers to recognize and engage with appropriate reading strategies. Part of the hard work of Bible interpretation stems from the need to give concerted attention to learning what would have been intuitive for the most part (learned from a young age) for the original audiences of the books of the Bible. By learning the contours of various biblical genres we not only gain knowledge the author was assuming for the original audience (and which is essential for proper understanding of Scripture), but we also appropriate a suitable reading strategy for what we are interpreting. Learning genres is an active endeavour by readers, just as using genres is an authorial praxis.

A text's genre suggests a strategy for reading that text, including the outcome of response the author intends to evoke in readers. This response takes the shape of whatever genre the author employs in communication. Since different genres are intentionally used to elicit different kinds of responses, we must listen carefully for fitting responses grounded in the text's generic shaping. Poetry is often chosen as a genre to express or evoke an emotive response. Whether expressing adoration, anger or grief, the psalmists choose poetry because it is eminently suitable for such expression. Our response then will not be adequate if we stop at a cognitive understanding of a psalm. The call is to respond holistically: emotionally, volitionally and cognitively.[112] In the end, anticipating the kind of impact a certain genre makes should be part of our generic reading strategy.

---

110. Collins, 'Morphology of a Genre', p. 10.

111. For a full treatment of authorial intention as an author's communicative intentions, see Brown, *Scripture as Communication*, ch. 2.

112. Cf. Vanhoozer, *Drama of Doctrine*, pp. 276–281.

Genre and the interpreter

It might seem redundant to comment on genre and *the interpreter* after our discussion of genre and *interpretation*. Yet it is the case that we as interpreters are not objectively detached or hermetically separated from the genre analysis we do. Interpreters, whether they want to or not, impact the interpretative process. They 'get in the way'. In relation to this chapter, interpreters bring a theory of genre to their reading of Scripture; they bring presuppositions about the genres of particular books of the Bible; and they bring an evaluative hierarchy of genre to their reading of the whole biblical canon.

The focus of this chapter has been on genre theory. One possible reaction to all this talk about genre theory is a questioning of theoretical deliberation itself. *'Is all this theorizing really necessary?'* Yet none of us comes to interpretation without a theoretical grid in place. It is the case that 'without some kind of theory, however unreflective and implicit, we would not know what a "literary work" was in the first place, or how we were to read it. Hostility to *theory* usually means an opposition to other people's theories and an oblivion to one's own.'[113] We all have a genre theory, whether implicit or explicit. I hope this chapter has not only clarified some current theoretical topics and issues, but has also made its readers more aware of their own theoretical assumptions about genre.

Presuppositions and genre

Not only do we as interpreters operate from our own genre theory, but we also routinely presuppose what we are reading as we come to any biblical book. We presuppose its genre and we apply a corresponding reading strategy to the book, often without conscious attention. We are probably most aware of our position in relation to the text (our initial genre guess and corresponding reading strategy) when we have misapprehended the genre in which a text participates. We become aware of our own faulty categorization precisely when we run into clues in the text that conflict with our initial genre hypothesis. We come, as we do to any text, with an implicit but full set of assumptions about it, including its genre type. These genre presuppositions come from the communities that have shaped our Bible reading (family, church, tradition etc.) and our own past readings of the text.

Schultz uses the book of Jonah to illustrate how one book can be identified

---

113. T. Eagleton, *Literary Theory: An Introduction*, 2nd ed. (Minneapolis: University of Minnesota Press, 1996), p. x. Cf. also Brown, *Scripture as Communication*, ch. 6.

by a broad range of genre categories. He lists the following categories that have been suggested for Jonah: '[F]able, didactic novel, prophetic legend, parable, midrash, allegory, prophetic confession', prophetic writing more broadly, or some mix of genres.[114] I would suggest that an interpreter's presuppositions come into play here as with other Bible books. We do not leave our assumptions at the door when we interpret the Bible. As interpreters, we bring with us our broader convictions about what the Bible is, including what particular books can and cannot be generically. Acknowledging this and as much as possible examining our presuppositions in the light of Scripture itself will be a helpful starting point for informed hermeneutical reflection.

Genre hierarchies

The topic of genre and ideology has been one significant area of discussion in recent genre analysis. One way ideology works itself out in the area of genre is through hierarchical ordering of genres. The history of genre theory has demonstrated that theorists and authors have preferred certain genres over others. From the ancient Greek preference for tragedy over satire to the elevation of poetry over novel in the nineteenth century, no era has been immune from establishing and then assuming genre hierarchies. And in spite of concerted efforts by contemporary genre theorists to raise our awareness of this issue, the preferential treatment of certain genres continues. The difference is merely in the favourite genre of the moment. As Fowler comments on genre hierarchy in literary criticism, 'Nor will it quite do merely to alter the hierarchy of kinds in favor of [more popular kinds of genres], as some . . . would like. Such paradigms of rank were always far too crudely schematic, too oblivious to variations in the temperament of readers.'[115] If the problem is an unreflective elevation of some genres over others, the antidote begins with an awareness of what preferences we as interpreters bring to what we read.

This seems especially important as we approach Scripture. Whether personally or culturally conditioned, most readers have 'favourite' genres in the Bible. Do we prefer and thus value more highly letters over narratives, because they are more 'didactic' and provide more straightforward theology (or so we think)?[116] Or are we partial to narrative, 'which has become for many the

---

114. Schultz, 'Form Criticism', p. 235.

115. Fowler, 'Future of Genre Theory', p. 303.

116. For the argument that narratives are didactic, that is, they seek to teach and are also quite theological in nature, see Brown, *Scripture as Communication*, pp. 161–162.

generic darling of the canon'.[117] In OT interpretation, the tendency to value certain genres over others is quite evident from the vantage point of some Christian readings of biblical law. 'Christian scholars have long tended to minimize the importance of biblical law', according to Damrosch.[118] Certainly, the tendency has been to elevate OT narrative over law, thereby dichotomizing the two. Yet by doing so, we risk a distorted view of the Pentateuch, which holds a central place for law within its broadly narrative parameters.[119]

As interpreters, we fool ourselves if we do not acknowledge our tendencies and even our actions in valuing some genres of the Bible over others. Yet a high view of Scripture would ask us to rethink such hierarchies. And the only way to affirm consistently the importance of all the Bible, with its manifold genres, is to recognize those parts or genres we are prone to devalue and turn our attention to them as well. In the process, we may be able to affirm with greater integrity that

> No one genre [of the Bible] is 'foundational'; *all* are necessary in order adequately to render the gospel. A Christian theology without apocalyptic, or prophecy, or wisdom, not to mention narrative, would be unthinkable. It follows that the biblical interpreter must be competent in more than one literary form, for it is precisely the canonical forms that mediate to the reader the capacity to see, taste, and feel *biblically*.[120]

Conclusion

This chapter has included a historical survey of genre theory, the elaboration of a definition of genre, and implications of these historical and definitional understandings of genre for interpreting the Bible. It has been one of my goals in this chapter to affirm the importance of genre awareness and analysis for interpretation of Scripture, while avoiding a simplistic view of what genre is and the issues it has raised in contemporary discussions. In the process, I have suggested the following as a definition for genre: *a socially defined constellation of typified formal and thematic features in a group of literary works, which authors use in individualized ways to accomplish specific communicative purposes.*

This definition, I believe, allows for an author's ability to *individualize cre-*

---

117. Vanhoozer, *Drama of Doctrine*, p. 273.

118. Damrosch, *Narrative Covenant*, 33.

119. Ibid., p. 34. Vogt, *Interpreting the Pentateuch*, forthcoming.

120. Vanhoozer, *Drama of Doctrine*, p. 285 (italics in original).

atively, while still granting that authors draw upon *conventional ways* of communicating so that readers will understand them. This definition identifies genre as a *purposeful activity*, while still affirming the presence of *generic features* in a text that lead readers to right understandings of its generic affinities. This definition also stays true to the *complexity and fluidity* of genres, while still affirming the *heuristic usefulness* of genre categories for interpreting texts.

Genre analysis, while certainly not the only skill required for scriptural interpretation, is a necessary one. While there is no guarantee that I shall rightly identify the genre of a biblical text, I cannot avoid the task of attempting to do so. In fact, I shall assign a genre identification to a text, whether I know it or not. By learning the contours of the genres represented in the Bible, I increase the likelihood of rightly identifying a text's genre, thereby drawing upon an appropriate reading strategy for it. By looking as closely as I am able at my predispositions about genre, whether my first-blush assignment of a genre to a text or the values I assign to various genres, I shall gain the crucial realization that my interpretation of a text is not identical to the text's message. This realization may just move me to humility and to interest in dialogue with others who also are serious about Bible interpretation. Both resulting attitudes would be eminently suitable for furthering reflection on genre within biblical studies.

Bibliography

ACHTEMEIER, P. J., '*Omne Verbum Sonat*: The New Testament and the Oral Environment of Late Western Antiquity', *JBL* 109 (1990), pp. 3–27.

AUNE, D. E., *The New Testament in Its Literary Environment* (Philadelphia: Westminster, 1987).

BAILEY, J. L., 'Genre Analysis', in J. B. Green (ed.), *Hearing the New Testament: Strategies for Interpretation* (Grand Rapids: Eerdmans, 1995), pp. 197–221.

BAILEY, J. L., and VANDER BROEK, L., *Literary Forms in the New Testament: A Handbook* (Louisville: Westminster John Knox, 1992).

BAKHTIN, M. M., *Speech Genres and Other Late Essays*, ed. C. Emerson and M. Holquist (Austin: University of Texas Press, 1986).

BOOTH, W. C., *The Rhetoric of Fiction*, 2nd ed. (Chicago: University of Chicago Press, 1983).

BROOKE-ROSE, C., 'Historical Genres/Theoretical Genres: A Discussion of Todorov on the Fantastic', *NLH* 8 (autumn 1976), pp. 145–158.

BROWN, J. K., 'Direct Engagement of the Reader in Matthew's Discourses: Rhetorical Techniques and Scholarly Consensus', *NTS* 51 (2005), pp. 19–35.

——, *Scripture as Communication: Introducing Biblical Hermeneutics* (Grand Rapids: Baker, 2007).

——, 'Silent Wives, Verbal Believers: Ethical and Hermeneutical Considerations in 1 Peter 3:1–6 and Its Context', *WW* 24 (autumn 2004), pp. 395–403.

BURRIDGE, R. A., *What Are the Gospels? A Comparison with Graeco-Roman Biography*, 2nd ed. (Grand Rapids: Eerdmans, 2004).

CAMPBELL, K. K., and JAMIESON, K. H., 'Form and Genre in Rhetorical Criticism: An Introduction', in K. K. Campbell and K. H. Jamieson (eds.), *Form and Genre: Shaping Rhetorical Action* (Falls Church, Va.: The Speech Communication Association, 1978), pp. 9–32.

COHEN, R., 'Introduction: Notes Toward a Generic Reconstitution of Literary Study', *NLH* 34 (2003), pp. v–xvi.

—— (ed.), *The Future of Literary Theory* (New York: Routledge, 1989).

COLIE, R., 'Genre-Systems and the Functions of Literature', in D. Duff (ed.), *Modern Genre Theory* (Harlow, UK: Longman, 2000), pp. 148–166.

COLLINS, J. J., 'Introduction: Towards a Morphology of a Genre', *Semeia* 14 (1979), pp. 1–20.

CONNORS, R. J., 'Genre Theory in Literature', in SIMONS and AGHAZARIAN, *Form, Genre, and the Study of Political Discourse*, pp. 25–44.

CROCE, B., *Aesthetic as Science of Expression and General Linguistic* (London: Macmillan, 1922).

DAMROSCH, D., *The Narrative Covenant: Transformations of Genre in the Growth of Biblical Literature* (New York: Harper & Row, 1987).

DAVID, C. W., *Oral Biblical Criticism: The Influence of the Principles of Orality on the Literary Structure of Paul's Epistle to the Philippians*, JSNTSup 172 (Sheffield: Sheffield Academic Press, 1999).

DERRIDA, J., 'The Law of Genre', tr. A. Ronell, *Critical Inquiry* 7.1 (autumn 1980), pp. 55–81.

DEVITT, A. J., 'Integrating Rhetorical and Literary Theories of Genre', *College English* 62 (July 2000), pp. 696–718.

——, *Writing Genres* (Carbondale: Southern Illinois University Press, 2004).

EAGLETON, T., *Literary Theory: An Introduction*, 2nd ed. (Minneapolis: University of Minnesota Press, 1996).

ELIOT, T. S., 'Tradition and the Individual Talent', in *Selected Essays* (London: Faber & Faber, 1932).

FARRELL, J., 'Classical Genre in Theory and Practice', *NLH* 34 (2003), pp. 383–408.

FEE, G. D., and STUART, D., *How to Read the Bible for All Its Worth*, 3rd ed. (Grand Rapids: Zondervan, 2003).

FOWLER, A., 'The Future of Genre Theory: Functions and Constructional Types', in COHEN, *Future of Literary Theory*, pp. 291–303.

——, 'The Life and Death of Literary Forms', *NLH* 2 (winter 1971), pp. 199–216.

FRYE, N., *Anatomy of Criticism: Four Essays* (Princeton: Princeton University Press, 1957).

GERHART, M., 'Generic Studies: Their Renewed Importance in Religious and Literary Interpretation', *JAAR* 45 (1977), pp. 309–325.

GIESE, JR., R. L., 'Literary Forms of the Old Testament', in D. B. Sandy and R. L. Giese, Jr. (eds.), *Cracking Old Testament Codes: A Guide to Interpreting the Literary Genres of the Old Testament* (Nashville: Broadman & Holman, 1995), pp. 5–27.

GOLDINGAY, J., 'Biblical Narrative and Systematic Theology', in J. B. Green and M. Turner (eds.), *Between Two Horizons: Spanning New Testament Studies and Systematic Theology* (Grand Rapids: Eerdmans, 2000), pp. 123–142.

HIRSCH, JR., E. D., *Validity in Interpretation* (New Haven: Yale University Press, 1967).

HOWARD, D., 'A Contextual Reading of Psalms 90–94', in J. C. McCann (ed.), *The Shape and Shaping of the Psalter*, JSOTSup (Sheffield: JSOT Press, 1993), p. 113.

JOBES, K. H., *1 Peter*, BECNT (Grand Rapids: Baker, 2005).

KLEIN, W. W., BLOMBERG, C. L., and HUBBARD, JR., R. L., *Introduction to Biblical Interpretation* (Dallas: Word, 1993).

LONGMAN III, T., 'Israelite Genres in Their Ancient Near Eastern Context', in M. A. Sweeney and E. Ben Zvi (eds.), *The Changing Face of Form Criticism for the Twenty-First Century* (Grand Rapids: Eerdmans, 2003), pp. 177–195.

———, *Literary Approaches to the Biblical Interpretation*, Foundations of Contemporary Interpretation 3 (Grand Rapids: Academie, 1987).

MILLER, C. R., 'Genre as Social Action', *QJS* 70 (1984), pp. 151–167.

MOWINCKEL, S., *The Psalms in Israel's Worship*, 2 vols. (Oxford: Basil Blackwell, 1962).

MURPHY, F. A., 'Revelation, Book of', in VANHOOZER, *Dictionary for Theological Interpretation*, pp. 680–687.

OSBORNE, G. R., 'Genre', in VANHOOZER, *Dictionary for Theological Interpretation*, pp. 252–253.

———, 'Genre Criticism – *Sensus Literalis*', in E. D. Radmacher and R. D. Preus (eds.), *Hermeneutics, Inerrancy, and the Bible* (Grand Rapids: Academie, 1984), pp. 165–190.

———, *The Hermeneutical Spiral: A Comprehensive Introduction to Biblical Interpretation*, 2nd ed. (Downers Grove: IVP, 2006).

PAVEL, T., 'Literary Genres as Norms and Good Habits', *NLH* 34 (2003), pp. 201–210.

PEARSON, B. W. R., and PORTER, S. E., 'The Genres of the New Testament', in S. E. Porter (ed.), *Handbook to Exegesis of the New Testament* (Leiden: Brill, 1997), pp. 131–165.

RICOEUR, P., 'The Hermeneutical Function of Distanciation', in *Exegesis: Problems of Method and Exercises in Reading (Genesis 22 and Luke 15)*, tr. D. G. Miller (Pittsburgh: Pickwick, 1978), pp. 297–320.

RUSSELL, D. A., *Criticism in Antiquity* (Berkeley: University of California Press, 1981).

SCHAEFFER, J.-M., 'Literary Genres and Textual Genericity', in COHEN, *Future of Literary Theory*, pp. 167–187.

SCHULTZ, R. L., 'Form Criticism and the Old Testament', in VANHOOZER, *Dictionary for Theological Interpretation*, pp. 233–237.

SIMONS, H. W., and AGHAZARIAN, A. A. (eds.), *Form, Genre, and the Study of Political Discourse* (Columbia: University of South Carolina Press, 1986).

STANTON, G., *Jesus of Nazareth in New Testament Preaching* (New York: Cambridge University Press, 1974).

STEIN, R. H., *A Basic Guide to Interpreting the Bible: Playing by the Rules* (Grand Rapids: Baker, 1994).

——, 'Is Our Reading the Bible the Same as the Original Audience's Hearing It? A Case Study in the Gospel of Mark', *JETS* 46 (2003), pp. 63–78.

TODOROV, T., *Genres in Discourse* (Cambridge: Cambridge University Press, 1990. [French original 1978]).

VANHOOZER, K. J. (gen. ed.), *Dictionary for Theological Interpretation of the Bible* (Grand Rapids: Baker, 2005).

——, *The Drama of Doctrine: A Canonical-Linguistic Approach to Christian Theology* (Louisville: Westminster John Knox, 2005).

VAN LEEUWEN, R. C., 'Wisdom Literature', in VANHOOZER, *Dictionary for Theological Interpretation*, pp. 847–850.

VOGT, P. T., *Interpreting the Pentateuch: An Exegetical Handbook* (Grand Rapids: Kregel, forthcoming).

WELLEK, R., and WARREN, A., *Theory of Literature* (New York: Harcourt, Brace, 1949).

WHITE, H., 'Anomalies of Genre: The Utility of Theory and History for the Study of Literary Genres', *NLH* 34 (2003), pp. 597–615.

WRIGHT, N. T., *The New Testament and the People of God* (Minneapolis: Fortress, 1992).

5. AMBIGUITY

David G. Firth

Introduction

There is a curious ambiguity to be found in the preface of the GNB. In it, we are told that a goal of the translation was to use language that was 'clear, simple and unambiguous'. Such a statement is not unique to this particular version of the Bible, since practically all of them make a similar claim. After all, since readers are supposed to be able to trust their translations, it is almost inevitable that they claim faithfully to represent the underlying Greek, Hebrew or Aramaic. But claiming to represent the intended meaning of the underlying text faithfully and then represent it unambiguously is ambiguous. Do these translators mean that they will introduce no new ambiguities? Or that they will resolve potential ambiguities in the underlying text and only present one option to their readers? If the translators' claim of faithfulness to the text is to be carried through, then ambiguities in the source text should be retained. But since translators normally claim to seek the meaning of the text they are translating, then it seems more common in modern translations that the potential ambiguity will be resolved by the translators, thus ensuring that modern readers are not confronted with the ambiguities so often found in the biblical text.

As a brief example, we can consider the last clause of Philippians 4:5.

A rather literal rendering of it would read, 'The Lord is near.'[1] Now, there are two broad possibilities for how one might interpret this clause. Either, Paul is emphasizing the nearness of the Lord to believers in the midst of conflict, so that their union in him should result in gentleness towards one another, or he is referring to the return of Christ, so that the reality of eschatological judgment provides a reason for this gentleness. Either is entirely possible because the word *engys* can mean 'near' in the sense of either space or time, just as can the English 'near'.[2] The GNB, however, translates this as 'The Lord is coming soon.' In this way, the ambiguity is resolved, and readers receive only one possible interpretation of this statement. This is not to offer a criticism of the GNB as it is certainly not the only translation to follow this approach,[3] and there are reasons why for certain readerships one might take this choice. But it serves to demonstrate what is meant by their avoidance of ambiguities.[4]

The underlying issue is perhaps a belief that ambiguity is something wrong, something to be avoided. Undeniably, there are contexts where the presence of ambiguity is highly undesirable. For instance, legal documents such as contracts or wills need to be written in such a way that there is only one reasonable interpretation that can be given, which is at least one reason why some legal documents are written in a form of arcane language that those untrained in the intricacies of the jargon find almost impenetrable. Instructions in certain processes also need clarity so as to avoid possible misunderstandings that could lead to flawed or dangerous outcomes. Anyone who has had the experience of assembling furniture that came 'flat packed for your convenience' will know just how frustrating ambiguous instructions can be. But that does not mean ambiguity itself is fundamentally wrong. It is a misunderstanding of genre to imagine that because

---

1. Unless stated otherwise, all Bible translations in this chapter are my own.

2. Cf. G. F. Hawthorne, *Philippians*, WBC 43 (Waco: Word, 1983), p. 182, for a list of scholars who have chosen either option. Hawthorne himself prefers the option of retaining the ambiguity, suggesting that Paul perhaps means that the Lord whose return is near is also near to believers. Similarly, P. T. O'Brien, *The Epistle to the Philippians* (Grand Rapids: Eerdmans, 1991), pp. 488–490.

3. E.g. LB.

4. If nothing else, this demonstrates the importance of readers comparing translations of the biblical text, preferably with versions that employ different translation principles, so as to recognize exegetical decisions a translation may have made. Such an approach wrests back the responsibility of interpretation to the reader away from the translator.

ambiguity is problematic in some contexts that it is necessarily problematic in all. Indeed, some genres can function precisely only because of the literary possibilities that ambiguity makes possible. The riddle, for example, is dependent upon ambiguity since it is the exploration of ambiguity (mixed with the reversal of expectations) that is meant to make the riddle funny. One of the most basic expressions of this in English is found in the nearly endless variations of the 'Knock, knock!' joke in which the ambiguity of homophonic sounds are explored. The use of ambiguity does not need to be as crass as this, but it is certainly true to say that ambiguity is a device by which texts can be made more interesting, since the ambiguities present are what draws readers into the text in order to explore the possibilities in meaning.

The location and value of ambiguity

The discussion so far has focused on ambiguity that might reasonably be considered to reflect the intent of the authors of texts, to the extent that this can reasonably be determined. Yet this is something that many literary critics would deny is possible, since it represents an example of the so-called intentional fallacy.[5] According to this approach, classically regarded as an expression of the new criticism,[6] one must interpret a text on the basis of its own internal evidence and not on the basis of any appeal to the author. Since one cannot claim to know the thoughts of an author apart from what is presented in a text, this view is unobjectionable. Nevertheless, many critics still recognize that an author has created the text, and done so with certain intentions, though we cannot necessarily determine if a single ambiguity is meaningful unless there are some elements in the genre being employed (such as the riddle) that require ambiguity for the text to be meaningful. Even the most carefully crafted of texts will occasionally generate an ambiguity without any necessary intention that the ambiguity is somehow meaningful. For example, it is not clear in 1

---

5. W. K. Wimsatt, Jr., and M. C. Beardsley, 'The Intentional Fallacy', *The Verbal Icon: Studies in the Meaning of Poetry* (Lexington: University of Kentucky Press, 1954), pp. 3–18, now available on line at
    <http://faculty.smu.edu/nschwart/seminar/Fallacy.htm>, accessed 6 Feb. 2008.
6. See D. Robey, 'Anglo-American New Criticism', in A. Jefferson and D. Robey (eds.), *Modern Literary Theory: A Comparative Introduction*, 2nd ed. (London: B. T. Batsford, 1986), pp. 73–91.

Samuel 16:21 whether Saul loved David or David loved Saul when David entered Saul's service, simply because the verb *wayye'ĕhābēnû* can have David as subject and Saul as object or vice versa. Either is possible, and defenders can be found for interpreting the verb either way.[7] Although it is possible that this is intended, nothing in the surrounding text makes anything of the ambiguity, so it is more likely that this is simply an example of the fact that some ambiguity is almost unavoidable in any substantial text. In the absence of any other textual evidence that seeks to make some capital of this, we should assume that this is not a piece of ambiguity that has any value in the art of the text.

Moreover, some points where the biblical text seems ambiguous to modern readers may be nothing more than evidence of a lack of historical understanding on our part. I well remember an earnest debate in a Bible study I attended in my teenage years in which we examined the parable of the talents (Matt. 25:14–30) and spent a considerable amount of time trying to decide if the 'talents' in the parable should be regarded as natural talents or spiritual gifts. The tradition of many English translations of effectively transliterating the Greek with 'talent' created an ambiguity for us simply because we did not realize that what was discussed in the parable was the transfer of large sums of money. Arguably, attention to the content of the parable should have prevented us from making this mistake, but had our translations followed the lead of the GNB at this point and simply referred to large sums of money,[8] then the issue would never have arisen. The language of the parable is unambiguous (at least at this point), but our lack of historical awareness in the use of that language created an ambiguity for us as readers.

Not all reader-initiated ambiguity is as innocent as this. One of the strong emphases of literary movements such as deconstruction and post-structuralism has been on the ways in which readers may themselves initiate ambiguities in a text. This approach takes the new criticism's denial of authorial authority one step further, denying the possibility that there is a single,

---

7. Cf. G. C. Wong, 'Who Loved Whom? A Note on 1 Samuel xvi 21', *VT* 47 (1997), pp. 554–556; and J. P. Fokkelman, *Narrative Art and Poetry in the Books of Samuel: A Full Interpretation Based on Stylistic and Structural Analyses*. Vol. 2: *The Crossing Fates (1 Sam. 13–31 & II Sam. 1)* (Assen: van Gorcum, 1986), p. 140. B. Green, *King Saul's Asking* (Collegeville: Liturgical, 2003), p. 65, accepts that Saul loves David, but in *How Are the Mighty Fallen? A Dialogical Study of King Saul in 1 Samuel* (London: Sheffield Academic Press, 2003), pp. 285–286, she argues that there is an intentional ambiguity here. A curious ambiguity thus arises in her reading!

8. The GNB has 'five thousand silver pieces' for 'five talents' etc.

determinative meaning, since the critic's task is to retain enough distance from the text so that rather than *deciphering* its meaning, the critic *constructs* meaning through the process of reading.[9] Jacques Derrida particularly exploited the possibilities created by this in order to create ambiguities through a close reading of a text that might otherwise be considered as resolved by the text's own structures. In this case, ambiguities unintended by the author, and not even necessarily elements within a text, can be generated.[10]

What this suggests is that ambiguities can be located in several places, though these are not always mutually exclusive. First, ambiguities may be found in the intention of the author, though one would need a range of elements within the text itself to indicate that there is meant to be any value in this ambiguity. However, where such evidence is available, then there is reason to believe that these are ambiguities that should be explored further because they are in some way important to the way the text is meant to be read. Secondly, ambiguities can also occur in the text without any intent on the part of the author. Such ambiguities are not necessarily to be understood as failures in composition, but as components of the text that should be treated as points to be resolved through exegesis rather than being elements that are meaningful for the interpretation of the text. Finally, ambiguities can lie in the realm of the reader, either because of a lack of the necessary interpretative skills or because of certain commitments in the processes of reading. Ambiguities generated through a lack of skill on the part of readers are best resolved through the theory of translation, while those wrought through the application of poststructuralist interpretations and deconstruction must be treated at other points, since their existence does not contribute to the art and enjoyment of the text itself, not least because they are often reading against the form of the text itself.

Of the three possible locations of ambiguity, only that which can in some sense be traced back to the intention of the author is of interest here because it is the only one of intrinsic value. Textual ambiguities simply inherent in the process of composition but unintended have no value in terms of the effects a

---

9. See P. V. Zima, *The Philosophy of Modern Literary Theory* (London: Athlone, 1999), p. 70, for the implications of this in the thinking of S. Fish.

10. The classic example is Derrida's treatment of Rousseau's use of 'supplement'. Rousseau regarded the written word as a supplement to speech, considering the spoken word to be central, but the written word to make up for its deficiencies. But Derrida then plays with the senses of 'supplement' in Webster's Dictionary to introduce ambiguities unintended by Rousseau. See J. Culler, *Literary Theory: A Very Short Introduction* (New York: Oxford University Press, 1997), pp. 9–12.

text is intended to generate.[11] Ambiguities generated by readers are of some interest, but since they are unique to each reader or group of readers, one cannot develop a comprehensive theory concerning their effect. On the other hand, ambiguities intentionally generated in the composition of the text are of interest precisely because they represent a means by which a text's author makes it more interesting and draws readers in to explore the elements of the text. To say this may seem to run foul of the intentional fallacy, and I have already indicated that there is nothing fundamentally objectionable in the claim that we cannot seek to determine the meaning of a text by appeal to the intent of the author. But this claim cannot absolutely rule out accessing the intent of the author. What it validly prevents is the claim that one can enter into the psychology of the author through criteria external to the text. Provided one works only by criteria established by the text itself, then there is no problem with seeking the author's intention, if it is recognized that it is only the intention as this can be reconstructed on the basis of the evidence of the text itself. Authors use a system of communication that can largely be analysed, and from this one can reasonably conclude that certain elements remain within the discernible intent of the author.[12] Hence, the existence of elements where the text itself plays with ambiguity and thus foregrounds it, either because the genre employed requires it or because the text makes reference to it, then one can reasonably assume that the ambiguity represents something intended by the author to be considered as a part of the communication of the text. Absolute rules for this cannot be given, but the general principle can be recognized.

The nature of ambiguity

Thus far, I have discussed ambiguity without providing any definition for it.

---

11. Readers, of course, still seek to decode such ambiguities, such as in 1 Sam. 16:21 whether Saul loved David or David loved Saul. But such ambiguities do not contribute to the poetics of the text.

12. Cf. K. J. Vanhoozer, *Is There a Meaning in This Text? The Bible, The Reader and the Morality of Literary Knowledge* (Leicester: Apollos, 1998), pp. 43–97, 201–280, for a discussion of the loss of the author and the possibilities of speech-act theory for recovering the authorial voice. For a more concise analysis, see N. B. McDonald, 'The Philosophy of Language and the Renewal of Biblical Hermeneutics', in C. G. Bartholomew, C. Greene and K. Möller (eds.), *Renewing Biblical Interpretation*, SHS 1 (Carlisle: Paternoster, 2000), pp. 126–133.

Although one can consider ambiguity from a range of perspectives, it will be sufficient for our purposes to take William Empson's definition. He defines it as 'any verbal nuance, however slight, which gives room for alternative reactions to the same piece of language'.[13] Hence, ambiguity occurs when there is an element within the language employed that allows various hearers or readers to understand it in a different way, and is quite distinct from vagueness, which is where language is insufficiently defined. In terms of the example from Philippians with which this chapter opens, it is possible to respond to Paul's statement that 'The Lord is near' in two ways, and depending upon which of these is taken, one will interpret him quite differently at this point. But it is also possible that one can conclude that Paul has intentionally used language capable of more than one response. If so, then as well as the two options mentioned, it is also possible that Paul wished to leave both of these possibilities open and not close off either. With such a brief statement, it is impossible to make a definitive assessment, but the very fact that we can make such an observation means that ambiguity can function in some quite distinct ways. Ambiguity may occur when a given text or utterance is capable of generating different responses, but the ambiguity itself will work in a number of different ways.

As well as providing a working definition of ambiguity, Empson has also developed a taxonomy for the different ways in which ambiguity may work. As is evident from the title of his seminal book, he has identified seven types of ambiguity, each of which he treats in successive chapters. However, the seven types are not absolutely discrete from one another, and the boundaries are sufficiently fluid that the different types frequently blur into one another. Indeed, it is common to find Empson musing on whether a specific example of ambiguity belongs in another type to the one in which he analyses it. Nevertheless, as long as it is taken as a taxonomy that broadly describes the options available rather than something that prescribes specific rules that define ambiguity, Empson's model is particularly helpful.

In spite of this, it has not been widely used in biblical studies, perhaps because so much of his work is given to particularly close reading of poetic texts rather than to developing the theory with which he worked.[14] Since he

---

13. W. Empson, *Seven Types of Ambiguity*, 3rd ed. (Harmondsworth: Penguin, 1960), p. 1. In addition to this, see also his *Some Versions of the Pastoral* (London: Chatto & Windus, 1935); and *The Structure of Complex Words* (Cambridge, Mass.: Harvard University Press, 1989).

14. E.g. P. R. Raabe, 'Deliberate Ambiguity in the Psalter', *JBL* 110.2 (1991), p. 213, notes Empson's work, but then makes no use of it in his examples of ambiguity in

famously claimed that 'a critic ought to trust his own nose, like the hunting dog, and if he lets any theory or principle distract him from that he is not really doing his job',[15] we should not be surprised by this. But it is true to say that the theory with which he works, greatly influenced by the pioneering approach of his teacher I. A. Richards,[16] lies in the examples given rather than in a clear exposition through which the examples can be understood. Moreover, not all of his examples stand up to close scrutiny, especially since he seems often to have quoted texts from memory, so that when the original texts were examined the pattern of ambiguity he analysed was not actually present. But these are flaws in his presentation, not in the underlying patterns he is able to discern.

Empson also rather stood against the flow in one important respect: he was always concerned with the intention of the author, even though he is often cited as one of those who pioneered the so-called new criticism.[17] As such, his work differs from those approaches that seek to open up fissures in a work by exploring what is not said. Nevertheless, his work remains important because it emphasizes the fact that playfulness in texts is not simply the prerogative of the reader – it is also something in which authors engage. Indeed, the fun of reading is often generated precisely because of the fact that authors will often engage in the intentional use of ambiguity, something for which Empson's taxonomy remains an indispensable tool.

Empson, as we have seen, identified seven types of ambiguity, though we can exclude from consideration his types five and seven.[18] These are situations where an author introduces an ambiguity only part of the way through the process of constructing a text (type 5) or where the ambiguity is an actual contradiction (type 7). These can be set aside from consideration on two grounds. First, if Empson's analysis of them is correct, then they do not contribute to the intended meaning of the text. They are essentially accidents in the process

---

Footnote 14 (*continued*)

    Psalms. The result is an intriguing collection of possible examples of ambiguity, but a collection that lacks theoretical tools to analyse the data further.

15. W. Empson, 'The Verbal Analysis', *KR* 12 (1950), p. 594.

16. I. A. Richards, *Practical Criticism* (London: Kegan Paul, Trench, Trubner, 1929).

17. E.g. N. Wolterstorff, 'The Promise of Speech Act Theory for Biblical Interpretation', in C. G. Bartholomew, C. Greene and K. Möller (eds.), *After Pentecost: Language and Biblical Interpretation*, SHS 2 (Carlisle: Paternoster, 2001), p. 76.

18. In *Seven Types of Ambiguity*, Empson addresses one chapter to each of the types he identified. A type 1 ambiguity is thus covered in his first chapter etc.

of textual communication. More fundamentally, however, they require an ability to enter into the psychology of the author to an extent beyond that which can adequately be recovered from the evidence of the text itself. We simply cannot know if an author became aware of the possibilities of a particular ambiguity only part of the way through composition, and so the fifth class must be ruled out. The seventh category of actual contradiction is also too vague to be useful, not least because it again requires too great a knowledge of the intent of the author. The problem is that we can determine the possible value of an ambiguity only on the basis of textual evidence, not on a psychological profile we construct as readers. In any case, since I have suggested that evidence for a meaningful ambiguity requires several textual clues, the type of one-off ambiguity Empson included in this class falls out of the range of items to be considered.

From the perspective of a workable theory of literature and poetics, we can conclude that five of Empson's seven types are of use in the analysis of ambiguity:

1. Details effective in multiple ways
2. Multiple possibilities with a single resolution
3. Simultaneous use of unconnected meanings
4. Alternative meanings combine to clarify author's intention
5. Apparent contradictions

We shall look briefly at each of these and their possible impact on the interpretation of shorter passages before offering a reading of certain aspects of 1 Samuel 21 – 22 in the light of the taxonomy as a whole.

Type 1 ambiguity: details effective in multiple ways

As is well known, it is possible for words, and larger details within a text, to draw on more than one possible meaning, which is perhaps the form of ambiguity most commonly considered.[19] While authors will typically eschew such activities due to the needs of clarity in communication, there are invariably points where using multiple possibilities for a particular expression or concept

---

19. See G. R. Osborne, *The Hermeneutical Spiral: A Comprehensive Introduction to Biblical Interpretation*, 2nd ed. (Downer's Grove: IVP , 2006), pp. 107–108. All of Raabe's examples in 'Deliberate Ambiguity' fall into this class.

makes for a more interesting text, one that draws readers in to explore its various elements. Often, the use of the multiple elements can have the effect of surprising readers who think they know the direction a text is taking, only to find themselves forced to think it through again in the light of the ambiguity. Making details within the text effective in multiple ways is thus an important tool in leading readers to assess and then reassess what they are reading. This should not offset the general semantic principle in the determination of meaning that the conclusion which contributes least to the meaning of the discourse should be selected because that which contributes least is that which will not include meanings not otherwise intended. Rather, it suggests that at times the multiple possibilities are themselves the minimum possibility.

This approach is particularly apparent in poetry in the OT, most notably through what is known as Janus parallelism.[20] This technique makes use of the fact that poetry in the OT most commonly expresses itself through a series of lines grouped because they are in some way parallel to one another. Classically, the forms of parallelism are described as synonymous, antithetic and synthetic, though it is now recognized that parallelism as a phenomenon is much more complex than this, and in Janus parallelism we have the phenomenon in which the parallelism seems to operate in two directions at once. The parade example of Janus parallelism is found in Song of Songs 2:12:

> The flowers have appeared in the land,
>> the time of pruning/singing has arrived,
> and the voice of the turtle dove is heard in our land.

The ambiguity developed here depends upon the possible meanings of the word *zāmîr*, which can variously mean 'pruning' or 'singing'. The reason for this is that most Hebrew words are constructed on the basis of a root consisting of three consonants, but because of certain limitations many roots are used for largely unrelated meanings. The existence of homophones and homographs is not unique to Hebrew, but it is a common feature of it. Normally, readers encountering these terms are quickly able to determine which sense of the word is intended, since the context makes this clear. But by means of Janus parallelism, the poet here is able to destabilize readers. The reference to the appearance of flowers in the opening line naturally leads one to

---

20. On this phenomenon, see W. G. E. Watson, *Classical Hebrew Poetry: A Guide to its Techniques* (Sheffield: JSOT Press, 1984), p. 59; and J. S. Kselman, 'Janus Parallelism in Psalm 75:2', *JBL* 121 (2002), pp. 531–532.

understand *zāmîr* as 'pruning', since this is the time that arrives with the flowers as the growth of plants needs to be cut back. But although this could relate to the voice of the turtle dove, the third line here makes more sense if the reference in the previous verse had been to the time of singing, since this is what the turtle dove does when it puts forth its voice. Although the two possible meanings of *zāmîr* here are clearly distinct, the poet is able to play with them so that both are brought to bear.[21] In the context of the song, the man employs the ambiguity to emphasize to the woman both that spring is the time for love to blossom and that he will continue to woo her. The ambiguity is not simply a clever literary device; it is a mechanism for enriching the ways in which the text communicates and readers are able to experience it.

Although common in the OT, the writers of the NT also make use of this type of ambiguity. As a technique, it is most common in John's Gospel. For example, in John 4:10 Jesus addresses the woman from Samaria, telling her that had she asked, he would have given her *hydōr zōn*. Although one can literally translate this as 'living water', the more common sense of the phrase would be 'potable water', because it was fresh or running. The contrast is with water drawn from a cistern, which would be rather brackish.[22] But there is also a significant body of references in the OT where the same phrase has a clearly metaphoric sense as living water (e.g. Jer. 2:13; Zech. 14:8), that is, as water which brings life (Ezek. 47:9).[23] As is common in John, Jesus is able to make use of the fact that the woman understands him to use the more common sense of the phrase as a means of drawing her into conversation, so that he is finally able to reveal that the living water he gives ultimately becomes a spring that rises up to eternal life (John 4:12–14).

In appreciating this type of ambiguity, one must take care to distinguish between forms of ambiguity that occur in the original languages and ambiguities generated by issues in translation. The examples we have looked at so far reflect situations where the words considered have semantically distinct meanings in the original languages. These must be distinguished from situations in which terms in Hebrew, Aramaic or Greek have a semantic breadth

---

21. D. Garret and P. R. House, *Song of Songs, Lamentations* (Nashville: Nelson, 2004), p. 159, thus argue that the translation needs to be 'the time for pruning and singing arrives', the expanded paraphrase being the only way to retain both elements.

22. G. R. Beasley-Murray, *John*, WBC 36 (Waco: Word, 1987), p. 60.

23. Cf. C. K. Barrett, *The Gospel According to St John: An Introduction with Commentary and Notes on the Greek Text* (London: SPCK, 1962), p. 195; and D. A. Carson, *The Gospel According to John* (Leicester: IVP, 1991), pp. 218–219.

that cannot be matched by a term in a language into which we translate the Bible. For example, in Psalm 24:4 we are told that the one who will ascend the hill of Yahweh will 'not lift up his soul to idols / what is false'. Although idolatry and falsehood can be seen as linked concepts in English, they are semantically distinct. But this is not the case in Hebrew, where the most obvious form of falsehood was idolatry. Similarly, in the vision of the valley of dry bones in Ezekiel 37 there is considerable play on the semantic range of the word *rûaḥ*, so that translators variously render it as 'wind', 'breath' or 'spirit' at various points throughout the chapter. John 3 makes the same play with *pneuma*, since the Greek term is largely equivalent to the Hebrew. But English lacks a word with this breadth, and so the range of translations is needed, and although this is a translational ambiguity, it is not something of interest here. These are still points where the author is playing with words, but they are playing within the one semantic range, not across multiple semantic domains.

Type 2 ambiguity: multiple possibilities with a single resolution

As a method of ambiguity, this is the opposite of the first. Type 1 ambiguity allows one detail to have more than one possible resolution, most commonly by playing with semantic domains. By way of contrast, this type deliberately leaves open a range of possibilities before ultimately leading to a single conclusion. As a device, this is commonly used in modern detective fiction where as many suspects as possible are left until the denouement. This type of ambiguity thus draws readers in so that they try to resolve that which is not stated, but for which a resolution is required for interpretation finally to take place.

Undoubtedly, the best example of this type of ambiguity occurs in Ecclesiastes, especially in the diverse ways in which the word *hebel* is used. The word is used with considerable frequency through the text, its thirty-eight occurrences representing just over half the total usage in the OT. In other places, it has the sense of vapour, though it is arguable that Isaiah 57:13 is the only place in the Bible where it is not used in a metaphoric sense.[24] If this is so, then the term was ripe for exploitation by Qoheleth,[25] since its use almost automatically leads readers to expect something more than a literal sense.

---

24. Though note Sirach 41.11.
25. Commonly translated as 'the Preacher' or something equivalent, it seems better to leave the title adopted by the book's main voice untranslated.

But what exactly does it mean? Most commentators provide a lengthy discussion of the meaning of *hebel*,[26] with a general though not universal preference for the idea that there should be a single translation for it throughout the book. As a result of these discussions, a range of possible translations is offered, such as 'enigma', 'meaningless', 'absurd' or 'ephemeral', as well as the familiar 'vanity' of the Authorized Version. We cannot resolve the question of what Qoheleth meant here, though the idea that he meant something in particular by the term seems reasonable, even if that may need to be represented by more than one term in English. This seems to be indicated by the prominence given to the term in the book's opening (1:2) and close (12:8), both of which insist that all is *hebel*. Through the book, Qoheleth has also provided a number of observations on things that conform to the category of *hebel*, each of which in some way enables the reader to resolve an otherwise perplexing term. But part of Qoheleth's art is that an exact closure is not given, so that as readers complete the book they have come to have a better understanding of what is meant by *hebel*, but perhaps not yet a final one, so that they are directed back to the start of the book to resolve the question. A range of possibilities for understanding the term is gradually narrowed down as one reads through the text, but since a central theme in the book is humanity's inability to understand absolutely, Qoheleth leaves the final definition of exactly what is meant by *hebel* dangling slightly beyond the reader's reach.

A narrative example of this type of ambiguity occurs in Jonah 3:4. In a five-word sermon (in Hebrew), Jonah cries out, 'Yet forty days and Nineveh will be overturned!' The key ambiguity here centres on the participle *nehpaket*, from the verb *hpk*. Although the verb means 'to change about', this change can be either positive or negative. It frequently refers to something being changed in the sense of complete destruction, especially in narratives relating to cities, and most notably in the account of the destruction of Sodom (Gen. 19:21, 25, 29; cf. Lam. 4:6). Given Jonah's own attitude towards the city, this may well be the sense he intends, though since he can proclaim only Yahweh's message (Jon. 3:2), he has no freedom to decide on the actual interpretation of his oracle. Yet at other points the 'change' that comes is one of deliverance and salvation,

---

26. Helpful discussions are provided by G. Ogden, *Qoheleth* (Sheffield: JSOT Press, 1987), pp. 17–22; T. Longman III, *The Book of Ecclesiastes* (Grand Rapids: Eerdmans, 1998), pp. 59–65; and M. V. Fox, *A Time to Tear Down and a Time to Build Up: A Rereading of Ecclesiastes* (Grand Rapids: Eerdmans, 1999), pp. 27–42. For a more detailed analysis, see D. C. Fredericks, *Coping with Transience: Ecclesiastes on Brevity in Life* (Sheffield: Sheffield Academic Press, 1993).

most obviously in Esther 9:1 (cf. Jer. 31:13). What is clear is that the situation in Nineveh cannot remain as it is. Clearly, the people of Nineveh understand the oracle to be announcing disaster, and so repent, giving evidence of this through a mass fast, the wearing of sackcloth and a turning away from evil and violence. Thus Yahweh relents of disaster towards them (Jon. 3:10). One could, therefore, understand Jonah's message to have failed: Yahweh has not destroyed the city. But the fact is that destruction is only one possible outcome from Jonah's preaching, because the city of Nineveh has fundamentally changed. What Jonah proclaimed as Yahweh's word has taken place. The multiple outcomes possible resolve themselves into a single outcome, which is part of the way in which this narrative holds our interest.

A similar example of this type of ambiguity occurs in Mark's Gospel, with its three predictions of the passion that prepare for the events of the last week in Jerusalem (Mark 8:31–33; 9:30–32; 10:32–34). In all three accounts, Jesus makes clear that he is on his way to Jerusalem, where he will suffer under the Jewish leadership and rise again after three days. But there is an ambiguity in the way in which this is announced in terms of the fact that 'the Son of Man will be handed over / betrayed into the hands of sinful men' (Mark 9:32; cf. 10:33 for the same ambiguity). There is, through all three predictions, levels of development, though what is clear throughout is Jesus' coming death and resurrection. There is no reference in the first prediction of Jesus being either betrayed or handed over, only that he will suffer, die and rise again. These three elements remain across all three, but there is the additional element in the second and third predictions that he will be either handed over or betrayed. The ambiguity here turns on the sense of *paradidōmi*, which can refer either to an act of betrayal (cf. Mark 3:19; 14:18–21), or, more neutrally, to being handed over (Rom. 8:32).[27] Earlier references in the Gospel narrative might lead to a preference being given to the option of betrayal, but since Jesus' language seems also to evoke Daniel 7:25, where the same verb is clearly a divine passive,[28] then an equally strong case can be mounted for such an interpretation here. Within the narrative, Jesus does not offer a conclusive explanation of this key verb, and its ambiguity may be one contributing factor (albeit a minor one) to the disciples' inability to understand what he is telling them. Readers coming to the Gospel thus do not know which of these possible resolutions will occur, and are thus led further into the text to discover that one

---

27. Cf. M. D. Hooker, *The Gospel According to St Mark* (London: A. & C. Black, 1991), p. 226.

28. See C. A. Evans, *Mark 8:27–16:20* (Nashville: Nelson, 2001), p. 57.

of the disciples will betray Jesus (14:18–21), a similar ambiguity subsequently resolved when Judas arrives in the garden, leading those who have come to arrest him (14:43).

Type 3 ambiguity: simultaneous use of unconnected meanings

This type of ambiguity is somewhat less common in the Bible than the first two, and is certainly more complex. It needs to be distinguished from the first type in that writers need to draw on and use multiple meanings inherent in words but without actually resolving them one way or the other. In the first type of ambiguity both possibilities are available but the text eventually makes a resolution, even if in the case of Janus parallelism the resolution is only temporary because of the ways in which the subsequent line will use the detail. However, just one sense is in use at each point, whereas in this type of ambiguity both elements are present throughout. The value of this type of ambiguity for an author is that it creates a means of disorientating readers who naturally look for a single resolution of the detail concerned. This disorientation is something readers seek to resolve as they continue to work through the text, though there may ultimately be a sense of pleasure from the point of recognizing the value of holding the unconnected meanings together.

An example of this can be found in Proverbs 25:15:[29]

> With patience can a ruler be seduced
>   and a soft answer can shatter bones.

There is nothing particularly ambiguous in the first line, but there is an intriguing example in the second with its reference to a soft answer being able to shatter bones. Taken as a whole, the proverb encourages courtiers to practise tact and diplomacy when dealing with rulers because these can prove to be powerful tools. But this still involves an ambiguity in terms of the nature of the answer given to the ruler. On the one hand, the answer is 'soft' (*rak*), a word that elsewhere means 'weak' (Gen. 33:13) or 'tender' (Deut. 28:54). That is to say, the 'softness' of this answer is linked with a lack of

---

29. On the details of this proverb, and the closely parallel 15:1, see W. P. Brown, 'The Didactic Power of Metaphor in the Aphoristic Sayings in Proverbs', *JSOT* 29.2 (2004), pp. 150–151.

forcefulness. On the other hand, this answer can shatter (*šbr*) bone (*gerem*) or even 'strength', since the word seems to have this sense in Genesis 49:14. That which shatters something is typically hard or violent, such as a weapon or a wild animal (1 Kgs 13:26; Ezek. 6:4–6), though it should be noted that the most common subject for the verb is Yahweh, for whom no weapon is stated. Nevertheless, by making this connection, the proverb is able simultaneously to treat the answer as something soft and lacking in force and something hard and forceful. The effectiveness of the proverb depends upon the fact that both meanings attach themselves to the answer given by the courtier.

This type of ambiguity is not dependent upon such paradoxes, though it is certainly one of its more common forms. Another example can be found in John 12:32, where Jesus declares, 'And I, when I am lifted up from the earth, shall draw all to myself.' Though the element of paradox is present in this statement, ambiguity is more important. In particular, attention needs to be focused on the verb *hypsōthō* (cf. John 3:14), which Barrett suggests was specifically chosen because of its ambiguity,[30] since it can refer either to Jesus' execution or to his ultimate exaltation. Although there is still considerable debate as to a possible Semitic background to the expression, it is worth noting that in Genesis 40:13 and 19 the heads of the butler and the baker are also 'lifted up', with one exalted and one executed.[31] Carson is more impressed by the links with Isaiah 52:13, where the Suffering Servant is exalted in his death.[32] Whichever option is taken,[33] the pattern for the Johannine use of this type of ambiguity may already have been established in the OT. In engaging with the text of John's Gospel, readers become familiar with this pattern of ambiguity and so learn to read Jesus' statement as referring both to the cross and to the glory he will have when he returns to the father. Death and exaltation are not elements typically held together,[34] but the ambiguity in 'being lifted up' allows these otherwise discrete semantic domains to work together. In this way, John is able to make clear through

---

30. Barrett, *John*, p. 356.
31. C. H. Dodd, *The Interpretation of the Fourth Gospel* (Cambridge: Cambridge University Press, 1953), p. 377.
32. Carson, *John*, p. 442.
33. For a survey of the issue and other possibilities, see Beasley-Murray, *John*, p. 214.
34. But note that J. Marcus, 'Crucifixion as Parodic Exaltation', *JBL* 125.1 (2006), pp. 73–87, has shown that it was a trope that had some currency in the ancient world.

Jesus that the way to glory is through the cross, itself an important element in John's teaching on discipleship.[35]

Type 4 ambiguity: alternative meanings combine to clarify author's intention

The fourth type of ambiguity occurs when an author deliberately leaves multiple alternative meanings open for a period and combines them only later so as to clarify their intention. In this case, the final combination is crucial, a combination that often occurs through the layering of various elements. Although this type of ambiguity can be seen in individual words and phrases, and is something of a stock in trade for Qoheleth (e.g. 9:11–18, where he explores wisdom as something both limited and powerful before resolving the ambiguity by pointing out that it can be undone by one sinner), it is perhaps more useful to analyse it through a slightly longer text. An intriguing example of this type of ambiguity occurs in Elisha's prophecy in 2 Kings 3, as recently noted by Westbrook,[36] when he argues that appreciating the presence of ambiguity is the key to the interpretation of the narrative, rather than the more traditional scholarly stock-in-trade of assuming that the text has been composed by a less than careful scissors-and-paste man.

The account has long been noted for the difficulties it poses, not least the fact that it appears to promise Israel victory over Moab, something that in fact does not happen after the Moabite king sacrificed his eldest son on the wall of the city so that 'great wrath came upon Israel' (2 Kgs 3:27).[37] At the point at which it seemed that the victory promised by Elisha came to pass, Israel was in fact defeated. However, as Westbrook has pointed out, there are actually some careful ambiguities in Elisha's prophecy, not least because of his own opposition to Ahab and his son Jehoram, which make it likely that he did not wish to see an attempt to reinstate Israel's control over Moab

---

35. On some of the wider issues of ambiguity in John and the reader's role in disambiguating the text, see P. M. Phillips, *The Prologue of the Fourth Gospel: A Sequential Reading* (London: T. & T. Clark, 2006), pp. 143–150.

36. R. Westbrook, 'Elisha's True Prophecy in 2 Kings 3', *JBL* 124.3 (2005), pp. 530–532. It should be noted that Westbrook does not consider the species of ambiguity, only that ambiguity is present.

37. D. J. Wiseman, *1 and 2 Kings* (Leicester: IVP, 1993), p. 202, points to a parallel expression in a Moabite inscription.

succeed.[38] In the light of this, Elisha's prophecy should be read with care, because its ambiguities make it easy to misunderstand, just as Jehoram does.

There are six sequential elements in Elisha's prophecy:[39]

1. Yahweh will fill the wadi with drinking water (addressing the immediate need).
2. Yahweh will give Moab into Israel's hand.
3. Israel will strike (*nkh*) every fortified city.
4. Israel will cut down every tree.
5. Israel will block all the wells.
6. Israel will spoil the fields with stones.

Notably only the first two elements refer to things Yahweh will do, with the rest referring to Israel. The order of these elements is somewhat unusual if Elisha is promising complete victory, because the actions of Israel in items four to six are all typical of what an army would do in an assault on a foe. In addition, the verb *nkh* is ambiguous. It can mean to 'strike' in the sense of completely destroy, which is the sense it has in 3:24 (cf. Josh. 8:21; 1 Sam. 17:35). But it can also mean to 'strike' in an inconclusive manner, as, for example, in Exodus 21:15, where a man is punished for striking either of his parents, irrespective of whether or not they died, or Numbers 22:23, 25, 27, where Balaam strikes his donkey, only to discover it is still well enough to answer him back.

The third element in the prophetic sequence can thus be interpreted in two distinct ways: either that there will be a total victory, or that Israel will strike Moab but not achieve any victory. However, the last three items are more typically elements of an assault rather than something that would be done after victory. This could suggest that the second interpretation is more likely, and the fact that the sign of the water in the wadi is offered as an indication of something even greater to come seems to suggest to Jehoram that total victory is that which is promised. The balance of the narrative then works with the two possible outcomes, leading to the point of Israel's defeat.

The important point to note in this instance is that ambiguity is operative at two levels. So far, I have focused more on Elisha's ambiguity as a speaker within the narrative. His own use of multiple possibilities for the verb *nkh* would best be analysed as an example of the second type of ambiguity, in

---

38. Westbrook, 'Elisha's True Prophecy', p. 531.
39. Ibid.

which there are multiple possibilities but a single resolution. However, Elisha is not the author of this narrative; he is presented as a character within it.

The fourth type of ambiguity that concerns us here is developed by the author of the narrative, though this is achieved by drawing on Elisha's own ambiguity. A key concern for the book of Kings, and the former prophets as a whole (Joshua–Kings), is the reliability of the authentic prophetic word. That which comes from Yahweh can be trusted to work itself out, and indeed this is the way in which Samuel is earlier shown to be a prophet of Yahweh (1 Sam. 3:19 – 4:1a). As such, the author here needs to show that Elisha's word does indeed come to pass: Israel 'strikes' (*nkh*) the Moabites and their cities (2 Kgs 3:24), and ultimately through its slingers, Kir-Hareseth (2 Kgs 3:25). What Elisha has promised has indeed come to pass. Elisha is a reliable prophet. On the other hand, prophets themselves are not necessarily to be trusted, as can be seen in the account of the man of God from Judah and the old prophet from Bethel in 1 Kings 13. Their message, when they speak as prophets, does indeed come to pass, but they are not themselves necessarily reliable characters, and the actual content of their words needs careful analysis if one is to avoid being taken in by them. Authority lies not in the prophets but in the authentic word they bring. The author of this narrative is able to achieve this through the ambiguity Elisha has created, but by means of a second level of ambiguity. The narrative thus needs to work out a seemingly ineffective prophecy, where Israel is in fact defeated, to force readers back to a careful reading of the prophecy itself to see that it promises rather less than might have been initially expected. The alternative possibilities latent within Elisha's prophecy as they are worked out enable the author's own contribution and use of ambiguity to be discerned.

Type 5 ambiguity: apparent contradictions

This final type of ambiguity occurs when an author deliberately places together statements or concepts that appear to contradict one another so as to invite readers to see the ways in which they mutually interpret one another and cohere so as to create a single meaning. It is important to note that the contradictions employed in this type of ambiguity are apparent, not actual. If this were not the case, then the contradictions would undermine the meaning of the text. Where this type of ambiguity occurs, it is common for the apparent contradictions to be placed close to one another in order to highlight the paradox seemingly created by the contradiction, though it is not necessarily the case that this will happen. Generally, signals in the text will point to the playfulness being employed. Once again, this technique has the effect of drawing readers into the world of the text so that they seek to disambiguate that which they read, so that the process of disambiguation is what brings them to a point of insight into the goals of the text.

The parade example of this type of ambiguity occurs in Proverbs 26:4–5:

> Do not answer a fool according to his folly,
>> lest you come to resemble him.
> Answer a fool according to his folly,
>> lest he become wise in his own eyes.

Unless one were to posit a different sense for the word 'answer' in each instance,[40] it seems clear that these proverbs are intended to operate as effective opposites. Given the close similarities in structure and vocabulary, it seems more probable that these verses should be translated as above. As such, these proverbs appear to give contradictory advice, the first advising against answering a fool, and the second insisting that a fool should indeed be answered. Each proverb thus has its own integrity and internal logic. The first insists that those who engage in discussion with the fool will simply be caught up in the fool's presuppositions. Once a false premise for an argument is accepted, then it is exceedingly difficult to break free from it. Therefore, one should not answer a fool on the terms set by the fool. By way of contrast, the second insists that the wise have a responsibility to answer the arguments of the fool because a fool who is not answered will become entrenched in folly, believing folly to be wisdom. The juxtaposition of these proverbs does not deny the insight each offers on its own. But by placing them side by side in this way the editors of this section of Proverbs have shown the partial nature of all proverbial wisdom.[41]

More than this, they effectively call upon the wise to recognize the importance of making the appropriate decision as to how wisdom is to be employed. The wise need to know both possibilities, but by means of this juxtaposition are warned that being wise is more than simply a matter of knowing some proverbial statements. It is also a matter of knowing how to choose the most appropriate strand of wisdom for the situation being encountered.[42] Indeed,

---

40. The root '*nh* could mean 'answer' or 'afflict', though in Eccl. 1:13 and 3:10 it seems to have the sense of 'be busy with'. Possibly the meaning in v. 4 is 'answer' and in v. 5 'afflict', so one does something different with each group. But to sustain such an interpretation one would need more clues than the text provides.

41. R. N. Whybray, *Proverbs* (Grand Rapids: Eerdmans, 1994), pp. 372–373.

42. Similarly, R. E. Murphy, *Proverbs* (Nashville: Nelson, 1998), p. 203.

one could argue that the effect of this juxtaposition of an apparent contradiction has the effect of causing readers to re-evaluate the whole of their
processes of interpreting any given proverb and its relationship to the rest of
the collection.

Although Proverbs illustrates the general principles behind this type of
ambiguity, its finest exponent is undoubtedly Qoheleth. So important is the use
of this technique that Fox has suggested that understanding the way contradictions work in Ecclesiastes is the starting point for understanding the book
as a whole.[43] Unlike Proverbs 26:4–5, Qoheleth does not simply lay his contradictions next to each other, with the possible exception of the antinomies laid
out in 3:1–8. The contradictions in the book have troubled numerous interpreters of the book, reaching back to the early rabbinic period, but it is now
generally recognized that they should be understood not as an example of confusion on Qoheleth's part, nor as something to be harmonized, but as an essential element in the way the book communicates.[44] To take but one example, in
Ecclesiastes 2:2 Qoheleth speaks rather dismissively of pleasure (*śimḥâ*), asking,
'What can it do?' Pleasure is simply one more element in the unresolved ambiguities of life that Qoheleth describes as *hebel*. Yet in 8:15 Qoheleth can praise
pleasure, because there is nothing better for someone in life than to enjoy all it
has to offer. The apparent contradiction here is marked, especially when the two
statements are placed next to one another as baldly as this. Yet Qoheleth also
provides limits as to the applicability of each statement. The first is in the midst
of an experiment that tries to answer the question of whether or not pleasure
provides something of ultimate value (Eccles. 2:1–11). The answer Qoheleth
reaches is that it cannot do so. As an absolute value, pleasure is limited. Yet, in
the context of the best way to live amid the vagaries of life, Qoheleth sees value
in pleasure. As with the example from Proverbs, the point Qoheleth wishes to
make is that both statements are appropriate given the right circumstances, but
by generating an apparent contradiction between them, he is able to create a
means by which readers are drawn to engage, question and wrestle with his text.
Qoheleth observes puzzling contradictions in the world, and by observing
them in this way, readers not only wrestle with the text, but are also forced once
more to wrestle with the ways in which they understand life.

John 7:8–10 provides another example of this type of ambiguity. Asked
about whether he is going to Jerusalem for the Feast of Tabernacles, Jesus says
in John 7:8, 'You go up to the feast. I am not going up to this feast because

---

43. Fox, *Time to Tear Down*, p. 3.

44. See especially, D. Ingram, *Ambiguity in Ecclesiastes* (London: T. & T. Clark, 2006).

my time has not yet been fulfilled.' In spite of this, in verse 10 we are told that after his brothers had gone up, then 'he also went up, not openly but in secret'. Given Jesus' emphasis upon truth in John's Gospel, this would seem a striking contradiction. Yet such patterns exist in John's Gospel.[45] At the wedding in Cana, Jesus declines to do a miracle on the grounds that his time has not yet come, but he still turns the water into wine (John 2:1–11). Some early copyists apparently felt the force of this contradiction and read his statement as saying he was 'not yet' going up (so NIV), so that a later journey would pose no difficulties. But the contradiction is only apparent, because Jesus has provided his own statement as to his programme. He will not travel at the direction of his brothers. Instead, his timing is controlled by God, which is why he must wait for the appropriate time. That is to say, his programme is not subject to human control, but must wait on the will of God. When Jesus does go, it is immediately clear that he is not acting on his brothers' programme since he goes in secret, waiting for the middle of the feast to begin to teach in the temple (John 7:14). The apparent contradiction here is thus an important element for John, because the surprise it creates forces us to re-evaluate Jesus' earlier statement, and to appreciate afresh the importance of God's timing for the things he does.

Understanding Saul through misunderstanding

Although the bulk of Empson's work examined the use of ambiguity in shorter poetic works, so that the more immediate pay-off from his work might be thought to occur in the Psalms and related texts, it is still able to contribute much to the study of narratives. The point to emphasize is that carefully constructed texts are able to draw readers in through various forms of ambiguity and in so doing enable them to engage more fully with the text. In the end, the text will normally disclose its appropriate resolutions, but the intention itself may well lie in retaining the ambiguity. Thus, although the examples of ambiguity considered so far have tended to look at verbal ambiguities, it is also possible to create ambiguity through narrative techniques. In this section, therefore, an extended reading of portions of 1 Samuel is given to show the value of Empson's taxonomy for this type of ambiguity. This, of course, is only one example of a phenomenon found across the Bible, but especially common in the OT narratives.

---

45. Barrett, *John*, p. 258.

Such a studied use of ambiguity has not normally been attributed to the books of Samuel.[46] By far the most common approach to this text has been to resolve apparent ambiguities, usually on the assumption that only one of the possible meanings the ambiguity generates was intended. There are indeed points where ambiguity exists in the text simply because of awkward details within it, a feature we would expect in most texts since authors are not always conscious of the fact that possible ambiguities exist within their work. For example, it is unclear in the MT whether it is Saul or Samuel who tears the cloak when Samuel leaves Saul in 1 Samuel 15:27. Such ambiguities occur frequently in many texts, but where we find a consistent pattern of ambiguities, then the possibility exists that the text has been deliberately framed in order to utilize ambiguity as a vital tool to pique the interest of readers.

The purpose of this section is to argue that just such a pattern exists in the characterization of Saul in 1 Samuel. Here he is consistently portrayed as misunderstanding potentially ambiguous statements. Indeed, through the ways in which Saul misunderstands, readers are brought to understand more clearly where his faults lie, because each example of misunderstanding points to his failure to accept that David is Yahweh's choice as his replacement. The examples we shall consider of this occur in 18:6–9, 20:24–34 and 22:11–17. In each case, the narrative voice in 1 Samuel presents a deliberately ambiguous speech, employing Empson's type 1 ambiguity in which certain details are able to be effective in multiple ways.[47] As we shall see, most scholars have sought to close off the intended meaning one way or the other, whereas the contention developed here is that the ambiguity is intentional and readers should therefore be aware that the dialogue is open to multiple possibilities. There is thus a distinction to be drawn between the experience of the characters within the narrative with respect to the ambiguity and the use made of it in the text. Saul's problem is that he invariably makes the wrong choice because of his obsession with the kingdom, but this is recognized only when this distinction is maintained.

David has slain his tens of thousands (1 Sam. 18:6–9)

The account of David's slaying of Goliath poses a host of narrative-critical issues we cannot address here.[48] Suffice it to say, the current form of the text

---

46. But see K. Bodner, *David Observed: A King in the Eyes of his Court* (Sheffield: Sheffield Phoenix, 2005), pp. 77–88.

47. Empson, *Seven Types*, pp. 1–47.

48. But see D. G. Firth, 'That the World May Know: Narrative Poetics in 1 Samuel 16–17', in M. Parsons (ed.), *Text and Task: Scripture and Mission* (Milton Keynes:

presents this account after the slaying of Goliath, though it is not necessarily immediately after it, since the narrative would seem to presume that David is already an established commander. Certainly, 1 Samuel 18:5 indicates that he has already taken on this role. Fokkelmann argues that the use of the singular *happĕlištî* refers specifically to the death of Goliath in that the plural is otherwise used to describe the Philistines as a group.[49] Although this is a significant point, David has already been described as a military chief for Saul, so it seems more likely that the reference is to battle with the Philistines generally, though with the singular perhaps highlighting the specific defeat of Goliath. In addition, David and Saul are met by women from all the towns of Israel. Even allowing for the hyperbole, such a greeting cannot be expected if they are only coming back to Gibeah after the death of Goliath. But however we take it, David is returning with Saul after success in battle. As they return, they are greeted by women whose actions are presented as replicating those of Miriam after the crossing of the sea (Exod. 15:20–21). The women's song is well known:

> Saul has slain his thousands,
>> and David his tens of thousands.
> (1 Sam. 18:7)

Although the women's song is well known, its meaning is disputed. Clearly, it is a victory song, but the question of its meaning hangs on the relationship between the two lines, since the song can either treat David and Saul essentially as military equals, or it may seek to belittle Saul. A good case can be made for either interpretation.

Those who read the text as belittling Saul point to the sense of intensification between the lines. Robert Alter, for example, highlights other examples of the technique of intensifying parallelism.[50] This is a common technique in Hebrew poetry in which the second line develops and intensifies the content of the first. Such a pattern suggests that the content of the second line must therefore go further than the first. Read in this way, the second line

---

Footnote 48 (*continued*)

   Paternoster 2005), pp. 20–32. In addition, these verses are absent from the Septuagint, though notably it presents a far more positive picture of Saul in this chapter than does the MT.

49. Fokkelman, *Crossing Fates*, p. 211.

50. R. Alter, *The Art of Biblical Poetry* (New York: Basic, 1985), p. 19; *The David Story* (New York: Norton, 1999), p. 113.

suggests the killing of a larger number of Philistines than the first, with the somewhat unusual change in subject suggesting that David has thus been much more effective than Saul. In short, on this interpretation, David is greater than Saul because the pattern of intensification suggests that the tens of thousands he has slain exceed the number of Saul's slain, who is assigned merely thousands. Since this is a common technique, this is a plausible way in which to read the song, and is certainly the option Saul himself takes. That is to say, Saul's interpretation of the song is possible, and operates within the frames of reference one would expect for such a text.

But this is not the only way in which the women's song can be understood. The difficulty with understanding the song as being an example of intensifying parallelism is that the combination of 'thousand' and 'ten thousand' is a stock pair in which there is frequently no discernible difference in meaning in parallel occurrences. Hence, McCarter points to Psalm 91:7:

> A thousand may fall at your side,
>   ten thousand at your right hand
> but [the pestilence] will not come near you![51]

In this example, clearly there is no intensification of meaning, so that both numbers are employed as shorthand for a very large number rather than providing any specific definition. If that is so, then both lines of the women's song may mean nothing more than that both Saul and David have slain many enemies.

The difficulty with this approach is that we have the change of subject between the two lines, which could suggest a distinction being drawn between Saul and David and that therefore the larger number does suggest a degree of intensification, provided it is understood in a more or less literal sense. But the alternative possibility, that this is an example of intensification, stumbles at exactly the same point because direct parallels of intensification with a change of subject are lacking. Because of this, David Gunn has argued that the song is intended to be ambiguous.[52] That is to say, the song can always be interpreted in both ways because the textual form does not close off either alternative. Gunn's view is highly plausible, but can be developed slightly by noting that the narrator records the women went out specifically to 'meet King Saul'

---

51. P. K. McCarter, Jr., *1 Samuel: A New Translation with Introduction and Commentary* (Garden City: Doubleday, 1980), p. 312.

52. D. M. Gunn, *The Fate of King Saul: An Interpretation of a Biblical Story* (Sheffield: JSOT Press, 1980), p. 119.

(18:6). Saul, and not David, was the focus of their celebration. The song itself remains ambiguous, but the narrative context suggests it was intended for Saul, and should therefore be interpreted positively. That is, the song is not belittling Saul but seeing him as the hero to whom David has attached himself. Without the narrative context, Gunn's approach would hold. But the context makes clear that the song does not promote David above Saul. In terms of Empson's taxonomy of ambiguity, the song itself contains a fundamental ambiguity of which the authors (the women) were unaware. But the narrator employs it differently, being fully aware of the multiple possibilities within it. Readers are thus drawn in to engage the text at different levels.

In spite of this, Saul interprets the song as a form of intensifying parallelism, displeased by the fact that David is said to have slain tens of thousands and he only thousands. Like the women, Saul fails to recognize the ambiguity of the song, and so draws a conclusion that the narrator indicates is false. And it is from a failure to understand an ambiguity that Saul begins to oppose David, because his misunderstanding leads to him understand David as the one who will replace him. There is, however, one further element of ambiguity inherent in all of this, because it is through this misunderstanding that Saul comes to understand correctly that David will be the next king. In drawing this element into the narrative, the text draws on Empson's second type of ambiguity, in which multiple possibilities come to a single resolution: in this case, the correct observation that David will succeed him, even if for the wrong reason. Thus irony and ambiguity come together.

David has slipped away (1 Sam. 20:24–34)

With David seen as his enemy, the narrative then records a number of attempts Saul made on David's life. Twice we are told Saul tried to kill David with his spear (18:10–11; 19:9–10), a story paralleled in this chapter when he attacks Jonathan (20:33). If nothing else, Saul is a poor shot with a spear, but these are all signs of his increasing desperation. Apart from this, the approaches in chapters 18–19 are largely parallel, except that Saul seeks to have David killed by indirect means in chapter 18, whereas his approach in chapter 19 is far more direct. Chapter 20 then recounts the story of how David is able to convince Jonathan that Saul intends to kill him. David encourages Jonathan to tell his father that David has asked for permission to attend a sacrifice in his own village rather than attend the New Moon feast with Saul,[53] something he would

---

53. The details of this feast are obscure, though it is known that the New Moon was an important time (Num. 10:10; 28:11–15). The fact that it ran over two days might

apparently have been expected to do. There were a range of possible reasons why David would miss the first day of this feast, and the narrative covers this fact by reporting some of Saul's self-talk, in which he justifies David's actions by reference to his having become unclean. There were a number of reasons why someone could become unclean, such as a nocturnal emission (Lev. 15:2), but most of these permitted a return to ritual cleanness on the following day. Touching a corpse was a more severe problem, since it resulted in a seven-day period of uncleanness (Num. 19:11), something that would be a constant problem for a soldier like David.

Nevertheless, it is clear that the second day's absence provided the key test that would prove to Jonathan that Saul intended to kill David, so the explanation offered for his absence could not provide him with seven days of uncleanness. The test required that David be eligible to attend on ritual grounds, so that the crucial component was that he had gone elsewhere when he was able to attend. Thus the reason on which Jonathan and David had agreed was that David had asked Jonathan for permission to attend an annual clan sacrifice in Bethlehem. Such an invitation would point to a clash of loyalties for David between his obligations to family and Saul. The nature of Saul's response would then demonstrate to Jonathan whether or not Saul really intended to kill David, perhaps because he would inevitably suspect that any point at which David was not with him was really an occasion when he was plotting against him.

True to David and Jonathan's expectations, Saul asked Jonathan where David was on the second night. Jonathan, however, changed the agreed wording, with changes then introducing elements of ambiguity that would again lead Saul to misunderstand what was being said. The agreed wording was that 'David earnestly asked leave of me to run to Bethlehem his city, for there is a yearly sacrifice there for all the clan' (20:6 ESV). But when asked by Saul, Jonathan resolves one ambiguity but adds another of great importance within the narrative flow of chapters 18–20. He deletes the verb 'run' (*rwṣ*) and replaces it with 'send' (*šlḥ*). In this way, he seeks to remove the possible implication that David has fled from Saul and that instead he has gone only because Jonathan has the authority to send him. Jonathan then offers an expansion on the original agreement by including a claimed order from one of David's brothers, adding that David could go only if he had found favour with Jonathan. This introduces a new ambiguity of authority in Jonathan's speech, one of which he is plainly unaware, but that the narrator is able to exploit.

---

suggest a combination with a Sabbath or simply that Israel's skills in astronomy were not sufficiently developed for an exact date.

Finally, Jonathan notes that David has asked to 'slip away' (*mlṭ*) and see his brothers. Here, more levels of ambiguity begin to open up. As was the case in 18:7, there are multiple ways in which this statement can be true. Although Jonathan seeks to present an essentially neutral statement about David, his changes to the agreed wording open up possible ambiguities that Saul will misunderstand, even though in doing so he will more truly understand the way in which David and Jonathan now relate to one another.

The key to this lies in the use of the verb *mlṭ*, a verb that has been a *Leitwort* through the preceding chapters.[54] The verb itself has a reasonably broad semantic range within the niphal (as here), from the relatively neutral 'slip away' (2 Sam. 4:6) to 'escape' (Judg. 3:29) or even 'be delivered' (Ps. 22:6). An important technique that is employed within the books of Samuel is garbled speech as a sign of distress.[55] Although Jonathan's speech is not garbled, it is certainly the case that his relative loquaciousness is a mechanism for portraying his nerves in this encounter with Saul, and it is by this means that the ambiguous verb slips in. His problems are compounded by the ways in which the verb has recently been used in 19:10, 12, 17 and 18. In each of those occurrences it was used with the meaning of 'escape' and always with reference to David. More specifically, it was the verb used by Saul himself at 19:17 when he confronted Michal and accused her of allowing David to escape. The neutral sense intended by Jonathan is not the sense Saul attributes to him, with the result that he accuses Jonathan of siding with David so that Jonathan's kingdom cannot be established. Once again, therefore, Saul's misunderstanding of ambiguous language is linked by him to the kingdom, indicating that he knows David is indeed his opponent for the throne.

The patterns of ambiguity employed here are consistent with 18:6–9. Jonathan's speech betrays an unwitting ambiguity, whereas the narrator employs it fully aware of the multiple senses possible. However, there is once again a situation in which multiple possibilities come together to a single resolution, because Saul's conclusions are actually correct about what Jonathan is doing. His reasoning may well be flawed, but the correct conclusion is still reached. Again, therefore, it is the employment of multiple levels of ambiguity that enable the ironies within the text to work.

---

54. A. H. van Zyl, *1 Samuël*, vol. 2, POut (Nijkerk: G. F. Callenbach, 1989), p. 58, points to the use of this verb as one of the key linking elements throughout 1 Sam. 18 – 20.

55. G. A. Rendsburg, 'Confused Language as a Deliberate Device in Biblical Hebrew Narrative', *Journal of the Hebrew Scriptures* 2 (1999). Available online at <http://www.arts.ualberta.ca/JHS/index.htm>, accessed 22 Jan. 2008, pars. 1, 6, 7.

The priests at Nob (1 Sam. 22:11–17)

The account of the slaughter of the priests at Nob is more complex than the preceding examples, though it will be seen to conform to the patterns previously employed. The whole of 1 Samuel 21:2–10 [ET 21:1–9] and 22:6–23 makes considerable use of ambiguity in recounting the events at Nob and their implications when Ahimelech is brought before Saul. For example, when David seeks Goliath's sword,[56] he asks whether there is a spear or sword under Ahimelech's hand (21:9 [21:8]), picking up a key term (*yād*) that runs throughout this section. Immediately before this, however, we are told that Doeg was in the sanctuary, 'detained' (*ně'ṣār*) before Yahweh. Why was Doeg there? The narrator chooses to leave this point unclear, since the verb *'ṣr* could mean either that Doeg was there because of the need to continue worship or that he was there under some restraint, perhaps as someone awaiting judgment in a criminal matter. All we know for certain about him is that he is a servant of Saul and an Edomite, a combination that indicates he will cause trouble.

The ambiguity in his characterization remains even in the description of the events in the sanctuary. In asking what is under Ahimelech's hand, David has also pointed to the place of the ephod (21:10).[57] Priests used the ephod when making formal inquiry of Yahweh, so Doeg possibly faithfully reports what he believes he saw occur. Nevertheless, almost all commentators have sought to resolve the ambiguity and therefore conclude either that Doeg lied in this matter,[58] or that he faithfully reported what happened.[59] Their conclusion on this point both shapes and is shaped by their interpretation of Ahimelech's speech to Saul in 22:11–14. Even the unusual reading of Reis, who argues that David and Ahimelech engaged in an extensive conspiracy, so

---

56. The question of what Goliath's sword was doing at Nob is itself problematic, since we have no account of how it arrived there, though the analogy to the capture of the ark by the Philistines highlights the fact that it was common practice to bring relics to the sanctuary of one's gods. Curiously, the sword is not mentioned again, which might suggest that there are other traditions concerning its use that the narrators of Samuel have chosen not to retain. Cf. S. Isser, *The Sword of Goliath: David in Heroic Literature* (Atlanta: SBL, 2003), pp. 34–37.

57. The words 'the ephod' are absent from lxx[B] but present in 4QSam[b]. The words *en himatiō* probably indicate that the translators conceived of the ephod as a garment. MT is to be retained. Cf. McCarter, *1 Samuel*, p. 348.

58. E.g. W. Brueggemann, *First and Second Samuel* (Louisville: Westminster John Knox, 1990), p. 159.

59. E.g. B. C. Birch, 'The First and Second Books of Samuel', in *NIB* 2: 1148.

their language throughout was coded agreement, still seeks to overcome the ambiguity narrative reticence has created.[60] Barbara Green seems to come closest to the view argued here when she says that 'the inquiry report is plausibly a report of what he saw'.[61] If the position taken here is correct, and the fact that scholars are otherwise divided on either side of the ambiguity could suggest that it is, then we can conclude that the narrator is intentionally creating a context fluid with ambiguity within this section of the narrative. None of this should be taken as presuming that Doeg is a neutral character. He is clearly concerned to give Saul the type of information he craves, and he might reasonably expect a suitable reward from Saul in the light of his claims about David not being able to reward his supporters. This can also be seen by noting what he omits as much as by heeding what he tells: there is, for example, no indication that David approached Ahimelech, nor a hint that David misrepresented himself to him. But on the key question of whether or not Doeg is truthful in reporting that Ahimelech has inquired of Yahweh for David, the narrative is prepared to leave the veil of ambiguity untouched.

Our primary concern, however, is with the events in 22:11–16, where once again Saul misunderstands a fundamental ambiguity. This time, however, the narrator will use this to show Saul's own failure as king. After Doeg's report, Saul summoned Ahimelech along with the rest of the priests from Nob to meet him, though clearly Ahimelech is his main point of focus as he dismissively addresses him as 'son of Ahitub', replicating his reference to David only as 'the son of Jesse' rather than naming him directly. Saul's accusation against Ahimelech comes in the form of a question, picking up on the three points Doeg has established. The heart of Saul's accusation is that Ahimelech has conspired with 'the son of Jesse' against him, with the specific elements of the conspiracy being that he has provided David with food, a sword and has inquired of Yahweh for him, all of which has enabled David to resist Saul, and indeed to rebel against him.[62]

Saul's accusation sets out the main issues to which Ahimelech must respond. Two of these points are beyond dispute: he has provided David with

---

60. P. T. Reis, 'Collusion at Nob: A New Reading of 1 Samuel 21–22', *JSOT* 61 (1994), pp. 59–73; cf. Bodner, *David Observed*, pp. 25–37.

61. Green, *How Are the Mighty Fallen?*, p. 355.

62. J. J. M. Roberts, 'The Legal Basis for Saul's Slaughter of the Priests of Nob', *JNSL* 25.1 (1999), pp. 21–29, has argued that Saul here invokes a standard practice in the ANE in which all divination oracles should be reported to the king, probably as a means of preventing rebellion.

both food and a sword. It is crucial for the narrative that Ahimelech cannot
know that David has misled him with his claims of being on a secret mission
for the king, but in any case Ahimelech cannot deny having provided these
things. But the question of whether or not he has inquired of Yahweh for
David is less clear. Certainly, there is nothing in 21:2–10 [MT 21:1–9] that clearly
indicates he has, though the possibility is not thereby excluded. But all we have
at this point is Doeg's testimony, and, as argued above, the narrator is content
to leave the question of the reliability of this testimony ambiguous here.
Accordingly, Ahimelech's response directly addresses only the question of
whether or not he has inquired of Yahweh for David, though there is probably an implicit defence in his opening question about David's status within
Saul's household of Ahimelech's right to give someone whom he believes is
serving the king both food and weaponry.

Ahimelech's speech is a carefully crafted piece, which employs rhetorical
questions rather than direct statements so as to avoid giving any direct offence
against Saul. This is also clear from the fact that he speaks of Saul in the third
person, using classical court language, so that he does not have to name Saul
directly. Finally, he speaks of himself as Saul's 'servant' (*'ebed*). Each of these
elements makes clear that Ahimelech is being extremely careful not to offend
Saul. The questions in verse 14 are used to suggest it was entirely appropriate
for him to assist David, but our central concern here is with the question in
verse 15, which can be understood in two distinct ways. The distinction here
lies in whether Ahimelech's response either denies making this inquiry for
David or admits to doing so, possibly in a routine manner.

Many commentators are struck by the unusual structure of his speech at
this point, but almost all also feel the need to resolve one way or another the
ambiguity created, with a clear majority believing that Ahimelech is here suggesting he has routinely inquired for David in the past.[63] Read in this way,
Ahimelech accepts that he has inquired of God for David in the past, while
his speech may also indicate that he accepts he has inquired of God for him
this time too. Understood this way, we would perhaps render his question
along the lines of 'Have I just begun to inquire of God for him today? Of
course not!' Robert Alter, however, argues for the alternative interpretation,
in which the condition set up by the question is hypothetical, so that we
would render it as something like 'Would I this day for the first time inquire
for him of God? Of course not!', so that in fact he is actually denying ever

---

63. E.g. R. Bergen, *1, 2 Samuel* (Nashville: Broadman & Holman, 1996), p. 229; Roberts,
'Legal Basis', p. 24.

carrying out an inquiry for David.[64] Edelman highlights the lack of a morph-
ologically defined condition verb form in Hebrew, which is why either translation is grammatically possible.[65] Ahimelech cannot, however, have meant
both of these things, though the presence of the ambiguity itself is important.

The question of which of these is intended by Ahimelech cannot be
answered on purely grammatical terms, but once again the context may
provide a clue for the reader. Ahimelech's defence does not address the issues
of the food or the sword, perhaps because they are indisputable.[66] The
opening component of his speech therefore asks Saul to consider David's
status and character as someone like Ahimelech would perceive him. In
essence, Ahimelech says that David's character and status are such that
it would only be natural that he would provide him with assistance.
Nevertheless, the only point of defence directly offered is in respect to the
question of the inquiry. That this point is defended might suggest that
Ahimelech believes he has been misrepresented to Saul. This seems clear
from the fact that he asks Saul not to accuse him in this matter (*'al yāśēm ha-
mmelek bĕ'abdō*). Such a request implies that Ahimelech believes the accusation to be false, that this is the one charge he can refute, even though he
acknowledges he would not have seen anything wrong in providing David
with support.

Ahimelech's problem is that he has left a fundamental ambiguity in his
response, so that his denial is also capable of being understood as a confession. Once again, Saul misunderstands an ambiguous statement that relates
to his status as king because it is his habit to interpret ambiguities in the way
most threatening to him. The forms of ambiguity employed here therefore
repeat those we have already seen. Ahimelech's ambiguity is an example of
unwitting speech under pressure, but this is intentionally employed by
the narrator because the multiple possibilities it opens up enable a fruitful
exploration of Saul's character. Saul in this chapter may not quite be the
paranoid figure presented by some commentators, but through the pattern
of misunderstood ambiguities we are able to come to a better understanding of him.

---

64. Alter, *David Story*, p. 136.

65. D. V. Edelman, *King Saul in the Historiography of Judah* (Sheffield: Sheffield Academic
    Press, 1991), p. 179.

66. Edelman, ibid., p. 178, assumes he intended to provide a fuller account, but this is a
    tenuous argument from silence.

Conclusion

The application of Empson's taxonomy of ambiguity is thus a useful tool in exploring both shorter phrases and extended narrative texts like these. It suggests a level of compositional skill and competence that also demands a great deal from readers who need to recognize both the ambiguities and the multiple ways in which they are being employed by the characters and the narrator. Readers need to develop the skill to appreciate the differences, though it may be that oral performance of these texts was also intended to highlight these points through intonation and the like.[67] However, it is unclear that we shall ever be able fully to recover the oral performance of these texts, so we may have to be content only with noting the ways in which ambiguities are employed both to engage readers and to generate interest in the narrative. In my last example, it also helps us understand the character of Saul because of the ways in which he misunderstands, with each new misunderstanding contributing to his own decline into violent retribution over the kingdom. So, through the ways in which the character of Saul is shown misunderstanding, readers are brought to a point of understanding.

Ambiguity is therefore not something to be feared by readers of the Bible as something to be removed in every instance. Rather, its presence can be a sign of a skilful writer who invites readers to enjoy and play with the text. A proper appreciation of the text thus requires both that we recognize the existence of this ambiguity and that we take time to note the ways in which it works. It is not enough simply to note that an ambiguity is present. The question must always be to ask what an ambiguity is doing, what its rhetorical force is. Noting the different forms of ambiguity can help us do just that, because appreciating the form used is the point at which we as readers are able to decode the goal of the ambiguity.

Bibliography

ALTER, R., *The Art of Biblical Poetry* (New York: Basic, 1985).

——, *The David Story* (New York: Norton, 1999).

BARRETT, C. K., *The Gospel According to St John: An Introduction with Commentary and Notes on the Greek Text* (London: SPCK, 1962).

---

67. Cf. A. F. Campbell, 'The Storyteller's Role: Reported Story and Biblical Text', *CBQ* 64 (2002), pp. 427–441, for an examination of this possibility.

BEASLEY-MURRAY, G. R., *John*, WBC 36 (Waco: Word, 1987).

BERGEN, R., *1, 2 Samuel* (Nashville: Broadman & Holman 1996).

BIRCH, B. C., 'The First and Second Books of Samuel', in *NIB* 2: 947–1383.

BODNER, K., *David Observed: A King in the Eyes of his Court* (Sheffield: Sheffield Phoenix, 2005).

BROWN, W. P., 'The Didactic Power of Metaphor in the Aphoristic Sayings in Proverbs', *JSOT* 29.2 (2004), pp. 133–154.

BRUEGGEMANN, W., *First and Second Samuel* (Louisville: Westminster John Knox, 1990).

CAMPBELL, A. F., 'The Storyteller's Role: Reported Story and Biblical Text', *CBQ* 64 (2002), pp. 427–441.

CARSON, D. A., *The Gospel According to John* (Leicester: IVP, 1991).

CULLER, J., *Literary Theory: A Very Short Introduction* (New York: Oxford University Press, 1997).

DODD, C. H., *The Interpretation of the Fourth Gospel* (Cambridge: Cambridge University Press, 1953).

EDELMAN, D. V., *King Saul in the Historiography of Judah* (Sheffield: Sheffield Academic Press, 1991).

EMPSON, W., *Seven Types of Ambiguity*, 3rd ed. (Harmondsworth: Penguin, 1960).

——, *Some Versions of the Pastoral* (London: Chatto & Windus, 1935).

——, *The Structure of Complex Words* (Cambridge, Mass.: Harvard University Press, 1989).

——, 'The Verbal Analysis', *KR* 12 (1950), pp. 594–601.

EVANS, C. A., *Mark 8:27–16:20* (Nashville: Thomas Nelson, 2001).

FIRTH, D. G., 'That the World May Know: Narrative Poetics in 1 Samuel 16–17', in M. Parsons (ed.), *Text and Task: Scripture and Mission* (Milton Keynes: Paternoster 2005), pp. 20–32.

FOKKELMAN, J. P., *Narrative Art and Poetry in the Books of Samuel: A Full Interpretation Based on Stylistic and Structural Analyses*. Vol. 2: *The Crossing Fates (1 Sam. 13–31 & II Sam. 1)* (Assen: van Gorcum, 1986).

FOX, M. V., *A Time to Tear Down and a Time to Build Up: A Rereading of Ecclesiastes* (Grand Rapids: Eerdmans, 1999).

FREDERICKS, D. C., *Coping with Transience: Ecclesiastes on Brevity in Life* (Sheffield: Sheffield Academic Press, 1993).

GARRET, D., and HOUSE, P. R., *Song of Songs, Lamentations* (Nashville: Nelson, 2004).

GREEN, B., *How Are the Mighty Fallen? A Dialogical Study of King Saul in 1 Samuel* (London: Sheffield Academic Press, 2003).

——, *King Saul's Asking* (Collegeville: Liturgical, 2003).

GUNN, D. M., *The Fate of King Saul: An Interpretation of a Biblical Story* (Sheffield: JSOT Press, 1980).

HAWTHORNE, G. F., *Philippians*, WBC 43 (Waco: Word, 1983).

HOOKER, M. D., *The Gospel According to St Mark* (London: A. & C. Black, 1991).

INGRAM, D., *Ambiguity in Ecclesiastes* (London: T. & T. Clark, 2006).

ISSER, S., *The Sword of Goliath: David in Heroic Literature* (Atlanta: SBL, 2003).

KSELMAN, J. S., 'Janus Parallelism in Psalm 75:2', *JBL* 121 (2002), pp. 531–532.

LONGMAN III, T., *The Book of Ecclesiastes* (Grand Rapids: Eerdmans, 1998).

McCARTER, JR., P. K., *1 Samuel: A New Translation with Introduction and Commentary* (Garden City: Doubleday, 1980).

McDONALD, N. B., 'The Philosophy of Language and the Renewal of Biblical Hermeneutics', in C. G. Bartholomew, C. Greene and K. Möller (eds.), *Renewing Biblical Interpretation*, SHS 1 (Carlisle: Paternoster, 2000), pp. 126–133.

MARCUS, J., 'Crucifixion as Parodic Exaltation', *JBL* 125.1 (2006), pp. 73–87.

MURPHY, R. E., *Proverbs* (Nashville: Nelson, 1998).

O'BRIEN, P. T., *The Epistle to the Philippians* (Grand Rapids: Eerdmans, 1991).

OGDEN, G., *Qoheleth* (Sheffield: JSOT Press, 1987).

OSBORNE, G. R., *The Hermeneutical Spiral: A Comprehensive Introduction to Biblical Interpretation*, 2nd ed. (Downer's Grove: IVP, 2006).

PHILLIPS, P. M., *The Prologue of the Fourth Gospel: A Sequential Reading* (London: T. & T. Clark, 2006).

RAABE, P. R., 'Deliberate Ambiguity in the Psalter', *JBL* 110.2 (1991), pp. 213–227.

REIS, P. T., 'Collusion at Nob: A New Reading of 1 Samuel 21–22', *JSOT* 61 (1994), pp. 59–73.

RENDSBURG, G. A., 'Confused Language as a Deliberate Device in Biblical Hebrew Narrative', *Journal of the Hebrew Scriptures* 2 (1999). Available online at <http://www.arts.ualberta.ca/JHS/index.htm>, accessed 22 Jan. 2008.

RICHARDS, I. A., *Practical Criticism* (London: Kegan Paul, Trench, Trubner, 1929).

ROBERTS, J. J. M., 'The Legal Basis for Saul's Slaughter of the Priests of Nob', *JNSL* 25.1 (1999), pp. 21–29.

ROBEY, D., 'Anglo-American New Criticism', in A. Jefferson and D. Robey (eds.), *Modern Literary Theory: A Comparative Introduction*, 2nd ed. (London: B. T. Batsford, 1986), pp. 73–91.

VANHOOZER, K. J., *Is There a Meaning in This Text? The Bible, The Reader and the Morality of Literary Knowledge* (Leicester: Apollos, 1998).

WATSON, W. G. E., *Classical Hebrew Poetry: A Guide to its Techniques* (Sheffield: JSOT Press, 1984).

WESTBROOK, R., 'Elisha's True Prophecy in 2 Kings 3', *JBL* 124.3 (2005), pp. 530–532.

WHYBRAY, R. N., *Proverbs* (Grand Rapids: Eerdmans, 1994).

WIMSATT, JR., W. K., and BEARDSLEY, M. C., 'The Intentional Fallacy', *The Verbal Icon: Studies in the Meaning of Poetry* (Lexington: University of Kentucky Press, 1954), pp. 3–18. Available online at <http://faculty.smu.edu/nschwart/seminar/Fallacy.htm>, accessed 6 Feb. 2008.

WISEMAN, D. J., *1 and 2 Kings* (Leicester: IVP, 1993).

WOLTERSTORFF, N., 'The Promise of Speech Act Theory for Biblical Interpretation', in
    C. G. Bartholomew, C. Greene and K. Möller (eds.), *After Pentecost: Language and Biblical
    Interpretation*, SHS 2 (Carlisle: Paternoster, 2001), pp. 73–90.
WONG, G. C., 'Who Loved Whom? A Note on 1 Samuel xvi 21', *VT* 47 (1997), pp. 554–
    556.
ZIMA, P. V., *The Philosophy of Modern Literary Theory* (London: Athlone, 1999).
ZYL, A. H. VAN, *1 Samuël*, 2 vols., POut (Nijkerk: G. F. Callenbach, 1988, 1989).

6. POETICS

Jamie A. Grant

Introduction

Poetic texts present their own challenges to the reader, regardless of their source language or cultural origin. Poetry is, quite simply, more difficult than prose. It is often associated with intensely figurative language, imagery not immediately obvious to the reader, sentence structures that go against the grain and a means of communication very different from that which the reader normally encounters. This is as true of the (primarily Hebrew) biblical poetic texts as it is of any other poetry. As a written communicative act the poetic fulfils its end in a unique way, therefore, any study of the poetic will inevitably differ from studies of the communicative effect of other types of literature.[1] However, this chapter is slightly different from the others in this volume for another reason. A primary concern in each of the chapters has been to engage with trends in secular literary studies and to examine their

---

1. Effectively, 'poetics' is that branch of literary criticism that deals with the techniques and means of communication specific to poetry. So there is a sense in which this chapter is asking and answering the same types of questions discussed in the rest of this volume: how we can best understand the fullness of communication found in the Bible's poetic books.

implications for our reading and understanding of the Bible. The primary foci of this chapter, on the other hand, are to consider recent literary approaches to the study of poetic texts that are unique to the field of biblical studies.

In particular, two trends need to be considered in any up-to-date discussion of the Bible and literary method: *canonical readings* of the OT's anthologies of poetry and advances in the understanding of *parallelism* (a key characteristic of Hebrew poetry). So we shall examine the significance of canonical approaches and their impact on our reading of the poetic books, and then turn our attention to the interpretation of Hebrew parallelism. Another aspect of this chapter that sets it apart from the others is that the issues under discussion are primarily relevant, in the main part at least, to the OT. In this volume we consistently try to apply the knowledge derived from advances in literary awareness to the whole Bible. However, because the Bible's poetry is found primarily in the OT, the discussions considered in this chapter are of greatest relevance to the field of OT studies. Having said that, I shall briefly discuss the poetic in the NT before the close of this chapter. First, I address the way in which new literary approaches affect the OT poetic texts.

Canonical approaches to poetic texts

While the general principles discussed below may be applied to all OT poetic texts, it is perhaps wise to take the book of Psalms as our main starting point, as the recent advances in the understanding of the Bible's poetry have been drawn mainly from study of Psalms. These principles can be (and have been) extended to other OT poetic texts, but the clearest route to understanding the canonical approach to biblical poetry takes Psalms as its starting point.

The canonical study of Psalms

Our understanding of the psalms has probably suffered as a result of its frequent presentation as the 'hymnbook of the Old Testament'. The psalter is often considered to be a collection of songs for worship and, undoubtedly, there is an element of truth in this idea – many psalms were probably sung in public or private worship in their original setting, just as they have been throughout the ages. However, one thing is certain, the psalter at some point became a canonical *book* of the OT, a book to be read, meditated upon and applied, just like any other.

The 'hymnbook' view of the Psalms has had a marginalizing effect upon our understanding of the OT's poetic texts. Many have had the idea that 'the psalter is not the place we go to find proper theology: these texts are (merely) poems'. This is partly to do with contemporary misconceptions about the value of the aesthetic. Modernity has tended to assume that anything significant should be explained 'factually', by our using propositional ideas. The poetic (with its use of metaphor, imagery and emotive description) is often considered to be insubstantial by comparison.[2] However, nothing could be further from the truth: the aesthetic and the didactic combine seamlessly in the Bible's poetic texts and, regardless of what the psalter may have been at various stages of its development, *it has become a book of the Christian canon* and as such teaches us theology, just like the more 'factual' books of the Bible.

As a book like any other, the Psalms (and the other anthological books of the Writings) have also been subject to the same editorial processes that can be observed in the remainder of the canon. Since Brevard Childs's *Introduction to the Old Testament as Scripture,*[3] the general principle that an editorial hand was at work in the formation of the final version of the canon has found broad acceptance with regard to the historical and prophetic books of the OT. However, discussion of the poetic books continued to focus on questions of genre and function within the cult and scholars were generally sceptical of any notion of editorial shaping in the poetic books. It was widely assumed that nothing other than the random compilation of disparate materials could be observed in the Psalms, Proverbs and Ecclesiastes, whereas Job, Lamentations and Song of Songs showed at least some degree of order. However, since the

---

2. The origins of this mindset go back to the Enlightenment itself. Perhaps the most influential critic of the value of the poetic was John Locke, in his 1689 work *An Essay Concerning Human Understanding* (published by Prometheus, 1994, but as a text in the public domain may be downloaded from various websites, e.g. <http://socserv.mcmaster.ca/econ/ugcm/3ll3/locke/Essay.htm>, accessed 6 Feb. 2006). Locke, for example, states that '[L]anguage is often abused by figurative speech . . . [I]f we would speak of things as they are, we must allow that all the art of rhetoric, besides order and clearness; all the artificial and figurative application of words eloquence hath invented, are for nothing else but to insinuate wrong ideas, move the passions, and thereby mislead the judgment; and so indeed are perfect cheats: and therefore, however laudable or allowable oratory may render them in harangues and popular addresses, they are certainly, in all discourses that pretend to inform or instruct, wholly to be avoided; and where truth and knowledge are concerned, cannot but be thought a great fault, either of the language or person that makes use of them.'

3. B. S. Childs, *Introduction to the Old Testament as Scripture* (London: SCM, 1979).

publication of Gerald Wilson's *The Editing of the Hebrew Psalter*,[4] which develops Childs's theories with regard to the psalter, an ever-increasing awareness of the canonical or editorial shaping of the final form of the Psalms and wisdom literature has arisen.

Editorial shaping in the Psalms

Since the key works of Gunkel[5] and Mowinckel,[6] study of the Psalms has been dominated by questions of literary genre and usage within Israel's public worship. Consideration of type and cult-function was so pre-eminent in study of the secondary literature that questions of editing in the psalms were almost entirely neglected. Westermann suggests that 'in laying the foundation for his interpretation of the Psalms, Gunkel above all had no interest in how the collection was handed down to us',[7] and this lack of interest in the formation of the psalter continued through several generations until the 1980s. However, in writing his chapter on the canonical shape of the Psalms, Brevard Childs asked a very pertinent question that ultimately led to a sea change in the study of the Psalms, namely 'Why is Psalm 1 the first psalm in the Psalter?'[8] It is not representative of the major genres of psalm, being neither a lament nor a hymn of praise. Equally, it seems unlikely that the first psalm was ever sung by the massed ranks of the covenant community at one of the great festivals, since it is a Torah/wisdom poem. Psalm 1, therefore, is insignificant either with regard to its genre or its function in Israel's cult, so why should it be chosen to head the book?

This initial question led naturally to a second: 'Why are there so many lexical and structural links between Psalms 1 and 2?' Neither poem is headed by a superscription (unusual in Book 1 of the psalter), both are bounded by an

---

4. G. H. Wilson, *The Editing of the Hebrew Psalter*, SBLDS 76 (Chico: Scholars Press, 1985).

5. H. Gunkel, *Introduction to the Psalms: The Genres of the Religious Lyric of Israel*, tr. J. D. Nogalski (Macon: Mercer University Press, 1998), originally published as *Einleitung in die Psalmen: Die Gattungen der religiösen Lyrik Israels*, GHAT 2 (Tübingen: Vandenhoeck & Ruprecht, 1933).

6. S. Mowinckel, *The Psalms in Israel's Worship*, tr. D. R. Ap-Thomas (Oxford: Basil Blackwell, 1962); this English text is a substantial revision of his earlier Norwegian work *Offersang og Sangoffer* (Oslo: Aschehoug, 1951).

7. C. Westermann, *Praise and Lament in the Psalms*, tr. K. R. Crim and R. N. Soulen (Atlanta: John Knox, 1981), p. 251.

8. Childs, *Introduction*, pp. 512–514.

inclusio grounded in the idea of 'blessing' (*'ašrê* is used in Pss 1:1 and 2:12), the verb *hāgâ* is key to each of the psalms (used of meditation on the Torah in 1:2 and the mutterings of rebellion in 2:1) and, among other links, the righteous, the wicked, the law, ideas of judgment and a perishing way all make an appearance in each poem.[9] Once these observations are made, the reader logically begins to question whether these connections are accidental or indications of purposeful editorial activity in the psalter. Have those who put the book of Psalms together as a book consciously chosen to put these poems alongside each other because of their similarity?[10]

This was the very issue Gerald Wilson, a student of Childs, sought to address in his *Editing of the Hebrew Psalter.* Having examined editing techniques apparent in collections of Sumerian hymns, Wilson went on to ask if such indicators of editorial influence are also apparent in the biblical psalms. The Sumerian hymnic collections contained several explicit indications of editing (e.g. the name of the scribe who gathered a collection), but Wilson also pointed out the presence of 'tacit' signs of editing (e.g. grouping hymns according to theme, or the similarity of their 'incipit' [first line]). Wilson argued that there are no explicit signs of editing in the psalter, but went on to show that there are many tacit indications of the grouping or ordering of psalms in the book.[11]

One of the first and most significant of these signs is seen in the above-mentioned placement of Psalms 1 and 2 at the head of the psalter. These poems are deliberately linked and seem to have been purposefully placed at the start of the psalter as an introduction to the wide diversity of material the reader will encounter within the collection as a whole.[12] It was a common practice in the ANE for the editors of anthologies of hymnic or poetic material to place an introduction at the head of the collection in order to provide the reader with a paradigm for the interpretation of the diverse materials that

---

9. See P. Auffret, *The Literary Structure of Psalm 2*, tr. D. J. A. Clines, JSOTSup 3 (Sheffield: JSOT Press, 1977); and J. A. Grant, *The King as Exemplar: The Function of Deuteronomy's Kingship Law in the Shaping of the Book of Psalms*, SBL, AB 17 (Atlanta: SBL; Leiden: Brill, 2004), pp. 60–65.

10. Of course, another option may be that one of these psalms was written to mirror the other, but this, of course, would be impossible to prove (Grant, *King as Exemplar*, pp. 60–70).

11. Wilson, *Editing*, pp. 9–10, 182–185.

12. J. C. McCann, *A Theological Introduction to the Books of Psalms: The Psalms as Torah* (Nashville: Abingdon, 1993), pp. 48–50.

follow.[13] By including Psalms 1 and 2 as an introduction to the canonical book, we see that the biblical psalter follows this pattern and thus points toward the subtle presence of editorial organization within it.

Once this introduction is observed, it soon becomes clear that there are other obvious indications of deliberate editorial activity throughout the book of Psalms. The division of the psalter into five books separated by doxologies is arguably the clearest indication that the order of the psalms is not entirely random.[14] It is possible that this was a deliberate attempt to echo the Pentateuch within the Writings, and the rabbis compared the 'five books of David' with the five books of Moses.[15] Regardless of whether this was the intent of the editors, the organization of the psalms into books is clearly not accidental but indicates deliberate editorial activity. In fact, it could be argued that the doxological division of the five books of the psalter is as close as we get to an indication of explicit editorial activity in the Psalms.

Another obvious sign of editing is seen in the incorporation of smaller groupings of psalms into the broader psalter as collections, for example the Songs of Ascent, Psalms 120 – 134. These psalms have not been dispersed throughout the book, like the laments, but their association with one another is retained by including them as a kind of mini-collection within the broader book. Furthermore, we can observe deliberate editorial structuring of such collections within the Psalms. Perhaps the best example of this is seen in the chiastic structure of Psalms 15 – 24. Patrick Miller points out that Psalms 15 and 24 are both entrance psalms that focus on questions of access into the temple; Psalms 16 and 23 are both psalms of comfort; Psalms 17 and 22 are powerful laments; Psalm 18 and (the linked) Psalms 20 and 21 are all royal psalms; thus leaving Psalm 19, a Torah psalm, as the central pivot of this collection.[16] Other indications of editing include the deliberate juxtaposition of

---

13. R. C. Van Leeuwen, 'The Book of Proverbs: Introduction, Commentary and Reflections', in *NIB* 5: 24.

14. G. H. Wilson, 'The Structure of the Psalter', in P. S. Johnston and D. G. Firth (eds.), *Interpreting the Psalms: Issues and Approaches* (Leicester: Apollos, 2005), pp. 230–231.

15. N. M. Sarna, *On the Book of Psalms: Exploring the Prayer of Ancient Israel* (New York: Schocken, 1993), p. 18.

16. P. D. Miller, 'Kingship, Torah Obedience and Prayer', in K. Seybold and E. Zenger (eds.), *Neue Wege der Psalmenforschung* (Freiburg: Herder, 1995), pp. 127–142. We shall return to think about this collection in more detail when we examine the application of the canonical approach to poetic texts below.

psalms apparently 'in conversation' with one another. For example, Psalm 90 (and the succeeding psalms in Book 4 of the psalter) seems to provide a response to the depths of despair found in the lament section of Psalm 89 (e.g. 89:40; cf. 90:14). The lament of Psalm 89 focuses on the demise of the Davidic monarchy and questions whether Yahweh is still in control of the destiny of his people. Psalm 90 responds with the voice of Moses, pointing out that Yahweh was the refuge and dwelling place of the people before king and temple existed and that he is still their Rock even although these institutions have been removed. The following psalms emphasize the continuing reign of Yahweh, and also encourage the people with the prospect of the future return of the Davidic king.[17]

So, while it is impossible to remove completely an element of 'randomness' from the psalter (claims for a transparent, logical ordering throughout the whole book go too far), there are many indications of extensive editorial activity within the Psalms.[18] Wilson summarizes the telltale signs of editorial activity in the psalter:

> I have been able to show (1) that the 'book' divisions of the Psalter are real, editorially induced divisions and not accidentally introduced; (2) the 'separating' and 'binding' functions of author and genre groupings; (3) the lack of a s/s [superscription] as an indication of a tradition of combination; (4) the use of *hllwyh* pss [praise Yahweh psalms] to indicate the conclusion of segments; (5) the use of *hwdw* pss [thanksgiving psalms] to introduce segments; (6) the existence of thematic correspondences between the beginning and ending pss in some books. All of these findings demonstrate the presence of editorial activity at work in the arrangement of the pss.[19]

The significance of editorial shaping in the Psalms

Reading the Psalms as a book has important implications for interpretation, primarily in terms of *context*. Traditionally, each psalm has been treated as an individual unit for interpretation purposes: these were contextless, hermetically sealed units as far as their interpretation was concerned. However, reading the

---

17. J. L. Mays, *The Lord Reigns* (Louisville: Westminster John Knox, 1994), pp. 124–125.
18. For a critique of the canonical approach to the psalms, see R. N. Whybray, *Reading the Psalms as a Book*, JSOTSup 222 (Sheffield: JSOT Press, 1996); and for a response to his criticisms of the method, see Grant, *King as Exemplar*, pp. 11–19, and David Howard's review of Whybray's book at <www.bookreviews.org/pdf/2475_1563.pdf>, accessed 22 Jan. 2008.
19. Wilson, *Editing*, p. 199.

psalms as a book means that, as with every book, passages fall within a context. Why are Psalms 1 and 2 the only psalms without a superscription in Books 1–3 of the psalter? Probably because Psalms 1 and 2 were meant to be read and understood together – as a joint introduction to the book of Psalms, an introduction that focuses on choosing a way of *Torah*-based devotion to Yahweh and absolute submission to his lordship. However, this double message is heard clearly only when we read these psalms in their canonical context.

Increasingly, scholars are becoming aware of the importance of context even within gathered, anthological books like the Psalms or Proverbs. Not that psalms cease to function as individual units for interpretative purposes; rather, it is that their context (the placement of any particular psalm within the psalter) impinges upon the interpretation of that individual unit.[20] It can therefore be argued that individual compositions within the psalter have limited interpretative autonomy: each is a literary unit in its own right (akin to any pericope within a narrative text), but the meaning found in each unit is often nuanced or influenced by its near neighbours or the collection within which it is found. To read and understand a psalm properly, we must be aware of its setting within any subcollection of which it may be a part, within its book and, indeed, within the whole psalter. We should pay particular attention to psalms that open or close books or that are central to a book.[21] Psalms are associated – resulting in an interpretative context – by way of their superscriptions (e.g. the Songs of Ascent again) or their opening/closing lines (e.g. the hallelujah commands found in Pss 111 – 117 or 146 – 150) or by theme (e.g. the 'Yahweh reigns' psalms, Pss 93 – 99). So, the position of a psalm within the psalter impacts how we read that poem.[22]

Method in discerning editorial context

Once it is established that editorial hands have in some sense shaped the poetic books, a secondary question must follow: '*How* can we discern the editorial shaping apparent in the Psalms and wisdom literature?' The basic thesis argued

---

20. R. E. Murphy, 'Reflections on Contextual Interpretations of the Psalms', in J. C. McCann (ed.), *The Shape and Shaping of the Psalter*, JSOTSup 159 (Sheffield: JSOT Press, 1993), pp. 21–28.

21. N. L. deClaissé-Walford, 'The Canonical Shape of the Psalms', in H. W. Ballard and W. D. Tucker (eds.), *An Introduction to Wisdom Literature and the Psalms: Festschrift for Marvin E. Tate* (Macon: Mercer University Press, 2000), pp. 93–110.

22. J. L. Mays, 'The Question of Context in Psalm Interpretation', in McCann, *Shape and Shaping*, pp. 14–20.

above is that editors have provided us, as readers, with a context for the interpretation of individual poems, proverbs, sayings and instructions. This context
inevitably influences our understanding of these individual literary units, so
how can we discern these frameworks for interpretation in the poetic books?

Continuing with the Psalms as our primary example, the foundational tenet
of a canonical approach to the psalter is that the ordering and placement of
the psalms is not entirely random, but that the book of Psalms has been
shaped by the work of editors in order to impact our understanding of individual poems. In order to discern editorial activity legitimately in the psalter,
ground rules have to be applied to prevent the misuse of the canonical
approach and its decline into rampant subjectivity. Gerald Wilson, as well as
being one of the originators of this method, also championed correct and
clearly defined methodology. Having highlighted the pitfalls of approaching
the psalter with a preconceived notion of the editorial themes to be found in
the book and then 'finding' psalms that fit this theory, he stated:

> My own preference is to work without a hypothesis . . . and to allow any sense of the
> structure that develops to derive from an intensive and thorough analysis of the
> psalms in question in terms of their linguistic, thematic, literary and theological links
> and relationships.[23]

Wilson suggests that editorial themes can be discerned from 'linguistic, thematic, literary and theological links and relationships' observed between
psalms. Psalms are linked in order to paint a fuller picture than is seen in their
individual parts. Content in context takes on a slightly different meaning. The
idea is that the theological concerns of the editors of the psalter's final form
are seen in the way in which they link psalms and also in their placement of
these psalms at key junctures throughout the psalter.

David Howard also provides helpful comment on canonical methodology
applied to the book of Psalms. His approach focuses on four areas of linking
that show concatenation between individual psalms or groups of psalms:
lexical, thematic, structural and genre connections.[24] Howard breaks these categories down further. Regarding lexical links we should look in particular for
'key-word' (*Leitwort*) links where the same word or phrase is repeated and for

---

23. G. H. Wilson, 'Understanding the Purposeful Arrangement of the Psalms: Pitfalls
and Promise', in McCann, *Shape and Shaping*, p. 48.

24. D. M. Howard, *The Structure of Psalms 93–100*, Biblical and Judaic Studies / University
of California, San Diego 5 (Winona Lake: Eisenbrauns, 1997), pp. 99–100.

thematic word links where the same concept is expressed using different words. Incidental links non-essential to both psalms may also appear, so we should be careful not to read too much into the repetition of the commonest of words. Thematic links are seen via lexical repetition and more generally linked concepts, or even in echoes and responses between psalms. For example, a question asked in one psalm may be answered in the following one (e.g. could 'The LORD is my Shepherd, I shall not be in want,' in Ps. 23:1 be a response to 'My God, my God, why have you forsaken me?' from Ps. 22:1?[25]), or a theme may be expanded upon throughout a chain of psalms (e.g. the *YHWH malak* psalms, Pss 93 – 99). Howard sees structural links as being particularly helpful when dealing with a group of psalms within the larger structure of the psalter and I discuss this further below. Both Wilson and Howard see genre as being of only limited importance as a tool for deriving thematic association between psalms; it can highlight certain interesting indicators (e.g. the possible transition between groups of psalms[26]), but it seems unlikely that the redactors of the psalter extensively used genre classification as an organizational tool: content, including the superscriptions, rather than type seems to have directed the editorial placement of the psalms.

There may be a certain degree of overlap in these categories. For example, thematic links often become apparent through the observation of lexical concatenation. Or, the use of the same word in consecutive psalms may indicate a structural connection as well as simple lexical linkage (e.g. the repetition of *'ašrê*, 'blessed', in Pss 1 and 2 forms a structural link, an inclusio, that goes beyond the simple repetition of words in successive psalms). However, these ground rules provide a reasonable framework within which the canonical approach can function. Seeking out such indicators of concatenation can help to define more clearly a context for the interpretation of individual psalms.

Collections, superscriptions and editorial context
As well as the indications of deliberate editorial association mentioned above, collections indicated by superscriptions are particularly significant for

---

25. Further discussion of the collection in which these psalms are found follows below in the section of worked examples. Unless stated otherwise, all Bible quotations in this chapter are from the NIV.

26. See Hossfeld and Zenger's discussion of 'corner psalms' (*Eckpsalmen*) and central psalms within a collection that, they suggest, may be marked by differences in genre from the surrounding psalms (F.-L. Hossfeld and E. Zenger, *Die Psalmen I*, NEchtB [Würzburg: Echter, 1993], p. 12).

discerning context. Obviously, lexical and thematic repetition is an essential feature indicating the deliberate association of juxtaposed psalms: where there is no repetition of words, ideas and motifs the reader makes no connection between neighbouring psalms.[27] However, an element of subjectivity in charting keyword links remains. Where does concatenation come to an end? Where did it begin? Sometimes linked groups of psalms have a clear beginning and end, but often this linking is more difficult to define. Book 1, for example, is so dominated by Davidic laments that it is difficult to define groupings within that broader collection.

It seems that if a proper definition of psalm groupings is key to the canonical approach to the study of the psalter, then the method of delimiting groups of psalms needs to be expressed clearly. Concatenation via linking techniques is not always sufficient to define a psalm grouping, so the reader should also look for indicators of editorial division, separation of groups of psalms from their broader setting. The whole idea of a psalm grouping implies *both* a conjunctive and a disjunctive literary function. On the one hand, the idea of a 'psalm grouping' implies a degree of connection between the psalms within that grouping and, logically, it in turn implies a degree of separation from the other neighbouring psalms that are *not* part of the grouping.[28]

Take the Songs of Ascent, Psalms 120 – 134, for example. How does this grouping impact Book 5 of the psalter? Clearly, they comprise a grouping, indicated, as is often the case, primarily by their superscription. Each of these fifteen psalms beings with the words *šîr hammaʿălôt*, 'A Song of Ascents', and there is evidence both from the psalms themselves and from extra-biblical material that these psalms were used in the temple during one of the great pilgrimage festivals. So there is good reason to see these psalms as a grouping, and, therefore, the editorial context for the interpretation of any one of these psalms is found within the collection – the emphases of the grouping shapes our understanding of each individual composition. What, therefore, are the implications for the rest of Book 5?

The conjunctive aspect of this collection provides a clear context for the interpretation of these psalms, but the disjunctive aspect also gives us indicators as to how we should read the psalms around about contextually. Psalms 119 and 135 are clearly not part of the Songs of Ascent; therefore, they fall within a different context. This leads us in turn to question the contextual

---

27. Howard, *Structure*, pp. 100–102; Wilson, *Editing*, pp. 182–197; Wilson, 'Understanding', p. 48; Mays, 'Question of Context', pp. 16–17.

28. Wilson, *Editing*, p. 199.

setting for these compositions. Looking for indicators of other groupings within Book 5, we see that Psalms 111 – 117 form a canonical collection because each of them either begins or ends with the hallelujah command (except Ps. 114, but it is possible that the hallelujah postscript to Ps. 113 was originally the superscript for Ps. 114). This clearly defined collection leaves Psalms 118 – 119 as a pairing designed to be read together, as evidenced by the lexical and thematic overlap in these psalms.[29] On the other side of the Songs of Ascent collection we see a group of Davidic psalms from 138 to 145, leaving the context for Psalm 135 to be found in relationship with Psalms 136 and 137.[30]

So we can see that collections are often marked by a common superscription or first line and that these collections help us to define the context for the interpretation of individual poems. Although the psalms within the collection are linked, at the same time they delimit the extent of the association and help us to see connections perhaps not otherwise immediately obvious.

The question of significant placement

Having outlined some of the principles for establishing context by way of lexical and thematic association, and having discussed the impact of collections on our reading of the text, it would probably be helpful to examine the question of significant placement within the psalter. Just what makes the placement of a psalm or a group of psalms particularly telling from an editorial perspective? At its most basic level the answer to that question is quite simple: we should pay particular attention to psalms or groups of psalms placed at the beginning, middle or end of one of the books of the psalter.

One of Wilson's observations on the editorial shaping of the psalter was to note the importance of the so-called 'seam' psalms, which come at the beginning and end of the five books of the psalter.[31] These positions have an obvious significance for our understanding of the thematic emphases the editors seek to highlight for the readers of the Psalms. The opening thoughts of a book, in a natural manner, set the tone for what follows, and it has been observed that the psalms that close the book divisions of the psalter often appear deliberately to echo the initial compositions.[32] Therefore, we should pay particular attention to the *beginning* and *end* of books as we seek to discern

---

29. Grant, *King as Exemplar*, pp. 175–180.

30. J. L. Mays, *Psalms*, Interpretation (Louisville: John Knox, 1994), p. 422.

31. Wilson, *Editing*, pp. 207–208.

32. N. L. deClaissé-Walford, *Reading from the Beginning: The Shaping of the Hebrew Psalter* (Macon: Mercer University Press, 1997), pp. 55–56.

editorial emphases. Furthermore, *centrality* within a book of the psalter is also considered to be significant. Zenger, referring to the placement of Psalm 119 in Book 5, states:

> According to the theological perspective of the fifth book of psalms which has the Torah Psalm 119 *intentionally placed in the middle of the composition*, the psalms are a means of opening oneself to the living Torah of YHWH – in accordance with the programme at the beginning of the Psalter, Psalms 1–2, and in accordance with the closing Hallel, Psalms 146–150, which interprets the recitation/signing of psalms as the actualization of the way of life (Torah) instilled in the cosmos.[33]

So, centrality within the respective books of the psalter also seems to be of importance in defining the points the editors of the psalter desired to stress. It may be that there is a single, central psalm that clearly lies at the very heart of one of the books (e.g. Ps. 119 in Book 5), and in other examples it appears to be a central collection (e.g. the Pss 15 – 24 collection in Book 1). However, the beginning, middle and end of the five books of Psalms should draw our attention, as these, in particular, seem to be the focus of editorial attention. It is, therefore, important to discern carefully what is being said both at the outset and the close of the five books of the psalter and also see if there is a central text or group of psalms. What is the thematic emphasis of the individual compositions or groups of psalms that lie in these positions? How might these themes shape our understanding of the book in which they are found or the psalter as a whole?

Some worked examples

As is our desire in this volume, it is appropriate to examine a few worked examples in order to give a fuller understanding of how this relatively new literary approach impacts the interpretation of individual poetic texts.

Psalms 1 – 2

Psalm 1 is a literary unit. Despite claims that Psalms 1 and 2 were once a single composition, Psalm 1 is a composition in its own right.[34] Brownlee, as others before him, suggests that the first two psalms of the psalter were originally a

---

33. E. Zenger, 'The Composition and Theology of the Fifth Book of the Psalter', *JSOT* 80 (1998), p. 102 (his emphasis).

34. Cf. W. H. Brownlee, 'Psalms 1–2 as a Coronation Liturgy', *Bib* 52.3 (1971), pp. 321–336, with J. T. Willis, 'Psalm 1 – an Entity', *ZAW* 91.3 (1979), pp. 381–401.

single composition. He comes to this conclusion having noted both early rabbinic association of the two psalms and the preponderance of lexical repetitions in Psalms 1 and 2. Willis, on the other hand, examines the inner strophic
structure of Psalm 1 and infers, correctly, that it is an entity in its own right.
This debate, which precedes the development of a canonical approach to the
biblical text, illustrates the value the method brings. Brownlee notices the
strong association between these neighbouring psalms and desires to draw out
the influence one text has on the reading of the other. In pre-Childs days, he
does this by suggesting that they were, in fact, at one point a single composition with a common *Sitz im Leben*. Willis, however, argues from structure that
Psalm 1 is a coherent whole and, therefore, must be seen in some way as separate from Psalm 2.

It seems most likely that Psalm 1 was originally written to be read as a psalm
in its own right. However, its placement alongside Psalm 2 (with all of the word
links, the Ps. 1:1/2:12 inclusio etc.) puts the poem very consciously into an
interpretative context. The two psalms are each individual compositions, but
their juxtaposition undoubtedly means that they are meant to be read in the
light of each other. They are autonomous texts, just like any other pericope,
but their interpretation is shaped by their context. So, although the two psalms
were never a single composition, they are each meant to be read and understood in the light of the other. Therefore, Psalm 1 speaks a message to today's
reader – a message about the avoidance of evil, the practice of the means of
grace, the blessings of being in right relationship with the living God and the
fact that life boils down to lifestyle choices. This is Psalm 1's message.
However, the editorial association with Psalm 2 provides each poem with a
context for their interpretation. So we should read and understand Psalm 1 in
the light of Psalm 2 and vice versa.

> The two psalms together call for a piety composed of obedience and trust that is
> fostered by the entire book. Delight in the torah and taking refuge in the Lord
> constitute the faith nurtured by the psalms. The psalms offer a 'way' and a 'refuge'
> in the midst of the wickedness and power of the world.[35]

So we have a dual message at the start of the psalter. Psalm 1 focuses our
attention on how to walk in the way of Yahweh. Psalm 2 points to Yahweh's
sovereign rule in every circumstance, encouraging the reader to take refuge in
his absolute authority. Contextually, these messages combine: walk in the ways

---

35. Mays, *Lord Reigns*, pp. 122–123.

of Yahweh, always remembering that he rules regardless of how circumstances may appear. This is the basic idea of the canonical reading of the psalms – the sum of the whole presents a message greater than the individual voice of the component parts.

Psalms 15 – 24

The consideration of Psalms 1 and 2 provides us with some illustration of how the canonical approach to poetic texts works. However, in order to see the full ramifications of this method (its 'cash value', if you like) we must also consider how the canonical method impacts larger collections of psalms within the book as a whole. The chiastic ordering of Psalms 15 – 24 is mentioned above and this collection provides a good foil to illustrate some of the more detailed workings of the canonical approach to anthological poetry. I have already mentioned some of the factors that link the psalms in this group. However, we must also consider the disjunctive functions at work in this psalm grouping: that is, how is this group of psalms distinct from its surroundings? It seems reasonable to expect that both of these characteristics should be present if we are to describe a set of juxtaposed psalms as a psalm grouping.

Pierre Auffret and Patrick Miller have pointed out that Psalms 15 – 24 constitute a collection of psalms arranged in a chiastic or envelope pattern.[36] They explain the interesting parallels of content between these psalms and suggest that this was actually an independent collection that was, at some later point, included as part of Book 1 of the psalter. Psalms 15 and 24 are both entrance Psalms, which discuss issues of righteousness and entrance into God's presence in worship – these two psalms demarcate the beginning and end of this psalm grouping. Psalms 16 and 23 are both psalms of comfort, which celebrate Yahweh's protection in the face of danger. Psalms 17 and 22 are both psalms of lament, which express the depths of despair and anxiety felt by the psalmist. Psalms 18 and 20 – 21 (many commentators highlight the close association between Psalms 20 and 21[37]) are royal psalms. What is more, they all appear to

---

36. P. Auffret, *La Sagesse a bâti sa maison: Études de structures littéraires dans l'Ancient Testament et spécialement dans les psaumes*, OBO 49 (Fribourg: Editions Universitaires, 1982), pp. 407–438; Miller, 'Kingship', pp. 127–142.

37. See e.g. Mays, *Psalms*, p. 90; J. C. McCann, 'The Book of Psalms: Introduction, Commentary and Reflections', in *NIB* 4: 757; H.-J. Kraus, *Psalms 1–59: A Commentary*, tr. H. C. Oswald (Minneapolis: Augsburg, 1988), p. 281. Older commentaries have also drawn attention to the links between these two psalms; e.g. A. F. Kirkpatrick, *The Book of Psalms* (Cambridge: Cambridge University Press, 1910), p. 106.

be kingship psalms connected with Yahweh's deliverance of his 'anointed one' in the context of battle. Psalm 19 is the central psalm in this chiastic pattern, a Torah psalm, and both Auffret and Miller suggest this indicates the thematic centrality of the Torah of Yahweh within this small collection.[38]

Thanks to this chiastic structure, Psalms 15 – 24 exhibit both conjunctive and disjunctive functions. The pairing of psalms at corresponding points from the outer markers to the focal point links the grouping internally. The entrance psalms bookend and thus set the limits of this subgroup, delimiting its boundaries by use of inclusio. An inclusio, by definition, indicates disjunctive function as well as conjunctive. The compositions on either side of the boundaries set by the inclusio are automatically understood to lie beyond the collection. So it is the combination of conjunctive links within a collection and disjunctive boundary markers that indicates the identity and extent of groups of psalms. The corresponding implications are clear. Psalm 16 should be read within the interpretative context of Psalms 15 – 24, but Psalm 14 finds its context outside that collection.

So how does the context of this grouping impact the interpretation of the individual compositions? First, the whole collection is framed in a Davidic setting by way of the superscriptions found throughout the grouping. This royal backdrop itself has implications for the interpretation of the individual psalms. Many of the psalms in the psalter probably originally found their setting in the royal court and were somehow connected to the king.[39] Over the years these psalms have been democtratized, removing the explicitly royal emphases and making them universally applicable to all believers. However, the king in the ANE was thought to have special rights of access to the deity. The king, as one of Yahweh's anointed ones, was an intermediary between God and the people, and was thus the visible vehicle of Yahweh's rule on earth. Yet here in Psalms 15 – 24, we see 'David' subject to the same conditions of access as any other temple-goer; we see him delight in divine comfort rather than the comforts of office; we hear his cries of dereliction, his prayers to Yahweh and his delight in God's Word. The king is the archetypal believer, an example for all others (or at least was meant to be).[40] The encouragement of

---

38. Auffret, *La Sagesse*, pp. 407–438; Miller, 'Kingship', p. 127.

39. See J. H. Eaton, *Kingship and the Psalms*, 2nd ed., SBT 32 (London: SCM, 1986); and J. A. Grant, 'The Psalms and the King', in P. S. Johnston and D. G. Firth (eds.), *Interpreting the Psalms: Issues and Approaches* (Leicester: Apollos, 2005), pp. 101–118, for further discussion.

40. This seems to be the implied emphasis of the kingship law (Deut. 17:14–20).

the royal background to these psalms is that every believer has the same access rights to Yahweh's throne and draws near under exactly the same conditions as the king himself. The democratization of the psalms humbles the royal figure and elevates the humble believer.[41]

There are other implications from a contextual reading. The bookends emphasize the holiness of God and what an awesome thing it is to have access into his presence. Therefore, they place the following discussion of the ups and downs of the life of faith in the context of an expectation of uprightness of character. The believing reader is reminded of the personal identity that should always mark the pursuit of Yahweh. This message is further emphasized by the centrality of the Torah in Psalm 19. So a lifestyle marked by holiness, devotion to the Torah and dependence on Yahweh is underlined at the beginning, end and pivot of this collection.

Other influences of a contextual reading include the movement we can chart from comfort (16) to lament (17) to prayerful dependence (18). There is rest and joy to be found in Yahweh, but that does not deny the reality of the ups and downs of life – even life with the Lord. So there is movement from joy in relationship with Yahweh to honest prayer in the face of difficulty to a reminder of the importance of prayer and of Yahweh's deliverance in response to prayer. This trajectory is, perhaps, even more poignant on the other side of the chiasm, where the reminder of the importance of prayer (20 – 21) is followed by bitter lament (22), which, in turn, is met with a reminder of the comfort to be found in Yahweh (23). This collection contains all of the rhythms of spiritual life and we are reminded of the movements between those spiritual and life experiences. Sometimes we transition from good place to hard one and are reminded also of the transition back again. The psalms of comfort should never be voiced to the exclusion of the laments, but equally the voice of complaint should never outweigh the reality of comfort, even if we do not feel it at a given moment.

Reading contextually means we read differently, and means we see more. The reader asks questions of the text that bring new light to the understanding of the particular poem.

Editorial shaping in Proverbs and Ecclesiastes

Many of the issues discussed above regarding the Psalms apply equally to the book of Proverbs. Obviously, the books of Job, Song of Songs and Lamentations, although written mainly in poetic form, are slightly different

41. Grant, 'Psalms and King', pp. 116–118.

from the Psalms in as much as they follow a fairly cohesive 'narrative' structure. Therefore, unlike the Psalms, their context has always been fairly readily discernible. However, Proverbs and Ecclesiastes are also made up of gathered poetic material, where questions of context, broadly speaking, were thought not to apply. In recent years, and in a manner somewhat analogous to the studies we have seen on the Psalms, several works have drawn attention to signs of editorial organization in Proverbs and Ecclesiastes also.

Proverbs

The problem of interpreting Proverbs, especially the main section of 'classical' two-line proverbs (Prov. 10 – 29), is well stated by Van Leeuwen:

> In these chapters we find discrete, entirely self-sufficient literary units . . . which are extremely terse in formulation and brief in compass . . . One is acutely aware that the briefer the literary unit the more difficult the interpretation. The problem is further complicated because the juxtaposed proverbs, to the modern, western mind at least, often appear to have very little to do with one another either formally or materially.[42]

Obviously, the individual proverbs of Proverbs 10 – 29 are even briefer literary units than those found in the psalms. Proverbs 1 – 9 and 30 – 31 contain longer groupings of proverbial statements (called 'instructions'), which provide a much clearer context for the interpretation of the individual proverb. However, chapters 10 – 29 consist of verse after verse of individual proverbial statements without obvious flow, progression of thought or context. The collections appear at first glance to be random, and for many years scholars assumed there was no purposeful ordering in this section.

The works of Ray Van Leeuwen, Knut Heim and others go a long way to dispelling the myth of the random collection of proverbs in the book of Proverbs. In a similar manner to the discussion of context in the psalms I have charted above, Heim argues that the proverbs in Proverbs 10 – 29 'have intentionally been arranged into small proverbial clusters to provide a context for interpretation, so that – taken together – they mean more than the sum of their individual parts'.[43] Proverbs as individual sayings have great power but, when

---

42. R. C. Van Leeuwen, *Context and Meaning in Proverbs 25–27*, SBLDS 96 (Atlanta: Scholars Press, 1988), p. 2.

43. K. M. Heim, *Like Grapes of Gold Set in Silver: An Interpretation of Proverbial Clusters in Proverbs 10:1–22:16*, BZAW 273 (Berlin: de Gruyter, 2001), p. 2.

taken out of context, these aphorisms can be abused or misused.[44] Therefore, it is important to remember from our perspective as readers of proverbial literature that meaning 'is always meaning-in-context'.[45]

Once again, from our perspective as those who seek to apply this new awareness of literary influence to the reality of reading and understanding the Bible, the most salient question is, 'How do we define these contextual clusters?'

Van Leeuwen observes that the communicative power of proverbs is effected through a process of 'accretion'. That is, each proverb is a basic building block and the overall message of the sage/editor is found in the addition of proverbial statements each upon the next to communicate a fuller message.[46] So proverbial statements *combine* to give this fuller meaning to each individual saying.[47] The definition of these 'proverb poems' is based on structural, poetic and semantic indicators. Structurally, Van Leeuwen points out that, although individual sayings and admonitions have a 'relative self-sufficiency' in their own right,[48] each proverb is in fact a 'paradigmatic building block' used by the author or editor to create larger poetic units.[49] So, from the perspective of poetics, it is clear that individual proverbial sayings

---

44. To this end, Bartholomew comments, 'Separated from their context in Proverbs, the sentences are more open to having different views read into them, and this can be dangerous. A proverb a day . . . may not always be helpful! . . . Recent decades have seen a series of studies showing that the proverbial sayings in Proverbs 10–31 are not context-less, as earlier scholars suggested, but that there are many signs of intertextual connections and careful editing of sections at least' (C. G. Bartholomew, *Reading Proverbs with Integrity* [Cambridge: Grove, 2001], pp. 5–6).

45. Heim, *Grapes of Gold*, p. 24.

46. Van Leeuwen, *Context and Meaning*, pp. 34–37.

47. Van Leeuwen, like Heim and the canonical-psalms scholars, suggests we gain something from contextual interpretation: 'In the combination and arrangement of these forms we may find that the meaning of the whole is more than the sum of its parts' (ibid., p. 37).

48. Ibid., p. 41.

49. Van Leeuwen, developing the ideas of Dundes, suggests that one of the main structural indicators to look out for is the idea of a Topic (T) followed by Comment (C) (*Context and Meaning*, pp. 47–51). This notion suggests that any given topic (e.g. money, speech, justice etc.) may be introduced in any given proverb and then commented upon in various ways throughout a string of proverbs until a new topic is introduced. (For more on Dundes's structuralist work, see his chapters 'On

are juxtaposed in such a way as to create proverb poems that, in turn, impact our interpretation of the individual sayings. So contiguous units within a broader poem provide 'commentary' on one another, and in doing so supply the reader with a context. At the word level, Van Leeuwen points out that the frequent repetition of similar words or concepts within juxtaposed proverbial statements indicates continuity and therefore context.[50] The beginning of a new topic (and ensuing comment) marks the next contextual poem for interpretative purposes.

Heim develops these observations in more detail, providing thorough criteria for the delimitation of editorial groupings within the book of Proverbs. He suggests that 'clusters' of proverbs are not to be discerned by observing clear beginning and end points of units, which can be hard to observe in the text, but by looking for formal links that associate proverbial sayings. So, the reader should watch out for the repetition of synonyms, word roots, sounds, consonants (etc.) in these clusters of proverbs. Heim argues that the movement between clusters is not marked by verses that clearly conclude a particular chain of proverbs. Rather, we should look out for a change in the linking device that bonds proverbs into groups (e.g. the movement from a speech-dominated cluster in Prov. 11:9–14 to a commerce-focused one in 11:15–21).[51]

> The primary criteria for the delimitation of proverbial clusters are consequently not boundary markers, as commonly thought, but linking devices (the 'twiglets' in the grape analogy). The focus should not be on what divides or separates groups from their environment, but on features which link and combine sayings into organic units. The most fundamental such device, of course, is repetition – repetition of sound and sense: consonants, word roots, words, synonyms, etc. The present study will make full use of the gamut of textual features that have previously been used for the delimitation of editorial groups, most of which focus on different kinds of repetition . . .[52]

Footnote 49 (*continued*)

the Structure of the Proverb' and 'Towards a Structural Definition of the Riddle', in *Analytical Essays in Folklore* [Paris: Mouton, 1975]. This work has also been picked up and adapted in biblical studies by Carole Fontaine in her *Traditional Sayings in the Old Testament: A Contextual Study* [Sheffield: Almond, 1982].)

50. Van Leeuwen, *Context and Meaning*, pp. 40–55.

51. Heim, *Grapes of Gold*, pp. 105–108.

52. Ibid., pp. 106–107.

So, once again, we see a growing trend to look for context for poetic texts within the OT's poetic anthologies. The placement of proverbs into poems and collections and then into a book automatically provides a context, and that context inevitably impacts interpretation.[53]

Ecclesiastes

Although it has not received the same degree of attention, a similar phenomenon can be traced in the study of Ecclesiastes. Until relatively recently Ecclesiastes has been viewed as the random thoughts of an unorthodox or disaffected sage. However, several recent studies have focused on the narrative flow that can be traced throughout the book and how this influences the interpretation of the (often confusing) individual poems, proverbial groups and other pericopes. Michael Fox has argued for the presence of a narrator in the text of Ecclesiastes who is seen in the introduction (1:2), conclusion (12:8) and at intervals throughout the text (7:27). Recognizing this, we are immediately drawn into material of a different type. These are not just the meanderings of a wisdom teacher. Rather, a story is being told by an author *about* the experiences, reflections and teachings of a sage called Qoheleth.[54] Now this is not narrative of the same type found in the historical books, but it is still story. Others have also picked up on the significance of the narrator for our understanding of the book as a whole.[55] Christianson focuses on the literary effect of framing a text with the words of a *narrator* (and the interplay of voices that follows) and also on the sequential *storyline* of Ecclesiastes. The effect of these two features is to provide context for the understanding of the poems and proverbs found throughout the book. Fox elaborates by pointing to the levels of narrativity in Ecclesiastes. Effectively, we read a story presented to the reader by a narrator who tells us about 'Qoheleth-the-reporter' (1:12 – 6:12), who reflects on his own experimental experiences and from the perspective of his now advanced years and 'Qoheleth-the-observer' (7:1 – 12:7), who undertook to investigate the central questions of the book reflectively.[56] Fox argues

---

53. We shall examine an example of the impact of contextual interpretation on a proverbial cluster below. For a critique of the canonical approach to Proverbs, see T. Longman III, *Proverbs*, BCOTWP (Grand Rapids: Baker, 2006), pp. 38–39.

54. M. V. Fox, *A Time to Tear Down and a Time to Build Up: A Rereading of Ecclesiastes* (Grand Rapids: Eerdmans, 1999), pp. 363–377.

55. See e.g. E. S. Christianson, *A Time to Tell: Narrative Strategies in Ecclesiastes*, JSOTSup 280 (Sheffield: Sheffield Academic Press, 1998).

56. Fox, *Time to Tear Down*, pp. 366–367.

that the postscript in Ecclesiastes 12:9–14 falls outside that framework, but it could equally well be read as the concluding voice of the narrator who introduces Qoheleth's thought in 1:1–11. The implications of these reading strategies from the perspective of poetics is that, again, we are given an interpretative context for understanding the layers of poetry within Ecclesiastes.

Worked examples from Proverbs and Ecclesiastes

Once again, we need to see something of the cash value of these approaches. Taking contextual awareness in the book of Proverbs first, how can awareness of proverbial clusters impact interpretation?

Proverbs 11

Heim suggests that Proverbs 11:1–14 forms a proverbial cluster, with 11:1 set apart somewhat from the verses that follow.[57] Proverbs 11:1 ('The LORD abhors dishonest scales, / but accurate weights are his delight'), therefore, provides the reader with an overarching 'Thought' (Yahweh loves trade justice and hates exploitation), followed by 'Comment' in the following verses. Heim's idea of co-referentiality[58] means this basic idea can be seen as influencing the interpretation of all that follows in the cluster: 'As such, the evaluation of characters and actions in the surrounding material is linked to the Lord's standards.'[59] So how does this contextual influence pan out in reality? In 11:2 'arrogance' and 'humility' are therefore paralleled with the divine standards of verse 1, as are 'integrity' and 'deceit' in verse 3. Exploitative behaviour (11:1) is a manifestation of an 'arrogance' (11:2) that places self-interest above equity towards others. Such behaviour ultimately will lead to 'disgrace' and 'destruction', whereas the 'humble' are 'guided' by the 'wisdom' of Yahweh's way. The value of contextual interpretation comes very clearly to the fore when we read Proverbs 11:4:

> Wealth is worthless in the day of wrath,
>   but righteousness delivers from death.

---

57. Heim, *Grapes of Gold*, pp. 134–137.
58. His suggestion is that a continuity of assessment may be applied even when there is an explicit change in the identity of the subject under discussion (e.g. the text moves from discussion of the 'fool' to discussion of the 'arrogant'). This change of subject does not necessarily imply a change of pericope (see e.g. ibid., pp. 81–82 and *passim*).
59. Ibid., p. 138.

This verse treated as an individual aphorism could mean no more than 'You can't take it with you.' However, contextually the verse takes on a slightly different hue. Whereas 'wealth' in the wisdom literature is morally neutral (and sometimes seen as one of several 'visible' affirmations of a wise lifestyle), in the context of this cluster we are probably meant to understand the type of wealth under discussion as wealth illegitimately gained. What is more, the contextual implication may be that the pursuit of such wealth will precipitate the 'day of wrath' more speedily, whereas those who reject ill-gotten gain are delivered from such temporal judgment. So, we see that a contextual interpretation of this verse offers the reader a fuller understanding than taking the proverb as an individual, contextless statement. The interpretative effects of this 'Thought' continue throughout this cluster until a new 'Thought' (questions of character in the business world) begins in 11:15. So we see that the placement of a proverb within a cluster impacts how we read it.

Ecclesiastes 1, 12

Awareness of the canonical structure of Ecclesiastes helps with understanding some of the big interpretative questions of the text. For example, dealing with the contradictions in the book of Ecclesiastes has presented problems for interpreters, both Jewish and Christian, throughout many generations.[60] However, a canonical awareness of the relationship between the narrator and the literary subject of the book, Qoheleth, enhances the reader's understanding of some of the complexities of the text.[61] The narrator's poem in Ecclesiastes 1:3–11 gives a foretaste of Qoheleth's reflections. Normally, the

---

60. See C. G. Bartholomew, *Reading Ecclesiastes: Old Testament Exegesis and Hermeneutical Theory*, AnBib 139 (Rome: Pontifical Bible Institute, 1998).

61. Of course, the textual identification of the narrator's voice and Qoheleth's does not deny the fact that the whole of Ecclesiastes may have been written by a single author. Fox suggests that 'The epologist speaks as "teller of a tale" who is telling about Qohelet by quoting his teachings. In my view, the words of Qohelet (1:3–12:7), the title (1:1), the motto (1:2; 12:8), and the epilogue proper (12:9–12) are all the creation of the same person, the author of the book, who is not to be identified with Qohelet, his persona. In other words, it is not that the epilogue is by Qohelet, but that Qohelet is "by" the epologist' (*Time to Tear Down*, p. 365). The true identity of the author(s) of Ecclesiastes and whether or not author and Qoheleth are, in fact, the same person are irrelevant to canonical analysis. In reading the final form of the book, we meet a narrator who presents the teachings of a wisdom teacher known as Qoheleth. This presentation of reality in the book

wisdom poems of the OT poetic texts provide balance and perspective amid the complexities of experiential reflection on the meaning of life and the true nature of wisdom.[62] Of course, the narrator's presentation of the Teacher's poem in Ecclesiastes 1 gives advanced warning that we should expect something quite different from this wisdom book.[63] The wisdom poem does not celebrate the rhythms of the created order but presents them as wearisome, grinding and somehow futile. What is more, Qoheleth's poem even anticipates and responds to possible counter-arguments (Eccl. 1:10), giving this passage 'a peculiarly argumentative or forensic quality of a sort unusual in Biblical literature'.[64] So, from a canonical perspective, how does the narrator's use of Qoheleth's wisdom poem at the start of the book impact interpret--ation? The effect is one of forewarning! The reader should not expect an easy journey through Qoheleth – here is an author who will take the familiar and make it seem foreign, an author who will challenge paradigms and force the reader to grapple with uncomfortable thoughts. So a canonical reading of Ecclesiastes starts us off with a third party's analysis and summary of Qoheleth's thought that warns us to expect the unexpected. While this does not necessarily make it easier to understand the ensuing contradictions of the book, they should not surprise us, for, canonically speaking, we have been warned!

Footnote 61 (*continued*)

> of Ecclesiastes has an effect on our reading and interpretation of the text as a whole. We read the prologue *as if* a third party were presenting the words of the Teacher. From the literary perspective, the self-presentation of the text means that we read the frame narrator as preparing the reader for the challenging words of Qoheleth, regardless of the fact that 'frame narrator' and 'Qoheleth' may be the same 'author'.

62. See e.g. Job 28, which provides a much-needed lacuna in the cut and thrust of debate in the speech cycles of the book of Job. The reader is drawn into the debate of chapters 4–27, and is left reeling by the complexity of the arguments and counter-arguments of Job and his friends. 'Who is right? Whose wisdom is true wisdom?' The wisdom poem of Job 28 provides a break in the argument and focuses the mind of the reader on the essential nature of wisdom as revealed by the Creator God. See A. Lo, *Job 28 as Rhetoric: An Analysis of Job 28 in the Context of Job 22–31*, VTSup 97 (Leiden: Brill, 2003).

63. Longman writes, 'The function of the prologue . . . is to set the mood for what is to follow' (*The Book of Ecclesiastes*, NICOT [Grand Rapids: Eerdmans, 1998], p. 59).

64. Fox, *Time to Tear Down*, p. 169.

However, the narrator does not stop with introduction; his voice is heard in the conclusion of Ecclesiastes as well.[65] Once again, a canonical reading of this book has important implications for interpretation. Just as the prologue warns the reader to expect a challenge from Qoheleth, so the epilogue (Eccl. 12:9–14) cautions the reader not to write the Teacher off as a maverick whom we can safely ignore. The prologue warns us of the coming challenge. We are told to brace ourselves for some difficult stuff. The core content of Ecclesiastes is every bit as difficult as the narrator's introductory summary implies, and so, quite naturally, the reader may be tempted to ignore the wisdom of Qoheleth as unrepresentative and somehow random: 'Why should we listen to the meanderings of one so disaffected and difficult to understand? He says one thing, but then contradicts himself? He seems to stand against the wisdom traditions we know and love . . . so why listen to him at all?'

'Not so fast!', responds the narrator. Let me close by telling you a little bit about this 'Wisdom Cowboy'. He is the one who has 'imparted knowledge to the people. He pondered and searched out and set in order many proverbs. The Teacher searched to find just the right words, and what he wrote was upright and true' (Eccl. 12:9–10). The canonical message of the epilogue is to affirm the 'orthodoxy' of Qoheleth's teaching. The narrator will not let the reader marginalize Qoheleth as some sort of crank. His teachings were 'just the right words'. What he wrote was 'upright and true'. So we are encouraged to go back again and revisit the text we would be happier to ignore.[66]

---

65. Longman, *Ecclesiastes*, pp. 274–284.

66. There is, of course, much debate about whether the epologist reads Qoheleth positively (Bartholomew) or negatively (Fox, Longman) or both positively and negatively. (At this point, I also choose to ignore the critical debate about how many epologists contributed to the epilogue of Ecclesiastes, because this is irrelevant to our discussion.) For me, the natural reading of Eccl. 12:9–10 is as a positive assessment of Qoheleth and his teaching. This, in turn, should flavour our interpretation of the following two verses (12:11–12), which are clearly ambiguous. It then logically follows that 12:13–14 is to be applied as an overall summary of Qoheleth's wisdom. Qoheleth is not one-dimensional and, in terms of the narrator's analysis, 12:13 is probably designed to imply limits to the value of the type of empirical and experiential wisdom practised by the Teacher and presented in Ecclesiastes. However, this caveat certainly should not be read as substantially detracting from the narrator's assessment of the overall worth or orthodoxy of Qoheleth's teaching. Bartholomew correctly argues that 'the narrator reads Qoheleth positively and at least as arriving at a point in agreement with fearing

The canonical effect of the prologue and epilogue in this book of wisdom poetry is profound. These bookends have a marked effect on interpretation.[67] We are told to expect challenge in the text, and challenge then follows, but, in conclusion, we are warned that we cannot just ignore this teaching. Qoheleth's voice must be heard. The reader must grapple with his thoughts regardless of the processing cost.

Conclusion

The poetic books of the OT all show signs that editors have somehow shaped their final form. The task of editorial criticism is to access the themes, concerns and emphases key to those who put together these books in the form we recognize today. Through careful study of the text, we see that the poetic texts are not isolated units that stand entirely on their own, but that they do in fact have a context drawn from the ordering of these collections. These contexts shape our understanding and interpretation of the individual texts found in the Psalms, Proverbs and Ecclesiastes. If we segregate poetic texts into their component parts and ignore the interaction between the texts within each book, then we miss out on the fullness of meaning to be found in these collections. The poetic whole of the final form of the book offers more than analysis of the individual parts on their own.

Reading Hebrew parallelism

Readers of the psalms and poetry of the OT often note that it does not rhyme. Perhaps the rhyming is lost in translation? But, of course, psalms do not rhyme in Hebrew (at least not often). While rhyme is often found in English-language poetry, the key dynamic of Hebrew poetry is *parallelism*: two lines held in poetic tension as a single unit. Awareness of how to read the parallelisms of Hebrew poetry is vital for full literary appreciation of the poetic books. As with the significant developments in our understanding of

---

Footnote 66 (*continued*)

God and keeping his commandments' (*Reading Ecclesiastes*, p. 170). Qoheleth may take the reader on a long and ponderous route through the ambiguities and complexities of life, but the narrator summarizes his conclusion thus: to fear God and follow his instruction is the wisest way to live.

67. Bartholomew comments that 'recognition of the literary craftedness of Ecclesiastes is crucial for its interpretation' (*Reading Ecclesiastes*, p. 229).

the OT poetic books that have developed out of the canonical approach, there have been substantial advances in our understanding of parallelism since the 1980s. Anyone undertaking research or study in biblical poetry should be well versed (if you will excuse the pun) in the art of interpreting parallelism.

Historical approach to parallelism

Essentially, parallelism is a 'compare-and-contrast' method that leads the reader into an ever-fuller understanding of the image being presented by the poet. The classical analysis of poetic parallelism was written by Robert Lowth (later Bishop of London) in 1753. Lowth was Praelector of Poetry at the University of Oxford from 1741 to 1752, and in 1741 he first delivered lectures on Hebrew poetry.[68] These lectures were later published in Latin in 1753 as *Praelectiones academicae de sacra poesi Hebraeorum* (Lectures on the Sacred Poetry of the Hebrews) and were first translated into English in 1787.[69] Lowth was one of the first scholars to focus on how parallelism set Hebrew poetry apart from other ancient forms of poetry, especially classical Latin and Greek poetry and his analysis of Hebrew parallelism was the classic statement on the subject for over 200 years. Lowth's observations of Hebrew poetics led him to suggest that there are three basic types of parallelism: synonymous, antithetic and synthetic.[70] Essentially, Lowth observed these three broad categories of parallelism within Hebrew. In *synonymous parallelism* the two lines[71] say essentially the same thing in a slightly different way (A = B). An *antithetic parallelism* holds opposite or contradictory ideas in tension (A ≠ B). *Synthetic parallelisms* occur where the second line of the parallelism adds

---

68. Lowth was as much recognized as a grammarian as a clergyman and biblical scholar.

69. The standard text available until recently was the 4th ed., published in 1839. However, this work has recently been reprinted as *Lectures on the Sacred Poetry of the Hebrews* (Whitefish, Mont.: Kessinger, 2004), and is available in the public domain at, for example, Google Books, <http://www.google.co.uk/ books?id=Y3 GsBHeX jmgC&pg=RA2-PR25&dq=Lectures+on+the+Sacred+ Poetry+of+ the+Hebrews&as_ brr=1#PRA2-PR20,M1>, accessed 22 Jan. 2008.

70. See the helpful discussion in S. E. Gillingham, *The Poems and Psalms of the Hebrew Bible*, The Oxford Bible Series (Oxford: Oxford University Press, 1994), pp. 69–88.

71. Each line of a parallelism is normally referred to as a 'colon' (pl. 'cola'), while a parallelism is often referred to as a 'bicolon'.

something to the first in a way that is neither synonymous nor contradictory
(A + B).[72]

It is relatively easy to illustrate the first two types of parallelism. Psalm 24:1
shows how synonymous parallelism works:

> [A] The earth is the LORD's, and everything in it,
>   [B] the world, and all who live in it . . .

Each line of the parallelism expresses essentially the same idea. The whole
earth belongs to Yahweh, complete with all it contains, and that notion is
restated in the second colon of the parallelism. Equally, it is relatively easy to
observe and understand the function of antithetic parallelism. Psalm 1:6 can
be used by way of illustration:

> [A] For the LORD watches over the way of the righteous,
>   [B] but the way of the wicked will perish.

The two lines of the parallelism basically reflect polar opposites. The way of
the righteous is the way of divine care, whereas the way of the wicked is sure
to perish – the two ideas are clearly contrary to each other; they present contrasting realities.

Definition of the third category of parallelism, however, is somewhat more
problematic. Lowth himself acknowledged that 'The variety in the form of
this synthetic parallelism is very great, and the degrees of resemblance almost
infinite: so that sometimes the scheme of parallelism is very subtle and
obscure . . .'[73] Exact definition of synthetic parallelism proved so elusive that
Lowth concluded that this category of parallelism includes 'all such as do not
come within the two former classes'.[74] Basically, any parallelism that was
neither synonymous nor antithetic was to be considered synthetic, simply
because it did not fit either of these two categories. Obviously, there are many
examples of parallelism that fit with the concept of synthetic addition or constructive parallelism. Psalm 10:1, for example:

---

72. Lowth further divided the category of synthetic parallelism (which he also referred
    to as 'constructive parallelism') into various subcategories because of the
    complexity and diversity of this type of parallelism. See ch. 19 of *On the Sacred
    Poetry of the Hebrews.*
73. Ibid., ch. 19.
74. Ibid.

[A] Why, O Lord, do you stand far off?
  [B] Why do you hide yourself in times of trouble?

The first line of the parallelism tells the reader that the psalmist feels somehow abandoned by God and the second colon gives us the added information that this apparent abandonment occurs during a time of trouble. Clearly, in this case colon B adds something to colon A in a constructive manner. However, the category of synthetic parallelism was from the outset somewhat problematic. As we shall see below, many parallelisms are neither synonymous nor antithetic, yet they cannot be legitimately described as constructive in a parallelistic sense. Categorization is always meant to function as an aid in ordering or assessment, but, even from the time of Lowth's writing, synthetic parallelism as a category was so broad that its value was questionable.[75]

However, Lowth's analysis was immensely profitable in terms of advancing scholarly understanding of Hebrew poetry and this approach was to hold sway with very little amendment until the rise in the application of literary theories to biblical studies that began in the 1980s.

Modern literary approaches to parallelism

More recent years have witnessed fairly substantial developments in the scholarly approach to Hebrew parallelism. Contemporary analyses, while often highly respectful of Lowth's thorough literary analysis of the function of Hebrew parallelism, questioned some of his conclusions. Several issues from On the Sacred Poetry of the Hebrews gave cause for concern, but two themes have dominated the revisions of the classical approach to Semitic parallelism. First, the category of synthetic parallelism is a 'catch-all' category that therefore runs the risk of becoming essentially meaningless – Line B almost always adds *something* to Line A, but can this always be defined as 'constructive' in a parallelistic sense? Secondly, few parallelisms are really synonymous – although changes in emphasis may only be slight, Line B seldom *simply repeats* the thought of Line A: something (no matter how slight) is normally added. Several key works in the 1980s sought to address this issue, of which the following have had a substantial influence on our understanding of how parallelisms work: James L. Kugel's *The Idea of Biblical*

---

75. It should be noted that Lowth himself was not entirely comfortable with this classification and was aware of the difficulties synthetic parallelism presented as a category (see n. 72, above).

Poetry,[76] Robert Alter's *The Art of Biblical Poetry*,[77] Adele Berlin's *The Dynamics of Biblical Parallelism*[78] and an article by David J. A. Clines called 'The Parallelism of Greater Precision: Notes from Isaiah 40 for a Theory of Hebrew Parallelism'.[79]

The problem of synthetic parallelism

It would, perhaps, be wise to highlight in more detail the limitations in Lowth's approach that have been addressed by these (and other) scholars before elaborating their suggestions for the revision and advancement they proffer.

First, that elusive category of 'synthetic parallelism'. The idea suggested by Lowth is that all parallelisms where the second line neither repeats (synonymous) nor opposes (antithetic) the content of the first line are in some sense synthetic – the second colon adding something to the first. In some cases, as in the example from Psalm 24:1 above, this idea seems to work quite well. However, in many cases where poetic lines are clearly held together in parallelistic structure, the relationship appears to be non-constructive in accordance with Lowth's suggestions. Take an example from the famous (and infamous) Psalm 137 (my tr.):

> [A] By the rivers of Babylon
>   [B] there we sat, also wept
>   [C] when we remembered Zion.[80]
> (v. 1)

Now, clearly there is some progression of thought in this verse, but is this really synthetic or constructive parallelism? The next verse raises the same question (my tr.):

---

76. J. L. Kugel, *The Idea of Biblical Poetry: Parallelism and Its History* (New Haven: Yale University Press, 1981).

77. R. Alter, *The Art of Biblical Poetry* (New York: Basic, 1985).

78. A. Berlin, *The Dynamics of Biblical Parallelism* (Bloomington: Indiana University Press, 1985).

79. D. J. A. Clines, 'The Parallelism of Greater Precision: Notes from Isaiah 40 for a Theory of Hebrew Parallelism', in E. R. Follis (ed.), *New Directions in Hebrew Poetry* (Sheffield: JSOT Press, 1987), pp. 77–100.

80. The Masoretes seemed to consider this verse a tricolon, indicated by the Masoretic division of the verse.

[A] Upon the willows in her [Babylon's] midst
   [B] we hung our lyres.
(v. 2)

A poetic narrative is unfolding before our eyes, but the relationship between the cola of each verse is actually very loose. Each new line is developing a new element of the 'narrative' rather than standing in particular relationship with the preceding line of the parallelism. So, yes, each colon adds something, but not really in the manner Lowth suggested. Many parallelisms fall within this category,[81] so either synthetic parallelism has to be expanded to such an extent that it makes its categorizing function worthless, or the classification of parallelisms needs to be reworked.

The problem of synonymous parallelism

Another foible of this categorization of parallelisms is illustrated by the example of a 'synthetic' parallelism given above, Psalm 24:1. There is a sense in which the cola stand in clear relationship with one another and in which something is added by the second line. However, even with such an example there are difficulties with regard to the precise definition of the type of parallelism. Is the psalmist adding a *new* thought in colon B of Psalm 24:1, or is he really *specifying* more detail with regard to the overarching thought of colon A? So is this a synthetic *addition* or is it a synonymous *specification*? The difference between the two can often be very slight. There is a difference between the cola of Psalm 24:1, but then can we ever really speak of entirely synonymous expression short of simple repetition? Synonyms seldom bear exactly the same meaning; therefore, besides questioning synthetic parallelism, we must also ask whether synonymous parallelism is a helpful category in itself.

The problems of categorization

These difficulties of categorization led first Kugel and then others to question the existence of strict categories of parallelism. Kugel noted with regard to the relationship between cola that 'one will be hard pressed to explain why

---

81. Gillingham, for example, points out that of the seven parallelisms in the much-
loved Ps. 23, only verse 2 reflects repetition that could be described as synonymous,
and none of the verses contrasts; therefore, the remaining parallelisms are all in
some sense 'synthetic'. Yet in the remaining examples, the second colon relates to
the first with a fairly wide degree of diversity; so in what sense is synthetic
parallelism a 'category'? (*Poems and Psalms*, pp. 75–76).

parallelism in some lines is so full and striking while in others it is so light, virtually non-existent'.[82] His observations on the text led him to the conclusion
that, simply put, the three categories of parallelism do not always work. So
Kugel goes on to challenge the long-established status quo by suggesting that
in reality 'Biblical parallelism is [either] of one sort "A, and what's more, B", or
a hundred sorts; but it is not three.'[83] In other words, Kugel suggests that all
parallelism is of the same very broad type in which the second line (in a wide
diversity of ways) advances the first, or, alternatively, there must be many
different categories of parallelism because so many verses reject (or at least do
not fall neatly within) Lowth's threefold categorization. Kugel's central point
is simply that B *in some way* always advances what we know from A. The ways
in which it does so are multiple and cannot be limited to three specific types
or categories of relationship between A and B.[84]

The key factor in this change of perspective with regard to the analysis and
categorization of the OT's parallelism is that the interpretative emphasis in
some sense shifts from Line A to Line B. Under Lowth's scheme of analysis,
Line A sets the tone and the question is always, 'How does Line B relate to Line
A?' By contrast, in Kugel's approach Line B sets the interpretative agenda
because the question asked must be, 'What is Line B doing to what we already
know from Line A?' Patrick Miller puts it succinctly: 'The paralleling or sec-
onding feature is the primary one.'[85] Basically, it is always Line B that is 'doing
something' in Kugel's analysis. *What* it is doing will vary. 'Parallelism employs
a complex of heightening effects used in combinations and intensities that vary
widely from composition to composition even within a single "genre".'[86] Line
B will always do something: sometimes B will be strongly linked to A and
neatly parallel the first colon, giving only slightly new information, and on
other occasions B will so heighten the impressions derived from A as to
develop the unfolding imagery of the parallelism radically.

Examples of heightening in line B
Robert Alter developed Kugel's theories through the careful examination of
the 'A, and what's more, B' principle at work in the poetry of the Hebrew Bible.
Alter had in the late 1970s been leading graduate seminars on Hebrew poetry

---

82. Kugel, *Idea of Biblical Poetry*, p. 49.

83. Ibid., p. 58.

84. We shall look below at examples that illustrate this point.

85. P. D. Miller, *Interpreting the Psalms* (Philadelphia: Fortress, 1986), p. 33.

86. Kugel, *Idea of Biblical Poetry*, p. 94.

at the University of California, Berkley, and had made observations similar to those Kugel later published.[87] Alter agreed with Kugel's basic theory regarding the interpretative crux being found in Line B, but felt that Kugel's understanding of the poetic in the OT was far too understated.[88] Expanding more explicitly on Kugel's ideas, Alter writes:

> In the abundant instances . . . in which semantic parallelism does occur in a line, the characteristic movement of meaning is one of *heightening* or *intensification* (as in the paradigmatic case of numerals), of *focusing, specification, concretization*, even what could be called *dramatization*. There is, of course, a certain overlap among these categories, but my concern is to point to the direction in which the reader can look for meaning, not to undertake an exercise in taxonomy. The rule of thumb then . . . is that the general term occurs in the first verset [Line A] and a more specific instance of the general category in the second verset [Line B].[89]

Hence, parallelism is now generally thought of as a technique whereby Line B in some way heightens or intensifies or expands upon the true statement of Line A. Hence, Clines refers to this phenomenon as 'parallelism of greater precision' because the paralleling line is the primary dynamic in the development of the ideas being presented to the reader.[90] Of course, this development occurs not only within the parallelism (normally a verse) itself but also with the addition of successive parallelisms. Not only do we witness development within the two-line structure of each verse, but there is dynamic development in each poem of the OT with the addition of each new parallelism. To

---

87. Alter, *Biblical Poetry*, pp. xi–xii.

88. Ibid., p. 4. Basically, Kugel suggests that the form of parallelism is much looser than Lowth suggested, and in the second part of his book seems somewhat to downplay the amount of actual 'poetry' that exists in the Hebrew OT. Kugel suggests rather that there is a type of continuum of loosely parallelistic structures that often represent no more than a type of heightened or prosaic rhetoric, as opposed to 'poetry proper'. Alter strongly rejects this aspect of Kugel's analysis, seeing rather many poetic parallelisms incorporated within narrative texts.

89. Alter, *Biblical Poetry*, p. 19 (emphasis mine).

90. Interestingly, Alter points out that this dynamic of heightening and intensification was observed by a German scholar responding to Lowth in 1782, but his observations went largely unnoticed. J. G. Herder noted that 'the two [parallel] members strengthen, heighten, empower each other' (Alter, *Biblical Poetry*, p. 11). Herder's work was called *Vom Geist der erbräischer Poesie* [On the Spirit of Hebrew Poetry] (Dessau, 1782).

understand Hebrew poetry properly we must grasp this idea of an ever more detailed picture being painted before our eyes with the addition of each paralleling line and each new parallelism. There is both beauty and meaning in this development. Parallelism has both aesthetic and semantic purposes. We are meant to admire the pleasing sense of symmetry found in each bicolon and, at the same time, to chart the development of the central ideas through the addition of detail to each image or idea.

Examples of poetic heightening

Alter highlights several examples of the different types of heightening or intensification he observes in the OT poetic texts. Proverbs 3:10 (my tr.) represents both specification and intensification:

> [A] Your storehouses will be filled with plenty,
> > [B] with new wine your vats will burst.

The movement from 'plenty' to 'new wine' *specifies* the crop in question, whereas the movement from 'being filled' to 'bursting' *intensifies* the imagery of God's provision for those who honour him. Other examples include *numerical intensification* (e.g. Prov. 6:16–19, which draws attention to that unexpected seventh behaviour that is also an abomination to Yahweh), *geographic specification* (e.g. Jer. 7:36, with the movement from 'cities of Judea' to the 'streets of Jerusalem') or *hyperbolic dramatization* (e.g. Ps. 18:42, where the psalmist's absolute victory over his enemies is presented as grinding them to dust, which is then poured out into the streets). Some of these heightening effects definitely overlap, as Alter himself suggests, but his observation of the intensification, specification and dramatization of various types between the lines of a parallelism provides a good starting point for understanding the heightening effect of parallelism.[91]

A via media?

Undoubtedly, Kugel, Alter and others are correct in their understanding of the dynamic function the second line in Hebrew parallelism performs and in their presentation of the weaknesses of Lowth's methodology. However, it is not without reason that Lowth's approach has acquired such broad acceptance and extensive application since *On the Sacred Poetry of the Hebrews* was first published. Students and scholars alike have found Lowth's categories helpful in the study of biblical poetry. Yet methodological limitations regarding Lowth's ideas

---

91. See pp. 18–26, 62–84 of Alter, *Biblical Poetry*.

clearly remain. But is there a *via media* between the old and the new?

Probably. Part of the problem of both the old and the new approach to parallelism is that the interpretative key to a parallelism does not lie primarily in Line A or Line B *but in their combination into a bicolon*. It is in the linking of these two expressions that a more complete thought is proposed. Neither line can be seen as the absolute driver for deriving the meaning of the verse. The poetic meaning is drawn from the two (or three) lines together that are held in creative tension. Clines notes the importance of this realization:

> Our study of the parallelism of greater precision has alerted us to something that is true of Hebrew poetry generally. The meaning of the couplet does not reside in A nor in B; nor is it in A+B (if they are regarded as capable of being added like 2+2 or 3+2). It is in the whole couplet of A and B in which A is affected by its juxtaposition with B, and B by its juxtaposition with A. The whole is different from the sum of its parts because the parts influence or contaminate each other.[92]

So where does that leave the interpreter with regard to biblical poetics? It leaves us drawing upon Lowth's observations where they are helpful and ignoring them where they are not. It also leaves us looking for heightening effects where they are to be found, but equally happy if no heightening is obviously present. Most of all it leaves us seeking to determine the value of *each parallelism as a whole*, gradually developing a word picture as colon builds upon colon and verse upon verse to present us with that communicative power and beauty that is unique to the poetic.

The poem as a unit

The reader will be immediately aware that this chapter has focused on poetics at a macro-level (canonical readings of poetic anthologies) and poetics at a micro-level (parallelism). This leaves us with an obvious gap: What about the analysis

---

92. Clines, 'Parallelism', p. 100. This deals helpfully with one of the main weaknesses of the modern approach to parallelism, where Line B is seen as the driving force of the parallelism. This approach does not deal well with the natural dynamic of the 'antithetic' parallelism (to use Lowth's categories), where the dynamic is found in the *contrast* between Line A and Line B rather than any heightening specific to Line B. It is as the two cola are read in contrast that the meaning is derived. Clines's insistence that the meaning of a parallelism is to be derived from the cola's relationship is helpful.

of the poem as a unit in itself? Parallelisms combine to form strophes, strophes (often) combine to form stanzas and stanzas are brought together to create poems. This is, indeed, a worthy area of study in itself but limits of time and space here do not allow for detailed analysis of the poem as a unit. In chapters of this type, inevitably one must be selective, and the decision to focus on canonical interpretations and parallelism reflects the significant movement there has been in these areas since the 1980s. In terms of the study of the poem as a unit there has not been the same sort of dynamic movement or radical change in recent years. The key ideas have remained largely the same in recent ideas.

Without dealing with this topic in any detail, the fundamental premise, then, is that parallelisms (as the basic unit of poetry) combine to form broader units (strophes or stanzas), which in turn combine to form poems. In the analysis of these broader units we become more aware of the flow of a poem, the foci of each section and, potentially, the 'rhetorical' thrust of the poem.[93] Several key studies continue to provide helpful guidance for the analysis of a poem's structure and its influence on interpretation.[94] These works provide a helpful starting point for studies in this area.

Poetry in the New Testament

Time, space and sense here do not allow for in-depth discussion of poetry in the NT. The main movements in the field of biblical poetics since the 1980s

---

93. It is a misnomer to describe the didactic purpose of a poem as 'rhetorical' in the strict sense (see chapter 7 in this volume). However, I use the word to make the point that poets often had a specific teaching purpose in mind when writing a poem, and awareness of the structure of the poem can help to get to the heart of that central aim.

94. Primary among the works looking at poetic structure are W. van der Meer and J. C. de Moor (eds.), *The Structural Analysis of Biblical and Canaanite Poetry*, JSOTSup 93 (Sheffield: Sheffield Academic Press, 1988); and J. P. Fokkelman's more recent *Reading Biblical Poetry: An Introductory Guide*, tr. I. Smit (Louisville: Westminster John Knox, 2001). Other helpful discussions include W. S. Prinsloo's 'text-immanent' approach to poetic structure (see his helpful 'Psalm 116: Disconnected Text or Symmetrical Whole', *Bib* 74 [1993], pp. 71–82), the introductory matter of S. Terrien's, *The Psalms: Strophic Structure and Theological Commentary*, ECC (Grand Rapids: Eerdmans, 2003); and L. A. Schökel's *Manual of Hebrew Poetics*, SubBib 11 (Rome: Pontifical Biblical Institute, 1988).

have occurred with regard to the more significant and substantial poetic collections of the OT. That there is Semitic poetry in the NT is beyond doubt,[95] but there are no *books* of poetry to be studied canonically, and understanding of the function of parallelism is drawn from the greater sample found in the OT and then applied to the poetic verses of the NT rather than vice versa. However, I hope that this analysis of the poetic in the OT (particularly with regard to the function of parallelism) may be useful to those seeking understanding of poetic texts in the NT also.

Conclusion

Study of the Bible's poetry has been a profitable and exciting area of research since the 1980s or so. Many of the schools of thought that have developed have substantially advanced our understanding of poetics and the function of poetry within the biblical text. These advances have also injected something of a new lease of life into the study of the Psalms and the wisdom literature, as well as other poetic texts.[96] Growing awareness of the editorial hand at work in the poetic books has led to a deeper understanding of the contextual interpretation of the otherwise sound-bite-like messages of poetry. Fuller understanding of the way in which parallelism (as we have seen, one of the key features of Hebraic poetry[97]) works has also led to deeper insight into the communicative intent of the Bible's poets. In biblical poetry, the aesthetic and the didactic combine with great power in order to convey a message that addresses the whole being of the

---

95. See Gillingham, *Poems and Psalms*, pp. 82–88, for a good discussion of how the main features of Hebrew parallelism are seen in many NT texts, particularly in Jesus' teaching (e.g. in the Sermon on the Mount). Other prominent examples of poetry in the NT include the Canticles in Luke (see e.g. R. Buth, 'Hebrew Poetic Tenses and the Magnificat', *JSNT* 21.1 [1984], pp. 67–83), individual verses throughout the NT and possible hymnic passages like Phil. 2:6–11 (although it should be acknowledged that there is some debate as to whether this passage is a hymn or some sort of 'high prose'; see G. F. Hawthorne, *Philippians*, WBC 43 [Waco: Word, 1983], pp. 76–79; cf. G. D. Fee, *Paul's Letter to the Philippians*, NICNT [Grand Rapids: Eerdmans, 1995], pp. 39–46).

96. Note e.g. the recent spate of commentaries on the books of Job and Lamentations.

97. Berlin describes the two primary characteristics of Hebrew poetry as *parallelism* and *terseness* (*Dynamics*, p. 5). The latter has not been addressed in this article, but is discussed elsewhere (see J. A. Grant, '"Szczęśliwy, kto . . .": Czesław Miłosz's Translation of the Psalms', *CBQ* 69.3 [2007], pp. 457–472).

reader. The advances of recent years equip the reader to grapple more fully with and to respond more completely to the Bible's poetic text.

Select bibliography

ALTER, R., *The Art of Biblical Poetry* (New York: Basic, 1985).

AUFFRET, P., *The Literary Structure of Psalm 2*, tr. D. J. A. Clines, JSOTSup 3 (Sheffield: JSOT Press, 1977).

——, *La Sagesse a bâti sa maison: Études de structures littéraires dans l'Ancient Testament et spécialement dans les psaumes*, OBO 49 (Fribourg: Editions Universitaires, 1982).

BARTHOLOMEW, C. G., *Reading Ecclesiastes: Old Testament Exegesis and Hermeneutical Theory*, AnBib 139 (Rome: Pontifical Bible Institute, 1998).

——, *Reading Proverbs with Integrity* (Cambridge: Grove, 2001).

BERLIN, A., *The Dynamics of Biblical Parallelism* (Bloomington: Indiana University Press, 1985).

BROWNLEE, W. H., 'Psalms 1–2 as a Coronation Liturgy', *Bib* 52.3 (1971), pp. 321–336.

CHILDS, B. S., *Introduction to the Old Testament as Scripture* (London: SCM, 1979).

CLINES, D. J. A., 'The Parallelism of Greater Precision: Notes from Isaiah 40 for a Theory of Hebrew Parallelism', in E. R. Follis (ed.), *New Directions in Hebrew Poetry* (Sheffield: JSOT Press, 1987), pp. 77–100.

DeCLAISSÉ-WALFORD, N. L., 'The Canonical Shape of the Psalms', in H. W. Ballard and W. D. Tucker (eds.), *An Introduction to Wisdom Literature and the Psalms: Festschrift for Marvin E. Tate* (Macon: Mercer University Press, 2000), pp. 93–110.

——, *Reading from the Beginning: The Shaping of the Hebrew Psalter* (Macon: Mercer University Press, 1997).

EATON, J. H., *Kingship and the Psalms*, 2nd ed., SBT 32 (London: SCM, 1986).

FOX, M. V., *A Time to Tear Down and a Time to Build Up: A Rereading of Ecclesiastes* (Grand Rapids: Eerdmans, 1999).

GILLINGHAM, S. E., *The Poems and Psalms of the Hebrew Bible*, The Oxford Bible Series (Oxford: Oxford University Press, 1994).

GRANT, J. A., *The King as Exemplar: The Function of Deuteronomy's Kingship Law in the Shaping of the Book of Psalms*, SBL, AB 17; Atlanta: SBL; Leiden: Brill, 2004).

——, 'The Psalms and the King', in JOHNSTON and FIRTH, *Interpreting the Psalms*, pp. 101–118.

——, '"Szczęśliwy, kto . . .": Czesław Miłosz's Translation of the Psalms', *CBQ* 69.3 (2007), pp. 457–472.

HEIM, K. M., *Like Grapes of Gold Set in Silver: An Interpretation of Proverbial Clusters in Proverbs 10:1–22:16*, BZAW 273 (Berlin: de Gruyter, 2001).

HOWARD, D. M., *The Structure of Psalms 93–100*, Biblical and Judaic Studies / University of California, San Diego 5 (Winona Lake: Eisenbrauns, 1997).

JOHNSTON, P. S., and FIRTH, D. G. (eds.), *Interpreting the Psalms: Issues and Approaches* (Leicester: Apollos, 2005).

KECK, L. E. (ed.), *The New Interpreter's Bible*, vols. 4, 5 (Nashville: Abingdon, 1996, 1997).

KIRKPATRICK, A. F., *The Book of Psalms* (Cambridge: Cambridge University Press, 1910).

KRAUS, H.-J., *Psalms 1–59: A Commentary*, tr. H. C. Oswald (Minneapolis: Augsburg, 1988).

KUGEL, J. L., *The Idea of Biblical Poetry: Parallelism and Its History* (New Haven: Yale University Press, 1981).

LONGMAN, T., III, *The Book of Ecclesiastes*, NICOT (Grand Rapids: Eerdmans, 1998).

McCANN, J. C., 'The Book of Psalms: Introduction, Commentary and Reflections', in *NIB* 4: 641–1280.

——, *A Theological Introduction to the Books of Psalms: The Psalms as Torah* (Nashville: Abingdon, 1993).

—— (ed.), *The Shape and Shaping of the Psalter*, JSOTSup 159 (Sheffield: JSOT Press, 1993).

MAYS, J. L., *The Lord Reigns* (Louisville: Westminster John Knox, 1994).

——, *Psalms*, Interpretation (Louisville: John Knox, 1994).

——, 'The Question of Context in Psalm Interpretation', in McCANN, *Shape and Shaping of the Psalter*, pp. 14–20.

MILLER, P. D., *Interpreting the Psalms* (Philadelphia: Fortress, 1986).

——, 'Kingship, Torah Obedience and Prayer', in K. Seybold and E. Zenger (eds.), *Neue Wege der Psalmenforschung* (Freiburg: Herder, 1995), pp. 127–142.

MURPHY, R. E., 'Reflections on Contextual Interpretations of the Psalms', in McCANN, *Shape and Shaping of the Psalter*, pp. 21–28.

SARNA, N. M., *On the Book of Psalms: Exploring the Prayer of Ancient Israel* (New York: Schocken, 1993).

VAN LEEUWEN, R. C., 'The Book of Proverbs: Introduction, Commentary and Reflections', in *NIB* 5: 19–264.

——, *Context and Meaning in Proverbs 25–27*, SBLDS 96 (Atlanta: Scholars Press, 1988).

WESTERMANN, C., *Praise and Lament in the Psalms*, tr. K. R. Crim and R. N. Soulen (Atlanta: John Knox, 1981).

WILLIS, J. T., 'Psalm 1 – an Entity', *ZAW* 91.3 (1979), pp. 381–401.

WILSON, G. H., *The Editing of the Hebrew Psalter*, SBLDS 76 (Chico: Scholars Press, 1985).

——, 'The Structure of the Psalter', in JOHNSTON and FIRTH, *Interpreting the Psalms*, pp. 229–246.

——, 'Understanding the Purposeful Arrangement of the Psalms: Pitfalls and Promise', in McCANN, *Shape and Shaping of the Psalter*, pp. 42–51.

ZENGER, E., 'The Composition and Theology of the Fifth Book of the Psalter', *JSOT* 80 (1998), pp. 77–102.

7. RHETORIC

Peter M. Phillips

Rhetoric used to be out of fashion. Even today, in public discourse it is characterized as 'spin' and in academic discourse marginalized in favour of more fashionable disciplines. Despite this, within the realm of biblical studies, rhetoric seems to be going through a major revival, to be the epicentre of '[a] near volcanic eruption . . . at the center of biblical interpretation'.[1] Key figures in the rehabilitation of rhetoric in biblical studies have been James Muilenburg, George Kennedy, Wilhelm Wuellner and Vernon Robbins; and within wider socio-literary studies, Chaim Perelman, Kenneth Burke, Ernesto Grassi and others.[2] Burke was an early advocate of the rehabilitation:

1. W. Wuellner, 'Biblical Exegesis in the Light of History and Historicity or Rhetoric and the Nature of the Rhetoric of Religion', in S. E. Porter and T. H. Olbricht (eds.), *Rhetoric and the New Testament: Essays from the 1992 Heidelberg Conference* (Sheffield: Sheffield Academic Press, 1993), p. 493.
2. For a discussion on the use of aspects of rhetoric in the Bible, and especially the NT, see G. A. Kennedy, *Classical Rhetoric and its Christian and Secular Tradition from Ancient to Modern Times* (London: University of South Carolina Press, 1980); *New Testament Interpretation through Rhetorical Criticism* (Chapel Hill: University of North Carolina Press, 1984); B. Mack, *Rhetoric and the New Testament* (Minneapolis: Fortress, 1980); M. Warner (ed.), *The Bible as Rhetoric: Studies in Biblical Persuasion and Credibility*

In part, we would but rediscover rhetorical elements that had become obscured when rhetoric as a term fell into disuse, and other specialized disciplines such as esthetics, anthropology, psychoanalysis, and sociology came to the fore (so that esthetics sought to outlaw rhetoric, while the other sciences we have mentioned took over, each in its own terms, the rich rhetorical elements that esthetics would ban).[3]

Despite the importance of rhetoric in ancient, medieval and renaissance education, throughout the reign of modernism rhetoric has been overwhelmed by other disciplines and by the hegemony of reason, leaving 'the science of speaking well' to be ridiculed as the pastime of the 'spin doctors'.[4]

(London: Routledge, 1990); D. F. Watson (ed.), *Persuasive Artistry: Studies in New Testament Rhetoric in Honor of George A. Kennedy* (Sheffield: Sheffield Academic Press, 1991); Bible and Culture Collective, 'Rhetorical Criticism', in *The Postmodern Bible* (New Haven: Yale University Press, 1995), pp. 149–186. James Muilenburg's Society of Biblical Literature Presidential Address on rhetorical criticism was later published as 'Form Criticism and Beyond', *JBL* 88.1 (1969), pp. 1–18. Good introductions to aspects of Wilhelm Wuellner's work can be found in W. Wuellner, 'Where Is Rhetorical Criticism Taking Us?', *CBQ* 49.3 (1987), pp. 448–463; 'The Rhetorical Genre of Jesus' Sermon in Luke 12:1–13:9', in Watson, *Persuasive Artistry*, pp. 93–118; and 'Biblical Exegesis', as well as the four articles in Part 1 of J. D. Hester and J. D. Hester (eds.), *Rhetorics and Hermeneutics: Wilhelm Wuellner and His Influence* (New York: T. & T. Clark, 2004). For Vernon Robbins's work on sociorhetorical criticism, see his own *Exploring the Texture of Texts: A Guide to Socio-Rhetorical Interpretation* (Valley Forge, Pa.: Trinity Press International, 1996). Other titles exploring some aspects of rhetoric and the Bible may be found in the bibliography. For a wider discussion of new approaches to rhetoric, see C. Perelman and L. Olbrechts-Tyteca, *The New Rhetoric: A Treatise on Argumentation*, Center for the Study of Democratic Institutions (Notre Dame: University of Notre Dame Press, 1969); C. Perelman, *The New Rhetoric and the Humanities* (Dordrecht: D. Reidel, 1979); K. Burke, *A Rhetoric of Motives* (Berkeley: University of California Press, 1969); E. Grassi, *Rhetoric as Philosophy: The Humanist Tradition* (University Park: Pennsylvania State University Press, 1980; repr. Carbondale: Southern Illinois University Press, 2001). For an intriguing discussion bringing in French Deconstruction and one of the architects of postmodernity, see G. Olson, 'Jacques Derrida on Rhetoric and Composition: A Conversation', *JAC* 10.1 (1990), pp. 1–21.

3. Burke, *Rhetoric of Motives*, p. xiii.
4. For a review of the history, see Kennedy, *Classical Rhetoric*; Wuellner, 'Biblical Exegesis'; and, from a philosophical viewpoint, Perelman, *New Rhetoric*, pp. 1–7;

Of course, this argument about the nature of rhetoric is ages old. Back in the fourth century BC, Plato famously despised the rhetoric of Gorgias and the other sophists, claiming that they spoke nothing of substance but simply peddled half-truths with pretty words.[5] Rather than explore the nature of rhetoric as a true art, Plato dismissed it as a form of flattery, a parody of the true art of justice; while justice sought truth, rhetoric simply dressed up falsehood, just as cosmetics pretends to make the body beautiful in a parody of the true beauty gained through gymnastics.

We see the same argument reflected in popular modern use of the term 'rhetoric'. An influential American political website at the turn of the millennium, Spinsanity (www.spinsanity.org) had as its strapline, 'countering rhetoric with reason'. The authors of Spinsanity focused their attention on what they deemed to be the manipulative rhetoric of the Bush administration. Their mission was to counter the use of spin and manipulation within contemporary mass media:

> Robust political debate is essential to democracy. Our national political discourse is an
> important part of the democratic process and serves as a critical check on those in
> power. We are therefore deeply concerned that our public political dialogue, largely
> expressed through the channels of the mass media, is becoming systematically
> dominated by sophisticated tactics of manipulation rather than norms of public
> reason. Despite widespread complaints about spin, no one is adequately documenting
> the full ramifications of this development to our satisfaction. Thus, our goal at
> *Spinsanity* is to use rigorous, non-partisan analysis to expose the use and intent of the
> simulated reason and public relations techniques that dominate political discourse,
> and to document how they are disseminated through the media. By exposing these
> tactics and demonstrating their pervasiveness, we hope to create a greater awareness
> of how spin operates and corrupts, and contribute to a healthy and vibrant political
> discourse.[6]

For the authors of Spinsanity, the manipulation and spin of the mass media was 'rhetoric', whereas their own promotion of a more straightforward and

---

Footnote 4 (*continued*)

    Grassi, *Rhetoric*, pp. 35–68. Note Quintilian's definition of rhetoric as *scientia bene dicendi*, *Institutiones* 2.15.38.

5. Kennedy, *Classical Rhetoric*, pp. 45–52.

6. Spinsanity's Mission Statement, <http://www.spinsanity.org/about/mission.html>, accessed 29 Sept. 2006.

common-sense analysis of political events was 'reason': rhetoric as wordplay without any sense of absolute truth. It is the very thing Plato makes Socrates criticize in Gorgias' sophistry. However, it is not clear how Spinsanity's rhetoric differs fundamentally from the Bush administration's rhetoric. The ultimate goal of both styles (Bush and Spinsanity, Gorgias and Plato/ Socrates) is to persuade – to influence, challenge and/or overturn the world view of their opponents – and as such both are forms of rhetoric. Spinsanity's authors view the world in ways diametrically opposed to those associated with the Bush administration and define this as a logical and ana- lytical world view, which they name 'reason'. In fact, their analysis is as rhetor- ical as Bush's rhetoric and their appeal to reason, as we shall see, reflects the first choice to be made in classical rhetoric: Does the orator choose 'logos' (an appeal to *reason*), 'pathos' (an appeal to *emotion*) or 'ethos' (an appeal to *character*)? Both Bush and Spinsanity were making an appeal to reason – the difference between them is not to be seen in terms of rhetoric but of world view. Indeed, from the perspective of the postmodern global village, both sides seem to have very similar world views and very similar techniques of rhetoric: both speak the same language, just with a slightly different dialect. However, both sides see the world with different eyes and believe their own world view to be the truth. Their rhetoric is based on their need to persuade others of the truth. Interestingly, Gorgias and the sophists had a different concept of truth where they were willing to suggest that absolute truth was simply unattainable and so sought to persuade people of the most reason- able version of it. So, for the sophists and their descendants, rhetoric is about persuading people to follow the most viable truth rather than declaring what was the absolute truth.[7]

The two mindsets classically come together in Plato's dialogue *Gorgias*, a dramatic retelling of a supposed conversation between Socrates and three sophist orators, Gorgias, Polus and Callicles. Socrates is invited to ask the orators any question he wishes and so begins a search for their definition of rhetoric. Socrates steers Gorgias towards an initial definition of rhetoric as that which deals with words and discourse. This is not good enough for Socrates,

---

7. See below for a further discussion of sacred rhetoric, or radical rhetoric that postulates one form of world view and denies all others; Kennedy, *New Testament Interpretation*, pp. 4–8; and *Classical Rhetoric*, pp. 29–31; Grassi, *Rhetoric*, pp. 102–114; J. Crafton, 'The Dancing of an Attitude: Burkean Rhetorical Criticism and the Biblical Interpreter', in Porter and Olbricht, *Rhetoric and the New Testament*, pp. 429– 442, 431–433.

and so he continues his interrogation of Gorgias and eventually Gorgias is pressed into praising rhetoric in these terms:

> *Gorgias*: What is there greater than the word which persuades the judges in the courts, or the senators in the council, or the citizens in the assembly, or at any other political meeting? If you have the power of uttering this word, you will have the physician your slave, and the trainer your slave, and the money-maker of whom you talk will be found to gather treasures, not for himself, but for you who are able to speak and to persuade the multitude.

> *Socrates*: Now I think, Gorgias, that you have very accurately explained what you conceive to be the art of rhetoric; and you mean to say, if I am not mistaken, that rhetoric is the artificer of persuasion, having this and no other business, and that this is her crown and end.[8]

So, Gorgias confirms his understanding that rhetoric involves persuasion but also a sense of gaining power over other people. The sophists were keen to show how people could be persuaded to follow an appropriate course of action by rhetoric rather than simply because it was the best way – many ways were the best way. Such thinking was anathema to Socrates (and Plato). Socrates unravels Gorgias' definition by suggesting that other arts also persuade and that Gorgias' limited definition of persuasion in the courts is itself meaningless. They agree together that rhetoric is to be limited to words and to persuasion and that it does not involve instruction. But this means that there has to be a distinction between persuasion and knowledge. Also, they agree that there are other arts which have persuasive qualities to them but that people can also acquire specific knowledge about these arts. Such arts can therefore be learnt and are not limited to persuasion. However, both agree that such knowledge should always be of more consequence than the orator's argument (reason vs. rhetoric), since someone trained in medicine, for example, should or could not be persuaded by rhetoric to do what he knows is wrong in his field.[9] Knowledge, therefore, is superior to persuasion. Of course, as a purely pragmatic sophist, Gorgias could accept this without needing to accept that

---

8. Plato, *Gorgias* 452e.

9. Derrida makes a similar statement in his conversation with Gary Olson, claiming that rhetoric should be taught within each academic discipline in a manner appropriate to that discipline. Derrida does not accept that rhetoric has a metacritical role.

such knowledge was always known – whereas the case of medical knowledge proves that knowledge can displace the need for rhetoric, in the public assemblies and law courts there was a healthy debate about what actually represented true knowledge. In these grey areas, the sophists argued that rhetoric had to operate while reason was uncertain.

The issue Socrates avoids, but Gorgias himself fleetingly suggests, is whether rhetoric is a part of a metacritical framework – in other words, is there something that transcends the individual arts and provides the persuasive elements in each? Since rhetoric has no knowledge content of its own (at least according to this dialogue), then it could be that it operates across medicine, art, politics, law and so on as the means of persuasion in each. Is there a common element of persuasion in an imposing temple building, a beautiful bronze statue, a gentle cure and a rousing call to arms, which is not so much to do with content as to do with the effect each has on its audience? If so, rhetoric does not have to be limited to doing clever things with words in law courts and it does not have to be subordinate to knowledge. Unfortunately, Socrates takes the conversation off in another direction. If rhetoric was allowed to have a metacritical role, then the priority of knowledge would have to be questioned and this was not something Socrates or Plato would have wanted to happen. So, instead, Socrates and Gorgias lament the fact that rhetoric often ends with people arguing over the truth. For Socrates this is the telling argument, since Plato has shown elsewhere in the dialogues that the only way to know the truth is through philosophical contemplation. As such, the dialogue turns to a discussion of dialectic as the more fruitful way to find the truth. Of course, this is Plato's world view. The issue remains of how Plato would then seek to convey this to the world at large. It is clear that in his teaching, his dialogues, his interaction with his community, he is as rhetorical as any other person in the ancient world. One of the most famous of Plato's works is Socrates' defence speech delivered at his trial. Although Socrates starts off with (a highly rhetorical) plea for the judges to forgive his plain-speaking, this speech is full of rhetoric and shows that both Socrates and Plato were themselves experts in rhetoric, although, in modern terms, they were clearly 'in denial' of this.[10]

Plato seems to have realized that in the *Gorgias* he had missed the point about rhetoric. In a later dialogue, the *Phaedrus*, he explores rhetoric as 'a kind of

10. Plato, *Apology* 17B, in *Plato with an English Translation*. Vol. 1: *Euthyphro, Apology, Crito, Phaedo, Phaedrus*, tr. H. R. Fowler, LCL (Cambridge, Mass.: Harvard University Press; London William Heinemann, 1914; repr. London: William Heinemann, 1960), pp. 68–69.

leading the soul' (c261a). This dialogue is a complex conversation between Socrates and a young admirer, set in the countryside where the two have been walking together. As such, persuasion between two individuals, two close friends, two lovers, is the main subject matter. In this dialogue, Plato does not confine his discussion to speeches made in the law courts or public assemblies, but suggests that rhetoric can be found also in interpersonal communication. This is a step towards a metacritical approach to rhetoric, an acknowledgment that rhetoric is about persuasion in general rather than just persuasion in the law courts and public assemblies. Socrates and Phaedrus trade speeches about whether it is better to be loved or to love, seeking to best one another, duelling over their friendship. Of course, throughout Socrates' contributions, rhetoric remains second best to philosophy. While exploring rhetoric much more openly than he had in the *Gorgias*, Plato still argues that the best orator is metaphysical: he will explore the true nature of the soul and the way different souls influence one another.[11] Words, then, are simply a means of expressing this metaphysical knowledge rather than influencing it,[12] and rhetoric must be the communication of what is important to the soul. As such, rhetoric still remains secondary to philosophical meditation and dialectic – all rhetoric does is to convey the outcomes of that higher discipline. In the end, Plato is a philosopher and his understanding is that true knowledge, the truth, can be gained only by a search for the reality of the truth in philosophy. The perfect orator must first be a philosopher in order that his rhetoric will be based upon the truth. Any concept that truth was negotiable and contextual and could be affected by verbal virtuosity was simply impossible for Plato's philosophical system.[13]

Although the *Phaedrus* moves closer to a metacritical conceptualization of rhetoric, it was up to Plato's student, Aristotle, to transform Plato's somewhat esoteric philosophy into the art of persuasion: 'So, let rhetoric be the ability to consider every possible means of persuasion . . . since rhetoric, so as to say, appears to be able to consider the means of persuasion in reference to any given subject.'[14]

Rhetoric for Aristotle was all about persuasion, although somewhat frustratingly he does not define what he means by this. In his system of causes, the

11. Plato, *Phaedrus* 271a5–b5, in *Plato*, vol. 1, pp. 550–551.

12. Kennedy, *Classical Rhetoric*, p. 57.

13. Perelman, *New Rhetoric*, p. 12.

14. Aristotle, *The Art of Rhetoric (Ars Rhetorica)*, tr. J. H. Freese, LCL (London: Heinemann; G. P. Putnam's Sons, 1926; repr. London: Harvard University Press, 1994), 1355b.

final cause of (the reason for) rhetoric is persuasion. This makes rhetoric a theoretical art, like poetics, which produced knowledge about persuasion: how to create persuasion in various situations, conditions and contexts. As such, Aristotle has moved away from his teacher's insistence on a separation between knowledge and persuasion. Rhetoric is in fact the discoverer of knowledge – albeit a limited form of knowledge concerning how to persuade others. What this knowledge includes is explored in the rest of the *Ars rhetorica* – a practical exploration of the overriding importance of demonstrable proof, an exploration of the three genres of rhetoric and of the various styles, modes of delivery and arrangement. As such, Aristotle's acceptance of rhetoric as a metacritical framework is compromised by the literary focus of the *Ars rhetorica*, in which there is little exploration of persuasion in the other arts, although there is some discussion of the role of certain textual genres and commonplaces in theatre and music – for example the role of the dramatic prologue.[15] However, the rhetorical nature of other disciplines is not explored in any depth.

While Socrates, Plato and Aristotle had been developing their understanding of rhetoric, others had created handbooks of rhetoric that explored the various rhetorical devices which could be used in the practical outworking of rhetoric.[16] Aristotle seems to have determined to explore the subject matter of these handbooks with a view to revising their content in terms of his own understanding of rhetoric. Plato had done the same in sections of the *Gorgias* and the *Phaedrus*. However, the move from Plato's metaphysics to Aristotle's pragmatism overemphasized the practical outworking of the body of knowledge rhetoric produces. In other words, Aristotle spends a good deal of time exploring the genres of rhetoric – judicial, deliberative and epideictic, along with the various commonplaces (devices) the skilled orator uses to increase the possibility of persuasion. The *Ars rhetorica*, therefore, becomes a practical exploration of the outcome of rhetoric rather than of the art itself; it codifies

---

15. P. M. Phillips, *The Prologue of the Fourth Gospel: A Sequential Reading*, Library of New Testament (New York: T. & T. Clark, 2006), pp. 39–44.

16. A good contemporary example is the *Rhetorica ad Alexandrum*, which circulated among Aristotle's works but was probably written by Anaximenes of Lampsacus in the middle of the fourth century. See Kennedy, *Classical Rhetoric*, pp. 22–23; M. Kraus, 'Ethos as a Technical Means of Persuasion in Ancient Rhetorical Theory', in T. H. Olbricht and A. Eriksson (eds.), *Rhetoric, Ethic and Moral Persuasion in Biblical Discourse: Essays from the 2002 Heidleberg Conference* (New York: T. & T. Clark, 2005), pp. 74–77.

the practice of rhetoric and turns the art into a theory.[17] This theory was focused especially on the role of the enthymeme – the proof of a particular argument.[18] As such, rhetoric moves towards that which can be proved or demonstrated. The domination of proof and of demonstrative discourse would later give rise to the Cartesian model of logical discourse as primary to rhetorical discourse and the abandonment of rhetoric in favour of reason.[19] At this stage, it is noticeable that the move is toward a textual development – towards rhetoric as the artful use of words rather than as a metacritical faculty of persuasion.

This move had a profound effect upon the historical development of rhetoric, since it was this aspect of rhetoric the later Roman orators adopted. The rhetorical works of Cicero and especially Quintilian centre not on the metacritical dimension of rhetoric but rather on the practical outworking of rhetoric. Indeed, it was Quintilian who defined rhetoric not in terms of persuasion but as the 'science of speaking well' (*scientia bene dicendi*).[20] This technical rhetoric becomes the norm within Greek and Roman society and rhetoric itself becomes associated almost completely with verbal/textual virtuosity.[21] This process has happened throughout history – a move from actual rhetoric to textual rhetoric, from oral practice to literary theory, in a process Kennedy and Wuellner both refer to as *letteraturizzazione* (literature-ization).[22] So, James

---

17. Wuellner, 'Rhetorical Criticism', p. 448.

18. G. A. Kennedy, *New Testament Interpretation*, p. 7; and *Classical Rhetoric*, pp. 60–81. See also C. Carey, 'Rhetorical Means of Persuasion', in I. Worthington (ed.), *Persuasion: Greek Rhetoric in Action* (London: Routledge, 1994), pp. 26–46.

19. Grassi, *Rhetoric*, pp. 112–114; D. Cohen, 'Classical Rhetoric and Modern Theories of Discourse', in Worthington, *Persuasion*, pp. 69–82, explores the various developments of classical rhetoric into modern and postmodern thinking.

20. Quintilian, *Institutiones* 2.15.38; Kennedy, *New Testament Interpretation*, p. 13.

21. Victor Bers refers to this as the difference between informal and formal rhetoric, or between 'rhetorical style' and '*rhetorikē technē*', in 'Tragedy and Rhetoric', in Worthington, *Persuasion*, p. 182; see also L. C. Alexander, *The Preface to Luke's Gospel: Literary Convention and Social Context in Luke 1.1–4 and Acts 1.1* (Cambridge: Cambridge University Press, 1993), pp. 65–66; P. Kern, *Rhetoric and Galatians: Assessing an Approach to Paul's Epistle*, SNTSMS 101 (Cambridge: Cambridge University Press, 1998), p. 7; M. Nanos, *The Irony of Galatians: Paul's Letter in First-Century Context* (Minneapolis: Fortress, 2002), pp. 322–331.

22. Kennedy, *Classical Rhetoric*, p. 5; and *New Testament Interpretation*, p. 3; Wuellner, 'Biblical Exegesis', p. 501.

Muilenburg, in his Presidential Address to the Society of Biblical Literature in 1968, did not call on the biblical guild to turn to rhetorical criticism because it was the theoretical art of persuasion or the philosophy of purposeful communication but because it would move the guild back towards an appreciation of the stylistics of the authors:

> What I am interested in, above all, is in understanding the nature of Hebrew literary composition, in exhibiting the structural patterns that are employed for the fashioning of the literary unit, whether in poetry or prose, and in discerning the many and various devices by which the predications are formulated and ordered into a unified whole.[23]

The result of this process, a rhetoric focused on literary production, will probably be the side of rhetoric most readers are already aware of. It is Aristotle and the subsequent handbooks that divide rhetoric into the three genres and that provide the various stages of creating a speech, the commonplaces and rhetorical devices that can be found on so many rhetoric websites.[24] But this form of rhetoric is what Kennedy calls 'secondary' rhetoric.[25] Primary rhetoric is the art of persuasion per se, usually experienced within a largely oral culture: the practice of rhetoric within a society, whether conceptualized or not. Secondary rhetoric is *handbook* rhetoric – the conscious development of primary (oral) rhetoric into a practical (textual) skill, fully conceptualized, with a developed theoretical framework, education system and supportive literature. To some extent, this secondary rhetoric is focused not on the oral delivery of rhetorical practice but on the exploration of verbal and textual virtuosity, often for its own sake. As such, it departs from the role of the orator and instead begins to look at the effect of rhetoric on its audience – a move away from oral skills to textual and literary skills. Whereas primary rhetoric is governed by the practicalities of delivering a speech, secondary rhetoric begins to focus on techniques of relieving tedium, identifying with the audience, creating good literature.

The Greek philosophical rhetoricians provided a bridge between the oral practice and the textual theory and seem to have maintained a foot in both

---

23. J. Muilenburg, 'Form Criticism', p. 8 (see n. 2 above); Perelman, *New Rhetoric*, p. 5.

24. Note e.g. G. Burton's *Silvae rhetoricae*, <http://rhetoric.byu.edu/>, accessed 23 Jan. 2008; R. Nordquist's *Glossary*, <http://www.nt.armstrong.edu/terms.htm>, accessed 23 Jan. 2008; and the quirkily named Rhetorosaurus site, <http://www.rhetorosaurus.co.uk>, accessed 23 Jan. 2008.

25. Kennedy, *Classical Rhetoric*, p. 5.

camps. At times, their interests focused on rhetoric's effect both on a gathered audience (*Gorgias*) and on individuals (*Phaedrus*), and the suggestion (*Gorgias*) and then assertion (Aristotle) that rhetoric is all about persuasion. However, in their discussion of handbook rhetoric and, especially in *Ars rhetorica*, the move towards a body of knowledge offering a technological explanation of rhetoric pushes the discussion decidedly towards secondary rhetoric.

Flowing from its importance within renaissance education, rhetoric has continued to be an important academic discipline within several European systems, and in the United States. As such, it is hardly surprising that secondary rhetoric is also part of the biblical guild's repertoire, with considerable energy being put into the development of rhetorical analysis of various biblical books. Following Muilenburg's call for a move towards rhetorical criticism, a number of scholars have demonstrated the presence of classical rhetorical features within biblical texts, such Hans Dieter Betz in his work on Galatians.[26] However, the guild's exploration of rhetoric still oscillates between primary and secondary rhetoric – between an analysis and exploration of the rhetorical commonplaces or devices and the exploration of the art of persuasion, of the power of the text. While the process of *letteraturizzazione* continues in the biblical guild, there is also a counterbalancing focus on the role of rhetoric as the art of persuasion, the exploration of the 'power' of the text and the determination of the author to persuade and alter world views.[27] It may be that in the new millennium this second focus is actually beginning to become more important than the first.

In his discussion of the role of rhetoric in Galatians, Philip Kern set up a more elaborate series of levels for rhetoric in the ancient world than simply primary and secondary rhetoric.[28] Kern argues that rhetoric was so essential to ancient (and modern) societies that it pervades all levels of social discourse. As such, Kern sets out the following hierarchy of levels:[29]

Level 1: strategic communication
Level 2: painting *oratory* statuary etc.

---

26. See D. F. Watson and A. J. Hausner (eds.), *Rhetorical Criticism of the Bible: A Comprehensive Bibliography with Notes on History and Method* (Leiden: Brill, 1994).

27. So, for example, the latest collection of papers from the 2002 Heidelberg conference, published in 2006, relates to the role of *ethos* and appeals to *ethos* within biblical texts and the focus is clearly on the ideological power of the text rather than on handbook rhetorical devices.

28. Kern, *Rhetoric and Galatians*, pp. 7–38; see also Phillips, *Prologue*, pp. 37–54.

29. Kern, *Rhetoric and Galatians*, p. 9.

Level 3: classical Ch'an rhetoric *Graeco-Roman rhetoric* etc.
Level 4: diatribe market language classroom language *handbook rhetoric* etc.
Level 5: species of handbook rhetoric: judicial, deliberative, epideictic

For our discussion here, Kern's categories need to be translated slightly into the language of strategic communication and encultured rhetoric:

Level 1: strategic communication
Level 2: rhetorical expression
Level 3: encultured expressions of primary rhetoric
Level 4: encultured expressions of secondary rhetoric
Level 5: subordinate divisions of secondary rhetoric and processes of *letteraturizzazione*

Level 1: strategic communication

Kern argues that rhetoric must be explored as strategic communication in general. In other words, rhetoric is not just something done with words but is a strategy at the very heart of communication between individuals, whether that communication is verbal or not. Of course, since a good deal of communication is non-verbal, this focuses our attention on the metacritical nature of rhetoric. This level of study had already been explored both by the ancient rhetoricians and modern scholars such as Perelman, Burke and Grassi. So, Wuellner (referring back to Perelman) states that rhetorical criticism 'takes us to "the social aspect of language which is an instrument of communication and influence on others"'.[30] Or, in Kennedy's words, 'rhetoric is that quality in discourse by which a speaker or writer seeks to accomplish his purposes'.[31] Similarly, Sternberg, in his appendix on 'Ideology, Rhetoric and Poetics' talks of rhetoric as embracing 'the whole discourse in its communicative aspect, as a set of means chosen and organized with an eye to an audience rather than to self-expression or pure making'.[32] In other words, rhetoric must not be limited to doing things with words. Rhetoric as the art of persuasion encompasses all forms of purposeful communication in the various media available for communication.

---

30. Wuellner, 'Rhetorical Criticism', p. 449, quoting from Perelman, *New Rhetoric*, p. 513.

31. Kennedy, *New Testament Interpretation*, p. 3.

32. M. Sternberg, *The Poetics of Biblical Narrative: Ideological Literature and the Drama of Reading* (Bloomington: Indiana University Press, 1985), p. 482.

Derrida and Grassi are wary of such broad definitions, since the expansion of rhetoric to include all strategic communication can be seen as a diminishing of the core role rhetoric has within specific acts of communication – if rhetoric is everything, then rhetoric is nothing.[33] The danger here is not to limit rhetoric but to make rhetoric so broad and so diffuse a phenomenon that it would be meaningless, subsumed into general theories of communication and social dynamics. However, in the quotation from Sternberg, there is a possible limit – the need for a contextual situation, the fact that rhetoric is interested not just in 'pure making' but rather that the 'making' is context-based; the 'making' is for an audience.[34] Admittedly, this is a fine distinction, since it could be argued that all communication is made for an audience, even if it is self-referential. But the point still stands: rhetoric is not just communication, but 'purposeful communication', communication within a specific context with a specific goal in mind.[35] This always means that, to some extent or other, rhetorical criticism needs to be a practical criticism rather than a theoretical criticism, since it is always interested in the interplay between the author–orator and the audience–reader.[36] So, Vernon Robbins's work in creating a socio-rhetorical criticism emphasizes the contextual nature of rhetoric, although not without creating its own handbook style.[37] Also the emerging science of sociolinguistics picks up this understanding of rhetoric by analysing the way in which different groups seek to share their world view both within and outside their own society through the manipulation of language.[38]

However, clearly there is still a long way to go before this understanding of rhetoric is fully grasped. For too long the biblical guild has paid homage to the

---

33. Olson, 'Jacques Derrida'; Grassi, *Rhetoric*, pp. xvii–xviii.
34. Wuellner, 'Rhetorical Criticism', p. 450; Olson, 'Jacques Derrida'.
35. Perelman, *New Rhetoric*, p. 7.
36. Kennedy, *New Testament Interpretation*, pp. 3–5; Wuellner, 'Rhetorical Criticism', p. 453; Perelman, *New Rhetoric*, pp. 11, 14; Burke, *Rhetoric of Motives*. For an introduction to and brief application of Burke's approach to rhetoric in terms of practical criticism, see Crafton, 'Dancing of an Attitude', in Porter and Olbricht, *Rhetoric and the New Testament*, pp. 429–442.
37. Robbins, *Exploring*; 'Rhetoric and Culture: Exploring Types of Cultural Rhetoric in a Text', in Porter and Olbricht, *Rhetoric and the New Testament*, esp. pp. 441–447.
38. M. A. K. Halliday, *Language as Social Semiotic: A Social Interpretation of Language as Meaning* (London: Edward Arnold, 1978), is the classic text, although a simpler

concept of the 'intentional fallacy', supposedly drawn from the work of Wimsatt and Beardsley,[39] by which we steer clear of attempting to work out what an author really meant. This has been seen as a move towards reading a text more objectively and more scientifically. Since we have no access to the identity or intentions of many of the biblical authors and since we cannot reconstruct those identities or intentions, the biblical guild has sought to bypass the role of the author through the development of *form criticism*, where cultural norms replace the author, or through *redaction criticism*, where other texts displace the author and create an author of the gaps, or through *literary criticism*, where the reader assumes more responsibility for the creation of a text's meaning. However, Wimsatt and Beardsley's discussion concerned speculation about external authorial intentions in poetry, and Beardsley himself later referred to the article as 'designedly subversive and unpleasantly provoking'.[40] The intentional fallacy sought to expose not the rhetorical purposes of the author, but the critic's

> reliance on external intention, gathered from the author's psychology or biography or 'revelations (in journals, for example, or letters or reported conversations) about how and why [he] wrote the poem – to what lady, while sitting on what lawn, or at the death of what friend or brother'.[41]

This exploration of the archaeology of a poem is decidedly different from the concept of authorial intention within a consciously rhetorical mode of communication. Rhetoric is intensely interested in authorial intention (or at least in a text-immanent intent if we cannot or will not speak of a specific author's intent), since it is so focused on the artful creation of a specific act of

---

introduction can be found in J. Holmes, *Introduction to Sociolinguistics* (London: Longman, 1992). There are also applications within biblical studies, esp. Bruce Malina's work; e.g. his 'John's: The Maverick Christian Group, The Evidence of Sociolinguistics', *BTB* 24.4 (1987), pp. 167–182. See Phillips, *Prologue*, pp. 57–71, for an alternative view on the sociolinguistics of the Fourth Gospel.

39. W. K. Wimsatt and M. C. Beardsley, *The Verbal Icon: Studies in the Meaning of Poetry* (Lexington: University of Kentucky Press, 1954), esp. the chapters entitled 'The Intentional Fallacy' (pp. 2–18) and 'The Affective Fallacy' (pp. 20–39).

40. Sternberg, *Poetics*, pp. 8–9, referring to M. C. Beardsley, 'Intentions and Interpretations: A Fallacy Revived', in M. Wreen and D. Callen (eds.), *The Aesthetic Point of View* (Ithaca: Cornell University Press, 1982), p. 188.

41. Sternberg, *Poetics*, p. 8, citing Wimsatt and Beardsley, *Verbal Icon*, p. 10.

communication intended to create or reinforce adherence to the author's point of view.[42]

What matters is where the argument goes from here. Aristotle's initial definition of rhetoric as 'the faculty of learning in each case the available means of persuasion' potentially places rhetoric at the metacritical level. However, we have seen that Aristotle then develops the practice of rhetoric within the terms of handbook rhetoric rather than exploring the more general concept of rhetoric as persuasion. However, contemporary theorists are rehabilitating rhetoric at this metacritical level – as a general concept of interpersonal communication that to some extent transcends the usual boundaries of historical-critical methodology, literary theory and hermeneutics.[43] Chaim Perelman rejects Aristotle's move towards *letteraturizzazione* by pointing to the effect of rhetoric as an act of speech:

> The distinction of the different genres of oratory is highly artificial, as the study of a speech shows. Mark Antony's famous speech in Shakespeare's *Julius Caesar* opens with a funeral eulogy, a typical case of epideictic discourse and ends by provoking a riot that is clearly political. Its goal is to intensify an adherence to values, to create a disposition to act, and finally to bring people to act. Seen in such perspective, rhetoric becomes a subject of great philosophical interest.[44]

Kenneth Burke moved the discussion in the same direction by suggesting that the chief means of persuasion was 'identification'.[45] Burke's philosophical foundation is that texts act, and in such a way as to 'entice others to agree with [them]'.[46] Burke calls this the 'dancing of an attitude' and it represents the way in which different aspects of a text (such as authorial intention, reception,

---

42. Kern, *Rhetoric and Galatians*, pp. 1–6; Phillips, *Prologue*, pp. 38–39; Perelman, *New Rhetoric*, p. 14. See also W. Booth, *The Rhetoric of Fiction* (Chicago: University of Chicago Press, 1961), pp. 149–168.

43. Kennedy, *New Testament Interpretation*, pp. 3–5; and *Classical Rhetoric*, pp. 5–6 and 108–119; Wuellner, 'Biblical Exegesis' and 'Rhetorical Criticism', esp. the opening comments on the link between literary theory and rhetoric, pp. 448–449; Robbins, 'Rhetoric and Culture', in Porter and Olbricht, *Rhetoric and the New Testament*, pp. 443–463; Hester and Hester, *Rhetoric and Hermeneutics*, esp. the essays in Part 1.

44. Perelman, *New Rhetoric*, p. 7.

45. Burke, *Rhetoric of Motives*; Crafton, 'Dancing of an Attitude', in Porter and Olbricht, *Rhetoric and the New Testament*, pp. 429–442.

46. Crafton, 'Dancing of an Attitude', p. 431; cf. Perelman, *New Rhetoric*, pp. 9–17.

intertextuality, social and historical influences and ideological connections) come together to change the perspective of the reader. Burke argues that this potential to change a reader's world view is the essential 'power' of the text, or how a text acts. His work goes on to show how this is effected through the reader identifying with or dissociating from the values expressed through the text. Burke's interest lies especially in the concept of 'identification', in that communication offers various opportunities for communicants to identify with one another, to agree that they will share viewpoints on at least some issues, that they will share 'consubstantiality' with one another.[47] As such, rhetoric embraces both persuasion and socialization, while also acknowledging the possibility of division and invective.[48] The role of a text, the 'power' of the text, especially a religious text, is to influence the way a reader sees the world – to persuade the reader that the text's world view or ideology is in fact the only way to see the world. Meir Sternberg expresses this concept well:

> As persuader, the rhetorician seeks not just to affect but to affect with a view to establishing consensus in the face of possible demur and opposition. Success has only one meaning and one measure for him: bringing the audience's viewpoint into alignment with his own.[49]

Level 2: rhetorical expression

Rhetoric as strategic communication attempts to mould another person's view of the world in which he or she lives; it invites its audience to reconsider their existing world view in the light of a world view promoted through strategic communication of one kind or another. However, in order to effect this potential change, and even to make the invitation to change, rhetoric has to be made real within the world in which we live: communicated, either between individuals or between the text and its audience, or through some other medium and its audience. It is important to acknowledge that this desire to communicate, to persuade, to influence does not have to be communicated or effected textually. So, Kern includes painting and statuary

---

47. Burke, *Rhetoric of Motives*, pp. 19–27.

48. Ibid., p. 46.

49. Sternberg, *Poetics*, quoted by Crafton, 'Dancing of an Attitude', p. 431. However, it is worth noting that Burke does not appear in Sternberg's bibliography or footnotes. See below on the rhetoric of sacred texts.

within his list of possible expressions, although without exploring the way in which these arts are themselves rhetorical. Different 'authors' will seek to persuade through different media: voice, text, visual arts, plastic arts, dramatic arts.[50] Just as a picture can paint a thousand words, so too architectural styles, musical forms and dramatic productions can act as rhetorical devices, as elements of strategic communication. As such, it is arguable that just about any artefact could represent a rhetorical strategy promoting a specific world view: 'As we go through life experiencing and enjoying music, clothing, architecture, food, and so forth, we are also participating in rhetorical struggles over what kind of society we will live in and what sort of people we will be.'[51]

The Bible contains numerous examples of non-verbal rhetorical expression. Our society, however, has become fascinated by the text and as such it is not surprising that text-based rhetoric dominates the discussion of rhetoric. Kern gives no examples of non-verbal rhetoric and Perelman urges against the development of theories of argumentation using non-verbal rhetoric. His argument is ideological: an argument must be active. Since non-verbal rhetoric relies on reception by an audience, it is therefore passive. A picture may paint a thousand words, but too many of these words rely upon the audience's subjective interpretation of the picture. Perelman concludes that non-verbal rhetoric cannot be used in a theory of argumentation other than as supporting evidence for a truly active argument.[52]

----

50. Kern, *Rhetoric and Galatians*, p. 8; E. Panofsky, *Meaning in the Visual Arts* (Garden City; Doubleday, 1955; repr. Chicago: University Of Chicago Press, 1983); E. Corbett, 'The Rhetoric of the Open Hand and the Rhetoric of the Closed Fist', *CCC* 20.5 (1969), pp. 288–296; R. Browne, 'Response to Edward P. I. Corbett, "The Rhetoric of the Open Hand and the Rhetoric of the Closed Fist"', *CCC* 21.2 (1970), pp. 187–190; R. Barthes, *Image, Music, Text*, tr. S. Heath (London: Fontana, 1977), esp. 'The Photographic Image' and 'Rhetoric of the Image', pp. 15–31 and 32–52; R. Amossy, 'Toward a Rhetoric of the Stage: The Scenic Realization of Verbal Clichés', *Poetics Today* 2.3 (1981), pp. 49–63; S. Meltzoff, 'On the Rhetoric of Vision', *Leonardo* 3.1 (1970), pp. 27–38; T. Eagleton, *Literary Theory: An Introduction* (Oxford: Blackwell, 1996), p. 107; D. Birdsell and L. Groarke, 'Toward a Theory of Visual Argument', *AA* 33.1 (1996), pp. 1–10; and D. Fleming, 'Can Pictures Be Arguments', *AA* 33.1 (1996), pp. 11–23.

51. B. Brummett, *Rhetoric in Popular Culture* (London: Sage, 2006).

52. Perelman, *New Rhetoric*; see also Fleming, 'Pictures', who strongly agrees that pictures in themselves cannot 'argue'.

However, most images are in fact artefacts just like texts – they are created by an artist with media other than words. As such, just as with texts, the artist will have chosen specific elements to include within the piece and will have moulded the image to create an effect of some kind or other, often with a specific audience in mind. Even the most pure art forms rely upon a mix of content, medium and form that seek to portray a message of some kind.[53] There is surely an analogy here with the orator's handling of words. Other artists simply use paint, canvas or stone rather than words. So, while expressing reservation, Robert Brown shows the possible extent of non-verbal rhetoric:

> The idea of non-verbal rhetoric has to be examined with care. The non-verbal arts which are mimetic (e.g. mimetic painting and dance, mime, silent films) can, like the arts of language, be employed for persuasion as well as delight. And they too employ signs as materials in the persuasive process. Other arts less directly involved in semiosis, like music, dancing, light shows, and the arts of costume and design, may be used in a quasi-rhetorical way to put an audience in the proper frame of mind; but they are usually controlled by or subordinated to a verbal or other semiotic process. Even architecture has been used rhetorically . . . All these it seems may legitimately be called non-verbal rhetoric because all are involved in a use of a semiotic system for persuasive purposes.[54]

We might want to query some of Perelman's logocentricity in his rejection of non-verbal rhetoric. Roland Barthes, among others, has explored the various levels of semiosis involved in pictures and in film,[55] and we shall explore below a biblical example of architecture as rhetoric. Created artefacts are expressions and, as expressions, promote the world view of their creator, whether intentionally or not. These artefacts are part of an individual's strategic communication and act as rhetorical expressions. On this basis it would seem legitimate to talk of the rhetoric of non-verbal communication. However, there is the danger of making rhetoric too all-embracing: that rhetoric becomes everything, and so nothing. Because of this, as we see in Perelman, some have sought to limit rhetoric to the verbal/textual in order to stop it colonizing the realms of aesthetics, politics, cultural studies and ideology. On the other hand, if rhetoric is strategic communication and not just

---

53. Panofsky, *Meaning*, pp. 38–50.
54. Browne, 'Response', p. 188.
55. Barthes, *Image, Music, Text*, pp. 46–51; cf. Amossy, 'Rhetoric of the Stage', p. 54.

playing with words, then how does a reader stop interpreting a non-verbal arte-fact as a sign? What are the limits of rhetoric?[56] How might such a non-verbal rhetoric work?

One of the key rhetorical strategies at work in this struggle, whether in verbal or non-verbal rhetoric, according to Perelman, is the creation of 'pres-ence'.[57] This strategy brings to the audience's attention that which may well be absent. The orator can do this, in verbal or textual oratory, through a whole series of devices the handbooks excel in describing. Indeed, a whole group of figures of speech, known under the umbrella terms of *enargia* (vividness), *hypo-typosis* (lively description) or *demonstratio* (vivid description), were developed to assist the orator to 'set things out in such a way that the matter seems to unfold, and the thing to happen, before our very eyes'.[58] These devices attempt to make the subject matter more 'real' for the audience, to encourage the audience to focus on them rather than upon other aspects that might well have negative implications for the argumentation process. For example, a defence lawyer may well use character witnesses to emphasize the social acceptability of the defend-ant. These character witnesses make 'present' the defendant's character and in turn 'background' other aspects of the case such as the prosecution's evidence. Different elements of strategic communication can therefore impact upon an audience by making one world view more present or relevant than another and so attracting the audience's allegiance to that world view.

This is a basic rhetorical strategy found both in societies that have concep-tualized their strategic communication (Hellenistic and Roman) and in those that remain preconceptual (Hebrew).[59] So, in his disputation concerning his own welfare or lack of it, Job and his friends foreground different aspects of reality. However, when God himself speaks (Job 38 – 41), he does not seek to justify his own actions or to provide some form of apology for what has hap-pened to Job. Instead, in a realization of much of what Elihu has previously argued, God pours forth a whole list of questions that focus upon his own character – especially as the eternal Creator. The questions are couched in terms of accusation:

---

56. It is interesting to see Jacques Derrida's confusion on this very topic, at one time talking of rhetoric as cultural phenomenon, rhetoric as everything, and then assuming that rhetoric is simply verbal/textual virtuosity. See Olson, 'Jacques Derrida', pp. 1–21.

57. Perelman, *New Rhetoric*, pp. 17–23.

58. Cicero, *Rhetorica ad Herennium* 4.68.

59. Kennedy, *Classical Rhetoric*, p. 120; Kern, *Rhetoric and Galatians*, pp. 8–9.

Have you ever in your life commanded the morning,
  And caused the dawn to know its place . . .?
Have you entered into the springs of the sea
  Or walked in the recesses of the deep?
(Job 38:12, 16 NASB)

If this text were part of Greco-Roman rhetoric, we would recognize the appeal to the character of the speaker (*ethos*) as well as the rhetorical device/commonplace known as *anacoenosis* or *erotema* (the use of interrogative questioning that does not expect a response from the audience but which assumes that the answer is obvious). There is no evidence, however, that the author of Job (whoever that was and whenever this text might have been written) knew any of the Greco-Roman handbook terms. In fact, some argue that Hebrew rhetoric is based on Egyptian or Assyrian rhetorical practices, which are much less understood than the Greco-Roman.[60] However, clearly the author was aware of modes of strategic communication and was able to deploy rhetorical devices in order to make present that which he thought would alter the audience's world view. Many other authors in the Hebrew Bible deploy similar strategies. The author of Job and authors of biblical books in general make use of standard rhetorical devices to make one world view more present than another, and so more real and acceptable to their audiences.

In the world view proposed in Job 38 – 41, God cannot be cross-examined, for he is the omniscient Creator, his actions are so beyond what can be expected of a human being as to be beyond reproach. As such, Job's response makes clear that he accepts the world view without question:

I know that you can do all things;
  no plan of yours can be thwarted.
You asked, 'Who is this that obscures my counsel without knowledge?'
  Surely I spoke of things I did not understand,
  things too wonderful for me to know.

You said, 'Listen now, and I will speak;
  I will question you,
  and you shall answer me.'

---

60. M. Roth, 'Rhetorical Criticism, Hebrew Bible', in J. Hayes (ed.), *Dictionary of Biblical Interpretation*, 2 vols. (Nashville: Abingdon, 1999), pp. 396–399; J. Breck, 'Chiasmus as a Key to Biblical Interpretation', *StVTQ* 43 (1999), p. 255.

My ears had heard of you
  but now my eyes have seen you.
Therefore I despise myself
  and repent in dust and ashes.
(Job 42:2–6 NIV)

Job capitulates to the presencing of a new world view: God's. He chooses
to identify with God and to bring his own understanding into line with God's.
This does not mean that Job's previous arguments have been answered, or that
the arguments put forward by Eliphaz, Bildad or Zophar have been answered.
To some extent, the presencing of God's character at the end of the disputation simply makes those arguments irrelevant. The outcome of Job's capitula-
tion is that God promises to punish Eliphaz, Bildad and Zophar, and to reward
Job. The message to the reader is clear: accepting God's world view as promoted in this text (Job 38 – 41) will ensure your welfare, whereas any attempt
to promote a world view contrary to this (e.g. Job's counsellors' speeches
earlier in the book) will result in punishment, although even this can be averted
by acquiescence to God's directives (Job 42:8).

While this example is limited to verbal rhetoric, examples of rhetorical
expression creating a sense of 'presence' using other media can also be found
in the Bible. A good example of non-verbal rhetoric within Israelite society is
the use of architecture. So, the development of the temple in both conceptual and actual form within David and Solomon's Jerusalem represents architectural rhetoric in terms of socio-political policy and in physical presence.[61]
First, the whole process of centralization of the Yahweh cult away from the
high places and into Jerusalem, whether or not that policy is fully imple-
mented, is an attempt to change the Israelite/Canaanite world view and to

61. S. J. de Vries, *I Kings*, WBC 12 (Waco: Word, 1985), pp. xxvi–xxix; S. Yeivin, 'Social,
    Religious and Cultural Trends in Jerusalem under the Davidic Dynasty', *VT* 3.2
    (1953), pp. 149–166. The literature on the interplay between sacred space, rhetoric
    and hermeneutics is gradually expanding. See e.g. M. Eliade, *Patterns in Comparative
    Religion* (New York: Sheed & Ward, 1958); P. Williams, 'Sacred Space in North
    America', *JAAR* 70.3 (2002), pp. 593–609; L. Jones, *The Hermeneutics of Sacred
    Architecture: Experience, Interpretation, Comparison*, 2 vols. (Cambridge, Mass.: Harvard
    Center for the Study of World Religions, 2000); J. Thomas, 'The Hermeneutics of
    Megalithic Space', in C. Tilley (ed.), *Interpretative Archaeology* (1993), pp. 73–97; Phillips,
    Prologue, pp. 1–6, 221–228; W. Brueggemann, *Mandate to Difference: An Invitation to the
    Contemporary Church* (Louisville: Westminster John Knox, 2007), pp. 9–40.

focus power and prestige at David's new capital at Jerusalem. This process of religious centralization, allied with the building projects within Jerusalem including the development of the palace/temple complex, represents the Jerusalem regime's attempt to control what is happening throughout Israel through the major societal marker institutions.[62] While the high places could operate independently of a Jerusalem hierarchy, allied to the older, pre-Davidic tribal structures, the centralization of worship into Jerusalem focuses power and social leverage into the hands of those in Jerusalem:

> Once the kingdom had been consolidated, the empire secured, and the city of Jerusalem turned into an increasingly pompous showplace for regal glory and power, Solomon took the logical, yet ultimately dangerous, step of building the temple. Clearly, the temple was meant to be recognized by the entire population of Israel, with its political dependencies, as the grand residence of Yahweh the champion God. Just as Solomon had adopted the Near Eastern ideology of the supreme resident God, with himself as king representing and serving the Deity, so did he adopt the Near Eastern concept of the temple as the divine residence.[63]

This concept was not limited to Solomon. Throughout the history of the post-Solomonic regime, we see various waves of centralization as the state becomes more and more threatened by external and internal pressures. It is the architectural reality and 'presence' of the temple/palace complex that provides some of the political and religious rhetoric for the domination of the Jerusalem elite over against the former tribal structures.

Secondly, the location, size and visual domination of the temple over the rest of Jerusalem provided a very present awareness of the wealth and power of the Jerusalem elite for those living in the city and, perhaps more importantly, for those making pilgrimage to the city. Here politics and religion provide visual architectural backing for the Jerusalem elite – an ostentatious show of their wealth, their piety as servants of Yahweh and their ability to dictate how Yahweh should be worshipped. Indeed, pilgrimage becomes a rhetorical tool

---

62. Interestingly, 2 Sam. 7 opposes this non-verbal rhetoric with its own verbal rhetoric about the role of the temple. The temple here is God's temple and is to bring glory only to God. In fact, it will be the establishment of God's house on these terms that will bring permanence and stability to the king's house (2 Sam. 7:13, 16, 24). Thus the text seeks to undercut the architectural rhetoric with a rhetoric of its own, and only the textual rhetoric survives physically.

63. De Vries, *I Kings*, p. xxvi.

in itself by bringing people to the very heart of this display of political power and wealth and by associating the regime's power/wealth with the nation's history and religious identity. Elites have been aware since the dawn of society that impressive and expensive architecture has a profound influence on the subordination of the masses, as shown, for example, in the ubiquity of elite Hellenistic and Roman archaeology at key sites throughout the extent of their empires. This sense of the rhetorical power of architecture even appears in a brief saying of Jesus concerning the obvious visibility of the city on the hill in Matthew 5:14, in which Jesus may be alluding to one of the Galilean centres of Hellenistic power, Sepphoris, built on a dominant ridge in light stone that reflected the sun. No one can hide a city on the hill – and the city was built on the hill and adorned by Herod Antipas specifically to make a rhetorical state-ment of power and wealth to the people of central Galilee.

Architecture, as the manipulation of space and landscape, is a rhetorical tool that presences power and wealth and so establishes the dominant world view: 'To call a space sacred asserts that a place, its structure, and its symbols express fundamental cultural values and principles. By giving these visible form, the sacred place makes tangible the corporate identity of a people and their world.'[64]

Of course, when a dominant world view is challenged, then a change in archi-tecture, a change in the visible proofs of domination, will also be effected along-side the regime change. We see this in the vicissitudes of the Jerusalem temple, (1) established by Solomon as a sign of God's presence and his (or the Jerusalem elite's?) authority in the tenth century, (2) its destruction by the Babylonians in their regime change in 586 BC, (3) its rebuilding under Zerubbabel in the late sixth century BC as a re-establishment of a legitimate Jewish regime in Jerusalem (albeit under the authority of the Persian overlord and so 'licensed' by them), (4) its extensive remodelling by Herod from 19 BC onwards as he sought to model his new regime on the lines of the Davidic past, followed by (5) the destruction of this temple by the Romans in AD 70 in their attempt to impose final control over the regime. Indeed, the discussions in the NT of the destruction and obso-lescence of the temple, alongside the apocalyptic revelation of a new temple, represent the same kind of rhetoric. Since the NT represents a new world view that, to some extent, replaces or modifies the old, a new architecture is needed – although this time that architecture is not instantiated within a physical build-ing but in the corporeality of Jesus and of his followers (Matt. 12:6; 27:40; Mark 13:1–2; 14:58; 15:29; Luke 21:5–6; John 2:19–21; 1 Cor. 3:16–17; Eph. 2:21).

---

64. J. Brereton, 'Sacred Space', in M. Eliade (ed.), *Encyclopedia of Religion*, vol. 12, p. 534, cited in Williams, 'Sacred Space', p. 595.

Level 3: encultured expressions of primary rhetoric

Kern's next level is to explore a specific enculturation of verbal rhetorical expression, Greco-Roman rhetoric. Although this level could refer to Persian statuary or early English hymnody or Polynesian architecture, Kern's ultimate goal is to narrow the discussion down to the textual rhetoric of Galatians and, as such, his emphasis is on textual rhetoric. This means Kern is now focused on the text and all other forms of rhetoric are barely mentioned from here on: we have 'move[d] from persuasive discourse employing words (level 2) to their employment within a particular milieu (level 3)'.[65] To some extent, this level represents a minor transition from rhetorical expression per se (primary rhetoric?) to encultured expressions of this (primary) rhetoric, through to an exploration of specific examples of encultured secondary rhetoric.[66] In other words, these three levels, together with the specificity of Level 5, represent the process of *letteraturizzazione*. The point that Kern is making here, however, is important. He is arguing that as a phenomenon of human (interpersonal and inter-group) communication, rhetoric is expressed in different cultures in different ways. Kern's example of this is to explore an ancient Buddhist form of rhetoric, known as Ch'an rhetoric.[67] However, much wider discussions could be held about the use of rhetoric in different cultures.[68]

The enculturation of strategic communication presents a number of potential difficulties for those exploring rhetoric in the Bible, since biblical material is drawn from several cultures and many different eras, some of which had conceptualized rhetoric and some of which had not.

First, the NT is written from within a broadly Hellenistic milieu in which rhetoric was widely developed in both primary and secondary forms. It is likely, therefore, that NT authors were aware of the primary rhetoric that was part and parcel of Hellenistic civilization. This exposure to rhetoric would enable them to pick up the general strategic nature of communication and to make use of general strategies of persuasion within their oral and textual discourse. Indeed, some NT authors may have been aware of secondary rhetoric to some extent and were able to employ recognizable rhetorical strategies within their

---

65. Kern, *Rhetoric and Galatians*, p. 9.

66. Kern himself shows some ambivalence at this level, stating that his use of the term 'Graeco-Roman Rhetoric' is special to this section of his argument and will be used with another elsewhere (ibid., p. 9, n. 5).

67. Ibid., pp. 10–12.

68. Kennedy, *Classical Rhetoric*, begins some of this exploration, pp. 6–9.

texts. However, we cannot therefore assume that handbook forms of rhetoric, with textbook standard devices and commonplaces, will naturally be found in NT texts. The reason for this is that textbook rhetoric tends to be a pedagogical tool rather than a literary reality – in other words, it is there as part of the secondary support to rhetoric, part of the teaching of rhetoric, rather than an expression of primary rhetoric. Indeed, those who practised elaborate and sophisticated rhetoric, as found in the textbooks, were often ridiculed. Their texts were highly polished pieces of art, often written up after the specific delivery of the speech and amended to become exhibitions of the art of rhetoric rather than practical, real-life examples of it.

This refining of rhetoric in elite literature should be contrasted with the more rough and ready pragmatism of the texts of the period, particularly when those texts were of relatively low status such as the NT books. So, Nils Lund complained that when biblical rhetoric is compared to refined Greco-Roman rhetoric, it is normally 'found wanting'; in other words, either the authors created crude or unfinished rhetorical devices, or they were not creating rhetoric at all but simply employing 'natural eloquence'.[69] Lund is seeking to find a textbook rhetoric or a polished rhetoric simply not present in this form of literature. But that does not mean the NT does not use Greco-Roman rhetorical devices and strategies.

Another contributory factor is that the NT also has links into Jewish culture and the Hebrew Bible. This means that the conceptualized rhetoric drawn from the Hellenistic milieu is heavily influenced by Hebrew/Jewish non-conceptualized rhetorical forms and styles. It is unlikely therefore that the NT would exhibit pure Greco-Roman rhetoric. But the picture is somewhat confused by a whole host of ideological arguments drawn from this cultural mix for and against the Hellenistic/rhetorical culture that forms the backdrop to the NT texts. So, Kennedy explores the way in which Paul, one of the most rhetorical of the NT authors, actually debunks rhetoric and philosophy by arguing that he will not use proofs (signs or wisdom) to proclaim the good news about Jesus (1 Cor. 1:22–25), that God chooses foolishness above wisdom (1 Cor. 1:26–31) and that in the end all things lie in God to be

---

69. N. Lund, *Chiasmus in the New Testament: A Study in Formgeschichte* (Chapel Hill: University of North Carolina Press, 1942), p. 8; cited in Kennedy, *New Testament Interpretation*, p. 11. See also Lund's two preliminary articles, which include some discussion of the history of chiasmus-chasing, 'The Presence of Chiasmus in the Old Testament', *AJSL* 46.2 (1930), pp. 104–126; and 'The Presence of Chiasmus in the New Testament', *JR* 10.1 (1930), pp. 79–93.

revealed (1 Cor. 2:6–13).[70] Such rhetoric does not follow the models set out
by the classical rhetoricians. However, in complete contrast to Paul's deconstructed rhetoric in 1 Corinthians, Galatians can be read as a classical rhetorical apology (with exordium, narration, proposition, proof and conclusion[71]),
with the rest of the Pauline corpus reflecting similar awareness of the rhetorical norms.[72] As such, in the Pauline corpus and in the NT in general, there is
a decidedly mixed approach to rhetoric. We shall not expect to find pure, theoretical rhetoric in these texts but rather living, vernacular fusion of primary
rhetoric drawn from both Greek and Hebrew rhetorical traditions.

Secondly, when we consider the rhetoric of the Hebrew Bible, it is unlikely
that the authors were even aware of the categories of Greco-Roman rhetoric.
As Kennedy says, it would seem that OT rhetoric remained preconceptual; in
other words, it existed, as countless scholars have shown, but no body of literature was developed as a means of teaching or standardization.[73] So, David
is commended as 'one who knows how to speak' (1 Sam. 16:18 my tr.), and the
ext clearly portrays David making use of rhetorical devices in his speech (1
Sam. 17:45–47; 24:8–15; 25:21–22; 2 Sam. 1:19–27). Plenty of other people in
the OT also offer similarly rhetorical utterances.[74] Rhetoric was an everyday
aspect of the strategic communication in Israelite society, although without the
development of a secondary rhetoric as with Greco-Roman literature. In other

70. Cf. Paul's argument in Galatians concerning the knowledge he has about the Jesus
    traditions: nothing has come from a human source; all has been revealed to him by
    God.

71. Kennedy, *Classical Rhetoric*, pp. 129–132; H. D. Betz, 'The Literary Composition and
    Function of Paul's Letter to the Galatians', *NTS* 21 (1975), pp. 353–379. For
    alternative readings of the rhetoric of Galatians, see Kern, *Rhetoric and Galatians*;
    and Nanos, *Irony of Galatians*.

72. E.g. M. Debanne, 'An Enthymematic Reading of Philippians: Towards a Typology
    of Pauline Arguments', in S. E. Porter and D. L. Stamps (eds.), *Rhetorical Criticism
    and the Bible* (Sheffield: Sheffield Academic Press, 2002), pp. 481–503; F. Long,
    'From Epicheiremes to Exhortation: A Pauline Method for Moral Persuasion in
    1 Thessalonians', in Olbricht and Eriksson, *Rhetoric, Ethic*, pp. 179–195; but see
    the bibliographies in Kern, *Rhetoric and Galatians*, and Nanos, *Irony of Galatians*, for
    further reading on Paul and rhetoric.

73. See his *Classical Rhetoric*, p. 120, and Bible and Culture Collective, *Postmodern Bible*,
    p. 173, for suggestions for further reading on this subject; D. G. Firth, 'Shining the
    Lamp: The Rhetoric of 2 Samuel 5–24', *TynBul* 52.2 (2001), pp. 207–208.

74. Roth, 'Rhetorical Criticism', p. 396.

words, Hebrew rhetoric seems to have been an expression of primary rhetoric – of the practical art that had not yet undergone the process of *letteraturizzazione* and become a theoretical art. This means that we do not have the specific categories to name the commonplaces, devices or tropes, or to analyse whether they conformed to any putative standards.

This does not prevent modern authors attempting to distil a handbook rhetoric out of the OT. So, Kennedy outlines a number of possible themes:

- an assertion of authority, 'the simple enunciation of God's truth'
- a focus on God as the active role in the effectiveness of rhetoric rather than the orator
- the lack of enthymematic argumentation – the truth is stated not proved
- the use of various forms of covenant speeches outlining the relationship between God and his people and comprising a narrative of what has happened, commandments concerning future action, along with threats or promises relating to the audience's response to these commandments
- the use of various prophetic and poetic forms[75]

These themes resemble elements of classical Greco-Roman rhetoric, but do not parallel it. Hebrew, or rather Judeo-Christian rhetoric, as Kennedy terms it, is only analogous to Greco-Roman rhetorical terminology. So, in the example above, I discussed the possibility of Job 38 – 41 being an example of Hebrew forensic rhetoric that includes examples of *anacoenosis* or *erotema* (rhetorical questions). I am not assuming here that the author of Job knew the difference between judicial, deliberative and epideictic rhetoric, or that he knew the rhetorical terms. What I am saying is that this *looks like* forensic rhetoric and *resembles anacoenosis*.

In his *Poetics of Biblical Narrative*, Meir Sternberg has gone much further than Kennedy by identifying fifteen rhetorical devices that make up what he calls a rhetorical repertoire for the Hebrew Bible. Unfortunately, Sternberg's rhetorical devices seem to be much more subjective than the Greco-Roman commonplaces and reflect the interests of narrative and reader-response criticism more than rhetoric, such as narrational evaluation, charged dramatization, informational redundancy, play of perspectives, analogical patterning, recurrence of key words, and pseudo-objective narration.[76]

---

75. Kennedy, *Classical Rhetoric*, pp. 121–122.
76. Sternberg, *Poetics*, pp. 475–481; on the dangers of reducing rhetoric to discourse, see Cohen, 'Classical Rhetoric', pp. 75–81.

Once again, it is possible to draw analogies between Sternberg's repertoire and classical Greco-Roman rhetoric. So, for example, we could note the similarities between Sternberg's *charged dramatization* and Greco-Roman rhetoric's *enargia* or *demonstratio*. Both involve intensifying the audience's focus on a specific event so that the audience notices aspects of that event that will persuade them, for example, of a character's moral standing or authority. However, that is not because Hebrew Bible authors knew of the Greco-Roman rhetorical device, but rather that they knew how to express themselves in Hebrew in a manner similar to *enargia*. The major problem with the majority of Sternberg's 'devices' is that they reflect elements of narrative or literary criticism rather than act as expressions of Hebrew rhetorical devices. This means that Sternberg's repertoire seems to cover narratology rather than rhetoric.

The fact remains that it is hard to reduce preconceptual primary rhetoric to a list of concepts – that is the whole point of calling it primary rhetoric as opposed to secondary rhetoric. It seems rather strange for the ancient primary rhetoric of the Hebrew Bible to be submitted to *letteraturizzazione*, reduced to handbooks of Hebrew rhetorical commonplaces by modern critics. If we cannot name and taxonomize the Hebrew devices, we are left with the need to use analogies to Greco-Roman rhetorical terminology that is already conceptualized. However, we need to recognize that such use can only be analogous, that Greco-Roman secondary commonplaces are only *similar* to Hebrew primary examples.

Thirdly, the interplay between conceptualized Greco-Roman rhetoric, non-conceptualized Hebrew rhetoric and ideological concerns about Hellenistic culture in general compounds the more fundamental issue raised earlier concerning the NT. The issue concerns the actual nature of biblical rhetoric itself: Is it rhetoric in terms of Greco-Roman definitions at all? So, classical Greco-Roman rhetoric focuses on three modes: *judicial* (rhetoric used in courts of law), *deliberative* (political or civil rhetoric) and *epideictic* (ceremonial rhetoric). Although specific sections of the Old and New Testaments could make use of each of these modes, for the most part the Bible is a different kind of rhetorical text.[77]

Burke, Grassi and Kennedy have all argued that in fact religious rhetoric is of a different nature to the rhetoric of demonstration set out by

---

77. Kennedy seems to agree with this point in his introduction, but then has three chapters exploring each mode of rhetoric as it relates to NT material (*New Testament Interpretation*).

Aristotle.[78] Whereas the main task of classical rhetoric was to state that which could be proved through the use of the enthymeme, in biblical rhetoric, statements are frequently made without the use of the enthymeme: they are not proved but simply taken as stated fact, as foundational. Kennedy calls this 'radical Christian rhetoric'. In other words, the Bible is a collection of rhetorical works that seek to persuade its readers/hearers that its world view (ultimately God's) is in fact the world view that matches reality and explains the world in which we live. It promotes that world view as the only acceptable world view. Grassi develops the concept of sacred rhetoric, which he argues is more important than rational discourse and that, in fact, precedes all rational discourse as its very foundation. Grassi suggests that the main characteristics of this sacred discourse are as follows:

- 'a purely directive, revealing or evangelical character, (never a demonstrating or proving function)'
- statements 'formulated without any mediation', 'in an imagistic way'
- metaphorical 'insofar as sacred language lends the reality of sensory appearances a new meaning'
- a claim to urgency
- an opposing viewpoint is deemed 'outrageous'
- its announcements claim to be outside time[79]

Grassi's main contention is that rational speech, established since Descartes as the main form of educated, 'critical' discourse in the West, is secondary rather than superior to rhetoric. Rhetoric is the visceral, experience-centred exploration of reality to which rational discourse provides a muted commentary. He argues that Descartes's shift from rhetoric to rationality, from passion to proof, fundamentally changed what it meant to be human. Rhetoric provides the way back into experience, into affective language, and needs to replace rational discourse as the mainstay of all discourse:

> Rational speech is that which strictly, 'mathematically' explains or 'infers' what is
> implied in the premises. This speech is 'monological' in its deepest structure, for it
> is not bothered by emotion or place or time determinations in its rational process;
> it follows the ideal of philosophizing that Descartes created for us.

---

78. Burke, *The Rhetoric of Religion: Studies in Logology* (Berkeley: University of California Press, 1970); Grassi, *Rhetoric*, ch. 5; Kennedy, *New Testament Interpretation*, pp. 6–12.

79. Grassi, *Rhetoric*, esp. pp. 102–114; cf. Kennedy, *New Testament Interpretation*, p. 6.

> Rhetorical speech on the other hand is a 'dialogue,' that is, that which breaks out
> with vehemence in the urgency of the particular human situation and 'here' and 'now'
> begins to form a specifically human order in the confrontation with other human
> beings. And because the material belonging to language consists in the interpretation
> of the meaning of sensory appearances – for the main thing is to order and form
> these – it is laden with figurative expressions, color, sounds, smells, tangibles.[80]

I have already discussed Nils Lund's arguments about the limitations of biblical rhetoric, namely that when biblical rhetoric is compared to Greco-Roman
rhetoric it is normally 'found wanting'. However, Grassi's argument suggests
that this is putting the cart before the horse. It is not that biblical rhetoric, in
the Old or the New Testament, is an imperfect representation of Greco-
Roman Rhetoric, but that biblical rhetoric is a form of sacred rhetoric that
transcends or precedes the demonstrative rhetoric established through the
Aristotelian traditions. In other words, we should not judge biblical rhetoric on
the same terms as Greco-Roman rhetoric, but should instead judge it in accordance with Grassi's discussion of sacred rhetoric as listed above. Any attempt
to use Greco-Roman terms can at the most only be analogous and will always
run the risk of making category errors in suggesting that biblical rhetoric is
seeking to demonstrate or prove something to be the case, whereas in fact biblical rhetoric is only ever interested in stating reality.

Biblical rhetoric as sacred rhetoric therefore proposes to its reader a new
perspective on the world. That perspective is ultimately not the author's perspective but God's perspective and the reader is, all the time, encouraged to
adopt this world view as the only viable world view on offer. We have already
seen that this is the case with the end of Job's deliberations, but it can also be
seen through the Gospel narratives. In the Gospels the world is seen through
God's eyes. The reader is given insights into human characters, into the
motives that make people act in certain ways (Matt. 9:4), into knowledge only
God can know (e.g. see below on the prologue in John 1, Nathanael's meeting
with Jesus in John 1, the discussion between Jesus and the Samaritan woman
in John 4), and see discussions and events no characters within the text
are allowed to see (e.g. the various 'private' meetings between Jesus and
Nicodemus in John 3 and Jesus and the Samaritan woman in John 4, where the
disciples are said to be absent, and the scene in Gethsemane where Jesus
specifically prays on his own [Luke 22:39–46]); in John's Gospel the reader is
able to hear God's voice when others hear only thunder (John 12:28–29); and,

---

80. Grassi, *Rhetoric*, p. 113.

throughout the Gospel records, the reader is taken back to prehistory (Matt. 1; John 1:1; 8:58) and forward into the future (Mark 13; Matt. 24). The point of view, in other words, takes the reader into a different perception of reality. In John's prologue, for example, the reader is shown what was 'in the beginning'; the reader is taken through a breathtaking sweep of history from creation to pre-Christian revelation of the light within the darkness, to incarnation to behold the grace and truth that come through Jesus Christ. This is a rhetorical process that establishes the point of view the reader is invited to adopt for the rest of the text. It establishes the identity of the main character, Jesus, and gives the audience privileged insights into his identity, which are not given to the other characters within the text. Moreover, with the use of the first person plural, the reader is invited into a community of belief, into a community that identifies itself with this world view. This text seeks to persuade and to change, to confirm or instil belief in Jesus that will give eternal life.[81] This is biblical rhetoric, that which seeks to persuade the reader of God's world view and to bring about conviction or faith (*pistis*) in that world view.

Levels 4 and 5: encultured expressions of secondary rhetoric, subordinate divisions of secondary rhetoric and processes of *letteraturizzazione*

Despite the characteristic of biblical rhetoric as sacred rhetoric, rhetorical studies of the Bible have tended to focus too much on the handbook explanations of classical Greco-Roman rhetoric with its fascination with rhetorical devices and commonplaces. This emphasis follows from Muilenberg's call for a focus on stylistics. Since the handbooks focus on how to deliver specific forms of speeches, usually in law courts or civic assemblies, it is questionable how much this form of rhetoric can relate to biblical rhetoric itself. However, it is easy to find breakdowns of Greco-Roman rhetoric into specific modes, tropes and commonplaces. Indeed, even though Kern acknowledges the limited application of handbook rhetoric for biblical rhetoric, he still spends twice as long exploring these levels of rhetoric as he has for the previous three.

Classical Greco-Roman rhetoric, as we have seen, is divided into three types – judicial, deliberative and epideictic. Speeches can be created to meet

---

81. Phillips, *Prologue*. John 20:31, of course, includes a famous text-critical issue concerning the tense of the verb 'believe', which can be rendered either as 'continue to believe' or 'come to belief'.

specific needs within each of these three modes. Each speech can make use of the three (Aristotelian) forms of proof: *ethos* (relating to the character of the speaker and his credibility), *pathos* (the effect of the speech on the audience) and *logos* (the content of the speech itself).[82] Each speech is composed by going through the five stages of rhetoric, here listed by their common Latin names and a brief description in English:

- *inventio*: planning the discourse, deciding what to include
- *dispositio*: the arrangement of the various parts into a coherent speech often into the classic fivefold structure:
  - *exordium*: introduction to the speech, preparing the audience
  - *narratio*: statement of the facts of the case or the history that lies behind the speech
  - *confirmatio*: the core of the speech where the argument is presented and proven, usually with weaker arguments used first
  - *refutatio*: a refutation of the opponent and his arguments
  - *peroratio*: a conclusion of the speech, including a restatement of the facts, an amplification of the arguments used and any final appeals to the speaker's credibility (*ethos*) or the audience's support (*pathos*)
- *elocutio*: the choice of the correct words, style, commonplaces and devices
- *memoria*: preparation for delivery, including commitment of the speech to memory
- *pronuntatio*: all aspects of delivery, control of the voice and use of gestures

Within each of these five stages, the handbooks offer a wealth of possible strategies and commonplaces. These commonplaces give ample opportunity for biblical scholars to hunt down specific examples in the biblical text, for example the hunt for the chiasmus. One problem with some of these common-place-specific explorations is that they assume they will find examples within the biblical material of handbook quality. However, as is the case with many supposed chiasmi in the Bible, the results are often hotly contended. The other issue is that often the handbook commonplaces are confused or oversimplified, for example the confusion between chiasmus (grammatical cross-parallelism, as in Matt. 7:6) and *antimetabole* (repetition of words in a reversed order as in 1 John 3:9).[83]

---

82. Kennedy, *New Testament Interpretation*, pp. 15–33; Carey, 'Rhetorical Means'.

83. See Lund, *Chiasmus in the New Testament*, pp. 74–93; 'Chiasmus in the Old Testament'; and Breck, 'Chiasmus as a Key'.

However, George Kennedy's attempt to revive rhetoric, especially within NT studies in the 1980s, emphasized the need to look at the broader aspect of rhetoric and to avoid the hunt for stylistic trophies. His oft-quoted process for rhetorical criticism takes account of the need to see Judeo-Christian rhetoric as categorically different from handbook rhetoric and focuses much more on biblical rhetoric as radical Christian rhetoric or the rhetoric of sacred discourse. As such, Kennedy makes little mention of commonplaces, although the process is clearly derived from the Hellenistic-Roman hand-books rather than from philosophical rhetoric. The process can be set out in five stages:

1. Define the rhetorical unit to be studied (e.g. the *pericope* or narrative section).
2. Identify the rhetorical situation of the passage (e.g. its *Sitz im Leben*).
3. Determine the species of rhetoric being used (e.g. judicial, deliberative or epideictic),[84] and the rhetorical arrangement (in terms of *dispositio*).
4. Identify the rhetorical techniques or style being used (in terms of *elocutio*).
5. Review the overall impact of the whole process.[85]

It is interesting to note Wuellner's version of Kennedy's scheme, which seems to focus far more on the opportunity to find commonplaces and specific links to Greco-Roman handbook rhetoric:

• the definition of the rhetorical unit
• the identification of the rhetorical situation
• the identification of the rhetorical disposition or arrangement
• the identification of rhetorical techniques or style
• the identification of rhetorical criticism as a synchronic whole[86]

However, Wuellner is also insistent that, throughout the process, the effects of the rhetorical devices need to be explored rather than the microscopic identification of every commonplace used and an extended discussion of how

---

84. Here is where Kennedy comes closest to secondary rhetoric.
85. Kennedy, *New Testament Interpretation*, pp. 33–38; see also Wuellner's discussion, 'Rhetorical Criticism', pp. 455–458; and Robbins's comments in 'Rhetoric and Culture', pp. 443–447.
86. Wuellner, 'Rhetorical Criticism', pp. 455–458, with a subsequent exploration of 1 Cor. 9 using the process.

the author learned to make use of the commonplace in the first place. He speaks of the need to appreciate 'the liberation of rhetoric contained, the liberation from the Babylonian captivity of rhetoric reduced to stylistics'.[87] Any attempt within biblical studies to make use of the process Kennedy developed needs to take pains to avoid the descent back into stylistics. Biblical rhetoric points beyond stylistics to a new perception of the world; it seeks 'to lure the participants into identifying with the rhetor or with a foundational aspect of the argument so that they can be transported to a new position'.[88]

Conclusion

This chapter has explored the philosophical development of rhetoric as the art of persuasion and has sought consciously to avoid defining biblical rhetoric in terms of classical Greco-Roman rhetoric. To some extent, the discussion of this form of rhetoric and its role within biblical studies has here been marginalized, and purposefully so. Rhetoric in the Bible must not be limited to the exploration of commonplaces and the hunting down of rhetorical devices so that they can be displayed in articles, complete with Latin name tag, like exhibitions in a Victorian museum.

Biblical rhetoric is first and foremost the art of persuading individuals and communities to accept the Bible's world view. This is a rhetoric with immense power in that it assumes that that world view is the only viable one for humanity to accept. Of course, that world view, or rather, the various elements of that world view are in dispute within our own culture. Many within our society do not wish to accept that world view, or to be told that there is only one world view. Many within the church appeal to alternative world views, leading to the rejection of aspects of the biblical picture or a reassessment of the validity of the biblical text as a whole or in part, or reject the notion of a single biblical world view in the first place. As such, future exploration of biblical rhetoric will need to explore the power, ideology and ethical viewpoint of the text.[89]

In the recent collection of essays emerging from the various conferences on rhetorical criticism, Wilhelm Wuellner has begun to explore the role of

---

87. Ibid., p. 457.

88. Kern, *Rhetoric and Galatians*, p. 9.

89. Bible and Culture Collective, 'Rhetorical Criticism'; Olbricht and Eriksson, *Rhetoric, Ethic*, D. Patte, *The Ethics of Biblical Interpretation: A Re-Evaluation* (Louisville: Westminster John Knox, 1995).

power and the sublime in biblical rhetoric.[90] He argues that, since rhetoric is about challenging and changing world views, one way of doing this is to raise the perspective of the readers above their normal humdrum existence and to explore the role of esoteric language in persuading the audience of the viability or attractiveness of the specific world view on offer. This technique or strategy was well known in ancient rhetoric and is the subject of a treatise supposedly by Longinus called *On the Sublime*.[91] Wuellner takes Longinus' discussion, along with Kenneth Burke's exploration into the 'goadings of mystery' to explore the way in which such goadings urge the reader to identify with the world view on offer in the text:

> A rhetorical approach [to the sublime] focuses on the esoteric, spiritual power of
> language, i.e. the megalegoria-level of human language. For Kenneth Burke that
> esoteric language is the ineffable, the unconscious, the subliminal dimension that
> is not identical with mysticism. What others called 'the power of religious texts,'
> Burke preferred to call 'the goadings of mystery' or 'the radiance of the [ineffable]
> divine' . . .[92]

Wuellner's comments are similar to those made by Ernesto Grassi.[93] Indeed, just as Grassi argues for the foundationalism of rhetorical discourse, so Wuellner seeks to reverse Gadamer's dictum that 'all religious systems are rhetorical' by asserting that 'all rhetorical systems are religious'. In other words, rhetoric promotes a specific world view by making use of language and symbolism that are foundational to human existence – by providing the foundation for human existence within community structures.[94] With this in mind, Wuellner argues that rhetorical critics must be seen as stewards of the diversity of the sublime, as diagnosticians of the power of the sublime, and as 'therapists committed to restoring health' to the communities in which they live.[95]

-----

90. See esp. W. Wuellner, 'Reconceiving a Rhetoric of Religion: A Rhetorics of Power
      and the Power of the Sublime', in Hester and Hester, *Rhetoric and Hermeneutics*,
      pp. 23–78.
91. See Aristotle/Horace/Longinus, in T. S. Dorsch (tr.), *Classical Literary Criticism:
      Aristotle's On the Art of Poetry, Horace's On the Art of Poetry and Longinus' On the Sublime*
      (London: Penguin, 1965).
92. Wuellner, 'Reconceiving', p. 53.
93. Although the extensive notes to this article make only one reference to Grassi.
94. Wuellner, 'Reconceiving', p. 34.
95. Ibid., p. 74.

Wuellner's thesis explores the sublime in terms of a liberal, therapeutic model. However, the assertion that rhetoric moves beyond the mundane, beyond the hunt for commonplaces, reminds us again of the foundational basis of rhetoric as strategic communication. Rhetorical criticism is therefore the analysis of the strategies of persuasion within a text – not just the manipulation of words for effect, but rather the manipulation of a world view and the way in which that world view is offered to the reader. It is the study of how the Bible seeks to offer the reader a new way of seeing the world, of establishing a new community, a new way of being human. Ultimately, rhetoric is not about doing fancy things with words. Rhetoric is about life per se, in that 'its chief concern is the formation of human existence'.[96] Or in the words, of John's Gospel, 'these have been written that you may believe that Jesus is the Christ, the Son of God; and that believing you may have life in his name' (20:31 my tr.).

Bibliography

ALEXANDER, L. C., *The Preface to Luke's Gospel: Literary Convention and Social Context in Luke 1.1–4 and Acts 1.1* (Cambridge: Cambridge University Press, 1993).

ALTER, R., *The Art of Biblical Narrative* (New York: Basic, 1981).

AMOSSY, R., 'Toward a Rhetoric of the Stage: The Scenic Realization of Verbal Clichés', *Poetics Today* 2.3 (1981), pp. 49–63.

ANAXIMENES (?), *Rhetorica ad Alexandrum*, tr. H. Rackham and W. S. Hett, LCL (Cambridge, Mass.: Harvard University Press, 1937; repr. London: Harvard University Press, 1994).

ARISTOTLE, *The Art of Rhetoric (Ars Rhetorica)*, tr. J. H. Freese, LCL (London: Heinemann; G. P. Putnam's Sons, 1926; repr. London: Harvard University Press, 1994).

BAR-EFRAT, S., *Narrative Art in the Bible* (Sheffield: Sheffield Academic Press, 1992).

BARTHES, R., *Image, Music, Text*, tr. S. Heath (London: Fontana, 1977).

BEARDSLEY, M. C., 'Intentions and Interpretations: A Fallacy Revived', in M. Wreen and D. Callen (eds.), *The Aesthetic Point of View* (Ithaca: Cornell University Press, 1982).

BERS, V., 'Tragedy and Rhetoric', in WORTHINGTON, *Persuasion*, pp. 176–195.

BETZ, H. D., 'The Literary Composition and Function of Paul's Letter to the Galatians', *NTS* 21 (1975), pp. 353–379.

BIBLE AND CULTURE COLLECTIVE, 'Rhetorical Criticism', in *The Postmodern Bible* (New Haven: Yale University Press, 1995), pp. 149–186.

---

96. Grassi, *Rhetoric*, p. 113.

BIRDSELL, D., and GROARKE, L., 'Toward a Theory of Visual Argument', *AA* 33.1 (1996), pp. 1–10.

BOOTH, W., *The Rhetoric of Fiction* (Chicago: University of Chicago Press, 1961).

BRECK, J., 'Chiasmus as a Key to Biblical Interpretation', *StVTQ* 43 (1999), pp. 249–267.

BROWNE, R., 'Response to Edward P. I. Corbett, "The Rhetoric of the Open Hand and the Rhetoric of the Closed Fist"', *CCC* 21.2 (1970), pp. 187–190.

BRUMMETT, B., *Rhetoric in Popular Culture* (London: Sage, 2006).

BRUEGGEMANN, W., *Mandate to Difference: An Invitation to the Contemporary Church* (Louisville: Westminster John Knox, 2007).

BURKE, K., *A Rhetoric of Motives* (Berkeley: University of California Press, 1969).

——, *The Rhetoric of Religion: Studies in Logology* (Berkeley: University of California Press, 1970).

BURTON, G., *Silvae rhetoricae*, <http://rhetoric.byu.edu/>, accessed 23 Jan. 2008.

CAREY, C., 'Rhetorical Means of Persuasion', in WORTHINGTON, *Persuasion*, pp. 26–46.

CICERO, *Brutus* and *Orator*, in *Cicero in 28 Volumes*. Vol. 5: *Brutus, Orator*, tr. G. L. Hendrickson and H. M. Hubbell, LCL (London: William Heinemann, 1939).

——, *De oratore*, Books 1–2, tr. E. W. Sutton, LCL (Cambridge: Harvard University Press, 1942).

——, *De oratore Book III* and *Partitione oratoria*, tr. H. Rackman, LCL (Cambridge, Mass.: Harvard University Press, 1942).

——, *Rhetorica ad oerennium*, in *Cicero in 28 Volumes*. Vol. 1: *[Cicero] Ad C. Herennium de ratione dicendi*, tr. H. Caplan, LCL (London: William Heinemann, 1954).

CLINES, D. J. A., GUNN, D., and HAUSER, A. (eds.), *Art and Meaning: Rhetoric in Biblical Literature* (Sheffield: JSOT Press, 1982).

COHEN, D., 'Classical Rhetoric and Modern Theories of Discourse', in WORTHINGTON, *Persuasion*, pp. 69–82.

CORBETT, E., 'The Rhetoric of the Open Hand and the Rhetoric of the Closed Fist', *CCC* 20.5 (1969), pp. 288–296.

CRAFTON, J., 'The Dancing of an Attitude: Burkean Rhetorical Criticism and the Biblical Interpreter', in PORTER and OLBRICHT, *Rhetoric and the New Testament*, pp. 429–442.

CROSSAN, J. D., *Jesus: A Revolutionary Biography* (San Francisco: HarperSanFrancisco, 1995).

——, *The Historical Jesus: The Life of a Mediterranean Jewish Peasant* (Edinburgh: T. & T. Clark, 1993).

CROSSAN, J. D., and REED, J., *Excavating Jesus: Beneath the Stones, Behind the Text* (San Francisco: HarperSanFrancisco, 2002).

DEBANNE, M., 'An Enthymematic Reading of Philippians: Towards a Typology of Pauline Arguments', in PORTER and STAMPS, *Rhetorical Criticism and the Bible*, pp. 481–503.

DORSCH, T. S. (tr.), *Classical Literary Criticism: Aristotle's On the Art of Poetry, Horace's On the Art of Poetry and Longinus' On the Sublime* (London: Penguin, 1965).

DOWNING, F. G., *Doing Things with Words in First Century Christianity* (Sheffield: Sheffield Academic Press, 2000).

EAGLETON, T., *Ideology: An Introduction* (London: Verso, 1991).

——, *Literary Theory: An Introduction* (Oxford: Blackwell, 1996).

ELIADE, M., *Patterns in Comparative Religion* (New York: Sheed & Ward, 1958).

FIRTH, D. G., 'Shining the Lamp: The Rhetoric of 2 Samuel 5–24', *TynBul* 52.2 (2001), pp. 203–224.

FLEMING, D., 'Can Pictures Be Arguments', *AA* 33.1 (1996), pp. 11–23.

GRASSI, E., *Rhetoric as Philosophy: The Humanist Tradition* (University Park: Pennsylvania State University Press, 1980; repr. Carbondale: Southern Illinois University Press, 2001).

HALLIDAY, M. A. K., *Language as Social Semiotic: A Social Interpretation of Language as Meaning* (London: Edward Arnold, 1978).

HESTER, J. D., and HESTER, J. D. (eds.), *Rhetorics and Hermeneutics: Wilhelm Wuellner and His Influence* (New York: T. & T. Clark, 2004).

HOLMES, J., *Introduction to Sociolinguistics* (London: Longman, 1992).

JONES, L., *The Hermeneutics of Sacred Architecture: Experience, Interpretation, Comparison*, 2 vols. (Cambridge, Mass.: Harvard Center for the Study of World Religions, 2000).

KENNEDY, G. A., *Classical Rhetoric and Its Christian and Secular Tradition from Ancient to Modern Times* (London: University of South Carolina Press, 1980).

——, *New Testament Interpretation through Rhetorical Criticism* (Chapel Hill: University of North Carolina Press, 1984).

——, *The Art of Persuasion in Greece* (London: Routledge & Kegan Paul, 1963).

KERN, P., *Rhetoric and Galatians: Assessing an Approach to Paul's Epistle*, SNTSMS 101 (Cambridge: Cambridge University Press, 1998).

KRAUS, M., 'Ethos as a Technical Means of Persuasion in Ancient Rhetorical Theory', in OLBRICHT and ERIKSSON, *Rhetoric, Ethic*, pp. 73–87.

LONG, F., 'From Epicheiremes to Exhortation: A Pauline Method for Moral Persuasion in 1 Thessalonians', in OLBRICHT and ERIKSSON, *Rhetoric, Ethic*, pp. 179–195.

LONGINUS, *On the Sublime*, in Aristotle, *The Poetics*, tr. W. Hamilton Fyfe and W. R. Roberts, LCL (Cambridge, Mass.: Harvard University Press; London: William Heinemann, 1932; repr. Cambridge, Mass.: Harvard University Press, 1991).

LUND, N., *Chiasmus in the New Testament: A Study in Formgeschichte* (Chapel Hill: University of North Carolina Press, 1942).

——, 'The Presence of Chiasmus in the New Testament', *JR* 10.1 (1930), pp. 79–93.

——, 'The Presence of Chiasmus in the Old Testament', *AJSL* 46.2 (1930), pp. 104–126.

MACK, B., *Rhetoric and the New Testament* (Minneapolis: Fortress, 1980).

MALINA, B., 'John's: The Maverick Christian Group, The Evidence of Sociolinguistics', *BTB* 24.4 (1987), pp. 167–182.

MELTZOFF, S., 'On the Rhetoric of Vision', *Leonardo* 3.1 (1970), pp. 27–38.

MEYNET, R., *Rhetorical Analysis: An Introduction to Biblical Rhetoric* (Sheffield: Sheffield
    Academic Press, 1998).

MUILENBURG, J., 'Form Criticism and Beyond', *JBL* 88.1 (1969), pp. 1–18.

NANOS, M., *The Irony of Galatians: Paul's Letter in First-Century Context* (Minneapolis:
    Fortress, 2002).

NORDQUIST, R., *Glossary*, <http://www.nt.armstrong.edu/terms.htm>, accessed 23 Jan.
    2008.

OLBRICHT, T. H., and ERIKSSON, A. (eds.), *Rhetoric, Ethic and Moral Persuasion in Biblical
    Discourse: Essays from the 2002 Heidelberg Conference* (New York: T. & T. Clark, 2005).

OLSON, G., 'Jacques Derrida on Rhetoric and Composition: A Conversation', *JAC* 10.1
    (1990), pp. 1–21.

PANOFSKY, E., *Meaning in the Visual Arts* (Garden City: Doubleday, 1955; repr. Chicago:
    University of Chicago Press, 1983).

PATTE, D., *The Ethics of Biblical Interpretation: a Re-Evaluation* (Louisville: Westminster John
    Knox, 1995).

PERELMAN, C., *The New Rhetoric and the Humanities* (Dordrecht: D. Reidel, 1979).

PERELMAN, C., and OLBRECHTS-TYTECA, L., *The New Rhetoric: A Treatise on Argumentation*,
    Center for the Study of Democratic Institutions (Notre Dame: University of Notre
    Dame Press, 1969).

PHILLIPS, P. M., *The Prologue of the Fourth Gospel: A Sequential Reading*, Library of New
    Testament (New York: T. & T. Clark, 2006).

PLATO, *Apology*, in *Plato with an English Translation*. Vol. 1: *Euthyphro, Apology, Crito, Phaedo,
    Phaedrus*, tr. H. R. Fowler, LCL (Cambridge, Mass.: Harvard University Press; London:
    William Heinemann, 1914; repr. London: William Heinemann, 1960).

——, *Gorgias*, in *Plato in Twelve Volumes*. Vol. 5: *Lysis; Symposium; Gorgias*, tr. W. R. M.
    Lamb, LCL (London: William Heinemann, 1925).

PORTER, S. E., and OLBRICHT, T. H. (eds.), *Rhetoric and the New Testament: Essays from the
    1992 Heidelberg Conference* (Sheffield: Sheffield Academic Press, 1993).

——, *Rhetoric, Scripture and Theology: Essays from the 1994 Pretoria Conference* (Sheffield:
    Sheffield Academic Press, 1996).

PORTER, S. E., and STAMPS, D. L. (eds.), *Rhetorical Criticism and the Bible* (Sheffield: Sheffield
    Academic Press, 2002).

QUINTILIAN, *Institutiones oratoriae*, 5 vols., LCL (Cambridge, Mass.: Harvard University
    Press, 2001).

RHETOROSAURUS, <http://www.rhetorosaurus.co.uk>, accessed 23 Jan. 2008.

ROBBINS, V., *Exploring the Texture of Texts: A Guide to Socio-Rhetorical Interpretation* (Valley
    Forge, Pa.: Trinity Press International, 1996).

——, 'Rhetoric and Culture: Exploring Types of Cultural Rhetoric in a Text', in PORTER
    and OLBRICHT, *Rhetoric and the New Testament*, pp. 443–463.

ROTH, M., 'Rhetorical Criticism, Hebrew Bible', in J. Hayes (ed.), *Dictionary of Biblical Interpretation*, 2 vols. (Nashville: Abingdon, 1999), pp. 396–399.

SPINSANITY, <http://www.spinsanity.com>, accessed 29 Sept. 2006.

STERNBERG, M., *The Poetics of Biblical Narrative: Ideological Literature and the Drama of Reading* (Bloomington: Indiana University Press, 1985).

THOMAS, J., 'The Hermeneutics of Megalithic Space', in TILLEY, *Interpretative Archaeology*, pp. 73–97.

TILLEY, C. (ed.), *Interpretative Archaeology* (Oxford: Berg, 1993).

VRIES, S. J. DE, *I Kings*, WBC 12 (Waco: Word, 1985).

WARNER, M. (ed.), *The Bible as Rhetoric: Studies in Biblical Persuasion and Credibility* (London: Routledge, 1990).

WATSON, D. F. (ed.), *Persuasive Artistry: Studies in New Testament Rhetoric in Honor of George A. Kennedy* (Sheffield: Sheffield Academic Press, 1991).

WATSON, D. F., and HAUSNER, A. J. (eds.), *Rhetorical Criticism of the Bible: A Comprehensive Bibliography with Notes on History and Method* (Leiden: Brill, 1994).

WILLIAMS, P., 'Sacred Space in North America', *JAAR* 70.3 (2002), pp. 593–609.

WIMSATT, W. K., and BEARDSLEY, M. C., *The Verbal Icon: Studies in the Meaning of Poetry* (Lexington: University of Kentucky Press, 1954).

WORTHINGTON, I. (ed.), *Persuasion: Greek Rhetoric in Action* (London: Routledge, 1994).

WUELLNER, W., 'Biblical Exegesis in the Light of History and Historicity or Rhetoric and the Nature of the Rhetoric of Religion', in PORTER and OLBRICHT, *Rhetoric and the New Testament*, pp. 492–451.

——, 'Reconceiving a Rhetoric of Religion: A Rhetorics of Power and the Power of the Sublime', in HESTER and HESTER, *Rhetoric and Hermeneutics*, pp. 23–78.

——, 'The Rhetorical Genre of Jesus' Sermon in Luke 12:1–13:9', in WATSON, *Persuasive Artistry*, pp. 93–118.

——, 'Where Is Rhetorical Criticism Taking Us?', *CBQ* 49.3 (1987), pp. 448–463.

YEIVIN, S., 'Social, Religious and Cultural Trends in Jerusalem under the Davidic Dynasty', *VT* 3.2 (1953), pp. 149–166.

8. DISCOURSE ANALYSIS

Terrance R. Wardlaw, Jr.

Introduction

What is 'discourse', and what is 'discourse analysis' in relation to the study of the Bible? Most linguists and discourse analysts agree that the discipline of discourse analysis is wide-ranging and problematic to define. One remarks:

> My anxiety . . . was only aggravated to realize in a fresh way that discourse analysis is about . . . *everything*! It is grammar and syntax, pragmatics and lexicology, exegesis and literary criticism. In short, fertile ground for undisciplined minds.[1]

Although discourse analysis is a vast discipline, the present discussion will follow the observation of others that this is not a drawback that results in confusion but rather an advantage to be exploited. It has been noted before that discourse analysis is capable of functioning as a hermeneutic for interpretation.[2]

---

1. M. Silva, 'Discourse Analysis and Philippians', in S. E. Porter and D. A. Carson (eds.), *Discourse Analysis and Other Topics in Biblical Greek*, JSNTSup 113 (Sheffield: Sheffield Academic Press, 1995), p. 102.
2. J. T. Reed, 'Discourse Analysis as New Testament Hermeneutic: A Retrospective and Prospective Appraisal', *JETS* 39 (1996), p. 223; J. B. Green, 'Discourse Analysis

Moreover, the broad scope of discourse analysis is an aid for disciplining the exegete to consider the many facets in which discourse meaning is constructed in its social context. There is indeed method to the seeming madness. As a theory, discourse analysis provides a broad and integrated analytical framework for moving from one mode of investigation to another without being accused of methodological eclecticism, since discourse analysis is by nature inter-disciplinary in order to capture the complexity of 'discourse'.[3] Moreover, the field of discourse analysis allows the exegete both to examine linguistic routines of biblical Hebrew and Greek, and to examine literary and rhetorical features of the text (stylistics) in its social context. This approach makes sense because 'syntax, semantics, and pragmatics are not neatly divided in actual texts but dynamically interrelate'.[4] Therefore, diversity is one of discourse analysis's great-est strengths.[5]

Moreover, the present discussion at key points emphasizes the manner in which recent sociolinguistic discussions of discourse analysis provide means for exposing the presuppositions of various interpreting communities when considering the influence of the reader and reading communities on the inter-pretation of the text. The exposure of the ideologies of text, interpreter and interpreting institutions is of some importance within any comprehensive hermeneutic approach.

If we may situate it in its historical context, discourse analysis is the latest in three phases of linguistic research since the mid to late nineteenth century.

---

and New Testament Interpretation', in J. B. Green (ed.), *Hearing the New Testament: Strategies for Interpretation* (Grand Rapids: Eerdmans, 1995), pp. 175–196. One may conceive of discourse analysis as a hermeneutic on the grounds that it considers a text from various viewpoints from the level of the morpheme up through the social environment. Therefore, it is a way of looking at a text and systematically describing its meaning in a comprehensive manner. Discourse theoreticians move outside the realm of linguistics in order to interact with other disciplines such as the philosophy of language, physiology and sociology in order to place their findings about the construction of meaning on a rather broad philosophical and empirical foundation.

3. R. T. Lakoff, 'Nine Ways of Looking at Apologies: The Necessity for Interdisciplinary Theory and Method in Discourse Analysis', in D. Schiffrin, D. Tannen and H. E. Hamilton (eds.), *The Handbook of Discourse Analysis* (Oxford: Blackwell, 2001), pp. 199–214.

4. Reed, 'Discourse Analysis', pp. 223–224.

5. See ibid., p. 224.

First, historical linguists (also known as comparative philologists) focused on the etymological analysis of individual words and the classification of language families such as Indo-European and Semitic during the late nineteenth century. Secondly, following Ferdinand de Saussure in the early twentieth century, linguists became more aware of contextual language use and meaning.[6] At this time it became popular for linguists and grammarians to focus on the sentence in grammatical analysis (e.g. the work of Noam Chomsky in the field of linguistics).[7] Thirdly, in the second half of the twentieth century several fields of research converged with the result that linguists began to examine language phenomena beyond the sentence. Researchers both realized how context influences sentence structure, and also became interested in stretches of language larger than the sentence. One may therefore describe discourse analysis as *the analysis of language and its use beyond the sentence, including the analysis of language situated in its social context.*[8] Moreover, one may describe 'discourse' as *a unit of speech (either oral or written) treated by interlocutors as a complete utterance.*[9]

The following discussion therefore presents general trends and the opinions of the key scholars in linguistic discourse theory, provides an overview of OT Hebrew and Greek NT discourse analysis, applies selected aspects of discourse analysis both to Exodus 15:22–27 and Matthew 5:1–12, and then concludes with a description of both the benefits of discourse analysis for exegesis and its drawbacks.

---

6. F. de Saussure, *Course in General Linguistics*, ed. C. Bally and A. Sechehaye, tr. R. Harris (Chicago: Open Court, 1986).

7. Grammars that focus on the sentence include W. Gesenius, E. Kautzsch and A. E. Cowley, *Gesenius' Hebrew Grammar* (Oxford: Clarendon, 1910); P. Joüon, S. J., *A Grammar of Biblical Hebrew*, SubBi 14.1, tr. and rev. T. Muraoka (Rome: Pontifical Biblical Institute, 2003); B. K. Waltke and M. O'Connor, *An Introduction to Biblical Hebrew Syntax* (Winona Lake: Eisenbrauns, 1990); J. H. Moulton and N. Turner, *A Grammar of New Testament Greek*, vol. 3 (Edinburgh: T. & T. Clark, 1963).

8. The social context of language includes the original social environment of an utterance or text, as well as subsequent interpretative communities. Social environment may include the speaker(s), the addressee(s) and those who may overhear.

9. See G. Brown and G. Yule, *Discourse Analysis*, Cambridge Textbooks in Linguistics (Cambridge: Cambridge University Press, 1983), p. 199; Reed, 'Discourse Analysis', p. 225.

Linguistic discussions of discourse analysis

Emergence

Most scholars recognize Zellig S. Harris as the first linguist to look beyond the sentence in his formal methodology, thus laying the parameters for those who followed.[10] First, he proposed that discourse analysis is concerned with linguistic description beyond the sentence.[11] This approach may lead to the analysis of the structure of a text or a type of text, or the role of elements within individual sentences under the influence of a text's overall discourse structure.[12] Secondly, discourse analysis is concerned with the relation of language to behaviour, that is, with language situated in its social context. As later researchers explored the nature of discourse, the manner in which a discourse influences the meaning or construal of individual words became clear. This approach contrasted with earlier views of the meaning of the sentence as the component of its lexical parts.[13]

Following Harris, discourse analysis has been a popular topic of conversation among Bible translators from the 1960s on, and within this context there have been many advances in both theory and method on the basis of data from a wide variety of languages across the globe.[14] Translators found that discourse analysis was necessary in order to acquire a grasp of such varied phenomena as 'mystery particles', text organization, information selection and the specialized use of verbs. Moreover, as he formulated tagmemic theory, Kenneth L. Pike looked beyond the sentence and extended the referential hierarchy to paragraphs, texts and social contexts (the 'behavioreme').[15] In building upon

---

10. Z. S. Harris, 'Discourse Analysis', *Language* 28 (1952), pp. 1–30.

11. Ibid., pp. 1–3.

12. Ibid., pp. 2–3, 30; Brown and Yule, *Discourse Analysis*, pp. 153–189; G. Ward and B. J. Birner, 'Discourse and Information Structure', in Schiffrin, Tannen and Hamilton, *Handbook*, pp. 119–137.

13. N. R. Norrick, 'Discourse and Semantics', in Schiffrin, Tannen and Hamilton, *Handbook*, pp. 76–99.

14. See e.g. R. E. Longacre and S. H. Levinsohn, 'Field Analysis of Discourse', in W. U. Dressler (ed.), *Current Trends in Textlinguistics*, Research in Text Theory 2 (Berlin: de Gruyter, 1978), pp. 103–122.

15. K. L. Pike, *Language in Relation to a Unified Theory of the Structure of Human Behavior*, 3 vols. (Summer Institute of Linguistics, 1954–60), esp. Part 1; *Tagmemics, Discourse, and Verbal Art* (Ann Arbor: University of Michigan, 1981), p. 3; K. L. Pike and E. G. Pike, *Text and Tagmeme* (Norwood: Ablex, 1983), p. 1. Tagmemic theory utilizes

these earlier insights, both Joseph E. Grimes and Robert Longacre developed their own theories and methods of discourse analysis for use by linguists in the service of Bible translation.[16] Although Longacre uses tagmemic theory as the basis for his approach, most discourse analysts today use other theoretical frameworks.

Whereas many British and American linguists speak in terms of 'discourse analysis', some continental linguists and those who follow their lead conceive of this enterprise as 'text grammar' or 'text linguistics'. János S. Petöfi defines a text as 'a sequence of spoken or written verbal elements functioning as a single whole, which is qualified according to some (mostly extralinguistic) criterion as being a "text"'.[17] De Beaugrande and Dressler aim to describe how texts function in human interaction, and define a text as a communicative occurrence that meets seven standards of textuality: cohesion, coherence, intentionality, acceptability, informativity, situationality and intertextuality.[18] In textlinguistics proper, the written and spoken text is the minimal free unit of

---

Footnote 15 (*continued*)

the basic unit of the 'tagmeme', an analytical structure containing four cells (or quadrants) within which the analyst may include various types of information, depending on the hierarchical level being analysed. Though popular in SIL (Summer Institute of Linguistics) circles from the 1960s to the early 1990s, enthusiasm has waned in recent years with the popularization of other theoretical approaches.

16. J. E. Grimes, *The Thread of Discourse*, JLSM 207 (The Hague: Mouton, 1975); R. E. Longacre, *An Anatomy of Speech Notions* (Lisse: Peter de Ridder, 1976); W. Pickering, *A Framework for Discourse Analysis* (Dallas: SIL, 1978). The most recent version of Longacre's theory is found in *The Grammar of Discourse*, Topics in Language and Linguistics, 2nd ed. (New York: Plenum, 1996). For more recent views of the use of discourse analysis for translation in general, see B. Hatim and I. Mason, *Discourse and the Translator* (Harlow: Longman, 1990); *The Translator as Communicator* (London: Routledge, 1997).

17. J. S. Petöfi, 'Towards an Empirically Motivated Grammatical Theory of Verbal Texts', in J. S. Petöfi and H. Rieser (eds.), *Studies in Text Grammar*, Foundations of Language Supplementary Series 19 (Dordrecht: D. Reidel, 1973), p. 205.

18. R.-A. de Beaugrande and W. U. Dressler, *Introduction to Text-Linguistics* (London: Longman, 1981), pp. 3–10. On reference and the interpretation of pronouns, see Brown and Yule, *Discourse Analysis*, pp. 190–222. On Coherence, see Brown and Yule, *Discourse Analysis*, pp. 223–270. On Cohesion, see J. R. Martin, 'Cohesion and Texture', in Schiffrin, Tannen and Hamilton, *Handbook*, pp. 35–53.

language.[19] Within this research tradition, text analysis focuses not only upon the printed text. Rather, text theory handles both co-textual and con-textual components (internal properties of the text, and text-external relations).[20] Thus analysis should account for both the production and the reception of texts; language-historical, form-historical and socio-historical relations; as well as criticisms and interpretations with given purposes.[21] One drawback to this approach is that non-specialists find the notation (borrowed from formal logic) to be incomprehensible and often unfruitful.[22]

Concerns in linguistic discourse analysis

More recently, discourse analysts have raised an increasing number of research concerns. In order to focus upon what is helpful for the analysis of the Bible, I shall narrow the following overview to the topics of discourse structure, pragmatics and the locus of meaning.

Discourse structure

The analysis of discourse structure focuses on the sequence of information, the overall form and the structural conventions of a given discourse (related to genre). Analysts seek to identify the form of a discourse because form communicates meaning, as does departure from form.[23] Two related concepts relate to the overall structure of a discourse. First, 'linearization' refers to the linear presentation of information, since what comes first influences the interpretation of everything else that follows.[24] Secondly, 'staging' is a more general term that refers to the relative prominence given to the theme or point of departure of a clause, sentence, paragraph, episode or discourse, and around which it is organized.[25] The manner in which information is organized around

---

19. W. U. Dressler, 'Introduction', in Dressler, *Current Trends*, p. 2.

20. Petöfi, 'Empirically Motivated', p. 223. See the various topics treated in T. A. Van Dijk (ed.), *Handbook of Discourse Analysis*, 4 vols. (London: Academic, 1985).

21. Petöfi, 'Empirically Motivated', p. 223.

22. For an example of this notation, see T. A. Van Dijk, 'Text Grammar and Text Logic', in Petöfi and Rieser, *Studies*, pp. 17–78.

23. See B. Johnstone, *Discourse Analysis* (Oxford: Basil Blackwell, 2002), pp. 63–110; Hatim and Mason, *Discourse*, pp. 164–191.

24. Brown and Yule, *Discourse Analysis*, pp. 125–133.

25. Ibid., pp. 134–152; cf. Grimes, *Thread of Discourse*; W. Chafe, 'The Analysis of Discourse Flow', in Schiffrin, Tannen and Hamilton, *Handbook*, pp. 673–687.

the topic or theme influences both interpretation and recall.[26] Moreover, larger structural considerations help one to account for the use of particular verb forms or particles at given points in a discourse, and sometimes explain lexical choice in the relation between structure and genre.

Pragmatics

Stephen Levinson defines pragmatics as 'language in use', and pragmatics is concerned with such issues as deixis, which is the way language encodes the context of an utterance or speech event (deixis of person, time, place, discourse or social status), speech acts, intertextuality, genre analysis and rhetorical analysis.[27] I shall now briefly describe the relation of some of these pragmatic considerations to discourse analysis.[28]

Speech acts[29]   As the influence of J. L. Austin's William James lectures at Harvard University (1955) began to spread, some linguists moved beyond the investigation of the relation of one sentence or proposition to another, and began to examine how speakers use language in order to do things.[30] As one component of pragmatic investigation, discourse analysts examine such contextual factors as reference, presupposition, implicature and inference in order to describe

---

26. Brown and Yule, *Discourse Analysis*, p. 134.

27. S. L. Levinson, *Pragmatics*, Cambridge Textbooks in Linguistics (Cambridge: Cambridge University Press, 1983), p. 5.

28. Some scholars prefer to distinguish these areas from pragmatics. However, since the present chapter is written from a linguistic perspective, all of these dimensions are categorized under the heading of 'pragmatics' – in keeping with the traditional linguistic categories of semantics, syntax and pragmatics. This distinction is especially important in the generative tradition (Noam Chomsky), and is now residual in cognitive linguistics and other circles as a help for specifying the aspect of language under discussion.

29. See chapter 3 in this volume.

30. J. L. Austin, *How to Do Things with Words*, ed. J. O. Urmson and M. Sbisà, 2nd ed. (Cambridge, Mass.: Harvard University Press, 1962); J. R. Searle, *Speech Acts: An Essay in the Philosophy of Language* (Cambridge: Cambridge University Press, 1969); H. P. Grice, 'Logic and Conversation', in P. Cole and J. L. Morgan (eds.), *Syntax and Semantics*. Vol. 3: *Speech Acts* (New York: Academic, 1975), pp. 41–58; Levinson, *Pragmatics*; Brown and Yule, *Discourse Analysis*, pp. 27–67; Hatim and Mason, *Discourse*, pp. 76–100; R. S. Briggs, 'The Use of Speech-Act Theory in Biblical Interpretation', *CR:BS* 9 (2001), pp. 229–276.

what speakers and audiences are doing.[31] Since language sometimes seems goal-directed 'it strikes us as appropriate to query a speaker's intentions and to use motive to account for text'.[32] The discourse analyst may ask, 'What is the speaker/author trying to accomplish by saying this in this way?' In particular, the speech act of a text is reflected through its rhetoric,[33] and some scholars maintain that without a pragmatic reading, the literary text cannot be realized.[34] Moreover, Daniel Patte suggests that the Bible is part of a religious act, and therefore this intentionality should be considered from the angle of speech-act theory in analysis.[35]

Intertextuality In traditional literary studies, intertextuality has to do with the relation of one text to another, or the manner in which one text presupposes another. 'Intertextual relations between texts and other texts enable people to interpret new instances of discourse with reference to familiar activities and familiar categories of style and form.'[36] However, for some sociolinguistic discourse analysts intertextuality is more than the relation of one printed text to another. In addition, intertextuality refers to the relation of assumptions, presuppositions, logical implications or entailments, and implicatures behind a text or discourse.[37] It is the struggle between the intertextual assumptions of various ideological positions that may be seen 'as partly a contention over the claims of their particular visions and representations of the world to having a universal status'.[38] Moreover, 'Seeking hegemony is a matter of seeking to universalize particular meanings in the service of achieving and maintaining dominance, and this is ideological work.'[39] In

---

31. Brown and Yule, *Discourse Analysis*, p. 27. For definitions of these terms, see ibid., pp. 28–33.
32. Johnstone, *Discourse Analysis*, p. 197. See ibid., pp. 196–226 (ch. 7).
33. Ibid., p. 210.
34. J. L. May, 'Literary Pragmatics', in Schiffrin, Tannen and Hamilton, *Handbook*, pp. 787–797.
35. D. Patte, 'Speech Act Theory and Biblical Exegesis', *Semeia* 41 (1988), pp. 85–102.
36. Johnstone, *Discourse Analysis*, p. 15. See ch. 5 (pp. 137–167) for her complete discussion of intertextuality. Also see N. Fairclough, *Analysing Discourse: Textual Analysis for Social Research* (London: Routledge, 2003), ch. 3 (pp. 39–61); Hatim and Mason, *Discourse*, pp. 120–137.
37. Fairclough, *Analysing Discourse*, p. 40.
38. Ibid., p. 45.
39. Ibid., p. 58.

other words, various sides in a debate ask which intertextual connections are universally legitimate, which are not, and how 'our side' may hegemonically dominate the other in shaping a consensus.

Genre analysis[40]   A genre is a conventional type of discourse or printed text categorized by how it represents the world.[41] M. M. Bakhtin defines speech genre as socially situated language use that reflects its environment through characteristic features of lexis, phrasing, grammar and compositional structure, and emphasizes that each sphere of language use develops its own stable types of utterances.[42] For discourse analysts, the notion of genre or register is based on the observation that 'often-repeated activities involving discourse give rise to relatively fixed ways of proceeding with the activities, and these ways of proceeding often include relatively fixed, routinized ways of talking ("registers") and types of texts ("genres," in one sense of the word)'.[43]

Rhetorical analysis[44]   One scholar recently defined rhetoric in relation to the Bible as 'those distinctive properties of human discourse, especially its artistry and argument, by which the authors of biblical literature have endeavored to convince others of the truth of their beliefs'.[45] However, discourse analysts in linguistics conceive of rhetoric as more than convincing others. In addition, rhetoric is both lexicalized and grammaticalized in order to negotiate power or position, in order to create solidarity or distance, in order to influence the attitude of another, or in order to incite the hearer to action. Moreover, rhetoric relates to the way an author structures a discourse in terms of genre or sequential strategy, the manner of intertextuality, and what the speaker or author is attempting to accomplish with a given discourse. Rhetorical analysis has been especially important to linguists interested in feminist or racial concerns in relation to ideology and institutional discourse (in particular, critical discourse analysis, described below).

---

40. See chapter 4 in this volume.
41. Johnstone, *Discourse Analysis*, p. 155.
42. M. M. Bakhtin, 'The Problem of Speech Genres', in C. Emerson and M. Holquist (eds.), *Speech Genres and Other Late Essays*, tr. V. W. McGee, UTPSS 8 (Austin: University of Texas, 1986), p. 60.
43. Johnstone, *Discourse Analysis*, p. 15. Also see Fairclough, *Analysing Discourse*, ch. 4 (pp. 65–86); Hatim and Mason, *Discourse*, pp. 138–164.
44. See chapter 7 in this volume.
45. C. C. Black, 'Rhetorical Criticism', in Green, *Hearing the New Testament*, pp. 256–277.

The locus of meaning

Reading traditions through history have located meaning variously. Traditionally in the West meaning was located in the author's intent, and a text meant what the speaker meant. Then new literary criticism posited that the meaning of a text is what the *text itself* means, and the focus moved to observing the structure and system of the text. Then more recently reader-response critics suggested that the meaning of a text is its meaning to its audiences. Some discourse analysts conclude that we may learn from all of these viewpoints, and therefore suggest that each perspective should be considered since the meaning of a text is in all of these places.[46] Indeed, '[a]n influential view of meaning among students of discourse in linguistics, rhetoric, and anthropology locates meaning in the abstract space between hearers, speakers, and texts, saying that meaning is "socially constructed", or "jointly produced" '.[47]

Sociolinguistic concerns in discourse analysis

Social constructionist discourse is one of the more prominent theoretical approaches toward discourse analysis to develop within the last couple of decades, and critical discourse analysis is one component of this school of thought that may benefit Bible scholars.[48]

Social constructionist discourse analysis

Social constructionists 'share the starting point that our ways of talking do not neutrally reflect our world, identities and social relations but, rather, play an active role in creating and changing them'.[49] Advocates of social constructionism maintain that (1) knowledge is based upon our ways of categorizing the world, and should not be treated as objective truth; (2) the ways in which we represent the world are historically and culturally conditioned; (3) knowledge is created through social interaction in which we construct common truths; and (4) the social construction of knowledge has social consequences.[50] Moreover, social constructionists

---

46. Johnstone, *Discourse Analysis*, p. 230.
47. Ibid., p. 231; see Fairclough, *Analysing Discourse*, pp. 10–11.
48. The following discussion leaves aside ethnographic and intercultural discourse, as well as post-structuralist French Marxist analysis. These approaches reveal much about the shift in meaning across registers and cultures.
49. M. Jørgensen and L. Phillips, *Discourse Analysis as Theory and Method* (London: Sage, 2002), p. 1.
50. Ibid. p. 5.

take as their starting point the claim of structuralist and poststructuralist linguistic philosophy, that our access to reality is always through language. With language, we create representations of reality that are never mere reflections of a pre-existing reality but contribute to constructing reality. That does not mean that reality itself does not exist. Meanings and representations are real. Physical objects also exist, but they only gain meaning through discourse.[51]

What may be the benefit of social constructionist discourse analysis in general? Perhaps one benefit is the emphasis on the critique of ideology, and in particular the use of research in this endeavour. In this tradition, critique is 'the unmasking of dominant, taken-for-granted understandings of reality' so that the researcher (or exegete) may arrive at a position 'from which he or she can discover what is otherwise taken for granted'.[52] For example, what assumptions of the interpreter's reading community are in conflict with the world view in the printed text?[53]

Critical discourse analysis

In turning to critical discourse analysis, Norman Fairclough is mainly interested in the grammatical and semantic analysis of texts.[54] Fairclough maintains that texts are social events with causal effects in bringing about change in knowledge, beliefs, attitudes and values.[55] Accordingly, the effect of texts in establishing, sustaining or changing ideology (representations of the world that establish, maintain or change social relations of power, domination or exploitation) is a major concern for critical discourse analysis (CDA).[56]

Critical discourse analysts maintain that ideology is circulated and reproduced through discourse: 'Ways of talking produce and reproduce ways of thinking, and ways of thinking can be manipulated via choices about grammar,

---

51. Ibid., p. 8–9.
52. Ibid., p. 176.
53. For methodological application, see ibid., pp. 175–212.
54. Fairclough, *Analysing Discourse*. Fairclough's work is based on M. A. K. Halliday's systematic functional linguistics (most recently, M. A. K. Halliday and C. M. I. M. Matthiessen, *An Introduction to Functional Grammar*, 3rd ed. [London: Hodder Arnold, 2004]), which is concerned with the relationship between language and the social character of texts. See also T. A. Van Dijk, 'Critical Discourse Analysis', in Schiffrin, Tannen and Hamilton, *Handbook*, pp. 352–371.
55. Fairclough, *Analysing Discourse*, p. 8.
56. Ibid., p. 9.

style, wording and every other aspect of language.'[57] For 'every utterance has an epistemological agenda, a way of seeing the world that is favored via that choice and not via others'.[58] Ideologies may be associated 'with discourses (as representations), with genres (as enactments), and with styles (as inculcations)'.[59] Within the social context of the church, one would presumably find that the circulation and reproduction of scriptural ideology is desirable (although not in terms of exploitation, but rather in terms of salvation). The tools of CDA are an aid for formalizing the interpretation of a text and making explicit the relation of genre and style to ideology. The formal identification of the ideology of a text may then be applied in various contemporary social contexts.

CDA makes no claim to objectivity in its methodology. In fact, the analytical questions put forth are motivated by the belief that texts have social, political, cognitive, moral and material consequences and effects.[60] CDA therefore aims to raise moral and political questions about contemporary societies. Some scholars have in the past accused evangelical scholars of not being 'objective', and thus of not conducting research along the lines of 'serious' scholarship. CDA therefore may resonate well both with the text of the Bible and with its evangelical interpreters. On the one hand, the canon is an ideological text whose very literary structure seems to aim toward social, political, cognitive, moral and material consequences in the world, and on the other hand, evangelical scholars tend to aim toward interpreting the text in this manner. Although Fairclough focuses on new capitalism, his programme seems adaptable to studying the Bible's discourse with an eye toward impacting contemporary society. The commitment of critical discourse analysis to social change is therefore theoretical grounding for focusing upon the application of the Bible to social change.

Moreover, it must be admitted that the application of Scripture is one of the greatest weaknesses in scholarly approaches to exegesis. Quite often application or implication questions are either never raised or are added as an afterthought. Therefore, the systematic and rigorous application of CDA as one methodological component in the discourse analysis of Scripture may function as a discipline for bringing focus back to the cosmomorphic force of the Bible. CDA assumes that scholarship is able to change the world, and aims to focus only on research questions and investigations that will potentially bring about social change. This may be a needed corrective in bringing scholars

57. Johnstone, *Discourse Analysis*, p. 45; cf. Fairclough, *Analysing Discourse*, pp. 12–14.

58. Johnstone, *Discourse Analysis*, p. 45.

59. Fairclough, *Analysing Discourse*, p. 9.

60. Ibid., pp. 14–15.

to ask interpretative questions that will in some way impact the world for the better.

At this point in the discussion, I now recapitulate my definitions of both 'discourse' and 'discourse analysis' before moving to an overview of previous work in discourse analysis of the Bible. One may describe 'discourse' as a unit of speech (either oral or written) accepted by interlocutors as a complete utterance. Moreover, discourse analysis is the analysis of language and its use beyond the sentence, and this includes the analysis of language situated in its social context.

Discourse analysis of Old Testament Hebrew and New Testament Greek

What have biblical Hebrew (henceforth BH) and NT Greek (henceforth NTG) discourse analysts investigated, and how have they gone about their task? The following survey aims to describe key features of research since the 1970s in order to answer this question. As the discussion will demonstrate, more work has gone into the analysis of discourse structure and text type in relation to the verb system than into any other dimension of discourse analysis. Moreover, it will be observed that OT scholars have been more interested in discourse analysis than their NT counterparts. At the same time, recent years have seen an increasing amount of work on discourse analysis in NTG.

One of the first scholars to consider discourse analysis in BH was Francis I. Andersen, who used tagmemic theory as theoretical grounding for moving beyond the sentence in his linguistic description.[61] He therefore provides a highly formalized representation of syntactic structure. In his functional approach, Andersen followed tagmemic concerns when he described grammatical relations from clauses to paragraphs. He therefore moved beyond the traditional focus on the sentence. Although his use of tagmemic notation has been criticized as incomprehensible to the non-linguist, Andersen's work remains a respected taxonomy of clause and paragraph relations and merits consideration by the Hebraist.[62] Following Andersen, work on BH discourse has proceeded at a quickening pace.

---

61. F. I. Andersen, *The Sentence in Biblical Hebrew* (The Hague: Mouton, 1974).

62. Other than F. I. Andersen, Robert Longacre is one of the few BH scholars to base his approach on tagmemic theory.

J. P. Louw first described discourse analysis in relation to NTG in 1973.[63] This approach grew in popularity among Bible translators and made its way into mainstream NT scholarship in the 1990s. What are some of the benefits of discourse analysis for NT research? Louw suggests that

> Many discourse considerations, especially para-linguistic and extra-linguistic concerns, can enable a reader to go behind a text. Going *beyond* a text involves a refusal to recognize the discourse constraints of a text. The closest one can get to this ideal is to take the linguistic syntax, which is perhaps the most objective feature of a text, as the point of departure that will constrain the overall process of discourse analysis.[64]

Grammatical and stylistic analysis

One of the greatest debates in BH discourse studies centres on the Hebrew verbal system in relation to text type and salience. Some scholars find that particular verb forms tend to collocate predictably in mainline or offline material in certain clause types, with verb rank (or hierarchy) changing from one text type to another, whereas other scholars suggest that particular verb forms are used in the same way across text types.[65] Sides entrench on the basis of their own theory and methodology.[66] Longacre takes a functional approach when

---

63. J. P. Louw, 'Discourse Analysis and the Greek New Testament', *Bible Translator* 24 (1973), pp. 101–106.

64. J. P. Louw, 'Reading a Text as Discourse', in D. A. Black (ed.) (with K. Barnwell and S. H. Levinsohn), *Linguistics and New Testament Interpretation: Essays on Discourse Analysis* (Nashville: Broadman, 1992), pp. 17–30. By 'para-linguistic' and 'extra-linguistic' Louw means factors such as the historical or social setting of a text (both its original setting and its context through history to the present).

65. 'Collocation' refers to the context (either lexical or syntactic) in which a word or type of word occurs. Mainline material in narrative text refers to those sentence types that tend to carry the story forward, whereas offline material refers to subordinate material or speech. Mainline and offline materials change from one discourse genre to another, and their nature has been debated.

66. In addition to the following works, see also R. Buth, 'The Hebrew Verb in Current Discussions', *JOTT* 5 (1992), pp. 91–105; A. C. Bowling, 'Another Brief Overview of the Hebrew Verb', *JOTT* 9 (1997), pp. 48–69; C. H. J. van der Merwe, 'An Overview of Recent Developments in the Description of Biblical Hebrew Relevant to Bible Translation', in *Contemporary Translation Studies and Bible Translation: A South African Perspective*, ActSup 2 (Bloemfontein: University of the Free State, 2002), pp. 228–245.

he outlines his tagmemic analysis of the BH verb system in accordance with
text type and salience structure (or verb rank) in his work on the Joseph story.[67]
In contrast, Nicacci follows more traditional grammatical classifications in his
form-based approach when he divides the verb system into nominal clauses
(e.g. *waw-X-qatal*) and verbal clauses (e.g. *wayyiqtol*),[68] which cut across
Longacre's various text types.[69]

BH discourse analysts have likewise investigated the nature of verbless
clauses,[70] focus structure,[71] comparative Semitic syntax,[72] particles,[73] participant reference,[74] and quotative frames.[75]

---

67. R. E. Longacre, *Joseph: A Story of Divine Providence. A Text Theoretical and
Textlinguistic Analysis of Genesis 37 and 39–48* (Winona Lake: Eisenbrauns, 1989),
chs. 3, 4.

68. This has classically been defined as waw consecutive and imperfect verbs in
traditional grammars.

69. A. Nicacci, *The Syntax of the Verb in Classical Hebrew Prose*, tr. W. G. E. Watson,
JSOTSup 86 (Sheffield: JSOT Press, 1990). Also see Eskhult, Dawson, Endo and
Heller in the bibliography below. Longacre has been critiqued by J.-M.
Heimerdinger, *Topic, Focus and Foreground in Ancient Hebrew Narratives*, JSOTSup 295
(Sheffield: Sheffield Academic Press, 1999). In relation, also see the Tübingen
school of discourse study: W. Richter, *Grundlagen einer althebräischen Grammatik* (St.
Ottilien: EOS, 1978–80); W. Groß, *Die Satzteilfolge im Verbalsatz alttestamentlicher
Prosa: Untersucht an den Büchern Dtn, Ri und 2 Kön* (Tübingen: Mohr, 1996); A. Disse,
*Informationsstruktur im Biblischen Hebräisch: Sprachwissenschaftliche Grundlagen und
exegetische Konsequenzen einer Korpusuntersuchung zu den Büchern Deuteronomium, Richter
und 2 Könige*, ATSAT 56 (St. Ottilien: EOS, 1998).

70. F. I. Andersen, *The Hebrew Verbless Clause in the Pentateuch*, JBLMS 14 (New York:
Abingdon, 1970); J. Hoftijzer, 'The Nominal Clause Reconsidered', *VT* 23 (1973),
pp. 446–510; C. L. Miller (ed.), *The Verbless Clause in Biblical Hebrew: Linguistic
Approaches*, Linguistic Studies in Ancient West Semitic (Winona Lake: Eisenbrauns,
1999).

71. Heimerdinger, *Topic, Focus and Foreground*; K. Shimasaki, *Focus Structure in Biblical
Hebrew: A Study of Word Order and Information Structure* (Bethesda: CDL, 2002).

72. G. Khan, *Studies in Semitic Syntax*, London Oriental Series 38 (Oxford: Oxford
University Press, 1988). Interestingly, the study of comparative syntax is on the
rise, whereas comparative semantic analysis (etymology) is on the decline.
Whereas syntactic structure is more objectively identified and analysed, the
semantic association of a word is the most unstable linguistic component when
moving from one speech community to another because of the ways

In the area of NTG grammatical analysis, discourse analysts have treated diverse topics such as the relation of overall discourse to Greek circumstantial participles,[76] constituent order in copula clauses,[77] conjunctions[78] and constituent order in relation to the article.[79] Perhaps the most comprehensive analysis of NT Greek from a discourse perspective to date is the coursebook of Stephen Levinsohn.[80] Levinsohn's *Discourse Features of New Testament Greek* covers a wide range of topics such as constituent order, sentence conjunctions, patterns of reference, backgrounding and highlighting, the reporting of conversation, and boundary features.

---

its meaning is affected by cultural and religious associations across social boundaries.

73. C. M. Follingstad, *Deictic Viewpoint in Biblical Hebrew Text: A Syntagmatic and Paradigmatic Analysis of the Particle kî* (Dallas: SIL International, 2001).

74. Longacre, *Joseph*, ch. 6; L. J. de Regt, *Participants in Old Testament Texts and the Translator: Reference Devices and their Rhetorical Impact* (Assen: van Gorcum, 1999); 'Macrosyntactic Functions of Nominal Clauses Referring to Participants', in Miller, *Verbless Clause*, pp. 273–296.

75. Longacre, *Joseph*, ch. 7; C. L. Miller, 'Reported Speech in Biblical and Epigraphic Hebrew: A Linguistic Analysis' (PhD diss., University of Chicago, 1992; rev. 1996 [with an afterword] 2003); 'Discourse Functions of Quotative Frames in Biblical Hebrew Narrative', in W. R. Bodine (ed.), *Discourse Analysis of Biblical Literature: What It Is and What It Offers*, SemeiaSt (Atlanta: Scholars Press, 1995), pp. 155–182; and 'Introducing Direct Discourse in Biblical Hebrew Narrative', in R. D. Bergen (ed.), *Biblical Hebrew and Discourse Linguistics* (Dallas: SIL, 1994), pp. 199–241.

76. P. Healey and A. Healey, 'Greek Circumstantial Participles: Tracking Participants with Participles in the Greek New Testament', *OPTT* 4 (1990), pp. 177–259.

77. J. C. Callow, 'Constituent Order in Copula Clauses: A Partial Study', D. A. Black (with Barnwell and Levinsohn), *Linguistics*, pp. 68–89.

78. R. Buth, '*Oun, De, Kai*, and Asyndeton in John's Gospel', in D. A. Black (with Barnwell and Levinsohn), *Linguistics*, pp. 144–161; K. Titrud, 'The Function of Kai/ in the Greek New Testament and an Application to 2 Peter', in D. A. Black (with Barnwell and Levinsohn), *Linguistics*, pp. 240–270.

79. S. H. Levinsohn, 'A Discourse Study of Constituent Order and the Article in Philippians', in Porter and Carson, *Discourse Analysis*, pp. 60–74.

80. S. H. Levinsohn, *Discourse Features of New Testament Greek: A Coursebook on the Information Structure of New Testament Greek*, 2nd ed. (SIL International, 2000).

Discourse structure, genre, intertextuality, rhetoric and speech acts

In looking beyond the sentence, the overall structure and flow of a discourse is key to understanding its meaning. One of the first analyses of discourse structure within the OT by a discourse analyst proper is Longacre's work on the flood narrative.[81] Within this investigation Longacre cut against the grain of traditional source-critical views by suggesting that the narrative is unified, that the supposed doublets are in fact overlay (a rhetorical device cross-linguistically attested in non-Western languages) and that there are no inconsistencies in chronology. Subsequently, the analysis of genre,[82] intertextuality,[83] rhetoric,[84] poetics[85] and speech acts[86] have been considered by BH scholars.

It seems that the most popular area of research for discourse analysts in NTG has been the structural analysis of various books. This includes analyses of units in Philemon,[87] the nature of paragraph patterns, cohesion in

---

81. R. E. Longacre, 'The Discourse Structure of the Flood Narrative', JAARSup 47 (1979), pp. 89–133; also see R. E. Longacre and S. J. J. Hwang, 'A Textlinguistic Approach to the Biblical Hebrew Narrative of Jonah', Bergen, *Biblical Hebrew*, pp. 336–358.

82. T. D. Andersen, 'Genealogical Prominence and the Structure of Genesis', in Bergen, *Biblical Hebrew*, pp. 242–266; N. A. Bailey, 'Some Literary and Grammatical Aspects of Genealogies in Genesis', in Bergen, *Biblical Hebrew*, pp. 267–282; E. R. Wendland, 'Genre Criticism and the Psalms: What Discourse Typology Can Tell Us about the Text (with Special Reference to Psalm 31)', in Bergen, *Biblical Hebrew*, pp. 374–414; and B.-K. Ljungberg, 'Genre and Form Criticism in Old Testament Exegesis', in Bergen, *Biblical Hebrew*, pp. 415–433.

83. P. C. Beentjes, 'Discovering a New Path of Intertextuality: Inverted Quotations and Their Dynamics', in L. J. de Regt, J. de Waard, and J. P. Fokkelman (eds.), *Literary Structure and Rhetorical Strategies in the Hebrew Bible* (Assen: van Gorcum, 1996), pp. 31–50; E. R. Wendland, 'Obadiah's "Day": On the Rhetorical Implications of Textual Form and Intertextual Influence', *JOTT* 8 (1996), pp. 23–50.

84. E. J. van Wolde, 'The Text as an Eloquent Guide: Rhetorical, Linguistic, and Literary Features in Genesis 1', in de Regt, de Waard and Fokkelman, *Literary Structure*, pp. 134–151; E. R. Wendland, 'Obadiah's Vision of "The Day of the Lord": On the Importance of Rhetoric in the Biblical Text and in Bible Translation', *JOTT* 7 (1996), pp. 54–86.

85. L. F. Bliese, 'The Poetics of Habakkuk', *JOTT* 12 (1999), pp. 47–75.

86. A. Warren, 'Modality, Reference and Speech Acts in the Psalms' (PhD diss., University of Cambridge, 1998).

87. A. H. Snyman, 'A Semantic Discourse Analysis of the Letter to Philemon', in P. J.

Philippians,[88] the theme and unity of Philippians,[89] and the analysis of 1 John.[90] Also, the role of intertextuality has been considered,[91] as well as the issues of text composition and the setting of interpretation.[92] Moreover, Ernst Wendland relates rhetorical analysis to text analysis in his work on 1 John.[93]

One may therefore conclude that the move in theoretical linguistics from focusing on the sentence to focusing on larger stretches of discourse has generated considerable discussion among exegetes, and has also sparked the reconsideration of some old problems. This approach resulted in more precise grammatical (and thus semantic) analysis of both the BH and NTG text at many points. Thus, now that we have a feel for the type of work that has been performed in BH and NTG discourse analysis, we may conclude that the BH and NTG grammarian or exegete who ignores a discourse approach neglects the cutting edge in linguistic analysis. With this in mind, we now turn to the application of discourse analysis to one OT and one NT passage.

Hartin and J. H. Petzer, *Text and Interpretation: New Approaches in the Criticism of the New Testament* (Leiden: Brill, 1991), pp. 83–99.

88. G. H. Guthrie, 'Cohesion Shifts and Stitches in Philippians', in Porter and Carson, *Discourse Analysis*, pp. 36–59. Also see H. Van Dyke Parunak, 'Dimensions of Discourse Structure: A Multidimensional Analysis of the Components and Transitions of Paul's Epistle to the Galatians', in D. A. Black (with Barnwell and Levinsohn), *Linguistics*, pp. 207–239.

89. J. T. Reed, 'Identifying Theme in the New Testament: Insights from Discourse Analysis', in Porter and Carson, *Discourse Analysis*, pp. 75–101; *A Discourse Analysis of Philippians: Method and Rhetoric in the Debate over Literary Integrity*, JSNTSup 136 (Sheffield: Sheffield Academic Press, 1997).

90. R. E. Longacre, 'Towards an Exegesis of 1 John based on the Discourse Analysis of the Greek Text', in D. A. Black (with Barnwell and Levinsohn), *Linguistics*, pp. 271–286.

91. E.g. C. D. Osburn, 'Discourse Analysis and Jewish Apocalyptic in the Epistle of Jude', in D. A. Black (with Barnwell and Levinsohn), *Linguistics*, pp. 287–319.

92. E. R. Wendland, 'A Tale of Two Debtors: On the Interaction of Text, Cotext, and Context in a New Testament Dramatic Narrative (Luke 7:36–50)', in D. A. Black (with Barnwell and Levinsohn), *Linguistics*, p. 121.

93. E. R. Wendland, '"Dear Children" Versus the "Antichrists": The Rhetoric of Reassurance in First John', *JOTT* 11 (1998), pp. 41–84; also see W. Wuellner, 'Rhetorical Criticism and its Theory in Culture-Critical Perspective: The Narrative Rhetoric of John 11', in Hartin and Petzer, *Text and Interpretation*, pp. 171–185.

Application

In order to exemplify the potential fruit of discourse analysis for exegesis, let us look at Exodus 15:22–27 and Matthew 5:1–12, using some of the tools and considerations presented above. We first consider the structure and form of the text, its pragmatics (including illocutionary force, intertextuality, genre and rhetoric), as well as various dimensions of the locus of meaning. In relation to the various loci of meaning, we briefly consider historical or cultural information (background knowledge) from the time of the reported narrative that may impinge upon interpretation, the historical situation and ideological concerns of the implied author, and the ideological concerns of various interpretative communities. Finally, we consider issues that the text may raise regarding social change (application) in keeping with the discussion of CDA.

Marah

We now therefore apply discourse analysis to the Marah incident in Exodus 15:22–27. The following discussion interacts with the work of C. Houtman in his Exodus commentary in order to demonstrate how one may apply discourse analysis to the canonical text, and how this application may contrast with a redaction-critical study of hypothetical prior forms of the text.[94]

Structure

The discrete unit of Exodus 15:22–27 consists of narrative materials, interpretative comments given by the narrator and direct speech. The flow of the unit is roughly as follows: (1) Moses and Israel set out from the Red Sea and travelled for three days in the wilderness of Shur without finding water (15:22); (2) at Marah they were unable to drink the bitter waters (15:23); (3) the people murmured against Moses (15:24); (4) Moses cried out to the Lord (15:25a), who

---

94. C. Houtman, *Exodus*, tr. S. Woudstra, vol. 2, HCOT (Kampen: Kok, 1996; orig. *Exodus*, Commentaar op het Oude Testament [Kampen: Kok, 1989]). Although the following interaction deals primarily with literary factors, the editorial committee for the HCOT is to be applauded for its emphasis on the historical embeddedness of the text (ibid., vol. 2, p. ix). I wholeheartedly agree with reading the text in relation to history. Moreover, the aspect of Houtman's work dealt with below focuses on the redactional concerns of his commentary. His consideration of a broad range of versional witnesses, Jewish exegesis, early Christian interpretation, and reception history (including art) remains helpful.

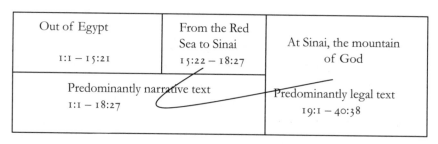

Figure 8.1 A representation of the book structure of Exodus; narrative materials are linked with instructional materials by means of lexical choice (the 'Torah' domain)

taught him (*yôrēhû*) about a tree that would make the waters sweet; (5) the Lord gave Israel a *ḥōq*, 'statute', and *mišpāṭ*, 'rule', and the Lord tested Israel (15:25b); and finally (6) the Lord warned Israel to obey his commands and statutes in order to avoid receiving the sicknesses of Egypt (15:26).

At book level, the Marah incident in 15:22–27 is one of the passages where predominantly narrative materials (chs. 1–18) are linked with predominantly legal ones (chs. 19–40; see fig. 8.1 above). This is accomplished lexically through the use of words from the semantic domain 'Torah' (*ḥōq*, 'statute', *mišpāṭ*, 'rule', *miṣwôt*, 'commands', 15:25–26), as well as the verb *yārâ*, 'to teach' (15:25), which is etymologically related to the noun *tôrâ*, 'instruction'. For example, *mišpāṭ*, 'rule' (21:1), *miṣwôt*, 'commands' (24:12) and *tôrâ*, 'instruction' (24:12), are found within the legal materials of Exodus 19 – 40. The exegetical significance of this observation is that the Marah narrative is a lens through which one may see the instructional materials that follow in chapters 19–40. Just as the Lord 'taught' (*yôrēhû* → *tôrâ*) Moses a tree that made bitter waters sweet (15:25a), the Lord will yet teach Israel a tree (Torah) that will heal life's bitter waters. In other words, obedience to the following Torah materials will make the sinfully bitter waters of life sweet (15:25b–26).[95]

In contrast with the preceding approach, which emphasizes the structural intent of the canonical text, Houtman follows the contemporary practice of

---

95. Regarding the symbolism and imagery in this passage, see D. Boyarin, 'Inner Biblical Ambiguity, Intertextuality and the Dialectic of Midrash: The Waters of Marah', *Proof* 10 (1990), pp. 29–48. Moreover, B. P. Robinson ('Symbolism in Exod. 15:22–27', *RB* 94 [1987], pp. 376–388) finds that early Christian symbolic interpretations which equate the wood with the cross are also valid. From a discourse perspective, canonical juxtaposition within the flow of a single discourse justifies these intertextual connections.

reading 15:22b–25a as belonging to one of the older layers (usually J), while reading 15:25b–26 as '(proto) Deuteronomic' or 'Deuteronomistic'.[96] There is therefore a literary or redactional disjunction between the first half of the passage and the second, which leads him to make no connection between the use of the verb *yārâ*, 'to teach', and *tôrâ*, 'instruction'.[97] Although he acknowledges centuries of traditional Jewish and Christian exegesis that recognize the legal concern of this text, in his own exegesis Houtman fails to interact in a meaningful way with either pre-critical traditions of interpretation or with Robinson's discussion of the text's unity and literary homogeneity, even though Robinson is cited in Houtman's bibliography.[98] He therefore concludes that traditional interpretations of the waters of Marah and the wood in relation to Torah and the cross are 'far removed from the original purport of 15:25a'.[99] Thus Houtman's discussion gives the impression that only the 'original' (pre-canonical?) meaning is valid, and fails to discuss other levels of meaning such as the place of this passage within the Torah or its relation to the NT. Even when he does move to a redaction-critical consideration of the link between the first and the second subunits of the passage, Houtman's disjunction between the ground event in 15:22–25a and the redactional interpretation in 15:25b–26 obscures the literary unity of and the information flow within the canonical text. Although he considers the relation between 15:22–25a and 15:25b–26, redactional concerns detract from Houtman's theological discussion and one suspects that an approach that focused more on the canonical form of the text would glean deeper theological insights.

Although Houtman assumes the scholarly tradition of source and redaction criticism, Robinson's argumentation and evidence regarding the literary unity of 15:22–27 seem more convincing. Robinson notes the thematic unity (security through obedience), the presence of wordplays throughout (*miyyam-sup, yāmim, mayim; šem, šam, śim, šāma', šāmar, mōsheh, mišpāt*), as well as both echoes of preceding passages and anticipations of those to come (*mārîm/miryam*, 15:20; *yārâ*, 15:4; *māḥālâ/mĕḥolât*, 15:20; *'elîmâ/ba'elîm/'elēmo'ab*, 15:11, 15; *lûn*, 16:2; *naśâ*, 16:4).[100] We may therefore conclude with Robinson that 15:22–27 'is thus found to *be* a carefully crafted artifact, with its several parts closely knit

---

96. Houtman, *Exodus*, vol. 2, pp. 304, 311.

97. Ibid., pp. 307, 311. At the same time, Houtman does interact with pre-critical traditions of exegesis in his discussion of lexical items.

98. Robinson, 'Symbolism', pp. 376–379.

99. Houtman, *Exodus*, vol. 2, p. 311.

100. Robinson, 'Symbolism', p. 378.

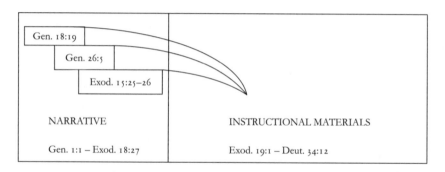

Figure 8.2 The lexical cohesion of narrative and legal materials within the Pentateuch

together through the use of elaborate word-plays, and the whole passage anchored to its context by the use of echoes and anticipations'.[101]

In turning to the overall structure of the Pentateuch, Exodus 15:22–26 joins Genesis 18:19 (*ṣāwâ*, 'to command'; *šāmar*, 'to observe'; *ṣĕdāqâ*, 'righteousness'; *mišpāṭ*, 'justice') and 26:5 (*šāma'*, 'to hear, obey'; *šāmar* 'to observe'; *mišmārâ*, 'observance'; *miṣwôt*, 'commands'; *ḥuqōt*, 'statutes'; *tôrôt*, 'instructions') as one of the three main passages in which the body of narrative materials in Genesis 1:1 through Exodus 18:27 are linked lexically with legal materials in Exodus 19:1 to Deuteronomy 34:12 (see fig. 8.2 above).[102] Thus the 'Torah' semantic domain provides structural cohesion between narrative and legal materials. The exegetical significance of this observation is that there seems to be authorial intent built into the structure of the text for the reader to interpret legal materials in the light of the adjacent narrative texts. Therefore, one is not doing violence to the text by reading passages such as the Marah incident in relation to legal materials. Rather, one is following the interpretative clues embedded within the text's own discourse structure. This observation suggests the appropriateness of interpreting other narrative texts such as the primeval history (Gen. 1 – 11), the patriarchal narrative (Gen. 12 – 50) and the exodus (Exod. 1 – 15) in relation to relevant legal texts in Exodus 19 – Deuteronomy 34 (*intertextuality*).

---

101. Ibid., pp. 378–379.

102. It is recognized that the unit from Exod. 19:1 to Deut. 34:12 does not consist of entirely legal materials, since there are also many narrative passages (e.g. the Balaam narrative in Num. 22 – 24). However, this generalization is made for the sake of describing the cohesion of these two text types as simply as possible.

Pragmatics

Next we examine how language is used within Exodus 15:22–27.

Deixis   How does language within Exodus 15:22–27 encode the context of this textual utterance, and what is the significance of these observations? First, the temporal deixis locates the situation after the incident at the Red Sea (15:22 relates to 13:17 – 15:21). At the outset of the story we are told that Israel set out from the Red Sea, and that Israel was in the wilderness for three days without finding water (15:22). This initial mention of the preceding deliverance therefore brings the reader to expect another miraculous act from the outset of the story. Three days without water legitimately results in desperation. This heightens the tension and emphasizes the significance of the present situation, sovereignly engineered by the Lord (*níssāhû*, 'He tested him', 15:25).

Secondly, the story occurs on the way from Egypt to Sinai, where Israel received Torah (15:22 – 19:1; spatial deixis). Thus with the first references to Torah after the Exodus (15:25–26) the reader receives a clue that obedience to the Lord's commands is Israel's appropriate response to freedom from slavery. When read typologically in larger canonical context, the Christian reader understands that freedom from the slavery of sin (Egypt) should result in obedience to the Lord's ethical commands (Sinai).[103]

Speech Act   What is the illocutionary force of Exodus 15:22–27? Or in other words, what is the author trying to do by including this narrative and reciting the events in this way? First, within the narrative world of Exodus and the Pentateuch, the author is teaching Israel that God may be trusted to work miraculous deliverance regardless of Israel's dire circumstances. Therefore, Israel is enjoined to trust the Lord in similar situations in the future. Secondly, the Lord is providing an analogy from real-world experience by which we may understand the nature of his commands: Torah turns sinfully bitter waters sweet. Therefore this text calls Israel as well as the church when this story is read as Christian Scripture in canonical context to a changed attitude. The Lord's commands are not burdensome drudgery, but lead to joy. Thirdly, related to the preceding point, Israel and the church are enjoined to obey the Lord's moral commands. If the reader is experiencing the bitterness of

---

103. This follows the sort of typological interpretation practised within the NT (Heb. 7:1–28). See G. von Rad, 'Typologische Auslegung des Alten Testaments', *EvT* 12 (1952–3), pp. 17–34; repr. *Gesammelte Studien zum Alten Testament 2* (Munich: Chr. Kaiser, 1973), pp. 272–288.

sinful disobedience, then this story is a call to obedience, with all of its sweet pleasures.

Intertextuality   How does Exodus 15:22–27 relate to other texts?[104] First, Boyarin has observed that this passage shares affinities with 2 Kings 2:19–22, where Elisha threw salt into the bitter waters of a town whose land was unproductive.[105] The tree from Marah (Torah) may therefore be compared with the salt of Elisha, and it should be noted that Elisha's salt made the waters pure. Thus the land of that city was productive again. Read typologically, the Torah is capable of making bad waters good, and it is able to bring fertility to a barren land. Secondly, Boyarin notes that the rabbis found a connection between the tree in Exodus 15:25 and Torah (Wisdom) in Proverbs 3:18 and 4:4, where Torah is referred to as a 'tree of life' able to bring life to whose who keep the Lord's commands.[106] Thirdly, Boyarin notes the paronomastic connection between *mārâ*, 'bitter' (the place name in Exod. 15:22–27), and the noun *morîm*, 'rebellious ones', in Numbers 20:10.[107] He therefore finds reason for interpreting Israel in a bad light within this passage. Israel did not trust the Lord to provide water in the wilderness, and therefore the use of this word, without stating so explicitly, implies that Israel is rebellious. Fourthly, the *'ēṣ*, 'tree', in 15:25 seems to echo the repeated use of this term in Genesis 2:16–17; 3:1, 2, 3, 6, 8, 11, 12, 17, 22, 24. In the garden (Gen. 2:4 – 3:24) both Adam and Eve disobeyed the Lord after being tempted by the serpent, and in Exodus 15:24 the people murmured against Moses (and the Lord) when they travelled three days without finding water. Moreover, whereas Adam and Eve 'died' when they were banished from Eden and from the tree of life (Gen. 2:17), the tree in Exodus 15:24 conversely is given by the Lord in order to turn bitter waters sweet to give life to those who drink. Therefore, in the Marah incident there seems to be a twofold reversal. Not only are the bitter waters made sweet, but this story points toward a reversal of the fall through obedience to the Lord's commands. Thus the Torah (reaffirmed by Jesus in Matt. 5:17–19) is metaphorically a tree able to restore life to a people morally and ethically dead.

---

104. The structural relation of this passage to the book of Exodus and to the Pentateuch as a whole is discussed above, and therefore will not be treated again here.

105. Boyarin, 'Inner Biblical Ambiguity', p. 38.

106. Ibid., p. 39.

107. Ibid., p. 40. Paronomasia is the use of words that sound the same but are etymologically unrelated (akin to homonymy).

In the sense in which some discourse analysts conceive of intertextuality, to what discourses (including social institutions) does this text relate? With reference to the discourse of some sectors in contemporary scholarship, is the Marah incident to be read in the light of source criticism, redaction criticism or transmission history (as with Houtman)? If so, then it is the task of the reader to split apart the 'seams' of the text, since the references to Torah may derive from a source separate from that of the narrative events themselves, from a later hand with an ideological purpose or from a later interpretative community. Given this approach, the focus becomes not so much the text as it stands, but rather prior hypothetical forms of this text. I find problems with this approach, since (1) this division of the ground narrative from its ideological interpretation does violence to the literary structure of the extant text, (2) no material literary finds objectify or support the claim that this narrative existed in another form at any point in Israel's history, and (3) there is no undisputed standard for discerning another authorial voice within the present text other than that of the implied author within the book of Exodus. Furthermore, reading the disjunctions in the text seems to turn the exegete's attention from theological reflection on the text as it stands to the possible meanings in earlier settings prior to redactional unity. In the case of Houtman's work, this seems to hinder his otherwise excellent theological discussion of present discourse flow.

By way of contrast, I choose to read Exodus 15:22–27 in relation to the church as a discourse community, and in particular to the evangelical segment of the church.[108] Seen in this light, the text in its canonical form is situated within and related to both the OT and NT, and Israel becomes a type for the body of Christ. Thus the Torah, which makes the bitter waters sweet within the Marah narrative, may be seen as the ethical commands of both the Old and New Testaments interpreted through Christ as the ethic for the church today. Therefore, this passage demonstrates to the church that the Lord's ethical commands can heal sinfully bitter waters and restore life as the *ekklēsia* wanders in a dry and barren wilderness. Any gospel that does not demand obedience to the Lord (Rom. 6) as the proper response to grace (freedom from slavery in Egypt) will therefore receive God's judgment through the diseases of Egypt.

---

108. It is recognized that there are many other discourse communities one may choose, such as orthodox Judaism, secular literary reading or a scientific (naturalistic) historical approach, to name a few.

Genre   See the discussion above on how Exodus 15:22–27 joins narrative with legal materials in order to create a hybrid genre (Torah).

Rhetorical analysis   How does the text seek to incite the reader to obey the Lord's commands? How does it achieve power or dominance? First, the entire situation begins with Hebrew lives hanging in the balance, needing water lest they die from thirst in the wilderness. The Lord intentionally tested Israel (15:25) by pushing them to the brink of endurance since many people would die after a few days without water. This situation indicates the significance of obedience since the text implicitly compares obedience to receiving water in a barren wilderness. This force casts itself upon the ideal reader, who may recognize that obedience to the Lord's commands is like receiving water when on the brink of death from thirst.

Secondly, the injunction to obey in 15:26 comes from the mouth of the Lord, who within the linear flow of the text is cast as the sovereign Creator (Gen. 1:1 – 3:24). By definition, then, the Lord retains the sovereign right to demand obedience.

Thirdly, emphasis on complete obedience to all of the Lord's commands is indicated syntactically through the use of the infinitive absolute plus a finite verb in the protasis of 15:26a (*'im šāmō'a tišma'*, 'if you indeed obey'). One synonym for obedience is stacked upon another with four synonymous phrasings used for a single idea: 'If you will diligently listen to the voice of the LORD your God, and do that which is right in his eyes, and give ear to his commandments and keep all his statutes . . .' (Exod. 15:26).[109]

Fourthly, the Lord states he will not send the diseases of Egypt upon them if Israel obeys him (15:26). This is an implicit promise to send the judgments from Exodus 7 to 12 upon Israel if they disobey.

Fifthly, with the intertextual connection between the banishment from the Garden of Eden (Gen. 3) and Marah, as well as the threat of plague in Exodus 15:26, the ideal reader recognizes that he too will fail to realize the fulfilment of entering the Promised Land. For the Israelites within the narrative world of Exodus, the threat of death from judgment rather than entering the Promised Land makes for strong rhetoric. For the ideal Christian reader today, the threat of death from judgment in contrast to entering the New Jerusalem in the context of obedience to the Lord's ethical commands also makes for strong rhetoric (Heb. 12:25–29; 13:14).

At this point Houtman's interpretation contrasts once again with a

---

109. Bible quotations in this chapter are from the ESV.

straightforward reading of the canonical text. Rather than following the flow of the Exodus narrative as it develops, Houtman's view on disparate redactional units impinges on his exegesis when he hypothesizes that the reference to the 'sicknesses of Egypt' in 15:26 refers to the general sicknesses in Egypt rather than to the plagues the Lord sent in chapters 7–10.[110] At least to me, the flow of the text suggests that 'the sicknesses of Egypt' in 15:26 refers to the preceding narrative account. Thus Houtman's interpretation flattens the rhetorical force of the text; the vivid narrative is dulled and the information sequence is broken.

Although the editors of the HCOT series state that primacy will be given to 'the final shape of the text',[111] an approach such as that of Robinson or Boyarin, which looks both to the discourse structure of the canonical shape of the text and to those communities who focus upon the canonical shape of the text, appears to produce deeper theological reflection. Exegesis that fails to give primacy to the structural integrity of the canonical text silences the authorial voice, flattens the theological development within the flow of discourse and, in the case of Exodus 15:22–27, dulls its rhetorical force. Whereas the information structure of the text assumes a given flow, source and redaction critical concerns appear to inhibit the theological interpretation of the text by reorienting the reader's focus. The reader's attention turns to hypothetical textual prehistories or 'unevennesses' in the text rather than grappling with its structural, illocutionary, intertextual, generic and rhetorical features.

The locus of meaning and ideology: author, text, reader

The issue of the locus of meaning in Exodus 15:22–27 is touched upon above with reference to intertextuality. In particular, with reference to which contemporary discourses is this text to be read? It is assumed that an author skillfully and faithfully embedded both intent and ideological position within the literary structure of Exodus, the Pentateuch and the Christian canon. Therefore, the present form of the canonical text faithfully conveys an author's intent, and fidelity to the text should consider each of these various levels of intertextual relationship (book, unit and, finally, inner-canonical workings). Therefore, loci of meaning reside at each of these textual levels. Since we no longer possess any form of the text other than that which tradition has handed down (if one ever existed), the canonical text is our best means for most objectively recognizing authorial intent. In the case of the Marah nar-

---

110. Houtman, *Exodus*, vol. 2, p. 308.
111. Ibid., p. x.

rative, various levels of intent may be recognized, among which are the following. First, the author and compiler of the canonical Pentateuch established the ideological context of this text in relation to Torah.[112] Secondly, the authorial intent of the church established the relation of this passage to Christian faith and practice through defining the canonical content of the Old and New Testaments.

With regard to the ideological position of Exodus 15:22–27, the author and text assume that the Lord speaks to people (15:26). Therefore, it is assumed that direct revelation is possible (which is the inciting event within the narrative world for the initial recording of this passage). Secondly, the ethical commands within the Torah derive directly from the Lord and faithfully reflect his will (15:26). Thirdly, the Lord is involved in people's lives (testing in 15:25). Fourthly, that this passage is found within the Christian canon indicates that the early church included it among other divinely inspired and normative texts.

However, the reader is still one factor in the construction of meaning that has not been discussed. I as reader–writer have chosen to relate Exodus 15:22–27 to traditional, evangelical discourse. Others may choose to relate Exodus 15:22–27 to the secular academy and subject this text to scientific (naturalistic and deistic) historical scrutiny under the assumption that God, in the sense of traditional Christian doctrine, does not speak. Still others may choose to relate this text to a discourse that lies somewhere between the two extremes, and that interprets the text on a continuum between these two disparate readings. Above all, no reading of this text is without its own philosophical and theological presuppositions, or without its own ideological leaning. The contemporary discourse within which the reader chooses to construct the meaning of the literary text of Exodus 15:22–27 determines not only the method by which one will read the text (conducting a canonical and literary reading of the present form, using source, redaction, tradition and reception criticisms, a feminist literary reading or a secular historical reading), but also whether readers will seek to align themselves with the ideology of the text or will use their own chosen ideology as a criterion for evaluating the ideology of the text.

Critical discourse analysis

What questions may we ask regarding the relation of Exodus 15:22–27 to contemporary discourses that may let this text speak in order to effect social

---

112. The present discussion, owing to insufficient space here, leaves aside the question of identifying the author(s), as well as the issue of when acts of authorship occurred.

change today? As an entry point into this discussion, how might the assumptions of Exodus 15:22–27 regarding ethical absolutes apply to struggles over power and moral positions within some mainline denominations in America and Europe today? Since CDA is concerned with the linguistic analysis of semantic or grammatical choices in stretches of spoken or written discourse, we therefore seek to identify one or two linguistic manifestations of church discourse power or rhetoric that are at odds with the preceding exegesis.

If we accept the ideology of the text at face value, then this passage suggests that the Lord does indeed speak, and that what was spoken in the past regarding ethical standards still applies today as the Pentateuch is read within a Christian context. This undercuts various denominational flirtations with speculative theology and arbitrary ethical standards as conceived within polity documents, as well as the practice of power by committees and administrators who ignore the Bible's ethics. The Lord speaks his will, and this is the ethical standard by which the church is to live, regardless of what human institutions may subsequently decide to enforce or regard as non-binding.

In particular, what lexis or rhetoric stands against receiving the Lord's commands as healing wood for life's bitter waters? First, one word that has been used in reference to individuals in the US who appeal to specific commands or texts of the Bible within the context of mainline denominational struggles over ethics is 'biblolatry'.[113] This semantic choice is a rather charged rhetorical tool by which appeal to the Bible is blended with the concept of idolatry. Presumably, reverence for God is distinct from revering what has traditionally been viewed as his Word, and the use of the word 'biblolatry' automatically equates an appeal to the canonical text with an act of disobedience toward God (thus shifting the charge of disobedience from those who advocate their own social agenda to those who appeal directly to the Bible). Set within the larger institutional context, the use of this term indicates that the denomination as an institution no longer acknowledges the Bible as authoritative, and therefore appeal to the Bible is illegitimate. Moreover, the use of this rhetoric is a charge that anyone within the denomination who appeals to the Bible is guilty of worshipping the canonical text as a god. This rhetorical choice therefore highlights the use of power within the denomin-

---

113. This lexical item (which originated with Samuel Taylor Coleridge) was used by one member of an ordination committee in a mainline denomination (spring 1997). Although the present discussion focuses only on particular phrases, a full CDA discussion would pick apart the lexis and grammar of a more complete transcribed or printed discourse.

ation in order to enforce a position at variance with the traditional Protestant and patristic emphasis on the authority of Scripture.[114] Furthermore, the appeal to an institutional norm at variance with the canonical text in some ways mirrors the state of the church and its use of authority or power to silence appeals to Scripture at the time of Martin Luther. Thus history is in the process of repeating itself, since some segments of Protestantism are devolving to a view of the Bible at variance with the traditional Reformation view.

Secondly, one occasionally hears the statement 'You need to spread your tent pegs a little wider.'[115] When used in response to an appeal to a particular command or text of the Bible, this rhetorical choice likewise indicates that those who appeal to the canon have unduly excluded other theological positions that do not recognize the normative authority of scriptural ethics. Moreover, it casts those who do appeal to the authority of the Bible as ignorant or unaware of other positions. Seen within the context of mainline denominational institutions whose administrators and committees emphasize inclusiveness and tolerance to such a degree that scriptural ethics are no longer binding, the assumption is that anyone who appeals to the Bible as an authority is ignorant! Thus advocates of tolerance take the high rhetorical ground and put the burden of proof on more traditional ethical views to demonstrate that they do in fact rest upon cogent theological formulation.

The Beatitudes

We now turn to one possible application of discourse analysis to the pithy and enigmatic Beatitudes in Matthew 5:1–12. Great care is taken in the preceding section to distinguish between each methodological step in the exegesis; however, the nature of the text in Matthew 5:1–12 is such that the write-up needs to collapse some steps in order to avoid an unduly long discussion.

Structure

The unit of Matthew 5:1–12 consists of two narrative verses (vv. 1–2), which provide the deictic viewpoint (context), and then follows with the Beatitudes themselves (vv. 3–12). Perhaps the most striking aspect of verses 3–12 is their characteristic structure, in which each Beatitude begins with the plural form

---

114. This statement by no means ignores the patristic emphasis on tradition in relation to the canon.

115. This was used in a committee meeting in spring 1993.

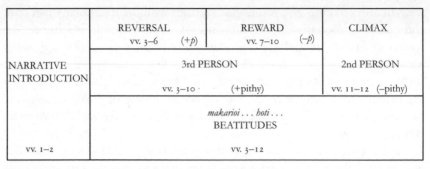

Figure 8.3 A representation of the structure of Matthew 5:1–12

of *makarios*, 'blessed' (Heb. *'ašrê*; Lat. *beatus*), and then follows with an apodosis consisting of a *hoti*, 'because, for', clause.

Verses 3–12 may then be further divided into two units. Verses 3–10 follow the identical pattern of *makarioi* + plural subject, *hoti* . . . (in the third person). Moreover, verses 3–10 are bound together by the inclusiatory phrase 'for theirs is the kingdom of heaven' in verses 3b and 10b. Then verses 11–12 are distinguished by a shift to the second person ('Blessed are you . . .'), the use of the imperative mood, and a longer form than the preceding Beatitudes.[116] Verses 3–10 may then be further divided into the subunits of verses 3–6 and verses 7–10. Verses 3–6 are characterized by the alliterative use of words with an initial *p* (in Greek: *ptōchoi, tō pneumati, penthountes, praeis, peinōntes*), and the content centres upon the reversal of the fortune of those who are oppressed.[117] Verses 7–10 lack this alliteration, and centre upon the reward yet to come for those who are righteous.[118] I specify the significance of this structure within the exegesis that follows (see fig. 8.3 above).

Pragmatics

We now turn to some preliminary remarks, then followed by a verse-by-verse exegetical discussion that considers relevant pragmatic concerns at the appropriate points (deixis, illocutionary force, intertextuality, genre, rhetorical analysis).

In the light of their non-transparent meaning, how may we rightly approach the Beatitudes? One writer captures the problem when he states that '[e]ach

---

116. M. A. Powell, 'Matthew's Beatitudes: Reversals and Rewards of the Kingdom',
    CBQ 58 (1996), p. 461.

117. Ibid., pp. 463, 475.

118. Ibid., p. 475.

beatitude is so short, so nearly cryptic, that it is easy – and tempting – for each commentator [or expositor] to add some of his own ideas . . .'[119] In reaction to this tendency in teaching and preaching, the present investigation attempts a reading from a discourse perspective by situating the Beatitudes within the textual flow of canonical discourse in order to provide a constraint on interpretation. This is a conscious interpretative choice regarding which intertextual connections are valid and which are not. In particular, the following discussion will use discourse analysis as a theoretical framework that justifies the observation of many scholars regarding the OT background and assumptions that inform the interpretation of the Beatitudes within the literary structure of the canon.[120] The aim here is to frame the basic discourse presuppositions behind the Beatitudes lest we inject our own cultural assumptions into the interpretation of such words as *praeis*, 'meek, humble' (v. 5), whose semantic network within the text is very different from that within various contemporary English speech communities (registers). Therefore, the following discussion chooses from the outset to limit valid exegetical observations to those that may be justified by appeal to canonical context (including its Hebrew OT or Aramaic and Greek translations), or to relevant historical background information that may inform the historical, linguistic and cultural assumptions of the text.

Narrative introduction (vv. 1–2) Within the overall flow of Matthew's Gospel the Beatitudes are situated in Jesus' Galilean ministry (temporal and spatial deixis, 4:23), and the text states that when Jesus saw the crowds he ascended the mountain (spatial deixis, 5:1). It has been observed before that this incident may echo Moses' ascent of Mount Sinai (Exod. 19 – 20), and this intertextual connection seems quite suggestive if valid.[121] First, within the context of the Sermon on the Mount (chs. 5–7), this suggests that Jesus' teaching is the fulfilment of that first given to Moses in the Torah (see 5:17–20). Therefore, there is basic continuity between Moses' teaching and that of

---

119. R. L. Harris, 'The Beatitudes: Teaching by Climax', *Presb* 30 (2004), p. 111.

120. As the following discussion hints, a canonical interpretation at the literary level is also justified on the historical plane, since the context of both the ground events and the composition of Matthew was steeped in OT background knowledge through acquaintance with Hebrew texts and/or Aramaic targums, the LXX and both the rabbinic and early Christian teaching of these documents within early worshipping communities.

121. D. A. Hagner, *Matthew*, 2 vols., WBC 33A, 33B (Dallas: Word, 1993), 1: 86.

Jesus, and this is artfully conveyed through the use of verbal echo. Secondly, there is also in some sense discontinuity between Moses' teaching and that of Jesus. Whereas the Israelites were earlier prevented from setting foot on the mountain as the Lord spoke to Moses (Exod. 19), the disciples and the crowd are now permitted to ascend the mountain in order to hear Jesus' teaching (5:1; 7:28). Therefore, whereas Israel formerly heard the Lord through the mediator Moses, the disciples and crowds now hear the voice of the Son of God directly (see 3:17). With the advent of the Messiah, the disciples and crowds are now permitted to enter the Lord's presence to a degree previously unknown. Whereas Israel was previously unable to see the Lord at the mountain, now 'Israel' is able to see God through the likeness of his Son.

The Beatitudes (vv. 3–12) First, in turning to the overall structure of the Beatitudes, the use of the formula *makarios . . . hoti . . .* is employed elsewhere within the NT (e.g. Matt. 13:16), but is rare outside it.[122] Therefore, this particular formula is characteristic to the NT, and the repeated use of this formula is a characteristic of Matthew 5:3–10 (relation to preceding and following genres). Thus what is the significance of this unique form? The formulaic pattern of many ancient texts served as an aid for memorization in an oral society within which printed materials were less widely available. It was quite common in that day for a teacher's lessons to be memorized, and various formulae aided this process. Therefore, the illocutionary force of the formulaic structure may be seen as an implicit call for Jesus' disciples to memorize this passage.

Secondly, since each Beatitude begins with the word *makarios*, 'blessed', what is the meaning and significance of this term? Both Zimmerli and Hagner note that the Greek word *makarios* may be conceived in terms of the Hebrew *'ašrê*, 'blessed'.[123] Without the copula (*hoti*, 'for'), *makarios* is found frequently in the LXX as the translation equivalent of *'ašrê*, (Pss 1:1; 2:12; 106:3 [LXX 105:3]; 119:1 [LXX 118:1]; Isa. 30:18). Moreover, the Hebrew term *'ašrê*, 'blessed', is used similarly in rabbinic literature (*b. Ḥag.* 14b; *b. Yom.* 87a). Zimmerli notes that whereas *barûk*, 'blessed', is used in relation to God, *'ašrê*, 'blessed', is used in relation to men.[124] Within the OT the word *'ašrê* (*makarios*) often refers to

---

122. Ibid., p. 89.

123. W. Zimmerli, 'Die Seligpreisungen der Bergpredigt und das Alte Testament', in E. Bammel, C. K. Barrett and W. D. Davies (eds.), *Donum Gentilicium: New Testament Studies in Honour of David Daube* (Oxford: Clarendon, 1978), pp. 12–15; Hagner, *Matthew*, vol. 1, p. 88.

124. Ibid., p. 12.

those morally righteous through obedience to the Torah (e.g. Ps. 1:1; Isa. 56:2), and within prophetic literature this word is sometimes used in relation to the change in times or dispensations (see the apocalyptic outlook in Isa. 30:18; 32:20; Dan. 12:12). Therefore, within the discourse flow of the canon (intertextuality), the marked repetition of *makarios*, 'blessed', in Matthew 5:3–12 seems to join other structural indicators in pointing toward a blessedness that derives from obedience to the Lord's commands. Moreover, the use of this term by Jesus may be an implicit claim for disciples to view his ministry in the light of the complex of ideas associated with its contextual use within prophetic apocalyptic. In other words, the prophesied time of blessing has now come.

Thirdly, when one compares Matthew's Beatitudes with similar statements in Luke's Sermon on the Plain (intertextuality), one notes that Luke's woe statements are missing from Matthew (Luke 6:24–26). Zimmerli suggests that Jesus is therefore emphasizing the positive nature of the newly revealed life-possibilities.[125] While Zimmerli is certainly correct regarding the positive tone of the Beatitudes, it seems there may be an additional factor to consider. If one remembers that the ground events the text portrays occurred in the context of persecution and that Matthew was composed both after and possibly during times of persecution, then the positive tone within this particular passage may be seen as Jesus' emphatic encouragement for those persecuted because of their obedience to him. Therefore, Matthew 5:3–12 remains especially relevant for believers today persecuted for faithfully following Jesus. This is an encouraging word that emphasizes the blessing of obedience in the face of hardship.

Verses 3–10 We now turn to select exegetical observations from Matthew 5:3–10. The cohesion of this unit is indicated by the inclusiatory phrase 'for theirs is the kingdom of heaven' in verses 3b and 10b, as well as by the use of the third person throughout.

Verses 3–6 As mentioned above, Matthew 5:3–6 is set apart through the alliterative use of *p* in the protasis of each verse (Greek: *ptōchoi tō pneumati, penthountes, praeis, peinontes*). Moreover, Powell argues that this subunit shares the common theme of the eschatological reversal of present injustice.[126]

---

125. Ibid., p. 15.
126. Powell, 'Beatitudes', p. 463.

'Blessed are the poor in spirit, for theirs is the kingdom of heaven' (Matt. 5:3). What is the meaning of 'the poor in spirit'? As Zimmerli, Hagner and Powell note, this phrase probably has in mind the OT concept of the *'anāwîm*, 'poor, oppressed', who are oppressed on account of their obedience and faithfulness to the Lord (see Pss 9:18; 40:18; 70:6; 86:1; Isa. 11:4; 29:19; 32:7; 57:15; 61:1; Amos 2:7; 8:4; Zeph. 2:3). For this segment of society, scriptural living led to poverty and persecution. Moreover, this phrase is found in the War Scroll from Qumran, where the community describes itself as 'poor in spirit'.[127] Since the Qumran community separated themselves in order to maintain purity, it is likely that the mainstream Jewish religious community in some sense persecuted them (whether overtly or through tacit marginalization). Thus the phrase 'poor in spirit' may have been a colloquialism that reflects an understanding of the *'anāwîm* as experienced in the years just preceding and following the advent of the Messiah. If so, then placing too much emphasis on the distinct phrase 'in spirit' may lead to overinterpretation.[128]

The 'kingdom of heaven' (God) implies the accomplishment of God's rule (6:10), and therefore the accomplishment of God's will is a blessing to those poor in spirit.[129] Seen within the flow of canonical discourse, God rules the land (1 Sam. 8:7), and the reference to Israel's lack of a king in Judges (17:6; 18:1; 19:1; 21:25) identifies Israel's failure to accede to divine kingship through obedience to the Torah. In ancient Israel, the establishment of the Davidic kingship (ideally) resulted in obedience to the Torah, and with Jesus' ministry comes the ideal Davidic king, who will once again bring obedience to the Law

---

127. 1QM 14.7; Zimmerli, 'Seligpreisungen', p. 19; Hagner, *Matthew*, vol. 1, p. 92. Powell fails to mention the reference from Qumran in his treatment of this phrase ('Beatitudes', p. 464), and this oversight seems to account for his interpretation of 'in spirit' as a peculiarly Matthean addition, when in fact it was part of the religious milieu Matthew reflects. Moreover, Powell cites several passages in Matthew which suggest that the phrase 'poor in spirit' does not refer to a group internal to Israel (ibid., p. 464). However, he fails to note that Matthew does include materials that distinguish the Jewish period of Jesus' ministry (15:21–28) from the post-Pentecostal Gentile expansion (28:18–20). Therefore, it may be more accurate to say that 'poor in spirit' in Jesus' day referred to a group internal to Israel, and that after Pentecost it refers to both Jewish and Gentile Christians ('Israel') afflicted on account of their righteousness.

128. See Powell, 'Beatitudes', p. 464.

129. Ibid., pp. 464–465.

of Moses with its correspondent justice (5:17–19). The word 'heaven' is used in this verse in order to avoid using the word 'God'. This accords with Matthew's Jewish background, and may be explained by the Jewish tradition that favours circumlocution in order to avoid taking the name of the Lord in vain (Exod. 20:7).

'Blessed are those who mourn, for they shall be comforted' (5:4). This verse is a striking echo of Isaiah 61:2 (LXX), which has traditionally been interpreted as a messianic passage (intertextuality).[130] Therefore, this beatitude should be seen as an implicit messianic claim that draws upon the original surrounding context from Isaiah, and thus Jesus ties his own teaching into Israel's messianic expectations. Moreover, this reappropriation of an OT text defines 'those who mourn' in terms of those who have been cast out of the land for their disobedience, followed by their joyful return from the judgment of exile. Therefore, in canonical context the comforting of those who mourn assumes the movement from judgment for sin to restoration. Cast in messianic terms, then, these are people who mourn because of the judgment they bear. Their comfort, then, consists in being welcomed back to Zion (see 9:9–13).[131]

'Blessed are the meek, for they shall inherit the earth' (5:5). Commentators tend to note the similarities between this verse and verse 3. [132] Like 'the poor in spirit', 'the meek' refers to the OT 'anāwîm, 'poor, oppressed, afflicted'. Therefore, the English translation considered alone may wrongly lead one to the conclusion that those who are passive are here lifted up as virtuous. However, seen within the flow of the OT context, 'the meek' instead refers back to those who suffer for obeying God's commands.[133] Moreover, verse 5 closely mirrors

---

130. Hagner, *Matthew*, vol. 1, p. 92.

131. Although Powell acknowledges the echo of Isa. 61:1–3, he fails to capture the significance of the manner in which this OT passage grounds the meaning of Matt. 5:4 within the canonical thought world. Instead, he concludes that this refers to those who sorrow in general. While one would not want to deny the reappropriation of a passage in a new context, one must at the same time recognize the original thought frame evoked when a passage is reappropriated.

132. Zimmerli, 'Seligpreisungen', p. 22; Hagner, *Matthew*, vol. 1, p. 93; Powell, 'Beatitudes', p. 466.

133. Although Powell acknowledges that the OT 'anāwîm lies behind the notion of the 'poor in spirit' and 'the meek' within the Beatitudes, he fails to recognize the full implications of this observation when he interprets the blessed as the unfortunate

Psalm 37:11 (LXX). This phrase assumes the OT passages where the Lord promises to give Canaan to Israel. As in the book of Joshua and in Psalm 37:9, 11, 22, 29, 34, those who trust and obey the Lord will inherit the land. In particular, Joshua 1:6–9 emphasizes obedience to the Torah in its entirety, as well as the connection between obedience and taking the land. However, in the context of Matthew 5:5, following Hagner, this becomes an eschatological promise regarding the messianic fulfilment of the regenerated earth (see Heb. 12:25–29).[134] Therefore, the poor and afflicted who suffer for their obedience to the Lord are encouraged because they will inherit the New Jerusalem.

'Blessed are those who hunger and thirst for righteousness, for they shall be satisfied' (5:6). If one likewise interprets verse 6 within the flow from OT to NT, then hungering and thirsting for *dikaiosyně*, 'righteousness', on the one hand may be interpreted literally in terms of passages such as Deuteronomy 8:3, 'man does not live by bread alone, but man lives by every word that comes from the mouth of the LORD'. Presumably, this passage was very real for Jesus, who quoted it in order to combat Satan's temptation during his forty-day fast. Likewise, the feeding of the five thousand (14:13–21) and the feeding of the four thousand (15:32–39) suggest that there is a literal element to this Beatitude. The crowds followed Jesus (as an example to us) and desired his teaching more than food. On the other hand, in Psalm 42:1–2, 9, the psalmist thirsts for the Lord within the context of oppression. This latter passage exhibits a metaphorical hungering and thirsting (deep longing) for the Lord to work an act of deliverance. The Hebrew words *sĕdāqâ*, 'righteousness' (Deut. 9:6; Ps. 5:8), and *mišpāṭ*, 'justice' (Mal. 2:17), were translated by the Greek word *dikaiosyně*, 'righteousness', in the LXX, and this usage lurks behind that of the NT. Righteousness in the OT is conceived in terms of obedience to the commands of the Torah. Therefore, those who fix their appetite upon obedience to the Lord will find their desires satisfied. First, they will find righteousness, and secondly, the Lord will provide for their physical needs.

Verses 7–10   Now we turn from the theme of the reversal of injustice to the theme of future reward.

'Blessed are the merciful, for they shall receive mercy' (5:7). What does it

---

Footnote 33 *(continued)*

in general rather than those persecuted on account of their devotion to the Lord ('Beatitudes', p. 469).

134. Hagner, *Matthew*, vol. 1, p. 92.

mean to be merciful? Seen within Matthew's field of discourse, showing mercy may include such acts as healing the sick (9:1–8, 27–31; 20:29–34), calling sinners back into fellowship (9:9–13), casting out demons (15:21–28; 17:14–20) and forgiving those who sin against us (18:21–35). Above all, mercy (along with justice and faithfulness) is one of the more important aspects of Torah (23:23). If Matthew plays upon the etymologically related word *eleēmosynē*, 'alms' (6:2–4; see Prov. 14:21; 17:5 [LXX]), then giving alms to and providing for the needs of the poor is also one dimension of showing mercy.[135] This is probably the case, since elsewhere Matthew reports Jesus' warning against letting traditional religious observances preclude showing mercy to those who are hungry (12:1–8). Those who perform such deeds of mercy will then likewise receive mercy from God in the coming kingdom.

'Blessed are the pure in heart, for they shall see God' (5:8). What does it mean to be 'pure in heart'? The intertextual relation between this verse and Psalm 24:3–5 (LXX 23:3–5) is often noted.[136] Within Psalm 24:3–5 it states that he who has clean hands, who has a 'pure heart' (*katharos tē kardia*), who does not lift up his soul to what is deceitful, and who does not swear deceitfully will receive a blessing from the Lord and righteousness from the God of his salvation. Moreover, this is the one who ascends the Lord's holy hill and stands in God's presence. The context of this verbal echo therefore suggests that a person pure in heart is one who obeys the Lord's commands. This results in the worshipper rightly standing in God's presence within the tabernacle or temple. Within Matthew, the writer emphasizes Jesus' teaching that purity does not consist merely in outward appearances of religiosity, but rather in righteous inner thoughts and motives from which outward deeds proceed (Matt. 23:1–39, esp. v. 26). Furthermore, Jesus is concerned with the purification of any uncleanness that prevents one from worshipping or entering the Lord's presence (*katharizō*, 8:1–4; 10:8; 11:5; 23:25, 26 // *katharos* in 5:8).

What does it mean that the pure in heart will 'see God'? Earlier within canonical discourse the Lord strongly warned Israel not to approach Mount Sinai to see him, lest they die (Exod. 19:21). Then when Moses asked the Lord to show him his glory (Exod. 33:18) the Lord responded that Moses would see the Lord's goodness; however, 'you cannot see my face, for man shall not see

---

135. Ibid., p. 93, notes that showing mercy to the needy became a key element in rabbinic ethics.

136. Zimmerli, 'Seligpreisungen', pp. 23–25; Hagner, *Matthew*, vol. 1, p. 94; Powell, 'Beatitudes', pp. 472–473.

me and live' (Exod. 33:20). Moreover, each year Israelite men were to appear before the Lord for the Feast of Unleavened Bread, the Feast of Weeks and the Feast of Booths (Exod. 23:17; 34:23; Deut. 16:16). Therefore, until the advent of the Messiah, no one could see the Lord and live. Worshippers came before the Lord's presence, but without seeing him. However, within the book of Matthew the Father declares that Jesus is his Son (3:17; 17:5), and therefore Jesus faithfully reveals the Lord's nature and likeness to a degree hitherto unknown (John 14:7–10; Heb. 1:3). Thus, as the messianic age dawns, there is a fundamental change in the knowledge of God that will eventually culminate in the Lord's pure-hearted servants fully seeing his face at the eschaton (Rev. 22:3–4).[137]

'Blessed are the peacemakers, for they shall be called sons of God' (5:9). In looking to the OT discourse from which this verse flows, only one related reference to the verbal form of *eirēnopoioi*, 'peacemakers', is found within the LXX version of Proverbs 10:10, where it states that 'he who boldly reproves makes peace' (RSV).[138] In its immediate context within Proverbs, the man of integrity is contrasted with the man who perverts his ways and winks the eye (Prov. 10:9–10). Therefore, the peacemaker rebukes those who are perverted and wink the eye (those who do not obey the Torah and thus do not work for social justice). This canonical intertextual connection provides further textual warrant for Powell's argument that 'peacemakers' refers to those who actively establish justice and *šālôm*, 'peace', on the earth.[139]

However, the immediate context within the Sermon on the Mount suggests that there may be more to the notion of 'peacemaker'. Zimmerli notes the connection of verse 9 with 5:38–48, where Jesus teaches that disciples are not to take revenge for evil deeds (vv. 38–39), to be involved in civil litigation

---

137. See Hagner, *Matthew*, vol. 1, p. 94. Powell ('Beatitudes', p. 473) notes Matthew's eschatological outlook in 13:43; 25:34.

138. However, in the MT this verse reads, 'but a babbling fool will come to ruin' (NRSV, fn.). RSV, NRSV, NBJ (1998) and NLT follow LXX within the main text (RSV, NRSV and NLT footnote the MT reading). The Vulgate, Luther, NIV, NBS (2002) and ESV follow MT (NBS footnotes the LXX reading). The *BHS* critical note at Prov. 10:10 indicates that the Syriac agrees with the LXX. The present discussion leaves aside the occurrence of the verbal form *eirēnopoiēsas* in Col. 1:20, since this occurrence refers to Jesus' work restoring our relationship to the Father, whereas the following discussion deals with the human element, in keeping with the sense of 5:9.

139. Powell, 'Beatitudes', p. 474.

(v. 40) or to hate their enemies (vv. 43–47).[140] In stark contrast, we are to promote peace by forgiving those who oppress, by giving what is asked of us and by praying for our enemies. This intertextual connection resonates with Hagner's reading when he posits a connection between the Zealots of Jesus' day and this Beatitude.[141] Hagner finds that this Beatitude refers to the downtrodden and oppressed for whom it was a temptation to usher in the kingdom of God violently through revolution in order to demonstrate that they were loyal 'sons of God'. Instead, we are to become peacemakers along the lines set out by Jesus in 5:38–48 in order to become 'sons of your Father who is in heaven' (5:45//5:9b). Thus to be a 'son of God' is to please the Lord (see 3:17; 17:5; 12:50).

To the contrary, Powell argues that 'peacemakers' does not refer to those who work for reconciliation (5:23–24//5:7) through a generosity of forgiveness (18:21–35). He points out Jesus' teaching that his peace does not mean peace in this sense of the word (10:34–36; see also 5:11–12; 10:21–22). Nevertheless, it does seem possible to read 5:9 in relation to both reconciliation and the establishment of social justice, since both of these intertextual connections find textual warrant.[142] Thus a polyvalent or polysemous reading of 5:9 recognizes both sets of intertextual connections without unduly foreclosing the ambiguity that seems to be built into the very structure of the Beatitudes as a whole. On the one hand, we are to respond peacefully when mistreated, in order to promote reconciliation (whether it be between us and the other party or between God and the other party), and on the other hand, full loyalty and obedience to Jesus may result in fractured family relationships (which are to be received in accordance with 5:38–48, but not encouraged on our part!).

'Blessed are those who are persecuted for righteousness' sake, for theirs is the kingdom of heaven' (5:10). Within Matthew's field of discourse, persecution was not foreign to the life of Jesus. In fact, Jesus' life begins and ends with victory over persecution (2:13–18; chs. 26–28). Likewise, Jesus warns his disciples of coming suffering and calls them to take up their cross (10:16–42). However, this is not suffering in general, but rather suffering 'for righteousness' sake'. In other words, faithful obedience to the Lord and one's pure heart result in suffering (see 10:16, 22). The one who faithfully endures persecution both is and will be blessed, in contrast with the one who falls away

---

140. Zimmerli, 'Seligpreisungen', p. 21.

141. Hagner, *Matthew*, vol. 1, p. 94. Hagner also notes the NT theme of 'peace' in Rom. 14:19; Heb. 12:14; Jas 3:18; 1 Pet. 3:11.

142. Powell, 'Beatitudes', p. 473.

(13:20–21).[143] In particular, the 'kingdom of God', both in its present and future dimensions, is the reward for those who endure persecution for Jesus' sake (see the preceding discussion of vv. 3, 5).

Verses 11–12   'Blessed are you when others revile you and persecute you and utter all kinds of evil against you falsely on my account. Rejoice and be glad, for your reward is great in heaven, for so they persecuted the prophets who were before you' (5:11–12). In moving from verses 3–10 to verses 11–12 there is both a shift in person, from third to second, and in mood, from indicative to imperative. Moreover, verses 11–12 break with the formulaic structure of verses 3–10 and expand on the theme of verse 10, persecution. What is the significance of this grammatical disjunction? Powell notes the relation between Hebrew parallelism and the overall structure of the Beatitudes, and one therefore wonders whether the shift in person and number may likewise reflect an underlying Hebrew stylistic convention.[144] It may be the case that Matthew's Greek here echoes the BH discourse phenomenon whereby the speaker or writer refers to the same participant with a change in grammatical person. Within prophetic discourse (e.g. Hosea), a change from non-face-threatening third person forms to second person at paragraph boundaries renews the audience's involvement (rhetorical entrapment).[145] Moreover, a shift in grammatical person (from third to second) may renew the audience's attention towards the end of a paragraph or at central and climactic points.[146] If so, then verses 11–12 are set apart as the most prominent material of the Beatitudes, and the space given to the theme of persecution in verses 10–12

---

143. See ibid., p. 474.

144. Ibid., p. 461.

145. L. de Regt, 'A Genre Feature in Biblical Prophecy and the Translator: Person Shift in Hosea', in J. C. de Moor and H. F. Van Rooy (eds.), *Past, Present, Future: The Deuteronomistic History and the Prophets* (Leiden: Brill, 2000), p. 250. De Regt follows R. Alter (*The Art of Biblical Poetry* [New York: Basic, 1985], p. 144) in describing this as 'rhetoric of entrapment'. Second-language discourse interference is not unheard of. For example, it is common for Korean and Chinese writers of English to structure an e-mail message in accordance with Korean or Chinese discourse conventions and put highlighted information at the end rather than at the beginning.

146. L. de Regt, 'Person Shift in Prophetic Texts: Its Function and its Rendering in Ancient and Modern Translations', in J. C. de Moor (ed.), *The Elusive Prophet: The Prophet as a Historical Person, Literary Character and Anonymous Artist* (Leiden: Brill, 2001), p. 231.

further emphasizes its importance. If so, then Powell's interpretation of the person shift as Jesus' distinction between the people whom he addresses and those whom he describes as blessed must be reconsidered.[147] Rather, Jesus addresses his disciples and hearers without distinction, and the person shift highlights the significance of the material within verses 11–12 rather than necessarily indicating different addressees. Moreover, if this is the manifestation of an underlying BH discourse phenomenon, then Hagner's argument is undercut that verses 11–12 derive from a different source, since it differs both in person and in form from the preceding eight Beatitudes.[148]

Within verses 11–12, Jesus therefore emphatically encourages his disciples to receive reviling, persecution and hurtful lies suffered for his sake with rejoicing. The reason given is that their future reward in heaven will be great (//vv. 3–10). Moreover, disciples who experience this kind of suffering for Jesus' sake are like the long line of prophets who likewise suffered for their faithful obedience throughout Israel's history (see 2 Chron. 36:16, Matt. 23:35, Heb. 11:32–38 regarding the possible discourse assumptions within the minds of Jesus' hearers and Matthew's addressees). To become Christlike, then, is to identify with Jesus, to take up one's cross, and to follow his pattern by obediently suffering for the sake of the kingdom (16:21–28; 17:22–23; 20:17–19; 24:9–14; chs. 26–28).

We are now in a position to describe some of the overall discourse and literary effects of the basic structure and style of the Beatitudes (rhetoric). First, why are they so enigmatically opaque? What were Jesus and Matthew attempting to do with this device? Since ambiguity forces the addressee or reader to wrestle with a given text, the basic structure therefore seems to draw the reader in, force the reader to pin down the meaning, and consequently both internalize and exemplify the text to a greater degree than if its meaning were more transparent. With greater reflection comes greater inner turmoil and greater sanctification as we are confronted by the text. Secondly, the movement from present distress to future reversal and reward is both an encouragement and an exhortation to remain steadfast in the face of persecution (illocutionary force). Present hostility will be reversed. Thirdly, within this text Jesus uses language of authority and power (rhetoric). He gives pronouncements that allow for no argument or rebuttal. They are forceful. They are given on the mountain by One in authority, one regarded as a teacher and one greater than Moses. Fourthly, at the end of verse 12 the sequencing of material leaves the reader thinking on the blessing of persecution, which is a call for a change of attitude.

---

147. Powell, 'Beatitudes', p. 469.

148. Hagner, *Matthew*, vol. 1, p. 95.

Persecution is not to be avoided at all cost, but rather to be embraced when necessary.

The locus of meaning and ideology: author, text, reader

Within the horizon of Jesus' first ideal addressees in the ground historical event depicted within the text, his teaching probably evoked intertextual associations to OT passages taught in the temple and synagogues, as well as recited in liturgy. References to persecution were seen in terms of the Roman occupation of Palestine. For Matthew's first addressees, persecution was probably seen in terms of both the life of Jesus and the Jewish and Roman persecution of early Christians. Intertextual connections to OT passages were probably based on the LXX.

However, Western readers today tend to be distant from overt or militant persecution, and therefore this dimension of the Beatitudes text remains opaque. Moreover, contemporary Western Christians tend to be far less acquainted with the OT than both Jesus' and Matthew's early audiences. Whereas both liturgy and culture were steeped in OT knowledge that rendered the Beatitudes more understandable, the voice of the OT in the church today tends to be drowned. In contrast to Western readers, however, contemporary reading communities in both the Middle and Far East may identify themselves more easily with the theme of persecution in Matthew 5:1–12. As the ideal reader constructs meaning, the text takes on a greater relevance and the ideological perspective of the text more readily realizes its intended function of encouraging believers to stand firm.

Critical discourse analysis

Since persecution is the most dominant theme of the Beatitudes, I now therefore ask several questions aimed at Western readers with a view toward social change.

Although overt or militant persecution is not so evident in the West, this does not mean that persecution in various forms does not exist. With this in mind we resume our discussion of 'biblolatry' and 'spreading your tent pegs', mentioned above, and scrutinize the institutional church (correspondent to the religious institution of Jesus' day). This enables us to ask how the Beatitudes may relate to the use of power as an attempt to intimidate believers or clergy who may call for a return to scriptural practices at key points where the church has in fact departed from the canonical text as an authoritative document. Where church praxis departs from traditional formulations based on the systematic searching of the canonical text aligned with the discourse of both the early church and the Protestant Reformation, have pastors or candidates seeking ordination been marginalized for failing to follow the drift of mainline denominations toward speculative theology, secular leadership principles, secular approaches to counselling, popular philosophy and the popular acceptance of other religions as equally valid with Christianity? Do pastors find themselves barred from positions of leadership within their denomination or tradition? Are candidates for ordination denied or in any way 'hassled' for adhering to Scripture and its traditional interpretation? Do seminary students with a bent toward more traditional interpretations of the Bible find themselves struggling academically when their work is equal to or of higher quality than that of students who receive better grades within academic institutions that inculcate non-scriptural beliefs and practices? The existence of various reactionary publications that are intended to encourage believers to remain faithful in the light of this type of persecution suggests that this is in fact the case.[149]

If so, then persecution is indeed rampant within Christian institutions in the West today, and the Beatitudes are both a call for contemporary disciples of Jesus to follow his example, as well as an encouragement that this situation will some day be reversed and a reward be given to those faithful to the end. Those who mourn will be comforted by God, those humbled by institutional power will inherit the earth, and those who hunger and thirst for righteousness will be satisfied. The merciful will be shown mercy from God, the pure in heart will see God, the peacemakers will be called sons of God, and those persecuted for their obedience to the Lord's commands will inherit the kingdom of heaven. We are called to stand firm in obedience to the Lord with great rejoicing when pursued in various ways and when evil lies are spread about us. The result of standing firm against denominational drift and institutional injustice will be a great reward in heaven as we join the company of the prophets who preceded us. However, although we are called to stand firm, we are not called to oppose corrupt institutions on their own terms. Rather, the Beatitudes are conceptualized within the discourse flow of the Sermon on the Mount. Therefore, we are to oppose corruption and injustice without returning evil for evil. Instead, we are to return good for evil (Matt. 5:38–42), love for hatred, and prayer for persecution (5:43–48). We are to be wise as serpents, innocent as doves, and always tempered by lovingkindness.

---

149. For an example of such a periodical, see 'Good News', a publication in the Wesleyan tradition, based in Wilmore, Kentucky (USA). Numerous similar publications represent more traditionally minded elements in other denominations. These publications provide an outlet for people marginalized from official denominational periodicals.

Conclusion

In the preceding discussion I outlined the major trends in linguistic discourse analysis, provided a brief overview of the reception of discourse analysis in Old and New Testament studies, and then applied discourse analysis to Exodus 15:22–27 and Matthew 5:1–12. We found that one may define 'discourse' as a unit of speech (either oral or written), which is accepted by interlocutors as a complete utterance. Moreover, 'discourse analysis' is the analysis of language and its use beyond the sentence, and this includes the analysis of language situated in its social context.

One may identify the following strengths in discourse analysis as a literary method. First, it has very broad concerns with a wide array of descriptive tools at the interpreter's disposal. Although both linguists and Bible scholars agree that discourse analysis is an interdisciplinary approach that is hard to define, I proposed that the broad concerns of discourse analysis mirror the complexity of language in its social context. Moreover, the broad concerns of discourse analysis are advantageous for the exegete in that it disciplines the interpreter to approach the text from many different angles in order to better understand its meaning(s). Secondly, the consideration of AUTHOR–TEXT–READER is a means for describing the influence of all three dimensions on the social construction of meaning without placing undue emphasis on one to the neglect of others. Thirdly, this approach disciplines the exegete to consider aspects of meaning that range from the present interpretative situation to the original social context of the text. Fourthly, the concern of discourse analysis for social context avoids the tendency of some literary critics to focus only upon the text. This approach both balances a concern for the text in its original historical setting, and raises our awareness of the text's contemporary social context.

Conversely, one may identify the following weaknesses in discourse analysis as a literary method. First, the technical language some discourse and text-analysts use is obscure to the non-specialist, as is their formal notation. Some have pointed out that this unnecessary complication could be avoided by using a purely literary analysis instead (poetics). Secondly, the wide range of concerns presents an array of theories the thorough discourse analyst must master in a rudimentary way in order to consider the various ways a text develops meaning. It is time-consuming to delve into speech-act theory, theories of intertextuality and genre analysis, grammatical analysis, issues of text history and so forth, in addition to the traditional discipline of historical-critical Old and New Testament introduction. Notwithstanding these weaknesses, advances in both theory and methods in discourse analysis offer much for the disciplined exegete who is willing to tackle a linguistic approach to the Bible in order to acquire an array of tools for engaging the text and attempting to hear it speak on its own terms to us today.[150]

Bibliography

ALTER, R., *The Art of Biblical Poetry* (New York: Basic, 1985).

ANDERSEN, F. I., *The Hebrew Verbless Clause in the Pentateuch*, JBLMS 14 (New York: Abingdon, 1970).

——, *The Sentence in Biblical Hebrew* (The Hague: Mouton, 1974).

ANDERSEN, T. D., 'Genealogical Prominence and the Structure of Genesis', in BERGEN, *Biblical Hebrew*, pp. 242–266.

AUSTIN, J. L., *How to Do Things with Words*, ed. J. O. Urmson and M. Sbisà, 2nd ed. (Cambridge, Mass.: Harvard University Press, 1962).

BAILEY, N. A., 'Some Literary and Grammatical Aspects of Genealogies in Genesis', in BERGEN, *Biblical Hebrew*, pp. 267–282.

BAKHTIN, M. M., 'The Problem of Speech Genres', in C. Emerson and M. Holquist (eds.), tr. V. W. McGee, UTPSS 8 (Austin: University of Texas, 1986), pp. 60–102.

SCHIFFRIN, TANNEN and HAMILTON, *Handbook of Discourse Analysis*, pp. 121–132.

BEAUGRANDE, R.-A. DE, and DRESSLER, W. U., *Introduction to Text-Linguistics* (London: Longman, 1981).

BEENTJES, P. C., 'Discovering a New Path of Intertextuality: Inverted Quotations and Their Dynamics', in DE REGT, DE WAARD and FOKKELMAN, *Literary Structure and Rhetorical Strategies*, pp. 31–50.

BERGEN, R. D. (ed.), *Biblical Hebrew and Discourse Linguistics* (Dallas: SIL, 1994).

BLACK, C. C., 'Rhetorical Criticism', in GREEN, *Hearing the New Testament*, pp. 256–277.

BLACK, D. A. (ed.) (with K. BARNWELL and S. H. LEVINSOHN), *Linguistics and New Testament Interpretation: Essays on Discourse Analysis* (Nashville: Broadman, 1992).

BLIESE, L. F., 'The Poetics of Habakkuk', *JOTT* 12 (1999), pp. 47–75.

BODINE, W. R. (ed.), *Discourse Analysis of Biblical Literature: What It Is and What It Offers*, SemeiaSt (Atlanta: Scholars Press, 1995).

BOWLING, A. C., 'Another Brief Overview of the Hebrew Verb', *JOTT* 9 (1997), pp. 48–69.

BOYARIN, D., 'Inner Biblical Ambiguity, Intertextuality and the Dialectic of Midrash: The Waters of Marah', *Proof* 10 (1990), pp. 29–48.

BRIGGS, R. S., 'The Use of Speech-Act Theory in Biblical Interpretation', *CR:BS* 9 (2001), pp. 229–276.

---

150. Many thanks to Keith Slater, an SIL linguist, for evaluating this chapter.

BROWN, G., and YULE, G., *Discourse Analysis*, Cambridge Textbooks in Linguistics (Cambridge: Cambridge University Press, 1983).

BUTH, R., 'The Hebrew Verb in Current Discussions', *JOTT* 5 (1992), pp. 91–105.

——, '*Oun, De, Kai*, and Asyndeton in John's Gospel', in D. A. BLACK (with BARNWELL and LEVINSOHN), *Linguistics*, pp. 144–161.

CALLOW, J. C., 'Constituent Order in Copula Clauses: A Partial Study', in D. A. BLACK (with BARNWELL and LEVINSOHN), *Linguistics*, pp. 68–89.

CHAFE, W., 'The Analysis of Discourse Flow', in SCHIFFRIN, TANNEN and HAMILTON, *Handbook of Discourse Analysis*, pp. 673–687.

COULTHARD, M., *An Introduction to Discourse Analysis* (London: Longman, 1977).

DAWSON, D. A., *Text-Linguistics and Biblical Hebrew*, JSOTSup 177 (Sheffield: Sheffield Academic Press, 1994).

DISSE, A., *Informationsstruktur im Biblischen Hebräisch: Sprachwissenschaftliche Grundlagen und exegetische Konsequenzen einer Korpusuntersuchung zu den Büchern Deuteronomium, Richter und 2 Könige*, ATSAT 56 (St. Ottilien: EOS, 1998).

DRESSLER, W. U. (ed.), *Current Trends in Textlinguistics*, RTT 2 (Berlin: de Gruyter, 1978).

ENDO, Y., *The Verbal System of Classical Hebrew in the Joseph Story: An Approach from Discourse Analysis*, SSN 32 (Assen: van Gorcum, 1996).

ESKHULT, M., *Studies in Verbal Aspect and Narrative Technique in Biblical Hebrew Prose* (Uppsala: Uppsala University Press, 1990).

FAIRCLOUGH, N., *Analysing Discourse: Textual Analysis for Social Research* (London: Routledge, 2003).

FOLLINGSTAD, C. M., *Deictic Viewpoint in Biblical Hebrew Text: A Syntagmatic and Paradigmatic Analysis of the Particle kî* (Dallas: SIL International, 2001).

GEE, J. P., *An Introduction to Discourse Analysis: Theory and Method* (London: Routledge, 1999).

GESENIUS, W., KAUTZSCH, E., and COWLEY, A. E., *Gesenius' Hebrew Grammar* (Oxford: Clarendon, 1910).

GREEN, J. B., 'Discourse Analysis and New Testament Interpretation', in GREEN, *Hearing the New Testament*, pp. 175–196.

—— (ed.), *Hearing the New Testament: Strategies for Interpretation* (Grand Rapids: Eerdmans, 1995).

GRICE, H. P., 'Logic and Conversation', in P. Cole and J. L. Morgan (eds.), *Syntax and Semantics*. Vol. 3: *Speech Acts* (New York: Academic, 1975), pp. 41–58.

GRIMES, J. E., *The Thread of Discourse*, JLSM 207 (The Hague: Mouton, 1975).

GROSS, W., *Die Satzteilfolge im Verbalsatz alttestamentlicher Prosa: Untersucht an den Büchern Dtn, Ri und 2 Kön* (Tübingen: Mohr, 1996).

GUMPERZ, J. J., 'Interactional Sociolinguistics: A Personal Perspective', in SCHIFFRIN, TANNEN and HAMILTON, *Handbook of Discourse Analysis*, pp. 215–228.

GUTHRIE, G. H., 'Cohesion Shifts and Stitches in Philippians', in PORTER and CARSON, *Discourse Analysis*, pp. 36–59.

HAGNER, D. A., *Matthew*, 2 vols., WBC 33A, 33B (Dallas: Word, 1993).

HALLIDAY, M. A. K., and MATTHIESSEN, C. M. I. M., *An Introduction to Functional Grammar*, 3rd ed. (London: Hodder Arnold, 2004).

HARRIS, R. L., 'The Beatitudes: Teaching by Climax', *Presb* 30 (2004), pp. 111–113.

HARRIS, Z. S., 'Discourse Analysis', *Language* 28 (1952), pp. 1–30.

HARTIN, P. J., and PETZER, J. H., *Text and Interpretation: New Approaches in the Criticism of the New Testament* (Leiden: Brill, 1991).

HATIM, B., and MASON, I., *Discourse and the Translator* (Harlow: Longman, 1990).

——, *The Translator as Communicator* (London: Routledge, 1997).

HEALEY, P., and HEALEY, A., 'Greek Circumstantial Participles: Tracking Participants with Participles in the Greek New Testament', *OPTT* 4 (1990), pp. 177–259.

HEIMERDINGER, J.-M., *Topic, Focus and Foreground in Ancient Hebrew Narratives*, JSOTSup 295 (Sheffield: Sheffield Academic Press, 1999).

HELLER, R. L., *Narrative Structure and Discourse Constellations: An Analysis of Clause Function in Biblical Hebrew Prose*, HSS 55 (Winona Lake: Eisenbrauns, 2004).

HOFTIJZER, J., 'The Nominal Clause Reconsidered', *VT* 23 (1973), pp. 446–510.

HOUTMAN, C., *Exodus*, tr. S. Woudstra, vol. 2, HCOT (Kampen: KOK, 1996; orig. *Exodus*, Commentaar op het Oude Testament [Kampen: KOK, 1989]).

JAWORSKI, A., and COUPLAND, N. (eds.), *The Discourse Reader* (London: Routledge, 1999).

JOHNSTONE, B., *Discourse Analysis* (Oxford: Blackwell, 2002).

JØRGENSEN, M., and PHILLIPS, L., *Discourse Analysis as Theory and Method* (London: Sage, 2002).

JOÜON, P., S. J., *A Grammar of Biblical Hebrew*, SubBi 14.1, tr. and rev. T. Muraoka (Rome: Pontifical Biblical Institute, 2003).

KHAN, G., *Studies in Semitic Syntax*, London Oriental Series 38 (Oxford: Oxford University Press, 1988).

LAKOFF, R. T., 'Nine Ways of Looking at Apologies: The Necessity for Interdisciplinary Theory and Method in Discourse Analysis', in SCHIFFRIN, TANNEN and HAMILTON, *Handbook of Discourse Analysis*, pp. 199–214.

LEVINSOHN, S. H., *Discourse Features of New Testament Greek: A Coursebook on the Information Structure of New Testament Greek*, 2nd ed. (SIL International, 2000).

——, 'A Discourse Study of Constituent Order and the Article in Philippians', in PORTER and CARSON, *Discourse Analysis*, pp. 60–74.

——, 'Participant Reference in Koine Greek Narrative', in D. A. BLACK (with BARNWELL and LEVINSOHN), *Linguistics*, pp. 31–44.

LEVINSON, S. C., *Pragmatics*, Cambridge Textbooks in Linguistics (Cambridge: Cambridge University Press, 1983).

LJUNGBERG, B.-K., 'Genre and Form Criticism in Old Testament Exegesis', in BERGEN, *Biblical Hebrew*, pp. 415–433.

LONGACRE, R. E., *An Anatomy of Speech Notions* (Lisse: Peter de Ridder, 1976).

——, 'The Discourse Structure of the Flood Narrative', JAARSup 47 (1979), pp. 89–133.

——, *The Grammar of Discourse*, Topics in Language and Linguistics, 2nd ed. (New York: Plenum, 1996).

——, *Joseph: A Story of Divine Providence. A Text Theoretical and Textlinguistic Analysis of Genesis 37 and 39–48* (Winona Lake: Eisenbrauns, 1989).

——, 'Towards an Exegesis of 1 John based on the Discourse Analysis of the Greek Text', in D. A. BLACK (with BARNWELL and LEVINSOHN), *Linguistics*, pp. 271–286.

——, '*Weqatal* Forms in Biblical Hebrew Prose', in BERGEN, *Biblical Hebrew*, pp. 50–98.

LONGACRE, R. E., and HWANG, S. J. J., 'A Textlinguistic Approach to the Biblical Hebrew Narrative of Jonah', in BERGEN, *Biblical Hebrew*, pp. 336–358.

LONGACRE, R. E., and LEVINSOHN, S. H, 'Field Analysis of Discourse', in W. U. Dressler (ed.), *Current Trends in Textlinguistics*, RTT 2 (Berlin: de Gruyter, 1978), pp. 103–122.

LOUW, J. P., 'Discourse Analysis and the Greek New Testament', *Bible Today* 24 (1973), pp. 101–106.

——, 'Reading a Text as Discourse', in D. A. BLACK (with BARNWELL and LEVINSOHN), *Linguistics*, pp. 17–30.

MACDONELL, D., *Theories of Discourse: An Introduction* (Oxford: Basil Blackwell, 1986).

MARTIN, J. R., 'Cohesion and Texture', in SCHIFFRIN, TANNEN and HAMILTON, *Handbook of Discourse Analysis*, pp. 35–53.

MAY, J. L., 'Literary Pragmatics', in SCHIFFRIN, TANNEN and HAMILTON, *Handbook of Discourse Analysis*, pp. 787–797.

MERWE, C. H. J. VAN DER, 'An Overview of Recent Developments in the Description of Biblical Hebrew Relevant to Bible Translation', in *Contemporary Translation Studies and Bible Translation: A South African Perspective*, ActSup 2 (Bloemfontein: University of the Free State, 2002), pp. 228–245.

MILLER, C. L., 'Discourse Functions of Quotative Frames in Biblical Hebrew Narrative', in BODINE, *Discourse Analysis of Biblical Literature*, pp. 155–182.

——, 'Introducing Direct Discourse in Biblical Hebrew Narrative', in BERGEN, *Biblical Hebrew*, pp. 199–241.

——, 'Reported Speech in Biblical and Epigraphic Hebrew: A Linguistic Analysis' (PhD diss., University of Chicago, 1992; rev. 1996, 2nd ed. [with an afterword] 2003).

—— (ed.), *The Verbless Clause in Biblical Hebrew: Linguistic Approaches*, Linguistic Studies in Ancient West Semitic (Winona Lake: Eisenbrauns, 1999).

MOULTON, J. H., and TURNER, N., *A Grammar of New Testament Greek*, vol. 3 (Edinburgh: T. & T. Clark, 1963).

NICACCI, A., 'On the Hebrew Verbal System', in BERGEN, *Biblical Hebrew*, pp. 117–137.

——, *The Syntax of the Verb in Classical Hebrew Prose*, tr. W. G. E. Watson, JSOTSup 86 (Sheffield: JSOT Press, 1990).

NORRICK, N. R., 'Discourse and Semantics', in SCHIFFRIN, TANNEN and HAMILTON, *Handbook of Discourse Analysis*, pp. 76–99.

OSBURN, C. D., 'Discourse Analysis and Jewish Apocalyptic in the Epistle of Jude', in D. A. BLACK (with BARNWELL and LEVINSOHN), *Linguistics*, pp. 287–319.

PATTE, D., 'Speech Act Theory and Biblical Exegesis', *Semeia* 41 (1988), pp. 85–102.

PETÖFI, J. S., 'Towards an Empirically Motivated Grammatical Theory of Verbal Texts', in PETÖFI and RIESER, *Studies in Text Grammar*, pp. 205–269.

PETÖFI, J. S., and RIESER, H. (eds.), *Studies in Text Grammar*, Foundations of Language Supplementary Series 19 (Dordrecht: D. Reidel, 1973).

PICKERING, W., *A Framework for Discourse Analysis* (Dallas: SIL, 1978).

PIKE, K. L., *Language in Relation to a Unified Theory of the Structure of Human Behavior*, 3 vols. (Summer Institute of Linguistics, 1954–60).

——, *Tagmemics, Discourse, and Verbal Art* (Ann Arbor: University of Michigan, 1981).

PIKE, K. L., and PIKE, E. G., *Text and Tagmeme* (Norwood: Ablex, 1983).

PORTER, S. E., and CARSON, D. A. (eds.), *Discourse Analysis and Other Topics in Biblical Greek*, JSNTSup 113 (Sheffield: Sheffield Academic Press, 1995).

POWELL, M. A., 'Matthew's Beatitudes: Reversals and Rewards of the Kingdom', *CBQ* 58 (1996), pp. 460–479.

RAD, G. VON, 'Typologische Auslegung des Alten Testaments', *EvT* 12 (1952–3), pp. 17–34; repr. *Gesammelte Studien zum Alten Testament 2* (Munich: Chr. Kaiser, 1973), pp. 272–288.

REED, J. T., 'Discourse Analysis as New Testament Hermeneutic: A Retrospective and Prospective Appraisal', *JETS* 39 (1996), pp. 223–240.

——, *A Discourse Analysis of Philippians: Method and Rhetoric in the Debate over Literary Integrity*, JSNTSup 136 (Sheffield: Sheffield Academic Press, 1997).

——, 'Identifying Theme in the New Testament: Insights from Discourse Analysis', in PORTER and CARSON, *Discourse Analysis*, pp. 75–101.

REGT, L. J. DE, 'A Genre Feature in Biblical Prophecy and the Translator: Person Shift in Hosea', in J. C. de Moor and H. F. Van Rooy (eds.), *Past, Present, Future: The Deuteronomistic History and the Prophets* (Leiden: Brill, 2000), pp. 230–250.

——, 'Macrosyntactic Functions of Nominal Clauses Referring to Participants', in MILLER, *Verbless Clause in Biblical Hebrew*, pp. 273–296.

——, *Participants in Old Testament Texts and the Translator: Reference Devices and their Rhetorical Impact* (Assen: van Gorcum, 1999).

——, 'Person Shift in Prophetic Texts: Its Function and its Rendering in Ancient and Modern Translations', in J. C. de Moor (ed.), *The Elusive Prophet: The Prophet as a Historical Person, Literary Character and Anonymous Artist* (Leiden: Brill, 2001), pp. 214–231.

REGT, L. J. DE, WAARD, J. DE, and FOKKELMAN, J. P. (eds.), *Literary Structure and Rhetorical Strategies in the Hebrew Bible* (Assen: van Gorcum, 1996).

RICHTER, W., *Grundlagen einer althebräischen Grammatik* (St. Ottilien: EOS, 1978–80).

ROBINSON, B. P., 'Symbolism in Exod. 15:22–27', *RB* 94 (1987), pp. 376–388.

SAUSSURE, F. DE, *Course in General Linguistics*, ed. C. Bally and A. Sechehaye, tr. R. Harris (Chicago: Open Court, 1986).

SCHIFFRIN, D., TANNEN, D., and HAMILTON, H. E. (eds.), *The Handbook of Discourse Analysis* (Oxford: Blackwell, 2001).

SCOLLON, R., and SCOLLON, S. W., 'Discourse and Intercultural Communication', in SCHIFFRIN, TANNEN and HAMILTON, *Handbook of Discourse Analysis*, pp. 538–547.

SEARLE, J. R., *Speech Acts: An Essay in the Philosophy of Language* (Cambridge: Cambridge University Press, 1969).

SHIMASAKI, K., *Focus Structure in Biblical Hebrew: A Study of Word Order and Information Structure* (Bethesda: CDL, 2002).

SILVA, M., 'Discourse Analysis and Philippians', in PORTER and CARSON, *Discourse Analysis*, pp. 102–106.

SNYMAN, A. H., 'A Semantic Discourse Analysis of the Letter to Philemon', in HARTIN and PETZER, *Text and Interpretation* (1991), pp. 83–99.

TITRUD, K., 'The Function of Καί in the Greek New Testament and an Application to 2 Peter', in D. A. BLACK (with BARNWELL and LEVINSOHN), *Linguistics*, pp. 240–270.

TUGGY, J. C., 'Semantic Paragraph Patterns: A Fundamental Communication Concept and Interpretive Tool', in D. A. BLACK (with BARNWELL and LEVINSOHN), *Linguistics*, pp. 45–67.

VAN DIJK, T. A., 'Critical Discourse Analysis', in SCHIFFRIN, TANNEN and HAMILTON, *Handbook of Discourse Analysis*, pp. 352–371.

—— (ed.), *Handbook of Discourse Analysis*, 4 vols. (London: Academic, 1985).

——, 'Text Grammar and Text Logic', in PETÖFI and RIESER, *Studies in Text Grammar*, pp. 17–78.

VAN DYKE PARUNAK, H., 'Dimensions of Discourse Structure: A Multidimensional Analysis of the Components and Transitions of Paul's Epistle to the Galatians', in D. A. BLACK (with BARNWELL and LEVINSOHN), *Linguistics*, pp. 207–239.

WALTKE, B. K., and O'CONNOR, M., *An Introduction to Biblical Hebrew Syntax* (Winona Lake: Eisenbrauns, 1990).

WARD, G., and BIRNER, B. J., 'Discourse and Information Structure', in SCHIFFRIN, TANNEN and HAMILTON, *Handbook of Discourse Analysis*, pp. 119–137.

WARREN, A., 'Modality, Reference and Speech Acts in the Psalms' (PhD diss., University of Cambridge, 1998).

WENDLAND, E. R., 'Genre Criticism and the Psalms: What Discourse Typology Can Tell Us about the Text (with Special Reference to Psalm 31)', in BERGEN, *Biblical Hebrew*, pp. 374–414.

——, 'Obadiah's "Day": On the Rhetorical Implications of Textual Form and Intertextual Influence', *JOTT* 8 (1996), pp. 23–50.

——, 'Obadiah's Vision of "The Day of the Lord": On the Importance of Rhetoric in the Biblical Text and in Bible Translation', *JOTT* 7 (1996), pp. 54–86.

—, ' "Dear Children" Versus the "Antichrists": The Rhetoric of Reassurance in First John', *JOTT* 11 (1998), pp. 41–84.

——, 'A Tale of Two Debtors: On the Interaction of Text, Cotext, and Context in a New Testament Dramatic Narrative (Luke 7:36–50)', in D. A. BLACK (with BARNWELL and LEVINSOHN), *Linguistics*, pp. 101–143.

WOLDE, E. J. VAN, 'The Text as an Eloquent Guide: Rhetorical, Linguistic, and Literary Features in Genesis 1', in DE REGT, DE WAARD and FOKKELMAN, *Literary Structure and Rhetorical Strategies*, pp. 134–151.

WUELLNER, W., 'Rhetorical Criticism and its Theory in Culture-Critical Perspective: The Narrative Rhetoric of John 11', in HARTIN and PETZER, *Text and Interpretation*, pp. 1710–1785.

ZIMMERLI, W., 'Die Seligpreisungen der Bergpredigt und das Alte Testament', in E. Bammel, C. K. Barrett and W. D. Davies (eds.), *Donum Gentilicium: New Testament Studies in Honour of David Daube* (Oxford: Clarendon, 1978), pp. 8–26.